Inside the Norton Utilities™

Rob Krumm

Introduction by Peter Norton

Brady
New York

BRADY

Simon & Schuster, Inc.
Gulf+Western Building
One Gulf+Western Plaza
New York, NY 10023

Distributed by Prentice Hall Trade

Manufactured in the United States of America

1 2 3 4 5 6 7 8 9 10

Library of Congress Cataloging-in-Publication Data

Krumm, Rob, 1951-
Inside the Norton Utilities / Rob Krumm.
p. cm.
On t.p. the registered trademark symbol "TM" is superscript following "Utilities" in the title.
Includes index.
1. Norton Utilities (Computer programs) 2. File management (Computer science) I. Title.
QA76.76.U84K78 1988
005.4'3—dc19 88-3935
ISBN 0-13-467887-7 CIP

DEDICATION

If she is Snow White, then I must be Grumpy.

Acknowledgement

I wish to extend my thanks to Brad Kingsbury, John Socha, and the people at Peter Norton Computing for their cooperation and advice.

Limits of Liability and Disclaimer of Warranty

Trademarks

Contents

Preface

The highest compliment I can give the programs discussed in this book, the Norton Utilities, the Norton Commander, and the Norton Editor is to say that I never go to an office without taking them. They are the basic toolkit you need to begin problem solving on an IBM PC or compatible.

While the programs are widely known, there has always been a reluctance to write books about "small" programs. Everyone wants to publish books about 1-2-3 and WordPerfect but programs like the Norton Utilities can play as important a role in a computer user's life as a major application.

The programs provided by Peter Norton Computing are outstanding examples of how simple, well designed utility programs can enhance any MS-DOS system and remove many of the delays and frustrations that arise when you work with MS-DOS by itself.

The purpose of this book is to explore the features and uses of these programs and to teach you how to get the most out of the programs and your MS-DOS system.

The book has 14 chapters divided into five major sections.

Section I: Fundamental Concepts

This section is designed as an educational discussion covering the fundamental concepts of DOS operations. In this section the Norton Utilities programs are used to explore MS-DOS so you can actually see the way DOS organizes disks. This section demonstrates how you can use the Norton Utilities programs to educate yourself about your computer.

Section II: Batch Files

Section II explores the use of batch files and how the Norton Utilities programs can be used to enhance DOS batch file operations. This section explores many DOS techniques, including methods of using the Norton Utilities to create a system of hard disk menus.

Section III: Everyday Tasks

This section covers the type of everyday operations in which the Norton Utilities programs can be used to improve your systems operation, such as file organization, searching hard disks, organizing directories, and file protection.

Section IV: Organizational Tasks

This section includes information on how to organize and protect your files.

Section V: Survival Skills

This section covers critical operations such as recovering lost files, unformatting hard disks, and finding and fixing disk errors.

Section VI: Other Programs

This section covers the Norton Commander, the Norton Editor, and the Norton Guides.

Each section is a complete hands-on, step by step instruction about using the utilities and other programs.

This book was written for Version 4.0 of the Advanced Edition of the Norton Utilities. If you have an earlier version you may find that some of the features described in this book will not be contained in that version.

Rob Krumm

Introduction

It is a true pleasure for me on behalf of all my colleagues at Peter Norton Computing to introduce this official guide to the whole assortment of utility software that we publish. Rob Krumm first wrote about The Norton Utilities in 1986 in *Getting the Most from Utilities on the IBM PC.* Since then we've gotten to know each other better, and our mutual respect and friendship have grown steadily.

While he was writing this book, Rob practically became part of the family at Peter Norton Computing. That's why you see on the cover not just me, but my good friend, co-author, and colleague, John Socha, the director of Research and Development at Peter Norton Computing. John is, of course, the co-author of *Peter Norton's Assembly Language Book for the IBM PC,* and he is also one of the most gifted and original software developers working today. Along with the whole Peter Norton team he worked closely with Rob Krumm to make this book a definitive guide not only to both versions of The Norton Utilities, but also to the Norton Commander, The Norton Editor, and the newest members of our product line, The Norton Guides.

Why did The Norton Utilities become such popular software? Well, industry wisdom has it that software becomes a standard either by providing superior capabilities or by solving problems that were previously unsolvable. In 1982, when I sat down at my PC to write Unerase, I was solving a common problem to which there was no readily available solution. Since then we've added to Unerase utilities to deal with common traps and pitfalls of computer operations. At Peter Norton Computing we've steadily expanded and improved these utilities to help you understand and control the computer better. With these products you control the whole environment beneath individual applications to manage your files, arrange your hard disk effectively, and to get yourself out of emergency situations caused by an accidental erase or delete command.

When I wrote *Inside the IBM PC* in 1984 I began it with these words:

> This is the beginning of a marvelous voyage of discovery into the secrets, wonders, and mysteries of the IBM Personal Computer and the family of computers that has grown up around it.

That book and the subsequent books have been one part of the shared voyage of discovery that I and millions of readers have undertaken. The growing family of utility products from Peter Norton Computing has been the other part. Now, for the first time, Rob Krumm brings both streams together to the benefit of both the readers and the more than one million users of Norton utility software. Rob has created the one book that should accompany every copy of our utility software. I recommend it unhesitatingly to everyone who has read one of my books or used any Peter Norton Computing software.

Peter Norton

SECTION I
FUNDAMENTAL CONCEPTS

The purpose of Section I is to provide the reader with a basic understanding of the concepts used throughout this book. These concepts underlie many of the operations and techniques that involve the use of the Norton Utilities, the Norton Commander, the Norton Editor, and the Norton Guides.

Each section contains a complete hands-on, step-by-step sequence of commands that address the specific topics being discussed. It is not strictly necessary to read Chapter 1 of Section I in order to perform the operations related to those topics. However, this section provides some background information that explains the basis upon which MS-DOS computers operate. The understanding of that is crucial to the education of any computer user. While there are many good books on MS-DOS on the market, the information supplied in this section is valuable for two reasons:

1. The information provides a conceptual basis for the operation of the Norton Computing programs discussed in this book. It is designed to touch on important themes and concepts expanded upon in other sections of the book.

2. By using the facilities of the main Norton Utilities program, this section includes a hands-on exploration of how disks store data. Because the Norton Utilities program enables you to display

information that DOS is not capable of displaying, you can gain insight into the structure and use of disks. That would not be possible if the subject of the book were limited to MS-DOS alone.

For those of you who want to skip this section and jump into specific operations right away, cross references to the information contained in this section are provided in various places throughout the book where allusions to these concepts are made.

1

MEMORY VS. STORAGE

It is not uncommon for people to become disoriented by the technical language they encounter when they begin to work with computers. Language is technical not necessarily because it contains strange new words, although there are some terms that are specific to computers. The majority of the problems with computer terminology arise from the use of some very ordinary words. The difference is that these words have a specific, narrow meaning as opposed to their broader, more general usage.

The most important terms in a computer-oriented vocabulary consist of some very ordinary words borrowed from the general lexicon. It is possible to start with the general meaning of these words and by some reflection arrive at a meaning approximating their technical use. The two most important terms to understand are **memory** and **storage** (albeit, information storage).

To demonstrate, let's begin with a simple question: "What are the dates of the Mexican-American War?" There are two ways you could respond to this question. If you knew the dates you could answer the question. But if you did not know the dates what could you do? The obvious method is to seek out some resource, such as an almanac or encyclopedia, and look up the information. Once the information is found you could answer the question.

The process just described is a common, everyday experience, which contains the outline of the distinction between what is meant by computer memory and computer storage. When the question is asked, the first step is to see if you carried that information in your personal memory. What characteristics does that memory possess? First, there is easy access. The information stored in your memory is easy to get. In fact, it seems to take little or no effort to access that information; it simply pops out.

However, not everyone can answer the question from memory—perhaps they have never been exposed to the information. More likely, they knew the information at one time but the information is no longer in their memory. What does this tell you about the nature of memory? Memory is subject to change—the second characteristic. The set of information contained in your memory today is different from what it contained 10 years ago or will contain 10 days from now.

This ability to change the contents of your memory is beneficial because it allows you to get rid of obsolete information and learn new, more significant information. Implicit in this idea is a third characteristic of memory. There would be no advantage to a changeable memory unless there was also a limit on the total amount of information the memory could hold. Because of this limit it is advantageous to discard some information in favor of other information.

Of course, human memory is not well understood. The exact limit of information is difficult to judge and some people claim humans subconsciously remember everything from womb to grave. But as a practical matter we accept the characteristics of memory as:

1. fast access
2. changeable
3. limit in capacity

What happens when you do not know the information and must seek additional information in a book? What sort of memory lies in a book? To answer that question you can compare the information stored in a book, on an audio or video tape, in a photograph, etc. with the characteristics associated with memory.

Begin with access, the first characteristic. Reading material from a book takes longer and is harder than simply remembering it. Also, the information stored in the book is useless by itself. It becomes useful only after it has been read (that is, placed into someone's memory.) Information stored in books, tapes, and other media, serve the purpose of providing information for memory. Until the information is transferred to a memory, the stored data has no meaning.

Is stored information subject to change the same way that memory is? The answer is no. In fact, the purpose of storage is to create a permanent reservoir of information. You would not expect ink to fade from a page the way the date of the Mexican-American War fades from your memory. Of course, permanence is a relative concept. Catastrophic events can destroy books or even words engraved in stone. But excluding such events, stored data is intended to be permanent.

The final characteristic is capacity. When considering stored information, it is clear that it is designed to be unlimited. (Unlimited, here, refers more to an economic definition than some cosmic infinity.) For stored information to be practical, a readily available, inexpensive, medium of storage is needed. For a long time, paper was the obvious choice. Today, electronic devices, such as computers, use a non-paper form of storage that serves the same purpose.

You can see that memory and storage are really reverse images of each other. Memory is fast, changeable, and limited, while storage is slower, permanent, and unlimited. This relationship between memory and storage applies to computers as well as human activity. Computer memory is hard to picture because it is usually not visible to the person using the computer. The memory consists of banks of memory chips located on the computer's main circuit board, or on expansion boards. The specific function of these chips is to hold information that is of immediate use to the computer.

Chips that perform this memory function are often referred to as **RAM**, which stands for Random Access Memory. Random Access refers to the method by which the computer retrieves information from memory chips. The term random, often misunderstood technically, has a common connotation of disorganization and haphazardness. However, in the computer context, random has come to mean multiple ways of accessing data, as opposed to a single order.

A good analogy can be made by exploring the differences between a novel and an encyclopedia. The novel is meant to be read from beginning to end. Starting in the middle or skipping around to different parts would be a misuse of the novel and fail to get the point across. When a system is designed to be read from beginning to end, with a single beginning and end point, it is referred to as a **sequential access** system. The encyclopedia, on the other hand, is designed to be read in small pieces, not from beginning to end. Reading the encyclopedia from beginning to end does not have an advantage over reading all the selections in some other order, dictated by your information needs. Because the encyclopedia can be read in an almost infinite number of sequences, it is a random access system.

The duration of human memory is uncertain, while the RAM memory used in microcomputers has a very definite duration cycle. The RAM holds information as long as there is a constant supply of power to the computer. When this supply is cut off, on purpose when you turn the machine off or by accident when there is a power failure, all the information in the memory is lost.

> Note that operations such as rebooting or resetting your computer will also wipe out the memory.

For this reason it is necessary to have a means of storing information. Computers can recognize a wide variety of stored information from many different devices including tapes, disks, optical character readers, and paper punch cards. In todays microcomputers, disks of varying types and capacities are almost the exclusive means of storing data. Remember that no matter what a disk looks like, hard or floppy, internal or external, local or remote network, they all serve the same function of storing information. The information on the disk cannot be used until it is loaded into the computer's memory in the same sense that information in a book is meaningless without a person to read it.

The advantages of stored information are many. For example, because memory can be changed easily, you can place different groups of information into the memory to conform to a specific task that you want to perform. When you are finished, the same memory can then be loaded with different information for another task. This ability gives both humans and computers much greater flexibility than would be possible with memory alone.

The terms **internal** and **external** memory are also used to refer to memory and storage. The difference in terminology is not important. What is important is the characteristic differences between the two types of information. Computer operations often involve a complex series of memory and storage operations. Keeping the distinction in mind will be helpful in understanding these tasks.

Data and Programs

So far, the term information has been used to describe the material stored in memory or on disk. Information falls broadly into two categories. The two categories appear in language as **verbs** (action words) and **nouns**, (words that represent **objects**.) This distinction quite naturally flows through into computer languages and structures. When a computer works with information it can be action oriented, that is, give instructions for operations, or object oriented, contain data that describes things. When a series of instructions are grouped together it is referred to as a **program**.

Computer programs are verb oriented because they are meant to carry out actions or operations. Today, most people purchase programs designed by other people rather than creating the programs themselves. Some programs provide means by which the user can create new actions, that is, verbs, by pasting the program's original verbs together in a new way. Such user defined commands are often called **macros**. Computer memory and storage can also record data about people, places, financial transactions, American history, and so on.

Like the pages of a notebook, disks can record either kind of information. Disks can hold programs as well as data. The same is true of the internal memory of the computer. In fact, it is always the case that the memory is holding some verbs (programs) and some objects (data). Data is usually entered by the people using the computer, although it is becoming more common to purchase some standard reference text such as dictionaries in disk-based format. Computer operations are always a combination of verbs acting on objects.

Disk Type

Disks play a crucial role in computer systems. They are the repositories for the accumulated information, verbs, and objects in the computer system. There are primarily two types of disks used in computers today, **hard disks** and **floppy disks**. The key distinction between the hard and floppy disk is that the hard disk contains nonremovable media, while a floppy disk system has two parts, a disk drive and a removable disk. The floppy disk got its name because it was made of a soft plastic called mylar. The disk was flexible enough to flop once it was removed from the drive. Hard disks are constructed of rigid aluminum. The important distinction between the disks is that hard disks are fixed into the disk drive and cannot be removed. In fact, hard disks are factory sealed units whose capacity is fixed when manufactured. Today, the average hard disk has a capacity of more than 20 million characters and some disks boast capacities in the area of 100 or 200 million characters. The capacity of floppy disks is much smaller than hard disks, an average 360,000 characters. However, the advantage is that the floppy disk can be removed and replaced with another. Today, 3.5 inch hard plastic disks are becoming more popular. These disks are not floppy but are classified as floppy disks because they are removable. Special drives allow you to insert and remove cartridges with capacities of 20 million characters. These are called removable hard disks because they have so large a capacity.

It might be better to classify disks as fixed or removable but the traditional names are hard to shake. The key to remember is that all disks, regardless of their type, serve the same purpose-to store information, programs and data, so that it can be loaded into the memory when needed.

Speed of Access

Another distinction between disks classified as hard and floppy is the speed at which the data is accessed. Hard disks characteristically have a much higher rate of transference of data between the disk and memory, usually 10 or more times faster than floppy disks. As with most technical specifications, you can measure the speed of a device in many ways. Disks can be timed for transfer rate, latency, seek time, and access time. Each measures one part of the operation necessary to move information between the memory and the disk.

One key number that helps provide some indication of the differences in the performance between hard and floppy disks is the number of rotations per minute, **RPM**. A record player spins an LP at 33.3 RPM. A floppy disk drive spins a disk at 300 RPM. A hard disk rotates at 3600 RPM. The faster rotation speed gives the hard disk much of its improved performance.

A Primer on Binary and Hexadecimal Numbers

The following section is provided for those readers that would like some background on the different types of notations used to express values in computers. Remember that **decimal**, **binary** and **hexadecimal** numbers are only different ways of expressing the same thing. The only variations are the forms in which the values are written. Since this is the case, understanding these numbering systems is a much simpler task than it sounds.

Number Systems

Why hexadecimal numbers? Why binary numbers? The answers to those question might be found by asking a more direct question: Why decimal numbers?

There is no special mathematical reason why a decimal system, that is, a numbering system based on ten digits—**0,1,2,3,4,5,6,7,8,9**—should be used instead of some other numbering system. The reasons are historical, cultural, and perhaps partly biological.

Most people are acquainted with another system of numbering, the system of Roman numerals, which works very differently from the one used everyday. In the Roman numeral system each digit has an exact value, no matter where it appears. For example in the Roman number II each I has a value of 1. The value of the number is arrived at by adding together each digit.

```
I + I = 2
```

In a Roman numeral system when a new digit is added, its position is irrelevant. The value of the number results from adding the values together.

```
I + I + I = 3
```

> Today, it is common to use IV as a Roman numeral for 4, and VI for 6. This is a modern practice. The Romans used IIII for 4, and either IV or VI would have represented 6.

In the decimal system, the orders in which the numbers appear, is quite significant. For example 123 has a very different value from 321 or 132. Why is order so significant? The reason is that the order in which the numbers are sequenced tells you their place value. Place value is something most people take for granted because it was learned early in their education. When you look at a number, you obtain its value by performing both addition and multiplication. First, each numeral is multiplied by its place value and then all the values are added together to arrive at the total value of the number.

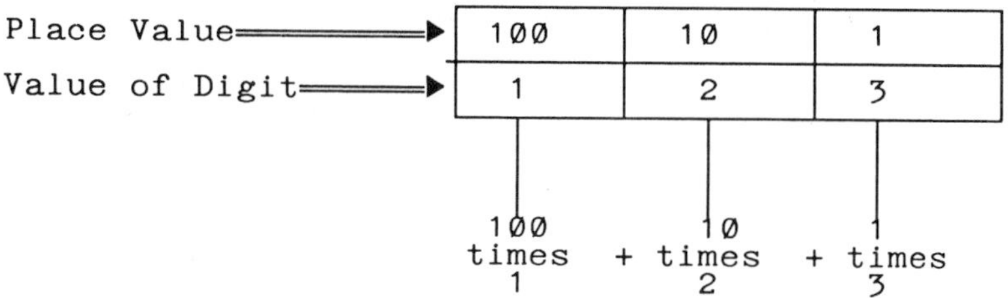

The concept of place values is based on the total number of digits used in a numbering system. There are ten numbers, 0,1,2,3,4,5,6,7,8, and 9, in the decimal system. The first place value is the ones place. The value of each of the following places is determined by multiplying by 10. Thus the values for place go from 1 to 10, 100, 1000, and so on.

But why must there be exactly ten digits? Why not 9 or 11? There actually is no reason why you could not construct a number system with any number of digits, as long as you had at least two. Thus, the simplest number system would be one that contained only two digits, 1 and 0. Such a system is called a binary system. In a binary system the place values are determined by multiples of 2 since there are only 2 digits. Thus, the value of each place doubles as you go to the left.

128	64	32	16	8	4	2	1

For example, if you wanted to write the number 27 in binary notation you would need to have one group of 16, plus one group of 8, plus one group of 2 and finally 1 group of 1.

16+8+2+1

To write a binary number you would place a 1 in the place value location where you wanted to add the value and a zero in the place value locations where you did not want the value added.

128	64	32	16	8	4	2	1
			1	1	Ø	1	1

The result is that the binary number 11011 is equal to the decimal number 27.

If your computer documentation requests the value of 100, be sure to question whether it is 100 decimal or 100 binary. Both systems share the 1 and the 0 characters, thus it is easy to get confused if you are not clear about which system of notation the information is describing.

Binary notation is very good at expressing computer operations because all computer operations are related to electronic switching elements. Like all switching mechanisms, computer operations have only two possible states, open or closed. These states can be represented by 0 for open and 1 for closed. A binary number has a direct one-to-one correspondence with the switch settings.

Binary digits, often referred to as "bits," are more cumbersome to read and write than decimal numbers. In many cases, an exact correspondence with the actual bits is not needed. You can summarize the value of long binary numbers by using the decimal values, which are shorter and easier to read. The decimal system is a higher level numbering system because it can represent larger values in fewer digits.

Decimal numbers have one disadvantage. Because they are based on a system of ten digits, there is no quick, simple way to convert between binary and decimal notation. It would be much simpler if the high level numbering system was a multiple of 2, which 10 is not. Because of this, computer scientists have tended to adopt a system that uses the increment of 2 closest to 10: 8 (octal notation) or 16 (hexadecimal notation).

In microcomputers, hexadecimal notation is the most widely used system. Since hexadecimal notation requires 16 digits and there are only 10 digits in the decimal system, it is necessary to add or invent some additional numbers. The traditional answer to this problem is to use the letters **A, B, C, D, E** and **F** as the six additional numbers.

Table 1.1. Decimal, Hexadecimal, and Binary Digits

Decimal	Hexadecimal	Binary
0	0	0
1	1	1
2	2	10
3	3	11
4	4	100
5	5	101
6	6	110
7	7	111
8	8	1000
9	9	1001
10	A	1010
11	B	1011
12	C	1100
13	D	1101
14	E	1110
15	F	1111

The hexadecimal system allows you to represent all of the binary numbers from 0 to 1111 with a single digit. Even more significantly, you can easily convert binary numbers to hexadecimal numbers. Below is an example of a binary number:

10110011

The first step in converting to hexadecimal is to break the number into groups of four digits each.

1011	0011

You can then match each four digit group with a hexadecimal digit.

Binary	1011	0011
Hexadecimal	B	3

Thus the hexadecimal number for 10110011 is B3. There is no quick conversion to the decimal number. To translate a hexadecimal number to a decimal number you must go through the process of multiplying each hexadecimal digit by its place value.

Hexadecimal	16	1
	B	3

Because B in hexadecimal notation stands for 11, the calculation is (11 times 16)+(3 times 1) which equals 179. You can see why going from binary to hexadecimal, or hexadecimal to binary, is much simpler than decimal conversion.

Bits, Bytes, and Words

Special types of notation, such as hexadecimal, are employed because they make references to actual computer data simpler and more direct, after you have gotten used to switching back and forth between different numbering systems.

In MS-DOS systems, and in most microcomputers, data is referred to in three ways. The smallest unit of data is the **bit**. A bit cannot be divided into a smaller unit because it represents a single switch setting inside the computer. All computer data is composed of bits. Normally, bits, representing single switches, are too small to be meaningful on the human level. When you work with a computer you are concerned with letters, numbers and other characters. The unit used to represent a single character is a **byte**. The byte is composed of eight bits, which together are used to represent a single character such as the letter A.

A byte is often said to be equal to the amount of space needed to store a single character. This is true but it can be misleading. Many applications such as spreadsheets or word processing programs always store information with additional data about its location, type, or format. For example, storing the number 1 in a spreadsheet cell will use up much more than a single byte because the spreadsheet program also records data about its location and format. In some instances it is common to use a unit of measure called a **word**. The term word has no grammatical meaning. Rather, it refers to two bytes of information taken together as a unit.

In the next chapter, the concepts discussed above will be put to use to explore the way disks operate. The Norton Utilities program will be used to see the operation of disk storage in a way not possible with DOS commands alone.

A Primer on Disk Structure

Disks, both hard and floppy, are organized in roughly the same way. The only difference between disks is the amount and number of features that they share in common.

All disks are divided into basic units of storage, called **sectors**. The amount of information stored on a disk is determined by the number of sectors that a disk contains. In theory, the size of the sector can vary. In practice, however, there is a remarkable conformity among MS-DOS computers. Each sector contains 512 bytes of information.

Disk sectors are created by dividing the disk into a series of concentric circles called **tracks**. The number of tracks on a typical floppy disk is 40, while a 20 megabyte hard disk will usually have over 600. (614 and 615 are common track numbers for 20 megabyte hard disks.) The disk is divided a second time, radially, by cutting the tracks into sections.

A floppy disk will usually have nine sectors on each track, while a hard disk will have seventeen sectors on each track. A disk will also have two sides, top and bottom, numbered 0 and 1. Hard disks actually consist of several disks stacked on top of one another, with space left between. A typical 20 megabyte disk drive contains two disk plates, sides 0 through 3.

You can calculate the total amount of space on a disk by multiplying the following:

```
sectors times tracks times sides by 512
```

For example, a floppy disk with 9 sectors per track, 40 tracks and two sides would be:

```
9 times 40 times 2 times 512 = 368,640
```

The capacity is referred to as 360K (kilobyte) per disk.

A hard disk with 17 sectors per track, 614 tracks and 4 sides would have a capacity of:

```
17 times 614 times 4 times 512 = 21,377,024
```

This would be referred to as a 20 megabyte disk. To keep track of the information on the hard disk, each sector is given a unique number. The first sector is 0, the second 1 and so on. A 360K disk will have 720 sectors, number 0–719. A 20 megabyte hard disk will have over 41,000 sectors.

The tracks and sectors are created by a process called **formatting**, which makes use of a special computer program called **FORMAT**. You cannot use a disk, hard or floppy, before it has been formatted.

When the format command is run, a disk will be divided into a number of tracks and sectors that must be numbered for identification. The format program also checks the integrity of the disk to make sure that all of the sectors will correctly accept data. If a defect is found the sector is marked unusable.

The complicated formatting process actually consists of two separate operations called low level and high level formatting. Low level (physical) formatting consists of placing electronic marks in the disk to imprint the physical locations of the tracks and sectors. Once the marking is in place, the high level formatting, also called logical formatting, organizes the sector's functions.

In MS-DOS computers, the two stage formatting of floppy disks is implemented with a single command, FORMAT. The same command, when applied to a hard disk, will perform only the high level formatting. The assumption is that the low level or physical formatting of the hard disk has already been done.

> Usually, low level formatting of hard disks is something the average user is never faced with. Suppose you wanted to perform a low level format on your hard disk. How would you do it?
>
> The supplier of the hard disk will usually provide a program that performs the low level format. IBM includes the program as part of the diagnostic disk.
>
> If you are using a compatible computer you may find that the program for formatting is not on a disk but built into the ROM on the hard disk controller card. To run this program you will have to use the DEBUG program to access the location in the memory where the program is stored. The typical address of a hard disk device is C800, such as with the popular Western Digital controller supplied with many hard disks.

The Role of DOS

The high level or logical disk formatting brings in the concept of the operating system. To understand what an operating system does, return to the analogy used to discuss memory and storage. If disk storage space is roughly analogous to a book, a disk drive is a sort of library in which data can be stored and then later retrieved.

As with a library, a record must be kept of which books are stored in the library and where they are located. A library without this type of organization is possible but not practical. The ancient library in Alexandria was reputed to have the finest collection of books in the world. But the scholars who gathered there seldom referred to the wisdom stored in the volumes because there was no organized retrieval system such as that used in modern libraries.

The same principles apply to disk storage. There must be a master librarian in the computer system responsible for keeping track of the data stored on the disk. The job requires constant attention because computers can save and then revise data very quickly. The master program that takes care of these library operations, as well as other crucial computer tasks, is called the operating system. **DOS** stands for **disk operating system,** which implies the type of storage device that will be used. **OS** or operating system is often used as well, usually on computers that can use different types of storage devices.

When DOS prepares a disk it builds new structures out of the sectors created by the low level format, during the high level formatting process. The first sector on the disk is called the boot sector. Then two other groups of sectors are set aside to hold information about the files stored on the disk. These two groups form a sort of card catalog for the disk. The two groups of sectors are called the **File Allocation Table** and the **Directory.** In this book you will use the Norton Utilities program to explore the structure of these areas in detail.

Once the areas of the disk needed for the card catalog—the File Allocation Table and the Directory—have been set aside, the rest of the disk is grouped into **data clusters**. A data cluster is the name given to the basic unit of storage on a disk. What is the difference between a cluster and a sector? Why are clusters needed?

The purpose of the cluster is to create a minimum allocation unit for data storage. Minimum allocation units are quite a common idea. For example, when you go to the market you cannot buy just one egg. Instead, the eggs are packaged in a minimum size carton that defines the minimum allocation unit.

The DOS librarian also has to consider what is the efficient minimum unit for disk storage. The amount of space defined as a cluster will vary in proportion to the size of the disk. On floppy disks, DOS usually allocates 2 sectors to each cluster:

```
512+512 = 1024
```

This means that the minimum allocation unit is 1,024 bytes of space. If you want to save a file with only 5 bytes, DOS will allocate 1,024 bytes for that file. On a hard disk, the total capacity is much larger, so the cluster size is increased. Typically, a hard disk will use a cluster size of 4 sectors, 4 times 512 or 2,048 bytes.

Once DOS has formatted a disk it is ready to receive data. It now has a structure in which to store data and record information about the data so that it can be retrieved. As part of the system, DOS requires that all data be given a name. The name, like a title of a book, is the logical handle by which a specific block of information can be located.

DOS recognizes three levels of organization in names for data, forming a hierarchy. For example, when you write an address on an envelope there are three parts that define the exact location:

1. State

2. City

3. Street

The largest unit is the state. Within the state is city and within city is the street. This type of system allows you to use the same street but in different cities or states. For example, the address below uses the same street name but are clearly different because they are related to a different city and state.

Pine Street, Philadelphia, PA

Pine Street, Walnut Creek, CA

The DOS logical naming system uses volumes, directories and filenames. Below is a typical name for a file:

```
c:\dos\ansi.sys
```

The name really consists of three parts. Each part corresponds to one of the three organizational levels recognized by DOS.

Volume	Directory	File Name
c:	\dos\	ansi.sys

A volume in DOS is one disk drive, hard or floppy. A directory is a unit that is smaller than a disk but larger than a file. It is a kind of file folder in which groups of related files can be gathered together.

In DOS, volumes contain directories, and directories contain files. On low volume disks, such as floppies, most users skip the directory level of organization. But it is important to remember that DOS creates at least one directory on each formatted disk, called the **root directory**. Note also the punctuation that DOS uses to identify the organizational parts:

C: Volumes are single letters with a colon.

\ The backslash is used to mark off a name of a directory. If no name is used with the \, the root directory is assumed.

Commands in DOS

The major functions of DOS take place behind the scenes. When you run programs such as word processors, spreadsheets or data bases, DOS performs a variety of tasks behind the scenes that allow those programs to operate. As a computer user you are not exposed to the details of those operations. However, the decision about what disk, directory and filename should be used for storing data are up to you. In addition, the tasks of maintaining this data library require you to manually enter specific instructions to DOS.

These instructions cover a wide range of operations from erasing old files, making duplicates, creating directories, copying programs from floppies to hard disks to making backups of data. You will have to tell DOS to load and execute programs.

Most people approach DOS commands and operations as if they were a list of specific commands to memorize. But a better way to look at DOS is as a language that consists of verbs and objects.

Grammar

Computer languages and command environments, like human languages, have a fundamental structure from which all the commands can be constructed. DOS works with six basic elements:

1. commands
2. delimiters
3. parameters
4. options switches
5. file specifications / wildcards
6. input/output devices

The most important rule is that all DOS entries must begin with a command. While every DOS command begins with a command word, it is usually followed by one or several of the basic elements above.

DOS commands are really the verbs of the DOS language. They represent the basic actions that DOS can perform and are divided into two major classifications:

1. **Internal Commands.** These commands are contained in the memory of the computer at all times when the DOS prompt is displayed. Because these commands are internal, no special disks or files need be present in the computer to execute an internal command.

2. **External Commands.** These commands are really small computer programs that are stored in disk files until they are needed. External commands are loaded each time they are requested and are erased from memory when the command is finished.

Both types of commands have their advantages and disadvantages. Internal commands are always available because they reside in the memory whenever DOS is active. However, internal memory is limited in a computer. If you increase the number of DOS commands that are resident in the memory of the computer, you decrease the amount of room that can be used for programs and their data.

External commands occupy internal memory only when they are being executed. Otherwise they reside in the external storage medium like other programs and data files. External commands make efficient use of the internal memory, but they are slower to execute than internal commands because they must be loaded into the internal memory each time they are used. In addition, the external commands must be stored on disk space that is immediately available to the computer or these commands cannot be executed. On floppy disk systems, where storage is limited, this can be a problem.

Internal Commands

Internal commands are the ones that are always available when the systems prompt is displayed. Naturally, they are the commands that you will need to use most frequently. Examples:

`CLS`	clears screen
`COPY`	transfers data from one device to another
`CHDIR` or `CD`	changes active directory
`DIR`	lists filenames
`ERASE` or `DEL`	deletes files
`MKDIR` or `MD`	creates directory
`PATH`	sets search path
`RENAME` or `REN`	renames a file
`RMDIR` or `RD`	removes empty directory
`TYPE`	displays files contents
`VER`	displays DOS version number

The commands listed above have one thing in common. They can be executed at any time that you see the DOS system's prompt. There is no need for any special disk to be present.

External Commands

External commands are not kept resident in the memory of the computer but are loaded from files stored on the disk when you request them. Thus if you ask for an external command and DOS cannot find the corresponding program file on the disk, the command will not operate. In order to access external commands you must make sure that they are available by copying the files from the DOS system's disk onto the disk you are using. DOS external commands are optional. Experience and need will indicate which external commands you require. Hard disk users often copy all the external command files onto the hard disk. Examples are:

`FORMAT`	prepares disks for data
`CHKDSK`	checks disk integrity
`EDLIN`	line editor program
`MODE`	selects output, screen modes
`BACKUP`	backup hard disk
`RESTORE`	restores backup files
`PRINT`	prints text files
`ASSIGN`	swaps drive designations
`TREE`	lists directories

```
SORT          sorts screen output
FIND          searches screen output
MORE          pauses screen display output
```

Parameters and Delimiters

Parameters are additional pieces of information added to commands, and fill the same role in DOS commands that the object does in human languages. Parameters indicate what will be effected by the command. For example, the command DEL deletes a file from the disk. However, simply entering DEL as a command to DOS is incomplete. DOS needs to know what you want to delete before it can carry out the command. To create a valid command you would have to supply a filename. Example:

```
DEL FORMAT.COM
```

The command has two parts: **DEL** is the command; **FORMAT.COM** is the parameter. Notice that there is a space between the command and the parameter. The space is an important part of the grammar of DOS; commands must be separated from their parameters by such delimiters. The space, in this instance, serves to delimit or punctuate the command. Without the delimiter the command would not be interpreted properly.

File Specification and Wildcards

There are times when you will find it advantageous to refer to files in a more general way. When you issue a command you may want to refer to more than one file at a time, so that the command entered can act upon more than one file.

For example, suppose there were 50 files on a disk that needed erasing. You might enter 50 commands, one to erase each file. However, the most convenient way would be to use a **wildcard**. The purpose of DOS wildcards is to refer to a group of files with a single command. DOS recognizes two special characters as wildcards: ? and *. The * is even more general than the ?. An * used in a filename indicates that any characters beginning at that position and continuing to the end of the filename or extension are acceptable. For example, entering *.PAY would refer to all files with a PAY extension.

```
MARY.PAY
MORRIS.PAY
JOE.PAY
SUE.PAY
```

```
WALTER.PAY
SAM.PAY
```

If you entered M*.PAY you would get

```
MARY.PAY
MORRIS.PAY
```

When * is used DOS does not care how many characters follow the specified characters. One of the most common wildcards is *.*. When *.* is used it tells DOS to use all the files contained in a directory. Most DOS commands and many programs allow you to enter file specifications with wildcard characters.

Options and Switches

Options affect how a command is carried out. They function as adverbs do in human languages, modifying the action of the command verb. Not all commands have options, but those that do have may have several. Options can be inclusive or exclusive of each other depending upon the command. If options are inclusive, they will function at the same time and produce a combined effect. The usual form for an option is a slash followed by a letter. DIR also has a /P option that pauses the listing when the screen is filled. This makes it easier to read the directory display. The command below shows how two options can be used at once.

```
DIR/W/P
```

The number of options varies with each command and some commands have no options at all. The options entered with / are also called switches because they turn on or off various features of the command.

Paths

If a disk has more than one directory, the path or pathname refers to the name of the file and the names of the directory and/or subdirectories that contain the file. Pathnames are needed to locate files that may be stored in various directories. When you instruct the computer to use a file on the disk the computer has to know what directory to look in. If you do not correctly identify the file and its pathname, the computer won't find the file. The term full pathname refers to the complete name of a file and the directories in which it is contained. For example:

```
\ACCOUNT\PAYROLL\WORKERS.88
```

This means that there is a file WORKERS.88 stored in the PAYROLL subdirectory of the ACCOUNT directory. Note that the pathname lists the items in descending order, generally with the filename coming last. The drive can be added to the pathname. Below is an example of the full drive and pathname of a file.

```
C:\ACCOUNT\PAYROLL\WORKERS.88
```

File Types

There are two basic types of files stored on computer disks.

Binary Files

Binary files are long sequences of numbers that contain coded information to be read directly by the computer. The microprocessor in your computer contains enough information to break the number sequence codes and interpret them as commands and or/data. Most programs are provided in the binary form. By convention, files that are program files carry either a COM or EXE extension.

Binary program files are microprocessor-specific. This means that a program written for an IBM PC will run only on a computer that has the same decoder set as the IBM.

If data is stored in a binary file it is likely that only the program and computer it was designed to operate with can understand the data.

ASCII Files

ASCII stands for the **A**merican **S**tandard **C**ode for **I**nformation **I**nterchange. This code creates files that are stored in a format common to many different programs and computers. Storage in ASCII format is usually less compact than binary storage. However, the advantage is that ASCII provides a common basis for the interchange of information.

As a computer user you will want to be aware of which programs work with ASCII files. Programs that can read and write ASCII files can exchange information with other programs that do the same. Programs that use only their own specially coded binary files are much more limited in sharing information.

ASCII provides 128 standard representations. These 128 ASCII characters include all of the characters shown on the normal keyboard, plus characters that represent special keys, such as <Esc>, <return>, and <Tab>. A file that is standard ASCII format means that any program that reads standard files can read and understand the information contained in that file. Therefore, the terms ASCII file, DOS text file, text file and ASCII standard file, all refer to the same thing. The IBM PC and compatible computers have a built-in character set that consists of 256 characters. The additional characters are those such as the accented e and the Greek letters used in mathematics. The entire set of characters, the 128 ASCII characters and the 128 other characters displayed by the IBM PC, is referred to as the **extended character set**.

All of the 128 standard ASCII characters can be represented with only seven bits. You can confirm this by calculating the number of possibilities with seven bits. Each bit can have only two options, ON or OFF. A seven-bit number can be arranged in 2 to the seventh power, or 128, different ways. But the eight bit structure used by the IBM PC allows you to represent data with eight bits. That means there are 2 to the eighth power, or 256, possible arrangements.

The Norton Utilities program have much in common with DOS commands. You will notice that the entry of Norton Utilities instructions work just about the same way as DOS commands using parameters, option switches and file specifications.

Setup for Working with This Book

In order to create a detailed, hands-on, interactive book about the Norton Utilities programs it is necessary to make some assumptions about the computer you are working with. Inevitably these assumptions will make some of the exact procedures presented in this book vary with the results on your computer.

This book assumes that you are working with a MS-DOS computer that has at least one hard and one floppy disk drive. The type of monitor you have is not particularly significant. The parts of the book that deal with menu batches assume that you are working with a single color (black and white if you have a color system).

The assumption is made that you are using a version of DOS 3.1 or higher. If you are using DOS 2 level, all of the operations in these sections will work but there will be some differences in the exact size and location of some files. These differences are noted in the text and should not cause you undue confusion.

The book also assumes that you have a copy of the Norton Utilities 4.0 Advanced edition. Section V deals with other products from Peter Norton Computing: the Norton Commander, the Norton Editor and the Norton Guides. You will probably want to read these sections even though you do not have the programs. The information contained is invaluable to potential solutions for problems and needs you might encounter.

Sections I through IV assume that you have loaded the Norton Utilities programs into a directory on your hard disk, called \DOS.

> Many users put their Norton Utilities programs in a sepatate directory, e.g. \NORTON. My personal preference is to place them in \DOS. The advantage is that you can access the programs by keeping a single path open to the \DOS directory.

This is a reflection of my own personal preference to place all my DOS utilities and Norton Utilities programs in the same directory. If you want to create this directory you can do so by entering the DOS command:

```
md c:\dos ↵
```

> If the message "cannot create directory" appears DOS is telling you that the directory already exists.

The assumption is made that you have already placed all the DOS utility programs supplied with your computer into this directory. The Norton Utilities program can be added to the directory by using the DOS copy command.
Example:

```
copy a:*.* c:\dos ↵
```

Repeat the command for both disks.

> If you have any of the other programs, the Commander, Editor, or Guides, they too can be loaded onto the hard disk. They will not be used until Section V, however.

In addition to placing the files on the hard disk, you must have access to the files. This means that a PATH should be opened to the \DOS directory using the DOS command PATH. To check the open paths, if any, enter

```
path ↵
```

If the path is not open at this time, open it by entering

```
path c:\dos; ↵
```

You should have this path open at all times while you are working. You might want to modify the AUTOEXEC.BAT file to include this command.

> If you are not familiar with AUTOEXEC.BAT see Section II, Batch Files.

With the Norton Utilities programs installed and the path open to the directory in which they are stored, you are ready to begin. This book assumes that you will begin working from the root directory of the hard disk. To change to that directory, enter

```
cd\ ↵
```

2

A HANDS-ON PRIMER ON DISK ORGANIZATION

The Norton Utilities programs provide a unique means by which you can inspect and analyze the operations of your computer when it comes to storing information on the disk. This means that you can see for yourself, not just read about the way a disk is actually organized.

Instead of discussing ideas of how a disk is used to store data, this section will present those ideas using hands-on exploration. The examples in this section use MS-DOS 3.2. If you have a different version of DOS, your screen and values will be slightly different, but the principles will remain the same. The first step is to format a 360K disk. If you are using a PC, XT or compatible, enter

```
format a: ↵
```

If you are using an AT or compatible with a 1.2 megabyte drive, enter

```
format a:/4 ↵
```

Answer the prompts that appear. When the disk has been formatted, you are ready to begin.

Examining Disk Structure

When you format a disk you are doing something very important: You are creating an organizational structure on the disk that will enable DOS to store information. To understand that structure and how it works, use the Norton Utilities to display information about the disk. Enter

`nu a:` ↵

The Norton Utilities main program menu appears.

```
The Norton Utilities  Advanced Edition  (C) Copr 1987, Peter Norton
            1:44 am, Sunday, December 20, 1987

                       Main menu

                     Explore disk
                     UnErase
                     Disk information
                     Quit the Norton Utilities

            View, edit, search, or copy selected item

Item type   | Drive | Directory name            | File name
Directory   |  A:   | \                         | Root dir
```

Figure 2-1

The program is divided into three parts: (1) **Explore Disk**, which allows you to explore in detail the exact information stored on the disk. You can also use these options to modify the information stored on the disk; (2) **unErase**, which contains a series of special commands and procedures that help you recover data from files that have been erased. (Unerasing is covered in detail in Section IV.); and (3) **disk information**, which displays summary information about the disk.

Disk Information

Your exploration of the disk will begin with the third option on the menu, disk information. Enter

d

The Disk Information menu consists of two parts: (1) **Map disk usage**, which displays a visual representation of the disk; and (2) **Technical information**, which lists the values for the current disk.
Enter

↵

The program displays a map of the disk.

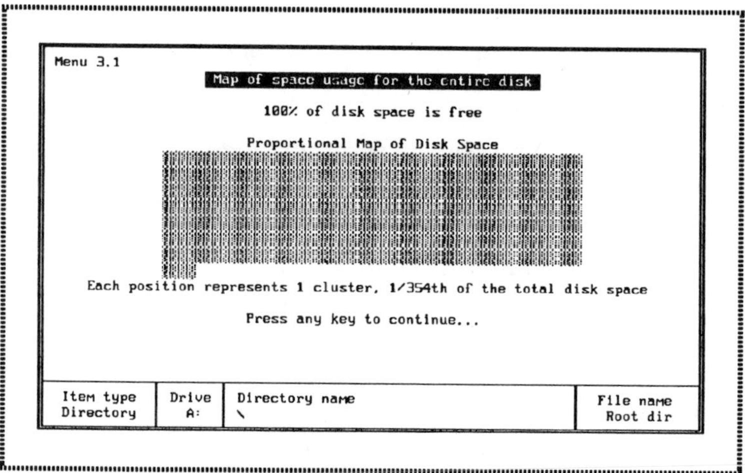

Figure 2-2

The map is designed to show which parts of the disk are used and which are free for new data. Because you have just formatted the disk, all of the data space is empty. As you add information to the disk, the map will change to reflect the locations in which data is stored. Display the technical information by entering

↵
t

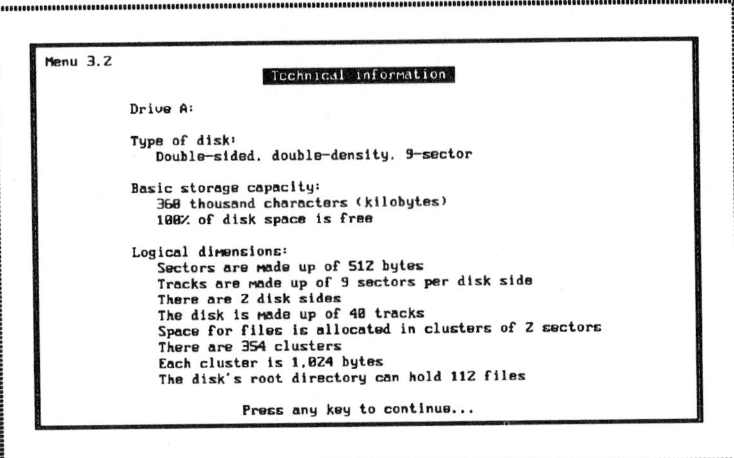
Menu 3.2

Technical information

Drive A:

Type of disk:
Double-sided, double-density, 9-sector

Basic storage capacity:
360 thousand characters (kilobytes)
100% of disk space is free

Logical dimensions:
Sectors are made up of 512 bytes
Tracks are made up of 9 sectors per disk side
There are 2 disk sides
The disk is made up of 40 tracks
Space for files is allocated in clusters of 2 sectors
There are 354 clusters
Each cluster is 1,024 bytes
The disk's root directory can hold 112 files

Press any key to continue...

Figure 2-3

The technical information screen lists three basic types of information about the disk: (1) **Type of disk**; (2) **Storage capacity**, which tells you the total capacity of the disk and what percentage is currently used for data storage; and (3) **Logical Dimensions**, which contains a number of special measurements that describe in detail how the storage capacity of the disk is organized.

The last group of values, the description of how a disk is organized, is very important. In this example, the values shown reflect the way DOS arranges a 360K floppy disk.

Sector Size

The sector is the basic unit of storage on a disk. In MS-DOS the size of the sector is determined when the disk is formatted. In almost all cases that size is 512 bytes. The sector is the smallest unit of storage on the disk.

> DOS is capable of dealing with a variety of sector sizes. The 512 byte sector size is the most commonly used size. Because compatibility is so important to the average user, almost all hardware and software suppliers recognize 512 as the standard size for sectors. Only rarely will you encounter an exception.

For more information on sector and tracks, you are referred to the earlier discussion on DOS, in this section.

Return to the main menu by entering

[Esc] (2 times)

Organization

The Norton Utilities program allows you to get a glimpse of the way the disk is organized. Enter

e
c
s

This displays the **Select Sector** menu, which allows you to display individual sectors. With this ability you can look at the actual contents of any of the sectors on the disk.

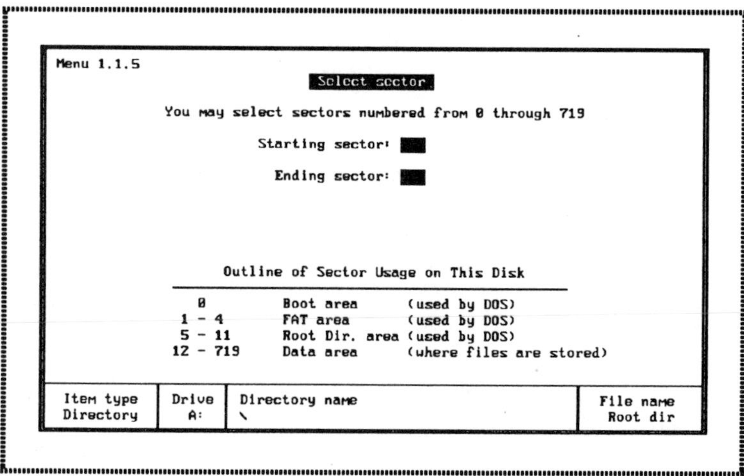

Figure 2-4

The bottom of the display shows that the disk is divided into four basic parts.

Boot Area

The boot area is the first sector on the disk. In the boot area DOS writes information about how the disk is organized. This enables DOS to work with a variety of floppy and hard disks with different capacities. Because each disk carries with it a description of its organization, DOS can adjust to disks of different sizes. The boot area takes up one sector.

FAT Area

FAT stands for File Allocation Table. This is an important table used by DOS to assign the disk sectors to various files. For each sector on the disk there is an entry in the file allocation table that tells DOS if the sector is in use by a file, and if so, which one. The size of the file allocation table will vary with the size of the disk. The larger the capacity of the disk, the larger the file allocation table must be to keep track of all of the sectors.

Directory

The directory is the area of the disk reserved for keeping information about the file stored on that disk. The directory stores the filenames, dates, size and other necessary information. Combined with the information stored in the file allocation table, the directory enables DOS to store and retrieve data from the disk. Keep in mind that damage to the file directory will make it difficult or even impossible to locate files.

Data Area

All the space on the disk left over after the boot, FAT, and directory areas, is data space. It is in these sectors that the actual information is stored.

Begin exploring the disk by looking at the boot sector. Note the entry should be the number zero, not the letter O. Enter

You have selected the boot sector of the disk. To display its contents, enter

e

The Norton Utilities program displays the information from the boot sector on the screen. Note that the display is broken into two parts. The left half of the screen shows the hexadecimal values for each byte. The right half shows the IBM character for that byte.

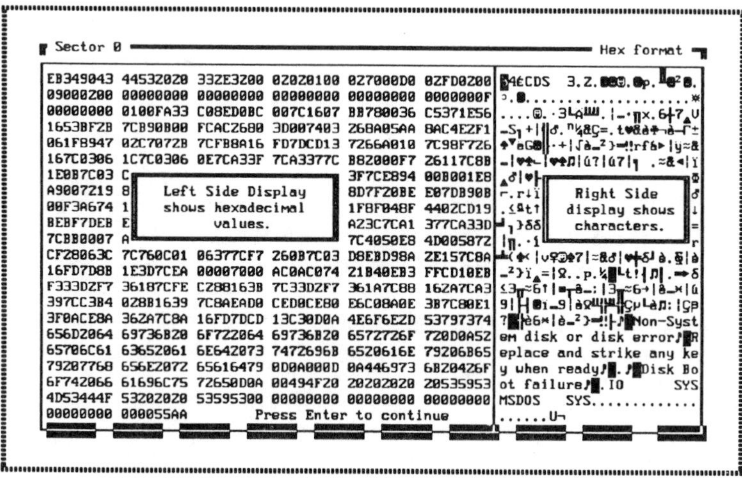

Figure 2-5

The information in the sector is numbered by each byte of information. The first byte is 0, the next 1, and so on. The Norton Utilities program keeps track of your cursor location by the byte number. If you look at the upper-right hand corner of the display you will see the byte to which the cursor is positioned.

You can switch between the hexadecimal and character displays by entering

`[Tab]`

The cursor jumps to the right side of the display. Use the arrow keys to change the location of the cursor. Enter

`[right arrow]` (3 times)

This places the cursor on byte 3. This is the place in the boot sector where the manufacturer's ID is placed. In the example the letter CDS stands for Cordata Data Systems. If you have an IBM version of DOS, your screen will show IBM. The ID also shows the version number of DOS used to format this disk. In this example, 3.20.

Following the ID section are a series of values that detail how this disk is to be organized. For example, the sector size is stored in bytes 11 and 12. You can locate these bytes by moving your cursor and watching the offset counter. In this case you will find that byte 11 holds the value of 00 and byte 12 holds the value 02.

These two bytes taken together form a single hexadecimal number that is equal to the sector size. The hexadecimal value is 0200. If you remember the discussion on hexadecimal numbers you will recall that the place values in hexadecimal notation are multiples of 16, not 10.

Place Value	4096	256	16	1
Hexadecimal	Ø	2	Ø	Ø

Translated to decimal value, 0200 is 2 times 256 or 512, which is exactly the value displayed in the Disk information. The Norton Utilities program reads the boot sector of the disk and displays the information in an easy to read format.

> You may wonder how it is that the number 0200 was used and not 0002, since byte 11 was 00 and byte 12 was 02. The answer has to do with the way values are read from the disk. When a value is composed of two bytes it is called a word. The first byte is called the low order byte while the second is called the high order byte. This is backwards from the human point of view since we tend to write numbers beginning with the highest place values on the left. Thus, if the data on the disk reads 01 F0, the hexadecimal values is F001.

If you look at the bottom of the sector you will see some messages you may have encountered while using your computer. It is in the boot track that the nonsystem disk message is stored. Also at the end of the sector are the names of the two hidden MS-DOS files. The program stored in the boot sector will search the disk for these two files when you boot your computer.

Now that you have looked at the boot sector, you will exit the Norton Utilities program. Enter

`[Esc]` (3 times)

How Files Are Stored

You can use your newly formatted disk to examine the changes that occur when you store a file. As an example, copy the COMMAND.COM file from your hard disk to the floppy disk in drive A. Enter

```
copy command.com a: ↵
```

> Copying the COMMAND.COM file to a formatted disk does not make that disk a bootable system disk. To be a bootable disk the two hidden MS-DOS files, the BIO and BDOS files, should have been placed on the disk with the SYS command before any files were copied to the disk. Keep in mind that the actual names of these files will vary with the computer you are using. IBM uses the names IBMBIO.COM and IBMDOS.COM while many MSDOS compatible computers use IO.SYS and MSDOS.SYS.

Restart the Norton Utilities program so that you can examine what changes, if any, have taken place. Enter

```
nu a: ↵
```

First, display the disk map. Enter

```
d
m
```

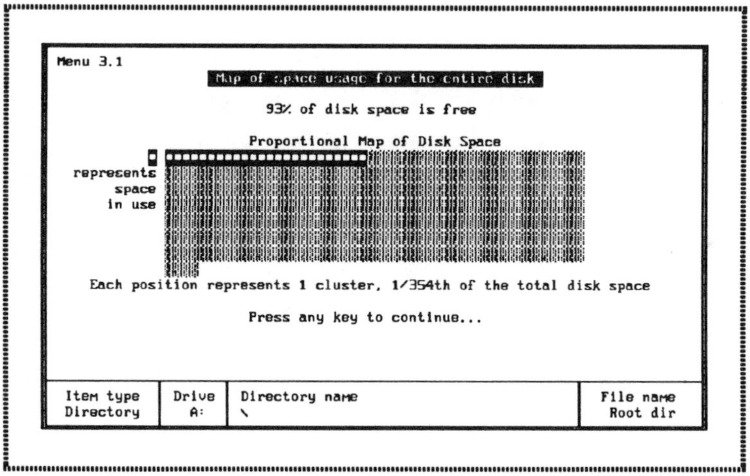

```
Menu 3.1
                 Map of space usage for the entire disk

                        93% of disk space is free

                     Proportional Map of Disk Space
            ▪
   represents
        space
       in use

   Each position represents 1 cluster, 1/354th of the total disk space

                     Press any key to continue...

 Item type | Drive | Directory name            | File name
 Directory |  A:   | \                         | Root dir
```

Figure 2-6

The map now shows that a portion of the disk, about 7 percent, is filled with data. Return to the main menu by entering

`[Esc]` (2 times)

The next step is to examine the directory and FAT areas to see how the new file was recorded. Enter

Display the contents of the directory by entering

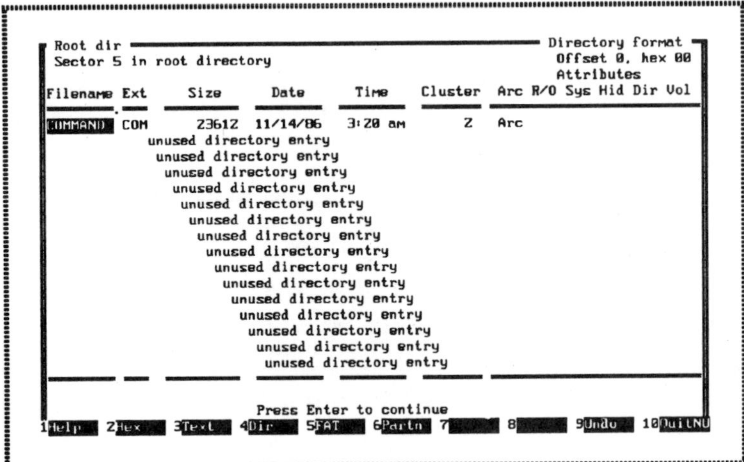

Figure 2-7

The directory display reveals the information that DOS stores about each file added to the disk.

1. **Filename.**

2. **Extension.**

3. **Size in Bytes.** It is important to note that the value recorded for the size of the file is different from the total amount of space used by the file. Because DOS allocates space by data clusters of a fixed size, it is unlikely that a file will end exactly at the end of a data cluster. More often, a file will end in the middle of the last data cluster, leaving some slack space at the end of the cluster that is not actually filled by the file. However, since the smallest unit DOS allocates to a file is a data cluster, no other file can use that slack space. The Norton Utilities program, FS (file size), does measure this space and the difference between the DOS file size and the actual space used by the file on the disk.

4. **Date & Time.** Date and time are taken from the system's clock at the time a file is created or modified.

5. **Cluster.** This is the number of the starting cluster of the file. In this example, the file begins at data cluster 2. If a file contains more than one cluster, the location of the other clusters is stored in FAT.

6. **Attributes.** Each file can be assigned one or more attribute. The attributes are archive, read-only, system, hidden, volume label, or directory. The archive, read-only, system, hidden, volume label, are discussed in detail in Section IV on unerasing. The directory attribute will be discussed in this section.

The current directory entry for COMMAND.COM shows that the first part of the file is stored in cluster 2 and that it has an archive attribute. The archive attribute is automatically assigned to a file when it is created.

In this case, copying a file also creates a new file which is marked for archive. The purpose of archive is to indicate which of the files should be backed up when the DOS backup program is used. BACKUP accepts a switch, /M, that selects only for files with an archive attribute.

The Norton Utilities program allows you to change the display mode of the data. In this case the Norton Utilities program automatically selects the directory display mode because the information on the disk is stored in the directory format.

The menu bar at the bottom of the screen shows the five display modes available.

F2 **Hex.** This mode displays the bytes stored on the disk in hexadecimal notation. This mode is the most literal display of information since it displays exactly what is stored on the disk.

F3 **Text.** This mode attempts to display information in a text format similar to a word processor or editor. In this mode, bytes that are not normally included in text files are ignored. Also, hex number 1A, 26 in decimal, is treated as an end of file marker.

F4 **Dir.** This format is used to display directory information in an easy to read format.

F5 **FAT.** This format is designed to display the file allocation table in a format that makes it easy to read.

F6 **Partn.** This format is used to show the partition table stored in the boot sector, sector 0, of a disk. The partition table is used to divide a hard disk into several separate sections. Most DOS users place all of the hard disk space into a single DOS partition.

Formats Hex(F2) and Text(F3) can be applied to any part of the disk. The other formats can only be useful when you are looking at the specialized areas on a disk such as the directory, FAT, or boot sector. Change to the hex display mode by entering

[F2]

In the upper left-hand corner, **Root dir** appears indicating that you are looking at the root directory of the disk. Below that the program reveals that the root directory begins in sector 5 of the disk.

Each directory entry consists of 32 bytes. The first 11 bytes are used to store the filename. You can recognize the filename COMMAND.COM as it appears in the right-hand panel.

```
 Root dir ──────────────────────────────────────────────── Hex format
                               ry                           t 0, hex 00
434F4D4D 414E4420 434F4D  ◄─── 000 00000000 0000841A  COMMAND COM ..........ä→
                          0 0000 000 00000000 00000000             ...........
00000000 00000000 00000000 0000 000 00000000 00000000 .......................
00000000 00000000 00000000 0000 000 00000000 00000000 .......................
00000000 00000000 00000000 0000 000 00000000 00000000 .......................
00000000 00000000 00000000 0000 000 00000000 00000000 .......................
00000000 00000000 00000000 0000 000 00000000 00000000 .......................
00000000 000000                              0000000 ....
00000000 000000  File Name expressed as hex  0000000 ....  File Name shown
00000000 000000  numbers.                    0000000 ....  as characters.
00000000 000000                              0000000 ....
00000000 00000000 00000000 00000000 00000000 00000000 ........................
00000000 00000000 00000000 00000000 00000000 00000000 ........................
00000000 00000000 00000000 00000000 00000000 00000000 ........................
00000000 00000000 00000000 00000000 00000000 00000000 ........................
00000000 00000000 00000000 00000000 00000000 00000000 ........................
00000000 00000000 00000000 00000000 00000000 00000000 ........................
00000000 00000000 00000000 00000000 00000000 00000000 ........................
00000000 00000000 00000000 00000000 00000000 00000000 ........................
00000000 00000000 00000000 00000000 00000000 00000000 ........................
00000000 00000000 00000000 00000000 00000000 00000000 ........................
00000000 00000000        Press Enter to continue      ........
1Help  2Hex  3Text  4Dir  5FAT  6Partn  7  8  9Undo  10QuitNU
```

Figure 2-8

The twelfth byte, the one following the filename, determines the attributes of the file. (A full discussion of the attribute byte is found in Section IV.) Another important part of the directory entry that you might want to locate is the value of the starting cluster.

Bytes 26 and 27 in the directory entry record the value of that cluster. The term offset refers to the byte's position relative to the beginning of the file.

> Remember that when counting bytes in a file it is traditional to begin with byte zero, not byte 1. This means that byte 26, referred to as offset 26 is actually the twenty-seventh byte in the file.

```
[down arrow]
[right arrow]
```
(4 times)

The offset counter shows 26. The twenty-sixth and twenty-seventh byte hold the first cluster assigned to this file. In this case the information reads 02 00. The bytes function as a word which means their order should be reversed to get their true meaning. Thus, the value stored is 0002 hex, a simple hex number to understand because it does not contain any letter values. 0002 is equal to the decimal value 2.

As you add new files to the disk, the directory will expand, listing each file and the necessary information. Since each entry is exactly 32 bytes long you can calculate the total number of filenames that can be stored in a sector.

```
512/32 = 16
```

This means that each sector in the directory can hold up to 16 files. When the disk is formatted, the root directory of the disk is assigned a specific number of sectors. In the case of a 360K floppy disk, 7 sectors are allocated for the directory.

```
7 * 16 = 112
```

The maximum number of file entries in the root directory of a floppy disk is 112. On a hard disk, DOS allocates more room for the directory. For example, DOS 3.2 will allocate 32 sectors for the root directory on a 20 megabyte hard disk.

```
32 * 16 = 512
```

A hard disk drive will hold up to 512 files in its root directory.

> If the root directory was the only one available on a hard disk, it would be quite common to run out of room in the directory before you had filled all the data space. Word processing often produces a large number of small files that would fill up the directory without using all of the disk space. The system of subdirectories in DOS 2 and 3 allows you to overcome the limit imposed by the size of the root directory.

Because each directory entry takes up the same amount of space, the next entry would begin at offset 32 (the thirty-third byte in the file). The third entry would begin at 64, the fourth at 96, and so on. You can also calculate the location of the starting cluster numbers. The first location is offset 26, thus the second address would be found at 26+32, 58.

Why would you want to make this type of calculation? Because it is by making these calculations that the Norton Utilities program changes the hex display into the directory display. The program is not magic, but a carefully constructed tool that helps you reveal the information coded onto the disk quickly and comprehensibly.

To watch a directory develop, add another file to the disk and then reexamine the directory. Enter

```
[Esc]  (3 times)
```

Place another copy of COMMAND.COM on A, but change the name so that DOS will create a new file, not copy over the previous file. Enter

```
copy \command.com a:sample.com ↵
```

Load the Norton Utilities program and display the directory.

```
nu a: ↵
↵  (4 times)
e
```

Now that there are two files in the directory you can see the amount of disk space taken up by the first file. The starting cluster number for SAMPLE.COM is 26. (Keep in mind that these exact locations will differ with different versions of DOS.) This means that all the clusters from 2 to 25, 24 clusters are used for COMMAND.COM. Since there are 1,024 bytes in each cluster you can calculate the amount of space allocated to a file.

```
24 * 1,024 = 24,576
```

The value calculated, 24,576, is larger than the size of the file, 23,612. You can now calculate the amount of slack space at the end of this file.

```
24,576 - 23,612 = 964
```

This means that there is 3.9 percent slack space in that file. The Norton Utilities program FS (file size) makes this calculation automatically as it lists files. (Once again keep in mind that your actual values may differ from the one shown here but the general principles still apply.)

Change the display to hex by entering

[F2]

This display shows you that the directory is really a stream of bytes, like all other disk information. What makes this a directory is the way that these bytes are interpreted. The figure shows where the starting cluster numbers are stored in the directory entries.

```
 Root dir                                                    Hex format
 Sector 5 in root directory                              Offset 58, hex 3A
434      414E4420 434F4D20 00000000 00000000 0000841A COMMAND COM ..........ä→
6E0 0200    0000 534      4C452020 434F4D20 00000000 n♪█.<\..SAMPLE  COM ....
000      000 841A 6E0 1A00                   00000000 ......ä→n♪█.<\.........
00000000 000 0000 000     00000000 0000000   00000000 .......................
00000000 000 0000 00000000 00000000 0000000  00000000 .......................
00000000 000 0000 00000000 00000000 0000000  00000000 .......................
00000000 000 0000 00000000 00000000 0000000  00000000 .......................
00000000 000 0000 00000000 00000000 0000000  00000000 .......................
00000000 000 0000 00000000 00000000 0000000  00000000 .......................
000                    000 00000000                   .................
000  Address for the   000 00000000  Address for the start  .................
000  start of COMMAND. 000 00000000  of SAMPLE.COM.         .................
000  COM.              000 00000000                   .................
000                    000 00000000 00000000 00000000 .......................
00000000 00000000 00000000 00000000 00000000 00000000 .......................
00000000 00000000 00000000 00000000 00000000 00000000 .......................
00000000 00000000 00000000 00000000 00000000 00000000 .......................
00000000 00000000 00000000 00000000 00000000 00000000 .......................
00000000 00000000 00000000 00000000 00000000 00000000 .......................
00000000 00000000 00000000 00000000 00000000 00000000 .......................
00000000 00000000 00000000 00000000 00000000 00000000 .......................
00000000 00000000         Press Enter to continue     ........
1Help  2Hex  3Text  4Dir  5FAT  6Partn  7  8  9Undo  10QuitNU
```

Figure 2-9

Looking at the directory raises one very important point. The directory gives a lot of information about the file. However, it does not indicate where the file data is stored after the first cluster. How can DOS tell which clusters, other than the first, belong to the same file? The answer lies in the third specialized area of the disk, the file allocation table.

File Allocation Table

The file allocation table, referred to as the FAT, is the part of the disk reserved for keeping track of which data clusters belong to which files, if the file contains more than one cluster of data.

Why bother with the FAT at all? It seems more logical to keep the information in the directory along with all the other data about the file. Doing that, however, runs into significant and ultimately defeating problems. Remember that the directory consists of a specific number of bytes, 32. How many of those bytes should be allocated to listing data clusters?

The problem is that you cannot tell which files will be large and which ones will be small. Many files begin small but grow. Others begin large and are reduced. If you wanted to include the list of clusters in the directory you would have to choose a fixed number of bytes in which to store the cluster numbers. That number would place a maximum size limit on the files. Also, files that do not need all the space for cluster numbers would still need to have the spaces left in the directory causing more slack space on the disk. To overcome this problem, DOS stores only the starting cluster number. Because every file must have at least 1 cluster, there is no slack space in the directory. The FAT takes over by creating a system of pointers that indicate where additional data for that file are stored. Return to the select file display. Enter

```
[Esc]
  c
  f
```

Highlight FAT area and press ↵. Display the FAT by entering

```
e
```

The Norton Utilities program automatically places the program into the FAT display mode. You can see that the FAT, even in this display mode, is not as clearly organized as the directory.

In some ways, the FAT is much simpler than the directory. The directory consists of a series of values. In the FAT there is one value for each of the data clusters on the disk. The values in the FAT can be one of three types:

1. **Zero.** If the FAT shows a zero it indicates that the data cluster is not in use by another file.

2. **Value.** If the FAT entry contains a value, it indicates two things. First, the value tells DOS that this cluster is in use by a file. Second, it points out the next data cluster that belongs to the same file.

3. **EOF.** EOF stands for end of file. This marker indicates two things. The first is that this cluster is used by a file. EOF tells DOS that this is the last cluster in the file.

> It is possible for the FAT to contain a value indicating that the cluster is bad. A bad cluster is one that is marked because of an error. It is not unusual to have some of these clusters on a hard or floppy disk. The marks are used to tell DOS not to attempt to use this area of the disk for data storage because that area of the disk appears to be unreliable. Bad clusters will cause you no problem and can be ignored. If you are using a floppy disk you may want to copy the files to another floppy as a precaution. If you have a hard disk there is little you can do.

If you look at the display you can see how this pointer system works. In the upper right corner of the display the number of the cluster represented by the first value is shown. In this case, it is cluster 2. The value in that position in the table is 3. This tells you that cluster 2 is in use by a file and that the file continues in cluster 3. Since you know from the directory that cluster 2 starts the COMMAND.COM file, you know that clusters 2 and 3 are part of the same file.

```
FAT area ════════════════════════════════════════════════ FAT format
Sector 1 in 1st copy of FAT                          Cluster 2, hex 0002

     3     4     5     6     7     8     9    10    11    12    13    14
    15    16    17    18    19    20    21    22    23    24    25 <EOF>
    27    28    29    30    31    32    33    34    35    36    37    38
    39    40    41    42    43    44    45    46    47    48    49 <EOF>
     0     0     0     0     0     0     0     0     0     0     0     0
     0     0     0     0     0     0     0     0     0     0     0     0
     0     0     0     0     0     0     0     0     0     0     0     0
     0     0     0     0     0     0     0     0     0     0     0     0
     0     0     0     0     0     0     0     0     0     0     0     0
     0     0     0     0     0     0     0     0     0     0     0     0
     0     0     0     0     0     0     0     0     0     0     0     0
     0     0     0     0     0     0     0     0     0     0     0     0
     0     0     0     0     0     0     0     0     0     0     0     0
     0     0     0     0     0     0     0     0     0     0     0     0
     0     0     0     0     0     0     0     0     0     0     0     0
     0     0     0     0     0     0     0     0     0     0     0     0
     0     0     0     0     0     0     0     0     0     0     0     0
     0     0     0     0     0     0     0     0     0     0     0     0
     0     0     0     0     0     0     0     0     0     0     0     0

                         Press Enter to continue
1Help  2Hex  3Text  4Dir  5FAT  6Partn  7  8  9Undo  10QuitNU
```

Figure 2-10

The next entry in the table represents cluster 3. It contains the value 4 indicating that it is in use by a file and the next data cluster used by the file is cluster 4. In this case the chain continues to the next cluster, and the next, until position 25.

You can use the [Tab] key to change the position of the highlight in the table to cluster 25. Enter

`[Tab]` (23 times)

The value displayed for this position is <**EOF**>. This end of file maker tells DOS that there are no more cluster for this file.

> The Norton Utilities program allows you to edit the values in the FAT table. This ability should be used only when you are sure that the file allocation table is in error and you know the modification you want to make. The implication is that only advanced users will want to make changes in the FAT table. If you should accidentally make a change, Norton Utilities will prompt you to save or discard the changes before they are actually written to the disk. By discarding the changes you will leave the FAT exactly as you found it.

The FAT display mode makes it easy to read and understand the FAT table. To see what the FAT would look like in raw bytes, enter

[F2]

The Norton Utilities program displays the FAT as it is actually stored on the disk.

```
 FAT area                                                  Hex format
 Sector 1 in 1st copy of FAT                          Offset 37, hex 25
FDFFFF03 40000560 00078000 09A0000B C0000DE0 000F0001
11200113 40011560 01178001 19F0FF1B C0011DE0 011F0002
21200223 40022560 02278002 29A0022B C0022DE0 022F0003
31F0FF00 00000000 00000000 00000000 00000000 00000000 1≡......................
00000000 00000000 00000000 00000000 00000000 00000000 ........................
00000000 00000000 00000000 00000000 00000000 00000000 ........................
00000000 00000000 00000000 00000000 00000000 00000000 ........................
00000000 00000000 00000000 00000000 00000000 00000000 ........................
00000000 00000000 00000000 00000000 00000000 00000000 ........................
00000000 00000000 00000000 00000000 00000000 00000000 ........................
00000000 00000000 00000000 00000000 00000000 00000000 ........................
00000000 00000000 00000000 00000000 00000000 00000000 ........................
00000000 00000000 00000000 00000000 00000000 00000000 ........................
00000000 00000000 00000000 00000000 00000000 00000000 ........................
00000000 00000000 00000000 00000000 00000000 00000000 ........................
00000000 00000000 00000000 00000000 00000000 00000000 ........................
00000000 00000000 00000000 00000000 00000000 00000000 ........................
00000000 00000000 00000000 00000000 00000000 00000000 ........................
00000000 00000000 00000000 00000000 00000000 00000000 ........................
00000000 00000000 00000000 00000000 00000000 00000000 ........................
00000000 00000000 00000000 00000000 00000000 00000000 ........................
00000000 00000000          Press Enter to continue    ........
1Help  2Hex  3Text  4Dir  5FAT  6Partn  7  8  9Undo  10QuitNU
```

Figure 2-11

The hex view of the FAT is much more complicated to read than the directory because the table is organized in groups of bits rather than bytes. DOS uses two types of FAT structures: 12 and 16 bit. Since 8 bits make up one byte, the 16 bit structure falls neatly into two byte pairs. But the 16 bit tables are used on high capacity hard disks. Most floppy disks, like the one in the example, have a 12 bit structure. The Norton Utilities make it unnecessary to decode the complicated 12 bit structure, however it might be interesting to try to decode a little bit of the FAT displayed on the screen.

Unlike the directory, the FAT begins with a value that acts as identification of the disk format. In this example the first byte is **FD**, indicating that this is a 360K disk. The first part of the actual file allocation table begins at offset 3. The 12 bit FAT table is not easy to decode because it is meant to be read by the computers microprocessor, which stores data in special areas called registers. The format that is most efficient for the microprocessor is not necessarily the easiest for a human to decode. As an example, take the first three bytes of the FAT in the illustration.

The FAT stores two values in each group of three bytes. To calculate the value of the bytes you need to rearrange the digits in a specific pattern as shown below.

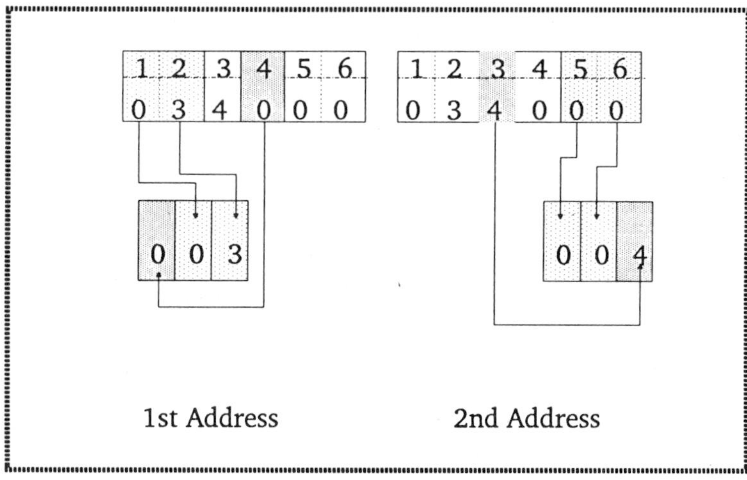

Figure 2-12

The first byte is followed by the fourth digit and the last byte is followed by the third digit. This complicated system works well on the microprocessor level and maximizes the amount of information that can be placed into the file allocation table area. The file allocation table determines the number of data clusters that you can have on a disk. A 12 bit table will limit the largest cluster number to FFF hex, 4095 decimal. In a 16 bit FAT, that value rises to FFFF hex, 65,535 decimal. Currently, DOS supports a maximum of 65,535 data clusters on a hard disk.

As mentioned earlier, disk manufacturers provide special software with high capacity hard disks (40 megabyte or more) that allow DOS to access drives with more than 32 megabytes.

FAT Problems

Unlike the directory, the FAT cannot be quickly or visually understood or analyzed. The only way to evaluate the information in the FAT is to follow the chain of values that link the data clusters together in files.

DOS provides the **CHKDSK** command to analyze the FAT. When you run CHKDSK the program does not actually check the disk space. Rather, it puts together the information in the directory with the information in the FAT to make sure that they match up. In checking the FAT against the directory, DOS will turn up two types of problems: lost clusters and cross-linked clusters.

Lost clusters are very much what their name suggests. These clusters have a value entered in their position in the file allocation table. However, none of the active files in the directory use this cluster. A lost cluster creates no active danger to existing data files. It does mean that DOS will not allocate this cluster to any new files because the value in the FAT is greater than zero.

A cross-linked cluster is a more serious matter. In this case, the FAT indicates the use of a data cluster by two or more different files. This situation is difficult because the data in the cluster should belong to one or the other of the cross-linked files. In the case of cross-linked data it is highly probable that one, or all the cross-linked files, have suffered damage.

You might wonder how lost clusters or cross-linked clusters occur. In general, these problems are the result of an interruption taking place while DOS is attempting to write information to the disk. The interruption can be the result of a hardware, software, or user error. For example, entering a [Ctrl/Alt][Del] reboot command while the computer is writing data to the disk can cause such problems. This has the same effect as a power failure. Errors can be caused if a program hangs up while writing data to the disk. Other errors are caused by problems with the hard disk itself.

The DOS program CHKDSK accepts a switch /F(fix) that causes the program to modify the FAT and directory in order to deal with lost clusters. Suppose that your computer lost power as it was writing a file from drive C to drive A.

> You can create just such an interruption as an experiment. The goal is to interrupt DOS while it is writing information to the disk. Timing is crucial in this experiment. The first step is to enter a COPY command, for example, copying a file from drive C to drive A. While the red light on drive A is lit, reboot the computer with [Ctrl/Alt][Del]. The effect will be to interrupt the normal DOS operation. If your timing is right you will create lost clusters on the disk in drive A. The example illustrated below was created by entering COPY \COMMAND.COM A:TESTING.COM and rebooting while the red light on A was lit.
>
> Getting lost clusters in this manner is a matter of luck, so be aware that the experiment might not succeed the first time.

> Also keep in mind that if you reboot your computer you will need to remove the disk from drive A and reset any paths necessary to gain access to the Norton Utilities programs.
>
> You will also have to delete the filename TESTING.COM from the disk in drive A. Why is that? The answer indicates how DOS actually goes about writing a file. When you copy a file, DOS first enters the filename into the directory. It then examines the FAT to determine what clusters are free for its use. DOS then writes the data into the clusters. When the writing is done it returns to the directory and completes the entry for that file by writing the location of the first cluster for that file and its size.
>
> This means that if DOS is interrupted while writing a file you will often see the name of the file in the directory with a size of 0 bytes. This is usually an indication of an interrupted file-writing process. It is possible that some or all of that file was actually written to the disk before the error occurred. Using the Unerase feature of the Norton Utilities program you might be able to recover part, or all, of this data. Section IV on Survival Skills details these operations.

The CHKDSK command when used with the /F(fix) switch will perform one of two operations on the lost clusters. For example, CHKDSK/F will display a message indicating the number of lost clusters and asking how you want to deal with the clusters. The following command would check the integrity of the FAT in drive A.

```
chkdsk a:/f ↵
```

If lost clusters are encountered, the program displays a message like this:

```
[C:\DOS]chkdsk a:f

24 lost clusters found in 1 chains.
Convert lost chains to files  (YN)?
```

The program offers you two choices. If you enter Y you are telling the program that you want to correct the problem by creating a filename in the directory that will correspond to the lost clusters. In that case, the FAT is left pretty much intact and the directory is modified by having a new filename or names added to it. The term chain refers to groups of clusters that are numbered consecutively in the FAT. The assumption is made that all consecutively numbered clusters should be placed into a single file. If DOS finds clusters that are not consecutive it counts each group as a separate chain and assigns a separate filename for each chain.

The file naming convention is to use the name FILE0000.CHK for the first chain of clusters, FILE0001.CHK for the second chain, and so on. Keep in mind that collecting the lost clusters into files does not free up any disk space. The purpose of the collected files is to allow you to examine the contents of the clusters to determine if you really want to preserve this data. If you do not intend to go through this trouble, it is better to select N.

If you enter N to the prompt, the program leaves the directory as it is and alters the FAT by setting all lost clusters back to a value of zero. This also resolves the problem of the lost clusters and in so doing releases all the data clusters to be used with other files.

Cross-linked clusters present a more difficult problem. When a disk contains cross-linked clusters the CHKDSK command will display a list of the cross-links and the files that they relate to. Example:

```
B:\COMMAND.COM
  Is cross linked on cluster 4
B:\SAMPLE.COM
  Is cross linked on cluster 4
```

The list will always contain pairs of entries, one for each file cross-linked to the same cluster. CHKDSK, even with the /F parameter, will not affect cross-linked clusters. The reason is that the disk directory or FAT provide no clues as to which file the cluster should belong.

The simplest way to get rid of the cross-links is to delete the files. If the files contain valuable data another solution is to copy both files to another name on the same disk, or preferably to another disk. Then, delete the cross-linked files and copy them back to their original disk or filenames. Keep in mind that while this will eliminate the cross-link, because DOS copies the cross-linked sector into both files, it does not mean that the files are undamaged. You will have to test the files to see which one, if either, still functions correctly.

One further note about CHKDSK and FAT problems. The CHKDSK program does not actually check the integrity of the clusters. It merely analyzes the FAT table. The Norton Utilities program **DT** (disk test) performs an actual test of the clusters on the disk. DT is discussed in Section IV, Survival Skills. Exit the Norton Utilities program by entering

`[Esc]` (3 times)

Directories

The previous exploration of the directory and file allocation table pointed out a weakness in the directory structure. Because the directory is fixed in size when the disk is formatted it limits the number of files you can place on a disk. The 112 file limit on a floppy disk is rarely a problem. But it is not unusual to want to store a thousand files on a hard disk. If the root directory were the only directory on the disk you would be limited to 512 files on a hard disk. (Former CP/M users may recognize this problem.)

With the release of DOS 2.0 and all subsequent versions, however, DOS can create additional directories on the disk. This structure has several benefits besides allowing more than 512 files on a disk. Directories help to organize files into logical groups so that operations can be performed more efficiently, as discussed in the beginning of Section I.

It might be interesting to look at exactly how the new directories are handled by DOS in terms of data clusters and the FAT. While directories are usually associated with hard disk drives, DOS will create them on any disk that has data clusters available. In this example, create a directory on drive A called SUBDIR. Enter

```
md a:\subdir ↵
```

Display a directory of the disk in drive A by entering

```
dir a: ↵
```

The directory shows SUBDIR with the <DIR> symbol in the listing.

```
Volume in drive A has no label
Directory of  A:\

COMMAND   COM     23612  11-14-86   3:20a
SAMPLE    COM     23612  11-14-86   3:20a
SUBDIR        <DIR]      12-29-87   6:28a
        3 File(s)  312320 bytes free
```

Copy a file into the new directory. Enter

```
copy command.com a:\subdir ↵
```

As discussed in the beginning of Section I, DOS allows you to create directories within directories. Create a directory under SUBDIR. Enter

```
md a:\subdir\subsubdir ↵
```

But what types of changes do these new directories make in the root directory and FAT? You can examine the changes using the Norton Utilities program. Enter

```
nu a: ↵
```

Display the root directory by entering

↵ (4 times)
e

The root directory display appear:

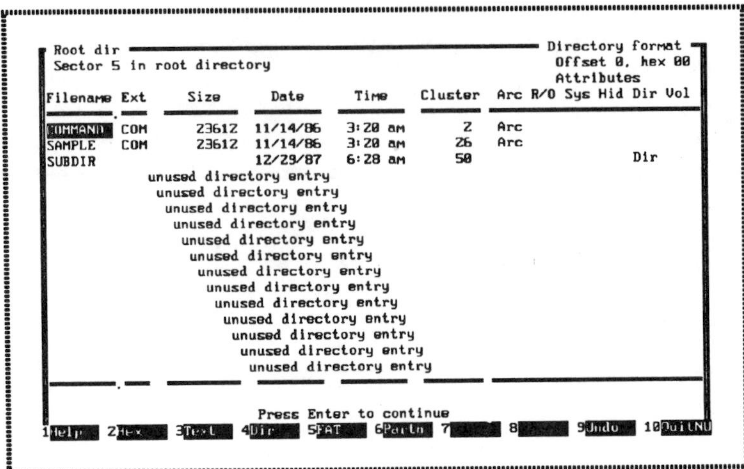

Figure 2-13

There are several points worth noting.

1. The directory is listed just like a file with a few minor exceptions. The directory entry has no file size. Also the attribute display shows **Dir** in the directory column. The directory is allocated a starting cluster number, 50, just like a file. When you create a directory you use up one data cluster, even if you never put any files in that directory. Note that you can add an extension to a directory. For example, OneWrite Plus, a popular accounting program, is usually installed directory named \ONEWRITE.PLS.

2. Remember that you made three additions to disk A, two directories and a file, but the root directory shows only one change, the addition of the SUBDIR directory. This is an indication that adding a directory expands the total amount of files you can have on the disk.

To get a more detailed look at the structure of a directory, display the contents of the SUBDIR directory. Enter

```
[Esc]
c ↵
```

Highlight the directory SUBDIR. Notice that the Norton Utilities program displays directory names in uppercase. Enter

↵
e

The program displays the contents of cluster 50 (this number may vary on your system), the SUBDIR directory.

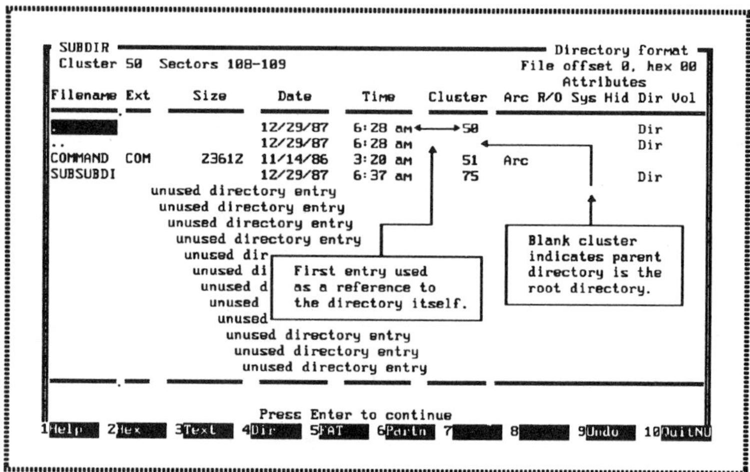

Figure 2-14

DOS automatically places two entries at the beginning of each data cluster, which will function as a directory. The names of the files are . (period) and .. (double period). The period entry is assigned to cluster 50 and represents the SUBDIR directory. The double period file indicates the location of the parent directory. In this case there is no value entered for the starting cluster indicating that the parent of this directory is the root directory. The third entry in the directory is a normal file entry, the file that you copied into the directory from drive C.

The two files, period and double period, make it possible to have the DOS tree-structured directory system. For example, the fourth entry in this directory is itself, another directory, SUBSUBDIR. This entry tells you that cluster 75 is allocated as a directory. If you were to examine the contents of cluster 75 you would find the period and double period files. In that case the period file would indicate the present directory in cluster 75, and the parent directory is located in cluster 50.

To confirm this hypothesis, change the display to show the contents of cluster 75 (note that your value may vary). Since you already know the cluster number you can select the data by entering that number. Enter

[ESC]
c
1

The Norton Utilities program asks you to enter the number or numbers of the clusters you want to display.

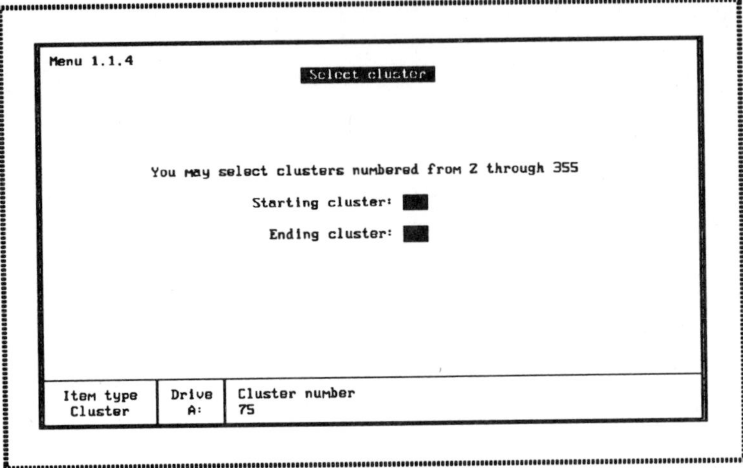

Figure 2-15

Enter

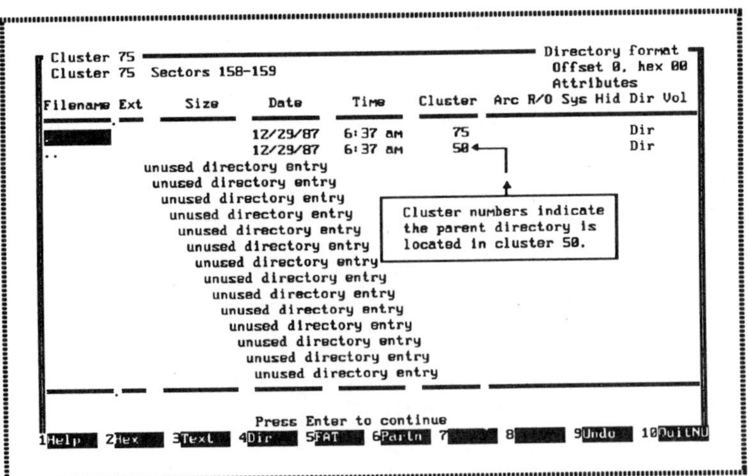

Figure 2-16

You can see that the guess was correct. DOS creates the illusion of a tree by linking each directory to its parent through the double period file. That is why it is necessary to have these files in each new directory you create.

It is important to keep in mind that even though you can have many directories, there is only one FAT table. Directories allow you to increase the total number of files stored on a disk but they do not increase the amount of space you have to store them in. Because each directory takes up a cluster that otherwise would be used for data storage, the directories decrease the total amount of data stored on the disk.

If you erase all the files in a directory, you will probably want to remove the directory as well, using the **RD** command. If you do not remove the directory the data cluster used for the directory will still occupy a cluster even though you have removed all the files.

> The statement that there is only one FAT on each disk is not strictly true. For example, you might try to calculate how much room is needed for a FAT that keeps track of all 354 data clusters on a floppy disk.
>
> In this section you learned that it takes three bytes to record two data clusters. That means each cluster requires 1.5 bytes. Multiply that by 354 and you get 531 bytes. Add in the three bytes for the FAT ID and you have 534 bytes. But DOS leaves 4 sectors (4 times 512 bytes = 2,048) for the FAT and actually keeps two copies of the FAT on the disk. For example, in the floppy disk used in these demonstrations, sectors 3 and 4 keep an identical copy of the FAT stored in sectors 1 and 2.
>
> Since the FAT is so important to the operation of the disk, you would assume that the second copy is used to backup the first copy of the FAT. This type backup was used in some CP/M systems. But Peter Norton states that DOS utilities such as CHKDSK do not make use of this second copy of the FAT. Perhaps, like other features in DOS, it was added for possible future use that was never implemented.

Exit the Norton Utilities program by entering

`[Esc]` (3 times)

Summary

This section is designed to provide a primer on the fundamental concepts employed by MS-DOS computers to store information on hard and floppy disks. It also demonstrates how the main Norton Utilities program allows you to peer beneath the surface and see exactly how a disk is organized. Below is a brief summary of the major ideas presented in this section.

Role of DOS. DOS, a master program, is used to oversee all of the operations on your computer.

Disk Organization. One of the primary roles of DOS is to organize and maintain data and program files on disk storage. DOS creates physical units, tracks and sectors, logical units, directories, file allocation tables, and data clusters.

The Purpose of the Norton Utilities. The Norton Utilities main program enables you to examine each of these structures directly. By using this program you can display disk information in a way that DOS normally will not permit. This ability is the basis for the Norton Utility programs. It allows you to manipulate the disk structures in ways that are easier and more powerful than the tools provided by DOS.

SECTION II
BATCH FILES

Batch files, one of the most powerful features of MS-DOS, allow you to create simple programs from text files containing DOS commands. With batch files you can automate a wide variety of operations that would otherwise require manual entry of a series of DOS commands.

In addition, as with most programming situations, the effect of a batch file often appears to be more than the sum of its individual commands. For example, one of the most important uses of a batch file is to build a menu that can help organize your computer. No single DOS command can create a menu, but by using a series of commands organized in a batch file you can create the effect.

When batch files are combined with some of the programs supplied in the Norton Utilities you will find that you can create a variety of useful tools that help make operation of your computer system easier for you or for others using your computer.

The first objective of this section is to show you how to create a number of useful batch file programs. The second objective is to teach you the basic principles behind DOS batch file creation so that you can develop your own ideas beyond the examples given in this section.

Getting Ready to Work

In order to perform the operations discussed in this section you will need access to the following files:

DOS Programs:
EDLIN.EXE(DOS 3) or EDLIN.COM(DOS 2)
FORMAT.EXE(DOS 3) or FORMAT.COM(DOS 2)

Norton Utility Programs:
NU (Norton Utilities Main Program)
SA.EXE (systems attributes)
ASK.EXE
TM.EXE (time mark)
BEEP.EXE
LP.EXE (line printing)
NI.EXE (Norton Integrator)

If you followed the instructions in Chapter 1 you should have all of these files copied to a directory called \DOS on your hard disk. In order to get access to these files you must make sure that a PATH has been opened to this directory. At the DOS prompt, enter

```
PATH c:\dos ↵
```

> You will also need access to DOS programs such as EDLIN. If they are stored in a directory different from your Norton Utilities programs you must open a path to both directories.
> Example:
>
> PATH c:\dos;c:\norton; ↵

If you copied these files to a different directory you should substitute the name of that directory for \DOS in the above command. Access to these programs will enable you to carry out the procedures outlined in this chapter.

> For information about Path and installing the Norton Utility programs see Chapter 1.

Safety Storage

The procedures used in this section create a new AUTOEXEC.BAT file. If you already have an AUTOEXEC.BAT in the root directory of your hard drive, make a copy of it so that you can restore the original after you have worked through this section. You can create a copy of the file by entering

```
COPY \autoexec.bat \saveexec.bat ↵
```

Should you later desire to restore this file to its original name, simply reverse the process by entering

```
COPY \saveexec.bat \autoexec.bat ↵
```

3

CREATING BATCH FILES

A common myth is the belief that in order to create DOS batch files you must use EDLIN, the line editor supplied with DOS. This myth results from the fact that most books covering batch files are books about DOS. The rationalization is that since every person who has DOS also has EDLIN, it is simpler to use EDLIN for batch file creation.

The truth is that a DOS batch file can be created by any program that creates ASCII compatible text files. The list of programs that create ASCII files involves almost every major computer application including most word processors. For example, you could create an ASCII text file with Lotus 1-2-3 by using the / Print File command. While this is not the best way to create batch files, it certainly can be done.

> When you create a text file with 1-2-3 you can suppress page formatting such as page breaks and margins by using the / Print File Options Other Unformatted command. This will produce an ASCII file without extra blank lines or spaces used for page formatting.

The most common ways to create text files such as batch files are listed below:

COPY CON: *filename*

This method requires no special programs and can be implemented whenever you have a DOS prompt. This approach uses the DOS COPY command to transfer text directly from the keyboard to a text file. Example:

```
copy con: autoexec.bat ↵
lotus ↵
[F6] ↵
```

The first line of this sequence tells DOS to copy the keystrokes entered from the keyboard into a file called AUTOEXEC.BAT. The second line enters the keystrokes l-o-t-u-s-↵ as the text of the file. The [F6] key is used to insert a [Ctrl/z] character into the file. In an ASCII text file the [Ctrl/z] character marks the end of the file. In this technique [F6] serves a dual purpose: it inserts the [Ctrl/z] at the end of the file and it signals DOS that you have completed the entry and wish to return to the systems level.

The advantage of this method of creating text files is that the DOS command, COPY, is memory resident and can be executed at any time. On the other hand, there is no way to edit text, that is, to make changes or corrections. In practice this method is used only to create the simplest files that consist of one or two modest commands.

EDLIN

The EDLIN (line editor) program is supplied with DOS. It is a popular way to create batch files because everyone has it available on their DOS disk. Keep in mind that EDLIN is a program, EDLIN.EXE (DOS 3 or higher) or EDLIN.COM (DOS 1 and 2). This means that the file must be available in the disk directory you are working in or is located in a disk and directory to which you have a path to DOS open. (For a full discussion of DOS paths, see Chapter 1.)

EDLIN is superior to COPY CON: because you can enter, revise, copy, even search and replace information. Another important capability of EDLIN is that you can insert special characters, such as control characters, into your files. As you will see, these control characters enable your batch files to use special attributes of your screen display (brightness or colors) and your printer (font and point size.)

Word Processing

Batch files can be created with word processing programs such as WordStar, WordPerfect, MicroSoft Word, and PFS Write. Word processing programs offer many editing advantages over EDLIN and are generally easier to use. Of course, since they are more complex programs they require more disk space and take longer to load than a simple editor like EDLIN. A word processor makes sense when you already have the program installed on your hard disk and are familiar with its use.

While all of these programs use slightly different file structures to store word processing documents, they also have commands that store the text as an ASCII text file.

WordStar

Create text files by using the N(on-document) command from the main menu. If you are using WordStar 2000 you must select the **UNFORM** format file when you create the document.

Word

To create a text file use the **Transfer Save** command. This command displays a menu with an option called **Formatted**. When Formatted is On, the text is saved as a Word Document. Change the setting to Off, and Word saves the file in ASCII text format. You may be prompted to confirm the loss of formatting if the text was originally created as a Word document. Simply enter Y and Word will proceed with saving the document.

WordPerfect

The [Ctrl/F5] command displays a menu that lists the WordPerfect options for saving text in ASCII format. Option 1 will create a text file. You can also create a text file using option 6.

The two options differ with respect to the way that paragraph text is treated. In option 1, a paragraph is saved as a series of individual lines of text, each one ending with a ↵ character. In option 6, WordPerfect saves all the text of a single paragraph as one long line of text and places only a single ↵ at the end of the paragraph. This file format is identical to the ASCII format created by Word. Note that the distinction affects text typed in paragraph form. Since batch files are always composed of single lines, this difference is irrelevant to batch file creation.

PFS Write

The [Ctrl/s] command allows you to specify ASCII as the file type. Enter [Tab] twice, then A. The file will be saved as an ASCII text file.

> Another technique by which text files can be produced from word processors involves sending a printout to a text file. The printer file can retain some word processing attributes such as indents and spacing. This technique is not usually applicable to batch files but will play a part in the development of text files used for display-oriented tasks. In the section on Norton Guide Databases you will learn how to create these files.

Norton Editor

The Norton Editor discussed in Chapter 7, is specifically designed for creating programs and batch files on the IBM PC. It combines a word processor-like interface with the speed and compactness of a line editor.

The AUTOEXEC Batch File

The AUTOEXEC.BAT file is special because of its relationship to the COMMAND.COM file. When DOS loads during the bootstrap routine, it automatically looks for a batch file called AUTOEXEC.BAT in the root directory of the disk from which it is booting. If such a file exists, the commands in the file are automatically executed.

The instruction to look for a file with exactly the name of AUTOEXEC.BAT is contained in the COMMAND.COM file. You can test this idea by using TS (Text Search), a program used to locate a specific group of characters on your disk. The program tells you what files on the disk contain that string of characters. (You will find more details about TS in Section III.) Test the concept that COMMAND.COM contains the name AUTOEXEC.BAT. Type

```
ts\command.com "autoexec.bat" ↵
```

The program will search the specified file and display the following:

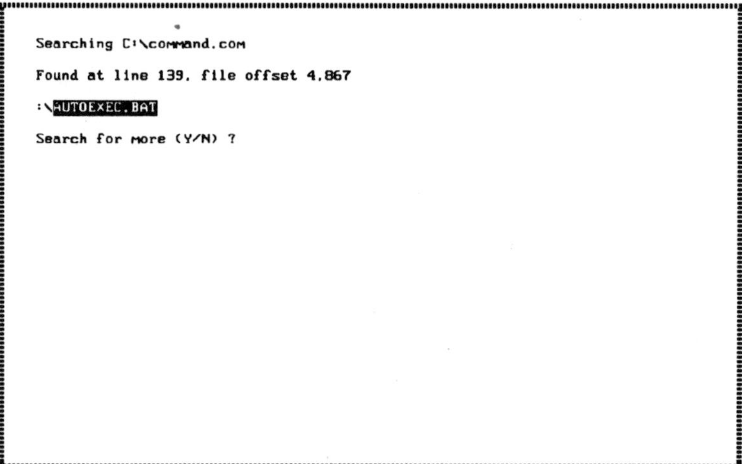
Searching C:\command.com
Found at line 139, file offset 4,867
:\AUTOEXEC.BAT
Search for more (Y/N) ?

Figure 3-1

The search confirms that COMMAND.COM carries within it the name of the batch file. In the illustration you can further see that a location within the file where the text can be found is also displayed.

> The COMMAND.COM file is called the "command interpreter". As implied by its name, this file contains the program that decodes the commands you enter at the DOS prompt. For example, the command PATH is a DOS Version 2.0 or higher command. That means that the version of COMMAND.COM supplied with DOS 1.0 does not contain information that will decode a PATH command. The COMMAND.COM supplied with DOS Version 2 and 3 do contain those instructions. For a full discussion of COMMAND.COM see Chapter 1.

The TS program displays the location as a line address, Line 139 and a byte location, offset 4,867. The address will vary depending upon the version of DOS you are using. These addresses can be used to locate the text if you want to change the entry. The program will search for more instances of the text by entering

y

When the search is completed, the program displays a summary of the search.

```
Searching C:\command.com

Found at line 139, file offset 4,867

:\AUTOEXEC.BAT

Search for more (Y/N) ? Y

Searching C:\command.com

Search Complete

1 file found containing the text "AUTOEXEC.BAT"

1 occurrence of the text "AUTOEXEC.BAT"

C:\>
```

Figure 3-2

The summary tells you that the text was found in the specified file, COMMAND.COM. This search confirms the notion that nothing happens in your computer system without a logical reason. The name AUTOEXEC.BAT is meaningful because the COMMAND.COM specifically refers to that name. The contents of the COMMAND.COM file control the default value for the name of the batch file that will be executed when the system boots.

Changing a System Default

It is possible to alter the COMMAND.COM file so that it will search for another filename instead of AUTOEXEC.BAT. This can be done by using the main Norton Utility program to load and revise the contents of COMMAND.COM. In order to perform this exercise safely, you should make a copy of the COMMAND.COM file first. Enter

```
copy \command.com \command.alt ↵
```

This creates a copy of the COMMAND.COM file under the name of **command.alt** (command alternate). To make changes in program files you can use the editing capacity of the main Norton Utility Program.

WARNING! The techniques you are about to learn will **permanently change the contents of a program file.** It is very easy to ruin a program file when you make alterations such as these. Never attempt to change a program unless you have another copy of it. If you are not sure, always make a copy of the file before you attempt to change it.

Load the main Norton Utility program by entering

nu ↵

The main menu appears.

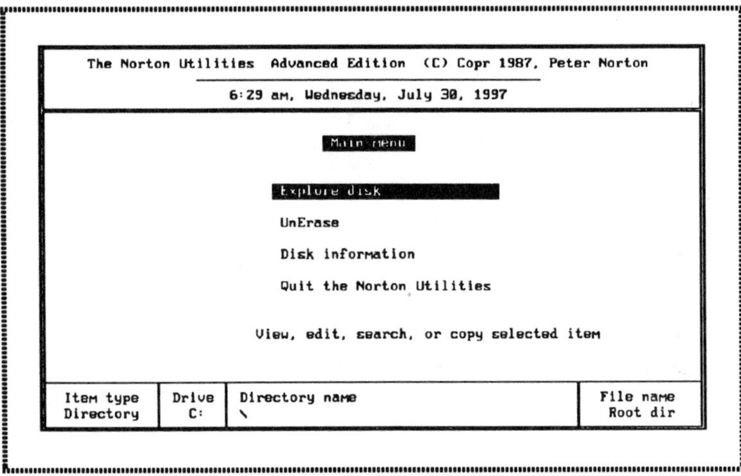

Figure 3-3

In this case you want to use the first option listed, EXPLORE DISK. Enter

The Explore Disk menu appears as shown on the following page:

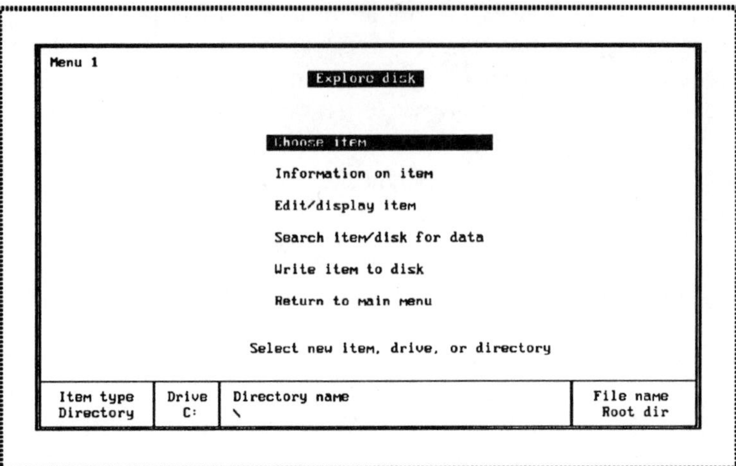

Figure 3-4

The first step is to select the item that you want to work with. Enter

c

The file to be changed is stored in the root directory of the disk. If you are not in the root directory, use the D command, change Directory, to select that directory. Enter

d

The program displays a diagram of the directories on the hard disk. (This display may be different from yours.)

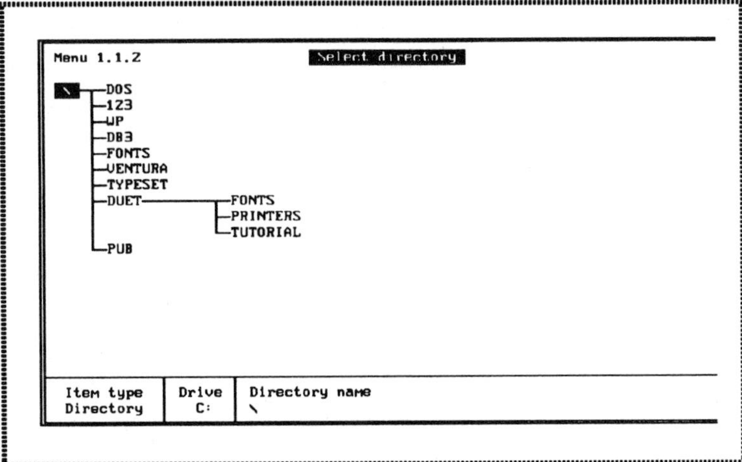

Figure 3-5

You can use the [up arrow] to position the highlight in the \, which stands for the root directory. When finished, enter

This places you back at the Choose Item menu. The highlight will automatically move to File. Enter

The program displays a list of the files and directories. The directory names appear in uppercase letters.

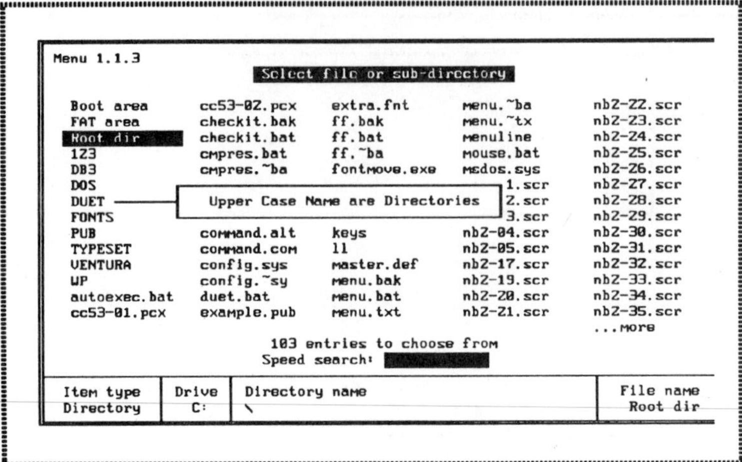

Figure 3-6

To locate the COMMAND.ALT file use the arrow keys to move the highlight or enter the name of the file. As you type the name of the file, the program will search the list and position the highlight to the first file that matches the characters you type. This is called "speed search" and is a very convenient feature. Enter

comm

The cursor jumps to the first file that matches those letters, probably COMMAND.ALT. If this is not the case, use the arrow keys to highlight the correct file. When it is highlighted, enter

↵

Now that you have selected a file, edit the contents by selecting the Edit/Display option. Enter

e

The program displays the contents of the file.

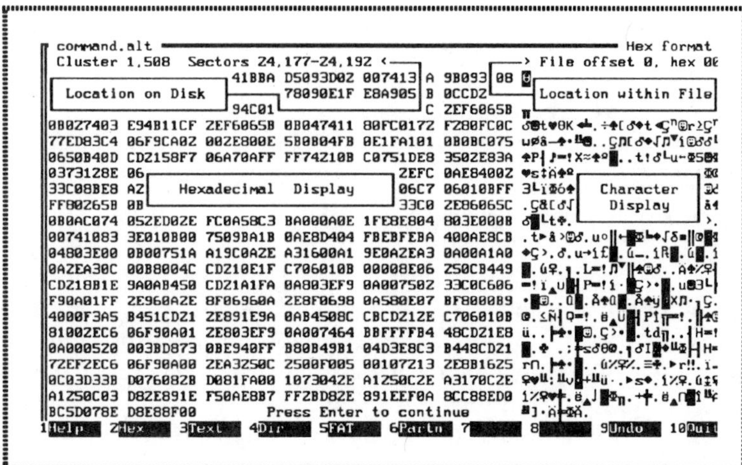

Figure 3-7

The display may seem quite strange at first, but a closer examination reveals that it discloses a great deal of information about the file in question.

At the very top of the screen the program reveals the name of the file on the left, and the display format type, also known as the **Hex display**, on the right. The Hex display was automatically selected by the program because the file contains the full range of binary code characters. Program files are written to be understood directly by the computer and seldom appear in a form readable to humans. In the case of this copy of the COMMAND.COM file, most of the information is structured as binary instructions meant for the computer to interpret.

When a file is loaded that is structured as a program, the Norton Utilities program displays the data in two ways:

1. The left side of the screen shows a numeric listing of the bytes contained in the file. The numbers are hexadecimal, not decimal, and are read as pairs, for example, **E9, DD, 0B, BA** and so on. Each pair represents the value of one byte. (For a complete discussion of the hexadecimal system see Chapter 1.) The screen displays the first 512 bytes, 1 disk sector, of the file's contents.

2. The right side of the screen is a listing of the equivalent screen characters. The IBM PC and compatible computers have a built-in set of display characters that correspond to most of the numeric values. Some values such as **00** and **FF** do not have any character equivalent and the program displays a dot in those positions. Remember that the character representations won't spell out anything you are familiar with because the file is meant as a program, not as a text file.

The second line on the display shows you more information about the file. On the left side of the line the program shows you the location of the file on the disk, for instance the starting cluster number 1,500 and the sector numbers contained in that cluster, 24,177–24,192.

> The exact location of the file on your computer will be different. You can find a complete discussion of disk organization in Chapter 1.

The right side of the line shows you the location of your cursor in the file. The position is listed as an **Offset value**. The term offset refers to the number of bytes from the beginning of the file. When you are at the beginning of a file the offset is 0, and if you move to the twelfth byte in the file the offset is 11. The offset is also shown in hex numbers as well as decimal. You can move through and edit the file in either the left or right panels. The program begins by positioning the cursor in the left panel. Enter

```
[Tab]
```

The cursor moves to the right panel. Enter

```
[Tab]
```

The cursor jumps back to the left panel. If you want to change data by entering the hexadecimal number value, use the left panel for editing. If you want to type in characters, as in a word processor, use the right panel. In this example the right panel is the appropriate one. Enter

```
[Tab]
```

To change the position in the file, enter

```
[right arrow]
```

The cursor moves to the next character. Note that the offset meter changes to 1 and that the highlight in the left panel moves to the second pair of numbers, 7D. In moving around a file you can use the following keys:

[Arrows]	Move one character or line in the direction of the arrow.
[Home]	The first sector or page of the file.
[End]	The last sector or page in the file.

[Pg Up]	The previous sector or page in the file.
[Pg Dn]	The next sector or page in the file.

In this example you want to find the character at offset 4,867, the value obtained by the TS program.

> If you are using a different version of DOS, the byte location will be different. For example, in DOS 3.1 the location will be 4,477. If this is the case, make the appropriate adjustments to the value specified in the commands.

Enter

`[Pg Dn]` (9 times)

The program displays the information that begins with byte 4,608 through 5,119, a total of 512 bytes.

```
 command.alt ━━━━━━━━━━━━━━━━━━━━━━━━━━━━━━━━━━━━━━━━━━━━━━━━━━━━━ Hex format
 Cluster 1,508  Sectors 24,177-24,192            File offset 4,609, hex 1201
72702031 3938312D 31393836 0D0A0D0A 00B01253 70656369 rp 1981-1986♪█♪█.░‡Spec
66696564 20434F4D 4D414E44 20736561 72636820 64697265 fied COMMAND search dir
63746F72 79206261 640D0A00 13135370 65636966 69656420 ctory bad♪█.‼‼Specified
434F4D4D 414E4420 73656172 63682064 69726563 746F7279 COMMAND search director
20626164 20616363 65737320 64656E69 65640D0A 003E1341  bad access denied♪█.>‼
63636573 73206465 6E696564 0D0A0077 134F7574 206F6620 ccess denied♪█.w‼Out of
656E7669 726F6E6D 656E7420 73706163 650D0A00 8913496E environment space♪█.ë‼I
636F7272 65637420 444F5320 76657273 696F6E0D 0A24496E correct DOS version♪█$I
76616C69 6420656E 7669726F 6E6D656E 74207369 7A652073 valid environment size
70656369 6669656 ┌──────────────────────────┐ 00000000 pecified♪█$/DEV/CON....
00002F43 4F4D4D4 │  File Names Stored in    │────────>../COMMAND.COM...:\AUTO
5845432E 4241540 │  COMMAND.COM file.       │ 00000E00 XEC.BAT......σ1..J└...⌡
434F4D53 5045433 └──────────────────────────┘ 00000000 COMSPEC==az/\ pdcA.....
00000000 00000000 00000000 00000000 00000000 00000000 ........................
00000000 00000000 00000000 00000000 00000000 00000000 ........................
00000000 00000000 00000000 00000000 00000000 00000000 ........................
00000000 00000000 00000000 00000000 00000000 00000000 ........................
00000000 00000000 00000000 00000000 00000000 00000000 ........................
00000000 00000000 00000000 00000000 00000000 00000000 ........................
00000000 00000000 00000000 00000000 00000000 00000000 ........................
00000000 00000000 00000000 00000000 00000000 00000000 ........................
00000000 00000000          Press Enter to continue    ........
1Help  2Hex  3Text  4Dir  5FAT  6Partn  7  8  9Undo  10Quit
```

Figure 3-8

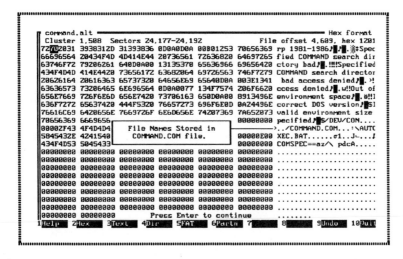

You can now see the \AUTOEXEC.BAT filename in the file. Because the Norton Utilities program allows you to edit the data as well as view it you can change the file specification. Move the cursor to the line that contains \AUTOEXEC.BAT. Enter

`[down arrow]` (10 times)

If your COMMAND.COM file is different you should deviate form the exact instructions in order to locate the correct bytes in your file.

Use the [right arrow] key to position the cursor on the letter A in \AUTOEXEC.BAT. Look at the File Offset counter at the top of the screen; it reads 4,867, the exact number of the offset location indicated by the *Text Search*. In this case the TS command provides you with a road map to find this text item in the file.

Note that the string actually begins with two characters, :\, before the name AUTOEXEC.BAT. The :\ is combined with the letter of the boot drive to create a full path name, e.g., C:\AUTOEXEC.BAT or A:\AUTOEXEC.BAT.

If it is true that this entry controls the way your system works when it boots, you should be able to change the name of the file specification and prompt your system to search for a different file when it boots.

People often are confused by the name AUTOEXEC (auto execute). Perhaps a name like SETUP or STARTUP would be better. As an experiment, change the name of the file to **SETUP.BAT.** Enter

```
setup.bat
[space bar]  (3 times)
```

Note that it was necessary to erase the final three characters that belonged to the old filename. The case of the letter, upper or lower, that you enter for the name of the file does not matter. The program displays the changed text in a different video (bold on monochrome systems) than the original data on the display to help you keep track of the changes you have made.

Any changes made have not been written to the disk but are being held in the computers memory. If you advance to another screen or exit from the editing mode, the program will display a screen that asks you if you want to save the changes. Enter

```
[Esc]
```

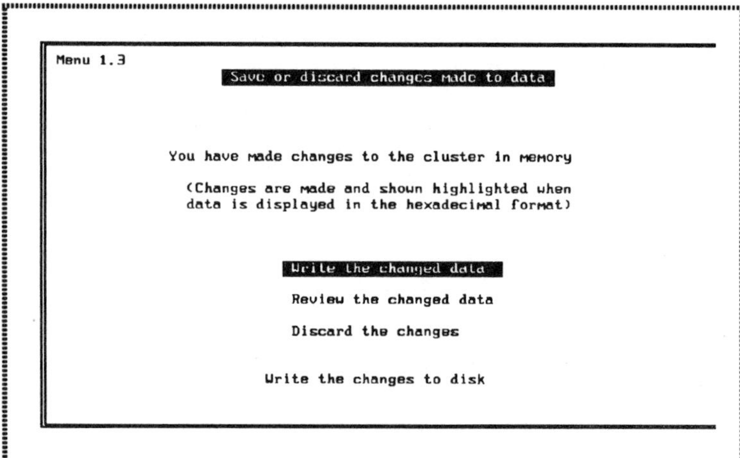
Menu 1.3
Save or discard changes made to data
You have made changes to the cluster in memory
(Changes are made and shown highlighted when data is displayed in the hexadecimal format)
Write the changed data
Review the changed data
Discard the changes
Write the changes to disk

Figure 3-9

You have three options:

Write. Save the changes to the file on the disk.

Review. Return to the previous screen to see the changes.

Discard. Ignore the changes and leave the disk file in its original form.

In this case you want to save the changes. Enter

```
w
```

The program flashes the message "Writing Changes . . ." for a moment while it rewrites the file sector. You are returned to the Explore Disk menu.

Now that you have created an alternate form of the COMMAND.COM file you can test it to see if it really works. Exit the Norton Utilities program by entering

`[Esc]` (twice)

You are now back at the operating system. In order to check your experiment you can substitute your alternate version of command interpreter file for the original. Since you expect your alternate version to search for SETUP.BAT it would be a good idea to create that file so that you can tell if the experiment has been successful.

First create a simple SETUP.BAT file. Enter

```
COPY CON: SETUP.BAT ↵
ECHO Experiment is a success ↵
ECHO The setup.bat file is found! ↵
[F6] ↵
```

Next, make a backup copy of the current COMMAND.COM file. Enter

```
copy command.com command.bak ↵
```

Now copy your alternate command interpreter file to the name COMMAND.COM. Enter

```
copy command.alt command.com ↵
```

If the concept is correct, when you boot the system it will look for the SETUP.BAT not the AUTOEXEC.BAT. Reboot your system by entering

```
[Ctrl/Alt][Del]
```

The screen will look like this:

```
C>ECHO Experiment is a success
Experiment is a success

C>ECHO The setup.bat file is found!
The setup.bat file is found!

C>
C>
```

Figure 3-10

This simple experiment shows that you that the Norton Utilities program has the power to change the basic setup of your system. As you proceed through this chapter you will learn more about how the utilities can be put to work to help get your hard disk system better organized. Before you go on, return your system to the way it was before the experiment, by simply copying the **COMMAND.BAK** file to the name COMMAND.COM. Enter

```
copy command.bak command.com ↵
```

> Note that if you have the Norton Utilities and DOS programs stored in a directory, you will need to open the path to that directory. Example: PATH C:\DOS;↵

Your system will boot up and search for AUTOEXEC.BAT once again. You might want to reboot your system before you go on.

Startup Options

The next section of this chapter will look at options presented by combinations of DOS procedures and Norton Utilities programs that can help you modify the way your system behaves when you turn it on. Most of the options are related to commands that you may want to include in your autoexec batch file, although they can work in almost any type of batch file.

CONFIG.SYS and the ANSI.SYS Driver

In Chapter 1 the concept of system configuration was discussed as it generally applies to MS-DOS systems. If you are not familiar with this concept you might want to review that chapter.

Certain of the features discussed later in this section depend upon the use of the ANSI device driver. This driver is supplied with MS-DOS in a file called ANSI.SYS. The reason for discussing this file now is that you will need to have the ANSI driver loaded in order for the utilities to operate properly. You can check to see if the ANSI.SYS driver is loaded by listing the CONFIG.SYS file in the root directory of your hard disk. Enter

```
type c:\config.sys ↵
```

This command lists the contents of the CONFIG.SYS file that are on your hard disk. This file is the one that loads the ANSI.SYS driver into memory when the system boots. Remember that just having the file ANSI.SYS on your hard disk is not enough. The CONFIG.SYS file, if any, must contain an instruction to load that driver into memory or it will have no effect.

If you get the message: File not found, you will need to create a CONFIG.SYS file. If you have a CONFIG.SYS it should contain a line that loads the ANSI.SYS driver. Examples:

```
DEVICE=ANSI.SYS
DEVICE=C:\DOS\ANSI.SYS
```

Assuming that the ANSI.SYS driver is in place, you are ready to continue.

Screen Attributes

There are two attributes that are apparent to all MS-DOS users: the screen display colors and the DOS prompt. With the ANSI.SYS driver loaded into the memory of the computer you can achieve a level of control over the default settings for these items. The DOS command **PROMPT** is used to select the type of system prompt that you want to display. The Norton Utilities program SA (Screen Attributes) allows you to change the color of the DOS screen display. If you do not have a color monitor, you can still use the attributes, brightness, reverse, underline and blinking, to alter your display.

The following creates an AUTOEXEC.BAT file that uses the Norton Utility and DOS programs. If you already have an AUTOEXEC.BAT, rename that file so that you can follow this procedure to create a new file but still have your original file to restore later. Enter

```
rename c:\autoexec.bat oldexec.bat ↵
```

Screen Color

The ANSI.SYS driver makes it possible to vary the screen colors, or in monochrome, attributes, that are displayed when DOS is active. The SA program provides a simple, direct means of selecting the display you desire.

The SA program issues special escape commands that the ANSI device driver recognizes as commands to change the screen display. In the next section you will learn how you can issue these escape commands within DOS and the Norton Utilities program, to liven up your screen displays.

The SA program allows you to control the following qualities of the screen displays:

Intensity. Intensity refers to how the characters are displayed. You can select BOLD or BLINKING.

Main Setting. There are three options, NORMAL, REVERSE or UNDERLINE.

Foreground/Background. These options allow you to set color on a color display.

For example, you can reverse the video (swap foreground and background colors) by entering

```
sa reverse ↵
```

To return to normal, enter

```
sa normal ↵
```

Note that NORMAL and REVERSE always assume that the colors are black (or whatever your monochrome display uses) and white.

Color screens can set combinations of WHITE, BLACK, RED, YELLOW, MAGENTA, BLUE, CYAN, or GREEN. If you have color, enter

```
sa bold red on white ↵
```

Notice that the bold attribute can be used only with the foreground color. Return the display to normal by entering

```
sa nor ↵
```

You only need to enter the first three letters, for example, yel for yellow, bli for blinking.

If you want to use the system attributes for DOS the best way to do that is to enter the command as part of your AUTOEXEC file. To create it with EDLIN, enter

```
edlin autoexec.bat ↵
```

Since this is a new file, begin with the insert command. Enter

```
i
```

The first line of this file is numbered as 1 and the first command is the SA command. Enter

```
sa bold ↵
```

EDLIN automatically creates a second line. To save the file as it is exit the insert mode.

```
[Ctrl/c]
```

Save the file with the e command.

```
e ↵
```

Execute the file by entering

```
autoexec ↵
```

You can execute the AUTOEXEC.BAT file at any time by entering the name of the file at the DOS prompt. The only thing special about AUTOEXEC is that the COMMAND.COM program searches for it when it loads. Other than that, AUTOEXEC.BAT is an ordinary DOS batch file and can be executed anytime you like.

You may notice that when the batch file is terminated, two DOS prompts appear. This is caused by the way EDLIN writes a file. Following each line, two characters, a carriage return and line feed (referred to by **CR/LF**) are inserted. At the end of a batch file another character, the end of file marker, is inserted. A file created with EDLIN will have all three characters at the end of a batch file. The presence of all three causes DOS to display a prompt twice instead of the single prompt you would expect. Later in this chapter you will learn how to eliminate the unwanted CR/LF characters at the end of a file written with EDLIN.

DOS Prompts

The DOS prompt refers to the characters that appear on the left side of the line when you are operating in DOS. The prompt's primary purpose is to indicate that the operating system is active, that is, COMMAND.COM is loaded into the memory and ready to receive a command.

The prompt also has a secondary purpose. It displays information about the current status of the system. The default value for the prompt is just two characters. To set the prompt back to its default setting, enter

```
prompt ↵
```

The prompt appears as a letter, corresponding to the current default drive, and a carat (>) added for readability sake. The latter has no special significance.

There are two ways to change the prompt display:

1. The **PROMPT** command. This command is used to specifically change the contents of the DOS prompt.

2. The **SET** command. The SET command controls a variety of DOS settings that are held in memory. The prompt specification is one of those settings and can be controlled with SET as well as the PROMPT command.

The commands are really two forms of the same command. Any changes made in one will affect the other.

Prompts are changed for two reasons:

1. To display more information about the system.

2. To make the prompt more readable.

The PROMPT command allows you to alter the text of the prompt by specifying special system's options that are referred to as meta strings. The term meta, used in this context, refers to a computer language in which special symbols or characters are used. Most of the commands in DOS consist of words, DEL AUTOEXEC.BAT, for instance. The term meta implies that special characters such as % $ &, etc., are used as well as words.

The meta strings recognized as part of the prompt are

$t system's time

$d system's date

$n current drive letter

$p current drive and directory

$v current version of DOS

$s leading space. (Spaces following the PROMPT command and before the text would normally be ignored. To have those spaces print as part of the prompt $s is used.)

$e escape character. (This allows you to enter escape commands that change screen attributes.)

$h erasing backspace. (This is used to erase characters displayed by a string, for example, time display 12:00:01, hh$h would erase the hundredths of a second portion of the display)

$g print > (The > would normally indicate a DOS redirection command)

$l print < (The < would normally indicate a DOS redirection command)

$b print | (The | would normally indicate a DOS filter command)

These meta strings can be combined with any other literal characters you desire. The most common type of prompt is one that displays the current drive and directory along with some characters for readability. The most common prompt is pg probably because the example appears in most DOS manuals. Enter

```
prompt $p$g ↵
```

The drive and directory appear followed by a >, C:\>. You do not need to use the $g. Enter

```
prompt [$p] ↵
```

This creates a prompt, [C:\]. You can also use the DOS SET command to create a prompt. The SET command is used to set a variety of DOS values. For example, to set the prompt with SET, enter

```
set prompt = $l$p$g ↵
```

The prompt appears as <C:\>.

Adding Special Characters

If you have worked with MS-DOS systems for any length of time you will have noticed that many programs display characters not found on your keyboard. The IBM PC uses a system of 255 characters for its display interface, yet a quick count tells you they are not all physically available. However, there is a trick by which you can type out most of those characters. The technique involves using the [Alt] key in combination with the numeric keypad. This method requires you to type the number that corresponds to the character that you want to display.

When you know the number of the character, enter it by holding down the [Alt] key and typing the digits on the numeric keypad. (The position of the [Num Lock] key does not affect this operation.) You should keep the [Alt] key down for all the digits, releasing it after the last digit is typed. The character will not appear on the screen until you have released the [Alt] key. Enter

```
[Alt/227]
```

The Greek letter Pi appears. Enter

```
[Alt/228]
```

The Greek letter Sigma appears. Since these characters do not represent a DOS command, start a new command line by entering

```
[Esc]
```

These special characters can be made part of your prompt if you desire. For example, the IBM character set contains several types of left and right pointing arrows, besides the < ($l) and > ($p). The following command uses characters from the IBM character set as part of the prompt. Enter

```
prompt [Alt/174]
$p
[Alt/175]
↵
```

This creates a prompt that contains characters not found on the keyboard.

```
C>prompt «$p»
«C:\»
```

Figure 3-11

Since they do not appear on the keyboard, the advantage of using special characters such as these is that they will not be mistaken for characters typed in by a user. Try another combination.

```
prompt [Alt/221]
$p
[Alt/222]
↵
```

The screen shows the new prompt.

```
C>prompt «$p»
«C:\»prompt ▌$p▐
▌C:\▐
```

Figure 3-12

Attributes in Prompts

The SA command makes use of special commands that the ANSI driver recognizes as instructions to vary the style of screen display. The SA command is a convenient way to enter those instructions, though not the only way. The general form of the ANSI command to change the screen display is

```
Escape [ #;#;.. m
```

The m must be a lowercase character and is an exception to the general rule in DOS operations that case is not significant. Entering M will cause the command to function improperly.

Escape stands for the [Esc] key character, while # stands for a numeric value that corresponds to the ANSI driver values for screen attributes and colors. The table below lists the available options:

Listing 3.1. ANCI Special Attributes

```
0  normal, white foreground, black background
1  Bold foreground color
5  Blinking
7  Reverse video (black on white)
8  Invisible (black on black)
```

Listing 3.2. ANSI Foreground Colors

```
30 black
31 red
32 green
33 yellow
34 blue
35 magenta
36 cyan 37 white
```

Listing 3.3. ANSI Background Colors

```
40 black
41 red
42 green
44 yellow
44 blue
45 magenta
46 cyan
47 white
```

The [Esc] key cannot be manually entered, however, because pressing [Esc] in DOS means that you want to cancel a command. To enter [Esc] as part of a specification, not a direct keyboard command, there must be a symbol for the keystroke that can be entered indirectly. The prompt command recognizes $e as a symbol for [Esc].

If you prefer a blinking prompt you can include [Esc][5m, (5 is the ANSI value for blinking) into your prompt command. If you substitute the $e symbol for [Esc] you get $e[5m as the keystrokes to be entered.
Begin by entering

```
prompt $e[5m
```

Now enter the symbols that display the directory name and > character.

```
$p$g
```

The last step is to return the screen display to normal text. Keep in mind that you want only the prompt to blink, not the command you enter. The ANSI value for normal is 0, making the command $e[0m. Enter

```
$e[0m ↵
```

The prompt appears as blinking text.

Figure 3-13

Notice that with this command any text entered by you or produced by a command will be normal. Enter

```
dir/w
```

The directory displays as normal text. When the prompt is redisplayed it appears as blinking text. It is important to remember to turn off a video attribute or the rest of the displayed text will also have that attribute.

Other Special Characters

There are about 27 characters in the IBM character set that have not been accounted for yet. They are the characters that match up to the [Ctrl-letter] combinations, such as [Ctrl/r], [Ctrl/o], and [Ctrl/z]. As in the case of [Esc], you cannot make a direct entry of these keys in DOS because DOS will take the entry of these characters as direct commands.

At first, this distinction may seem confusing. What is the difference between entering a key like M and entering [Ctrl/m]? The answer has to do with the two basic operations performed when you type: input and output.

For example, when you press the A key, DOS accepts the input and immediately tells the computer to place the matching character on the screen at the next available position. This is such a commonplace experience that ordinarily you don't give it much thought.

However, DOS does not treat all of the possible key combinations this way; some combinations trigger a different response. For example, when you press the [Esc] key, DOS interprets that keystroke as an instruction to ignore any previous characters and begin a new command entry. When you enter one of these special key combinations, DOS does not place the corresponding character onto the screen. In the case of [Esc], DOS places a \ and a new line on the screen, not the character symbol for [Esc].

It may interest you to know that some of the special keys on your keyboard, [backspace], [Tab] and ↵, duplicate functions that can be implemented by using [Ctrl/letter] combinations. The roots of these combinations lie deep in the origins of the ASCII coding system. For example, the combination of [Ctrl/m] issues a carriage return command, exactly the function that the ↵ key plays in DOS. Enter a simple command like the one below.

```
dir
```

Instead of pressing ↵, enter

```
[Ctrl/m]
```

The command executes exactly as it would if you had entered the ↵ key. In fact, to the computer, the [Ctrl/m] combination and the ↵ key are the same instruction. This is also true of the [backspace] key and the [Ctrl/h] combination. Enter

```
dirx
```

To erase the x you could use the [backspace] key. Instead, enter

```
[Ctrl/h]
```

This keystroke duplicates the same commands as the [backspace] key. Now execute the command by entering

```
Ctrl/m]
```

This demonstrates that the [Ctrl/letter] combinations (and [Esc]) are interpreted as keystroke commands by DOS. When they are entered, some action takes place. No characters or symbols appear on the screen, as is the case with normal alphanumeric characters. Like all characters in the IBM set, however, these control combinations do have special symbols assigned to them and you can access them, albeit indirectly.

The strategy is to use some program that has a method of recording the [Ctrl/letter] combinations and storing them in a text or batch file. Then you can print the file, including the [Ctrl] characters and the symbols that correspond to them. Both the EDLIN and Norton Editor programs allow you to make this type of entry. The Norton Editor method is discussed in Section V but its use parallels the EDLIN example very closely. Since the assumption in this chapter is that you may own only the Norton Utilities and DOS, an EDLIN example will be given.
Create a file called SYMBOLS. Enter

```
edlin symbols ↵
```

To add new lines to the file, enter the Insert command.

```
i ↵
```

EDLIN responds by displaying 1:* indicating that it is ready for you to enter the first line of the file. Enter

```
The character for [Ctrl/a] is
        [space bar]
```

So far everything has been simple, straight forward typing. But now you need to enter the character equivalent to [Ctrl/a], indirectly. First, you must enter a keystroke command that tells EDLIN of your intention to add a [Ctrl] character to your file. Enter

```
[Ctrl/v]
```

The characters ^V are inserted to show that you have prepared the way for entry of a control character. Entering an uppercase letter will prompt EDLIN to store the combination as a single [Ctrl] character. (Remember that the letter must be an uppercase character for this technique to work.) Enter

```
A ↵
```

The screen will look like this:

```
C>edlin symbols
New file
*i
        1:*The character for [Ctrl/a] is ^VA
        2:*
```

Figure 3-14

EDLIN is ready for another line. Enter

```
The character for [Ctrl/b] is
        [space bar]
```

Enter the [Ctrl/v] command.

```
[Ctrl/v]
   B
   ↵
```

You could continue this way until you have filled out all 26 letters. But you can see that the lines are all much the same except for two characters. A situation like this is built for a program like the Norton Editor. Since the assumption is that you do not have this program, EDLIN has some commands that can help. Exit the insert mode by entering

```
[Ctrl/c]
```

The first command is the COPY command. For example, you might simply want to copy the text of line 1 to line 3. To do so you would enter a command preceded by three numbers. In this example the command reads 1,1,3C. The first two numbers (1,1) tell EDLIN which lines to copy. In this case, line 1 through line 1. (Specifying line 1 as the beginning and the end is necessary because EDLIN expects two numbers.) The third number is the line number for the copied line, in this case, number 3. The C is the actual command, COPY. Oddly, EDLIN places the command letter after the line value, not before. In DOS, as in most other programs, the command verb, COPY, would precede the names of the items to be copied. Enter

```
1,1,3c ↵
```

Note that EDLIN did not visually confirm the copy. To see the new line, enter

```
3 ↵
```

There are two observations to make. First, the copy command worked, and second, the ^VA now appears as ^A. The indirect entry method has placed a [Ctrl/a] into the file.

Instead of typing in the characters, you can use [F1] to copy them. Enter

```
[F1]    (24 times)
```

Replace the letter a with the letter c. Enter

```
         c
[F1]  (5 times)
```

The final step is to enter the [Ctrl/c] character. Enter

```
[Ctrl/v]
c
↵
```

Enter another line into this file:

```
4i ↵
The character for [Ctrl/g] is
[space bar]
[Ctrl/v]
G
↵
```

Save the file by entering

```
[Ctrl/c]
e ↵
```

Display the contents of the file using the DOS TYPE command. Enter

```
type symbols ↵
```

The screen will look like this:

```
C>edlin symbols
New file
*i
         1:*The character for [Ctrl/a] is ^VA
         2:*The character for [Ctrl/b] is ^VB
         3:*^C

*1,1,3c
*3
         3:*The character for [Ctrl/a] is ^A
         3:*The character for [Ctrl/c] is ^VC
*4i
         4:*The character for [Ctrl/g] is ^VG
         5:*^C

*e

C>type symbols
The character for [Ctrl/a] is ☺
The character for [Ctrl/b] is ☻
The character for [Ctrl/c] is ♥
The character for [Ctrl/g] is

C>
```

Figure 3-15

Notice the symbols that appear for the control characters. At the same time, notice that no symbol appears for [Ctrl/g]. [Ctrl/g] is auditory, not visual, and caused the beep that sounded when you typed your file. In the ASCII code system, [Ctrl/g] was used to ring the bell on the Teletype machine and still serves the same function on a microcomputer today. You can see that it is possible to add sound, as well as visual items, to batch files.

The last step in this cycle is to add a PROMPT command to the AUTOEXEC.BAT file. Enter

```
edlin autoexec.bat ↵
        li ↵
```

Echo Off Command

The ECHO OFF command, a very common command placed at the front of a batch file, is used to suppress the display of the commands being executed. For example, in your current batch file, the SA BOLD command appears on the screen. With the ECHO OFF, the command would still be executed, but it would not appear on the display, presenting a cleaner appearance. Enter

```
echo off ↵
```

The ECHO command can be used in a variety of ways in batch files; ECHO OFF is only one of the variations. Others will be presented as this section progresses.

For the next entry, the prompt command, we will combine a number of the special strategies discussed so far in this chapter. Begin by entering a simple directory display command:

```
prompt $P
```

The next character in the prompt is a blinking one and you will have to enter an [Esc] command. Enter

```
$e[5m
```

The blinking character will be the one used for [Ctrl/p], the solid arrow. To enter a [Ctrl/p] into the prompt command, use the [Ctrl/v] method.

```
[Ctrl/v]
   P
```

Finally, turn off the blinking and return the text to the same value as set by the SA command, BOLD.

```
$e[0m ↵
path c:\dos; ↵
```

Save the file by entering

```
[Ctrl/c]
  e ↵
```

Execute the AUTOEXEC batch file. Enter

```
autoexec ↵
```

The batch sets the screen attribute, BOLD, and creates the prompt with the solid arrow blinking.

4

INTERACTIVE BATCH COMMANDS

The next step in organizing a hard disk is to create a menu program. The menu is designed to help users execute the programs stored on the hard disk, eliminating the need to poke around the disk looking for programs and files. The menu program is usually automatically displayed by the AUTOEXEC.

There are many ways to create menus. The Norton Utilities program provides a simple but powerful command called ASK.EXE. This makes it possible to create a menu or series of menus on your hard disk, which can help execute programs, format disks, backup files and set printer attributes.

The ASK command fills a gap in the DOS batch file command set. Without the ASK program, DOS has no way of asking and capturing the users response. With ASK, you can create interactive menus and submenus that will present a full automated interface for anyone who turns on the computer.

The ASK Command

The ASK command cannot operate by itself. It has meaning only within a batch file, and in conjunction with special batch file commands IF, ERRORLEVEL, and GOTO. The combination of these commands with ASK allows you to create batch files that function as interactive menus.

A menu batch file consists of the following parts:

1. Display a screen which lists the choices for the user. This can be done by using the type command to display a text file that lists the menu options.

2. Use the ASK command to capture the users selection.

3. Use the IF, ERRORLEVEL, and GOTO commands to execute a specific set of batch operations corresponding to the user's selection.

4. Run the menu batch again after the selected program has terminated.

The basic menu will require you to create two files: one for the batch commands and the other for the text of the menu screen. Begin with the batch file. Enter

```
edlin menu.bat ↵
```

Place EDLIN into the insert mode by entering

```
i↵
```

The first command in the menu batch file, ECHO OFF, suppresses the display of the commands while the batchfile is running. Enter

```
ECHO OFF↵
```

The next command in the file clears the display so that the menu screen begins at the top. Enter

```
CLS↵
```

Once the screen has been cleared you can display the menu text file. Although you have not created the menu yet, anticipate that you will create the file and use the name MENU.TXT. The TYPE command displays the contents of text files on the screen; use it to display the menu text. Enter

```
TYPE menu.txt↵
```

The menu text is displayed and you can use the ASK program. The ASK program does three things:

1. Pauses the batch file and waits for the user to enter a single character.

2. Displays a prompt for the user to read.

3. Sets the DOS errorlevel setting according to the users response.

When programs terminate, DOS allows them to issue a special code stored in a specific part of the memory (called the AL register.) Not all programs take advantage of this feature in DOS. Among the DOS utilities, BACKUP and RESTORE will set the errorlevel to 1 if they fail to complete the backup or restore operation.

This errorlevel code provides a method by which batch files can check to see if the previous command worked or failed. The ASK program capitalizes on the idea of errorlevel codes by placing an errorlevel code based on a users response into memory. Below is a typical ASK command:

```
ASK "Enter A, B or C", abc
```

The **"Enter A, B or C"** displays a text prompt on the screen. The letters that follow, abc, tell the ASK command what responses the user is allowed to make. If the user enters a, the errorlevel is set to 1. If the user enters b, the errorlevel is set to 2, and so on, up to level 9.

In this example, imagine that you want to create a menu with 6 choices. You will number the choices 1-6 and add a 7th choice for exit, e. Enter

```
ASK "Enter your choice"
    [space bar]
```

Before you end the command, you might want to add something to get the users attention. Remember that all the characters inside the quotation marks will be sent to the screen display. You can include control characters and ANSI escape character sequences. For example, suppose that you wanted to end the prompt with a flashing arrow, like the one used in the system's prompt display. You can include the same command in this string.

Note that the $e meta command for Escape cannot be used in the ASK command. The meta string applies only to a few specific DOS commands such as PROMPT. When using EDLIN you can add an Escape character to any text line indirectly by entering the [Ctrl/v][. Also keep in mind that the ANSI commands require [Esc][. In EDLIN the entry will look like ^V[[. Make sure that you enter both [characters when they are needed.

The command for blinking text is [Esc][5m. Enter

```
[Ctrl/v]
   [
   5m
```

To insert the solid arrow character, ▶, into the text use the [Ctrl/v] method once again. Enter

```
[Ctrl/v]
   P
```

Now turn off the blinking text. Enter

```
[Ctrl/v]
[
0m
```

For good measure you can include an audio prompt. Remember that [Ctrl/g] output as part of a text file will cause a beep to sound. Enter a [Ctrl/g] into the ASK command prompt.

```
[Ctrl/v]
G
```

Complete the ASK command with the closing quotation marks and the list of acceptable responses.

```
", 123456E↵
```

You have completed the first section of this batch, the portion that displays the menu and accepts the user's response. Keep in mind that the ASK command also filters out all unspecified responses. When you specify 123456E, you tell ASK to refuse to accept any other entries.

The screen will look like this:

```
C:\>EDLIN menu.bat
New file
*i
        1:*ECHO OFF
        2:*CLS
        3:*TYPE menu.txt
        4:*ASK "Enter your choice^V[[5m^VP^V[[0m^VG", 123456E
        5:*
```

Figure 4-1

Testing Errorlevels

The next section of the batch file is the portion of the program that uses the errorlevel setting to determine which group of batch commands should be executed. This effect is achieved by using the IF-GOTO command, listed below:

```
IF errorlevel 1 GOTO program1
```

The command is a conditional statement. If the current errorlevel value stored in the memory is 1, then jump to PROGRAM1. Note that there is no space between PROGRAM and 1. PROGRAM1 is simply a user defined term, not a DOS command such as GOTO, or errorlevel.

In order to remind you what user-defined terms, such as PROGRAM1, mean, DOS allows you to create labels within a batch file that identifies part of the batch file. To create a label, simply type a colon followed by the name of the label. Example

```
:PROGRAM1
COPY a:*.*  c:
```

When DOS executes a GOTO command, it searches the rest of the batch file for a label that matches the name in the GOTO instruction. When it finds the label :PROGRAM1, DOS executes the commands following that label, in this case, COPY a:*.* c:

In this example you want to set up seven programs to correspond to the seven entry numbers. The figure below shows the general structure of this type of batch file. There are four major sections. The first part displays the text of the menu; then users enter their selections.

The program then evaluates the entry and branches to the program label that corresponds to the selection. When the selected group of commands is completed the program re-runs the menu starting the process over again.

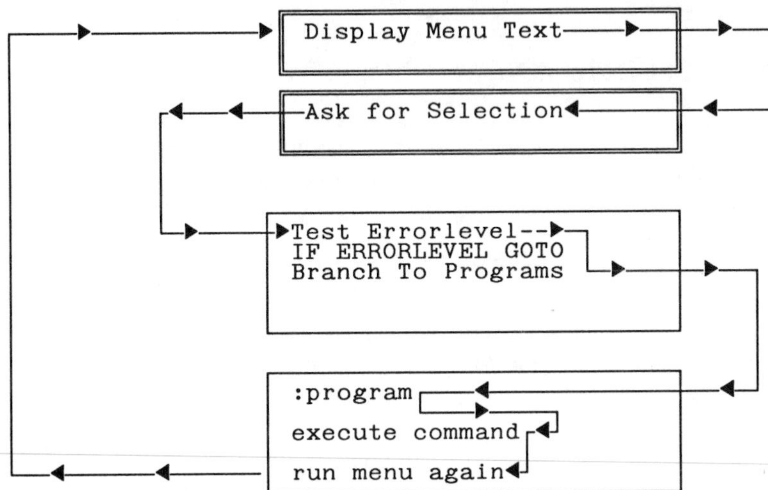

The diagram shows several important features of this technique. First, you can see a series of IF commands that test the value of the errorlevel. Notice that the test is arranged in descending order beginning with the highest errorlevel, 7, and going to the lowest errorlevel, 1. The labels that correspond to each of the errorlevels are arranged in ascending order beginning with PROGRAM1. The diagram shows that if the number 2 is entered, the errorlevel is set for 2, which in turn executes the commands following that label.

Note that the GOTO command does not stop DOS from executing commands in the labels following the first one. For example, if a GOTO command jumps to PROGRAM2, DOS will continue to execute PROGRAM3, PROGRAM4, etc., unless something is done to terminate the batch file. In the case of the menu program the problem is solved by running the menu batch again following the last command for each program.

Record a series of IF-GOTO commands in descending errorlevel. Enter

```
IF errorlevel 7 GOTO program7↵
```

Continue the entry until the batch file looks like Figure 4-2.

```
C:\>EDLIN menu.bat
New file
*i
        1:*ECHO OFF
        2:*CLS
        3:*TYPE menu.txt
        4:*ASK "Enter your choice^V[[5m^VP^V[[0m^VG", 123456E
        5:*IF errorlevel 7 GOTO program7
        6:*IF errorlevel 6 GOTO program6
        7:*IF errorlevel 5 GOTO program5
        8:*IF errorlevel 4 GOTO program4
        9:*IF errorlevel 3 GOTO program3
       10:*IF errorlevel 2 GOTO program2
       11:*IF errorlevel 1 GOTO program1
       12:*
```

Figure 4-2

Program Labels

The next section of the batch file lists the actual commands that you want carried out when you select one of the values for errorlevel. The most common use of menu choices is to execute programs. Suppose that you have WordPerfect, Lotus 1-2-3 and dBASE III Plus installed on your hard disk. You would like to execute those programs from this menu.

Begin by creating PROGRAM1, which will execute WordPerfect. Enter the label, remembering that the label is indicated by typing a colon first. Enter

```
:program1↵
```

record the commands you would normally enter into DOS. The example assumes that 1-2-3 is stored in the \123 directory on your hard disk.

The first lines in the program clear the screen and display a message telling the user what program is loading. This display is helpful because some programs take a few moments to load. The message confirms to users that they have selected the correct application and should wait while the software loads into memory. To enhance the disk, you can include an ANSI Escape code to make the word **Loading** blink. Enter

```
CLS←
ECHO
[Ctrl/v][[5m
Loading
[Ctrl/v][[0m
[space bar]
Lotus 1-2-3←
ECHO Please Wait ................
```

The screen will look like this:

```
C:\▸EDLIN menu.bat
New file
*i
        1:*ECHO OFF
        2:*CLS
        3:*TYPE menu.txt
        4:*ASK "Enter your choice^V[[5m^VP^V[[0m^VG", 123456E
        5:*IF errorlevel 7 GOTO program7
        6:*IF errorlevel 6 GOTO program6
        7:*IF errorlevel 5 GOTO program5
        8:*IF errorlevel 4 GOTO program4
        9:*IF errorlevel 3 GOTO program3
       10:*IF errorlevel 2 GOTO program2
       11:*IF errorlevel 1 GOTO program1
       12:*:program1
       13:*CLS
       14:*ECHO ^V[[5mLoading^V[[0m Lotus 1-2-3
       15:*ECHO Please Wait ..................
       16:*
```

Figure 4-3

Now enter the actual commands required to load the program:

```
cd\123←
lotus←
```

To finish your work, you must supply the commands that will execute after the 1-2-3 session has been completed. Return to the root directory and execute the menu batch file once again. Enter

```
cd\←
menu←
```

The basic format for each program entry has been established:

1. Load the desired program. This usually consists of an ECHO command that confirms to the user the selection they have made. Then change to the appropriate directory and execute the application program.

2. Redisplay the menu. This is done by changing the directory back to the root and running MENU again.

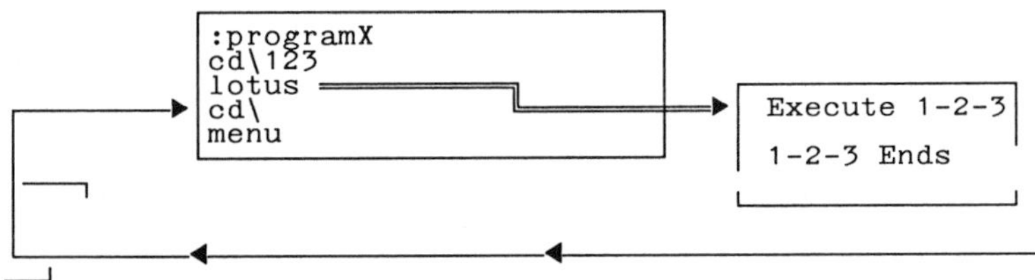

By repeating this structure for programs 2, 3, 4, etc., you will construct a batch file that can carry out any one of seven possible actions.

Since ASK will not set an error level higher than 9, this type of menu is limited to a total of nine different options. However, you can create a series of submenus that can extend the menu options infinitely, as you will see later in this chapter.

Complete the batch file as shown below.

Listing 4.1. File MENU.BAT

```
ECHO OFF
CLS
TYPE menu.txt
ASK "Enter your choice ^V[[5m^VP^V[[0m^VG", 123456E
IF errorlevel 7 GOTO program7
IF errorlevel 6 GOTO program6
IF errorlevel 5 GOTO program5
IF errorlevel 4 GOTO program4
IF errorlevel 3 GOTO program3
IF errorlevel 2 GOTO program2
IF errorlevel 1 GOTO program1
:program1
CLS
ECHO ^V[[5mLoading^V[[0m Lotus 1-2-3
ECHO Please Wait....................
cd\123
lotus
cd\
menu
:program2
```

(Continued)

Listing 4.1. File MENU.BAT *(Continued)*

```
CLS
ECHO ^V[[5mLoading^V[[0m WordPerfect
ECHO Please Wait....................
cd\wp
wp
cd\
menu
:program3
CLS
ECHO ^V[[5mLoading^V[[0m dBASE III Plus
ECHO Please Wait....................
cd\db3
dbase
cd\
menu
:program4
cd\
menu
:program5
cd\
menu
:program6
cd\
menu
:program7
cls
ECHO Menu Terminated - DOS now Active
```

Notice that programs 5 and 6 above have not yet been filled out and contain only the commands CD\ and MENU. Entering the latter commands in advance is allowed because they are part of any option you create. Program 7 has no commands except a CLS (clear the screen) and an ECHO that displays the message.

Save the text by entering

[Ctrl/c]
e↵

The basic structure of the batch file you just created can be used in many situations. You might want to create a file that contains only the outline of a menu batch without any specific commands. This file, like the one below called SAMPMENU.BAT, (sample menu), can simply be copied and edited whenever you want to create a menu.

Listing 4.2. File SAMPMENU.BAT

```
ECHO OFF
CLS
TYPE sampmenu.txt
ASK "Enter your choice ", 12345678E
IF errorlevel 9 GOTO program9
IF errorlevel 8 GOTO program8
IF errorlevel 7 GOTO program7
IF errorlevel 6 GOTO program6
IF errorlevel 5 GOTO program5
IF errorlevel 4 GOTO program4
IF errorlevel 3 GOTO program3
IF errorlevel 2 GOTO program2
IF errorlevel 1 GOTO program1
:program1
cd\
menu:
program2
cd\
menu
:program3
cd\
menu
:program4
cd\
menu
:program5
cd\
menu
:program6
cd\
menu
:program7
cd\
menu
:program8
cd\
menu
:program9
cls
ECHO Menu Terminated - DOS now Active
```

If part of your job is to create menus for several computers you will find that keeping this generic menu format batch file will save you time.

Using Supplied Batch Files

The previous section assumes that you know the exact commands to use in order to load a program from DOS. While this is the case with many applications, some programs require you to enter special parameters and switches as part of the loading command. To make this type of command simpler, the manufacturer will usually create a batch file of its own during the installation process.

For example, the Ventura Desktop Publisher program requires a rather complicated command sequence to operate. Example:

```
assign b=d
cd\fonts
rim
clear
CD C:\VENTURA
DRVRMRGR VP %1 /S=SD_WY705.EGA/M=32
assign
```

In the above command the /S switch sets the program for a specific screen display (in this example a Wyse 700 high resolution monitor) while the /M switch selects the mouse driver.

To avoid asking the user to enter this long command, Ventura creates a batch file called VP.BAT during the installation process. The user can start Ventura by simply entering VP.

However, be careful not to include batch file commands such as VP in your menu batch file program. Calling another batch file such as VP.BAT from your menu program causes DOS to continue reading batch commands fromVP, not MENU, after the application has been terminated.

When DOS executes batch files it can work with only one batch at a time. Thus when you load a batch file from within a batch file, the former batch, MENU, is terminated and the new batch, VP, takes its place. Since VP.BAT does not include explicit instructions to execute the MENU batch, the batch process terminates without going back to the menu.

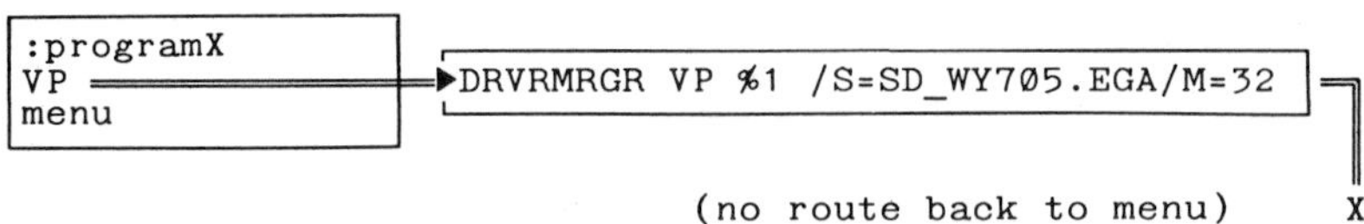

If you want to integrate commands already stored in batch files into menu programs you must enter or copy the commands from the existing batch file into the proper program label area in the menu batch.

To determine what the contents of the batch file are you can use the TYPE command. Example: TYPE vp.bat

To print the contents of a batch file use the DOS redirection feature. Example: TYPE vp.bat>PRN

EDLIN does not have the ability to insert the contents of a batch file directly into the file you are editing. However, many editing and word processing programs do have such commands. The Norton Editor discussed in Section V allows you to copy the lines from a file without having to retype them.

When you type the lines of the batch file into your menu program, your menu selection behaves just like the other batch did in terms of executing the application. On the other hand, because it is integrated into the Menu batch, it will redisplay the menu after the application has been terminated.

Creating the Text File

The menu program is actually ready to run at this time. The only missing element is the text of the menu display that will be stored in the file MENU.TXT. Although you can operate the menu batch without the text on the screen you have to rely on memory for the numbers that correspond to the menu choices. With the creation of the MENU.TXT file you have a visual reminder.

The MENU.TXT file can be any standard ASCII text file and need contain no special DOS batch commands. It is simply a file of text to be displayed on the screen. It can be created with any word processing program, text editor, or other program that outputs an ASCII text file.

You can include the entire IBM character set and even use ANSI [Esc] commands to change the color or attribute of the text items.

In the example below a simple menu display will be created. You might want to add characters that form lines and boxes, thus making the display more complex and interesting for the people using it.

Begin the creation of the text file by entering

```
edlin menu.txt↵
```

Place EDLIN into the insert mode by entering

```
i↵
```

Since this is a text file that will be displayed with the TYPE command you do not have to enter any special commands, only the text you want to display.

Pressing↵ creates blank lines. Enter

↵ (4 times)

On line 5 enter a title for this menu and then a few more blank lines.

IBM PC PROGRAM MENU↵
↵ (3 times)

The next line holds the menu option for program 1, Lotus 1-2-3. First, indent the text by adding spaces to the line.

[space bar] (5 times)

To make the number stand out from the rest of the text you can insert an ANSI [Esc] command to print the number as black on white. The [Esc] command value 7 reverses the video. Enter

```
[Ctrl/v]
[7m
1.
[Ctrl/v]
[0m
```

Now enter the name of the program that option 1 will execute. Enter

```
[space bar]
Lotus 1-2-3 Release 2.01↵
```

Repeat the command for WordPerfect and dBASE III Plus. Your screen should look like this:

```
C:\>edlin menu.txt
End of input file
*i
        1:*
        2:*
        3:*
        4:*
        5:*IBM PC PROGRAM MENU
        6:*
        7:*
        8:*     ^V[[7M1.^V[[0M Lotus 1-2-3 Release 2.01
        9:*     ^V[[7m2.^V[[0m WordPerfect Version 4.2
       10:*     ^V[[7m3.^V[[0m dBASE III Plus Version 1.1
       11:*
```

Figure 4-4

Option 4, 5, and 6 are currently not used. Entering numbers into the menu makes it easy to add options later on. Enter

```
[space bar]  (5 times)
      [Ctrl/v]
        [7m
        4.
      [Ctrl/v]
        [0m
        ↵
```

Repeat the command for options 5 and 6. The final entry on the list is the EXIT command. Enter

```
[space bar]  (5 times)
      [Ctrl/v]
        [7m
        E.
      [Ctrl/v]
        [0m
Exit Menu - Activate DOS↵
```

The menu is 14 lines long at this point. By adding blank lines you will cause the ASK command's prompt to appear lower on the screen. Enter

↵ (6 times)

The complete file will look like this:

```
IBM PC PROGRAM MENU

      ^VP[7m1.^VP[0m Lotus 1-2-3 Release 2.01
      ^VP[7m2.^VP[0m WordPerfect Version 4.2
      ^VP[7m3.^VP[0m dBASE III Plus Version 1.1
      ^VP[7m4.^VP[0m
      ^VP[7m5.^VP[0m
      ^VP[7m6.^VP[0m
      ^VP[7mE.^VP[0m Exit Menu - Activate DOS
```

Save the file by entering

```
[Ctrl/c]
  e↵
```

You are now ready to execute. Enter

```
menu↵
```

The screen will look like this:

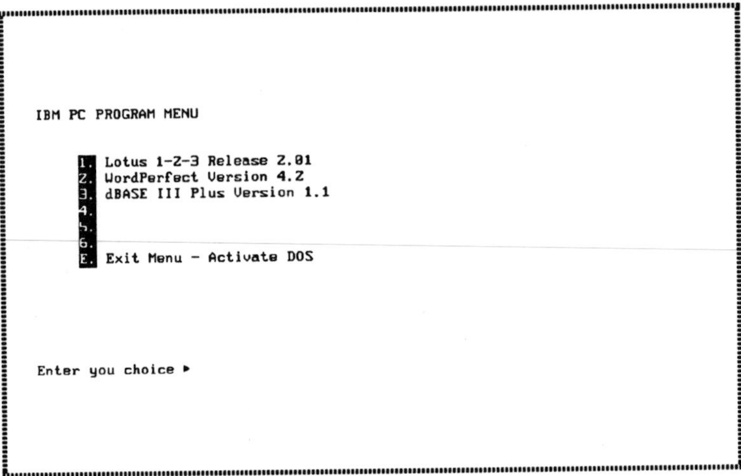

Figure 4-5

Notice that all the special ANSI commands added to the batch create the visual effects, such as reversed text and the audio effect of the beep.

You can now test out the menu program by entering the options numbers. No ↵ is necessary; entry of the number alone is sufficient. When you are finished testing the menu, use option E to exit the menu and return to DOS.

The Turnkey System

Now that you have created the master menu for your disk you can create a turnkey system to present it. A turnkey system is one that automatically displays a menu, such as the one you designed, each time the computer is booted.

You can produce a turnkey system by first creating an AUTOEXEC.BAT file to execute the MENU batch. Begin by deleting the AUTOEXEC.BAT file you created earlier in this chapter. Enter

```
del autoexec.bat↵
```

Now use EDLIN to create a new AUTOEXEC batch file. Enter

```
edlin autoexec.bat↵
i↵
```

The first line in the batch is the ECHO OFF command. Enter

```
ECHO OFF↵
```

The next line sets the DOS prompt. To make the prompt more interesting, insert ANSI Escape commands to incorporate a blinking arrow. Enter

```
PROMPT $p$e[5m
[Ctrl/v]
P$e[0m↵
```

The next command is a PATH command to ensure access to crucial files. In this case a path to the \DOS directory is needed because that is where the ASK.EXE program is being stored. Enter

```
PATH c:\dos↵
```

> You might want to include other directories besides \DOS in the path command. Opening a path to a word processing program is convenient, especially if that program can edit ASCII text files. This means that you can use your word processor instead of EDLIN to edit batch files. Example: PATH c:\dos;c:\word;

Time and Date

If you have an AT or compatible computer, the time and date for the system will be automatically inserted when you boot the system. If you have a PC- or XT-type computer you will have to insert the date and time manually when the system boots.

> If you have an PC or XT system that contains a clock card used to automatically set the time and date for DOS, you should include that command in this AUTOEXEC. For example, if you purchased an AST board that contains a clock, AST provides a program called ASTCLOCK.COM on a disk enclosed with the board. This program should be copied to your hard disk (the \DOS directory is a good place).
>
> You will then need to add a line to the AUTOEXEC.BAT file that reads:
>
> ASTCLOCK

If you are using a computer like the PC or XT that does not have a built-in clock/calendar enter the following commands into your batch. AT or compatible users will not need these commands.

```
DATE↵
TIME↵
```

Starting the Menu

The last command in the batch is the one that executes the MENU batch. Enter

```
menu↵
```

Entering the MENU as the last command in the AUTOEXEC batch file creates the turnkey effect. The booting of the system is a daisy chain response in which DOS calls the COMMAND.COM file. The COMMAND.COM file, as you discovered in this chapter, contains an explicit instruction to execute a file called AUTOEXEC.BAT. The AUTOEXEC.BAT file that you just created contains an instruction to execute your menu batch file.

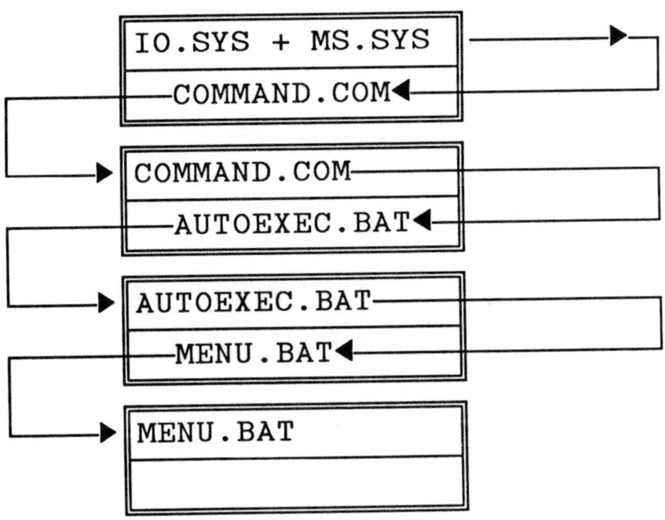

In its turn, the MENU batch leads to the applications programs stored on the hard disk. Save the file by entering

```
[Ctrl/c]
e↵
```

To test the effect of the batch files, warm boot the system by using the following combination of keys:

`[Ctrl/Alt/Del]`

When the system boots it will automatically display the menu. If you included the TIME and DATE commands, you must enter the time and date before the menu will appear:

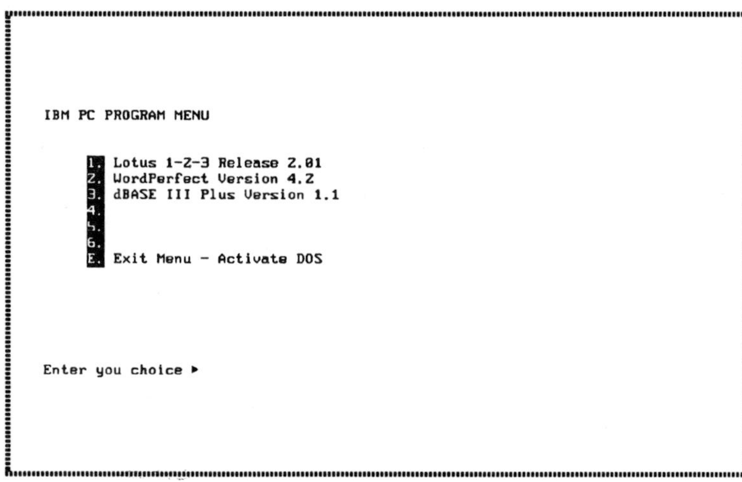

IBM PC PROGRAM MENU
1. Lotus 1-2-3 Release 2.01
2. WordPerfect Version 4.2
3. dBASE III Plus Version 1.1
4.
5.
6.
E. Exit Menu - Activate DOS
Enter you choice ►

Figure 4-6

When you have finished with the menu, exit to the operating system by using the E option.

5

ADVANCED MENU OPERATIONS

In the previous chapter you learned how to use the ASK program to create interactive batch files that have a look and feel similar to normal applications programs you use on your computer. The Norton Utilities program contains other programs that can be utilized from DOS batch files to enhance the basic menu batch you have created.

Creating a Time Log System

Included in the Norton Utilities package is a program called Time Mark (TM.EXE). The Time Mark program is an electronic stop watch that can be used to time various activities. In this chapter you will learn how Time Mark can be added to your menu to create a system that automatically records on the computer, the usage of applications.

To learn more about TM, enter

```
tm↵
```

The current date and time appear on the right side of the line. To place that display on the left side of the line, enter

```
tm/l↵
```

TM can be used with two arguments, START and STOP, which create a stop watch effect. Enter

```
tm start↵
```

The date and time are displayed again, but the difference is that the date and time have been stored in the memory. Enter

```
tm stop↵
```

This command prompts the program to output the amount of time that has passed since you started the timer, below the date and time display.

The timer commands can be used to time all types of operations. For example, to determine how long it takes to check the disk using the CHKDSK command, create a simple batch file. Enter

```
edlin checkit.bat↵
i↵
```

Begin by starting the Time Mark time. Use the /N switch to suppress the time and date display. Enter

```
tm start/n↵
```

Next, enter the command you want to execute, the CHKDSK command:

```
chkdsk↵
```

Finally, display the elapsed time. Note that using the /N switch with the STOP parameter suppresses the time and date display but displays the elapsed time. The /L parameter tells TM to place the elapsed time figure on the left side of the display. Enter

```
tm stop/n/l↵
```

Save the file by entering

```
[Ctrl/c]
i↵
```

Execute the batch by entering

```
checkit↵
```

The screen will look like this:

```
C:\>checkit

C:\>tm start/n

C:\>chkdsk
Volume CS 40         created Jan 1, 1980 12:05a

 21331968 bytes total disk space
    57344 bytes in 3 hidden files
    81920 bytes in 10 directories
 10919936 bytes in 487 user files
 10272768 bytes available on disk

   753664 bytes total memory
   620768 bytes free

C:\>tm stop/n/l
6 seconds
C:\>
C:\>
```

Figure 5-1

The batch file displays the time it took to execute the CHKDSK command.

The TM commands allows you to enter a text string that serves as a comment. The comment prints before the elapsed time and helps you identify what the elapsed time refers to. To add a comment to the CHECKIT batch file, enter

```
edlin checkit.bat↵
```

Change line 3. Enter

```
3↵
```

Enter the TM command with a comment:

```
tm stop "Checking this disk took "/l/ n↵
```

To clean up the batch display, insert an ECHO OFF command at the beginning of the batch. Enter

```
1i↵
echo off↵
[Ctrl/c]
```

Save the revised batch by entering

```
e↵
```

Execute the program by entering

```
checkit↵
```

The screen will look like this when the batch has completed its run.

```
C:\>checkit

C:\>echo off
Volume CS 40        created Jan 1, 1980 12:05a

 21331968 bytes total disk space
    57344 bytes in 3 hidden files
    81920 bytes in 10 directories
 10919936 bytes in 487 user files
 10272768 bytes available on disk

   753664 bytes total memory
   620768 bytes free
Checking this disk took  6 seconds
C:\>
```

Figure 5-2

Creating a Log

Suppose that instead of placing the text on the screen, you wanted to write the output of the TM to a text file that would serve as a log. Each time the CHECKIT batch was run, the TM command would record when it was done and how long it took.

The strategy of this change is to take advantage of the DOS redirection commands to redirect the output of the TM command to a disk file. Redirecting the output in this way creates the desired time log. Keep in mind that DOS uses two types of redirection commands when it comes to files, > and >>. Look at the command below:

```
tm stop > use.txt
```

The command creates a text file called USE.TXT that contains the information normally placed on the screen by the TM program. However, this type of redirection has a serious drawback for creating the time log because it overwrites any existing data stored in USE.TXT each time it is executed. A better solution is to use the >> redirection command. This command creates a new file if none exists, but appends the text onto the end if the file already exists. Example:

```
tm stop >> use.txt
```

The >> command causes the USE.TXT file to expand each time you execute the batch. Using this redirection command creates an ongoing log of activity. To see how this works, change the CHECKIT batch so that it creates a text file log rather than a screen display. Enter

```
edlin checkit.bat↵
4↵
```

The TM command accepts a special parameter called /LOG. the /LOG parameter tells TM to insert CR/LF characters that would not normally be sent to the screen display. The /LOG parameter is used when the output is going to be captured as part of a text file. Enter

```
tm stop "Disk Checked on"/l/log>>use.txt↵
```

Save the revised batch file by entering

```
e↵
```

Execute the batch file. Enter

```
checkit↵
```

This time the output of the TM STOP does not appear on the screen. Instead it is stored in a text file called US E.TXT. Check for this file by entering

```
dir *.txt↵
```

The directory should show at least two files, MENU.TXT and USE.TXT. Take note of the size of the file, which is approximately 70 bytes. Execute the batch again. If the logging concept is working correctly the USE.TXT file will increase in size. Enter

```
checkit↵
dir *.txt↵
```

The file size has increased. To see the contents of the file use the type command. Enter

```
type use.txt↵
```

The screen will display a log showing when the CHECKIT batch was executed.

```
C:\>type use.txt

Disk Checked on 5:15 am, Wednesday, December 2, 1987
6 seconds

Disk Checked on 5:18 am, Wednesday, December 2, 1987
6 seconds

C:\>
```

Figure 5-3

Multiple Timers

Each time a TM STOP command is issued the time that is displayed is set back to zero. For example, once you use the TM STOP command to display the elapsed time on the screen, you cannot use the command to store the text in a file. If you used the TM STOP to create the file log, you would not be able to display the value on the screen.

The solution lies in the program's ability to start and stop up to four timers independent of each other. This is useful in timing separate operations. It can also be used to time the same event two ways: one for screen display, the other for disk file logging.

The /Cn switch is used to create different times. The n can be a number from 1 to 4 indicating the number of the timer. When TM is used without a /Cn, the program assumes that you want to work with timer 1. As an example, set two timers. Enter

```
tm start /c1↵
tm start /c2↵
```

You can stop each one independently. For instance, to stop timer 2, enter

```
tm stop /c2↵
```

Timer 1 is still active and accumulating time. To stop that timer enter

```
tm stop /c1↵
```

Logging Activity from the Menu

Now that you have looked at the TM command you are prepared to modify the MENU batch to automatically create a log of application usage. The basic idea is to start two timers whenever an item is chosen from the menu. The first timer will display the elapsed time to the user, while the second will record the date and elapsed time in a disk file.

The way to implement this is to add commands in the MENU.BAT file that start and stop the timers as the selections are made from the menu. Begin by editing the MENU.BAT file.

```
edlin menu.bat↵
```

The editing that you are about to do assumes that you have created the MENU.BAT exactly as shown below. The line numbers are added for reference purposes only.

Listing 5.1. File MENU.BAT

```
ECHO OFF
CLS
TYPE menu.txt
ASK "Enter your choice ^V[[5m^VP^V[[0m^VG",
123456E
IF errorlevel 7 GOTO program7
IF errorlevel 6 GOTO program6
IF errorlevel 5 GOTO program5
IF errorlevel 4 GOTO program4
IF errorlevel 3 GOTO program3
IF errorlevel 2 GOTO program2
IF errorlevel 1 GOTO program1
:program1
```

(Continued)

Listing 5.1. File MENU.BAT *(Continued)*

```
13.  CLS
14.  ECHO ^V[[5mLoading^V[[0m Lotus 1-2-3
15.  ECHO Please Wait....................
16.  cd\123
17.  lotus
18.  cd\
19.  menu
20.  :program2
21.  CLS
22.  ECHO ^V[[5mLoading^V[[0m WordPerfect
23.  ECHO Please Wait....................
24.  cd\wp
25.  wp
26.  cd\
27.  menu
28.  :program3
29.  CLS
30.  ECHO ^V[[5mLoading^V[[0m dBASE III Plus
31.  ECHO Please Wait....................
32.  cd\db3
33.  dbase
34.  cd\
35.  menu
36.  :program4
37.  cd\
38.  menu
39.  :program5
40.  cd\
41.  menu
42.  :program6
43.  cd\
44.  menu
45.  :program7
46.  cls
47.  ECHO Menu Terminated - DOS now Active
```

Suppose you want to log the usage of 1-2-3. In the current MENU.BAT file, line 17 executes 1-2-3; but before that program is loaded, the timers should be started. Begin by inserting lines beginning at 17. Enter

17i↵

You are now ready to create the timers. In this example, timer 1 is used for screen display, while timer 2 is used to store data into the time log file. Enter

```
TM START /C1/N↵
TM START /C2/N↵
    [Ctrl/c]
```

The next step is to display and store the elapsed time information when the user exits the application. To see where that should be inserted, use the list command (l) to display the section of the batch file you are working in. Enter

```
l↵
```

The screen will look like this:

```
*L
     8: IF errorlevel 4 GOTO program4
     9: IF errorlevel 3 GOTO program3
    10: IF errorlevel 2 GOTO program2
    11: IF errorlevel 1 GOTO program1
    12: :program1
    13: CLS
    14: ECHO ^[[5mLoading^[[0m Lotus 1-2-3
    15: ECHO Please Wait...................
    16: cd\123
    17: TM START /C1/N
    18: TM START /C2/N
    19:*lotus
    20: cd\
    21: menu
    22: :program2
    23: CLS
    24: ECHO ^[[5mLoading^[[0m WordPerfect
    25: ECHO Please Wait...................
    26: cd\wp
    27: cd\
    28: menu
    29: :program3
    30: CLS
*
```

Figure 5-4

Because you inserted two commands into the file, the command to run LOTUS has been moved to line 19. Therefore you should insert the TM STOP commands beginning at line 21, just before you return to the menu. Enter

```
21i↵
```

The SET Command

In order to create a meaningful log of activity on your computer you should store the name of the application that was run, as well as the time information. This can be done by placing a comment in each of the TM STOP commands. Examples:

```
TM STOP "Lotus 1-2-3" /C1/L
TM STOP "WordPerfect"/C1/L
TM STOP "dBASE III Plus"/C1/L
```

Notice that the three commands are the same except for the text in the comment area. Below is a generalized form of the same command. Observe that %program% is used in place of the text of the comment.

```
TM STOP "%program%" /C1/L
```

In DOS, %program% is called a parameter. (A parameter is a symbol for a specific text string.) The question of how to assign a meaning to a parameter is answered by the use of the DOS command, SET, which allows you to define a parameter. The definition is stored in the memory of the computer and remains there until you remove the parameter with a SET command, or reboot the system. Parameters created with SET are not stored on the disk and disappear when the computer is turned off or rebooted.

Below, the SET command is used to define the parameter PROGRAM as the text "Lotus 1-2-3 Version 2.01." Both the TM commands that follow refer to the PROGRAM parameter. DOS will place the text of the PROGRAM parameter into any command that has %program% inserted in it:

```
SET program=Lotus 1-2-3 Version 2.01
TM STOP "%program%" /C1/L/N
TM STOP "%program%" /C2/L/LOG>>timelog.txt
```

In this case the parameter technique can help you avoid a lot of typing. First, you need only type the name of the program once for each set of commands. Second, since each set of TM commands is exactly the same, you can simply copy the line instead of manually typing each one. All you need to do to is enter a SET command that changes the meaning of PROGRAM.

To implement this system, the command on line 21 should be a set command. Enter

```
SET programLotus = 1-2-3↵
```

The next two lines consist of TM commands that include the text parameter created with the SET command. The first one stores the usage information into the time log file. Enter

TM STOP "%program%" /C1/L/LOG>>timelog.txt↵

The next command displays the elapsed time information on the screen for the user to see. Enter

TM STOP "%program%" /C2/L/N↵

To give the user the opportunity to see the elapsed time, use the DOS PAUSE command. This command pauses the batch file and displays the message "Press any key to continue." Enter

PAUSE↵

You have now setup the MENU to time the use of 1-2-3. To review your progress, use the list command (L) to display the change made in the batch file.

[Ctrl/c]
l↵

The screen display will look like this:

```
*l
        14: ECHO ^[[5mLoading^[[0m Lotus 1-2-3
        15: ECHO Please Wait...................
        16: cd\123
        17: TM START /C1/N
        18: TM START /C2/N
        19: lotus
        20: cd\
        21: SET program = Lotus 1-2-3
        22: TM STOP "%program%" /C1/L/LOG>>timelog.txt
        23: TM STOP "%program%" /C2/L/N
        24: PAUSE
        25:*menu
        26: :program2
        27: CLS
        28: ECHO ^[[5mLoading^[[0m WordPerfect
        29: ECHO Please Wait...................
        30: cd\wp
        31: wp
        32: cd\
        33: menu
        34: :program3
        35: CLS
        36: ECHO ^[[5mLoading^[[0m dBASE III Plus
*
```

Figure 5-5

The next step is to repeat the commands for the other applications in your menu, such as WordPerfect and dBASE III Plus. Since you can copy the commands just created exactly as they are to other parts of the MENU batch, this should go easily. Only the SET command needs to be changed to reflect the name of the application.

While EDLIN is rather primitive as compared to full-powered editors like the Norton Editor, you can still copy lines. The C command accomplishes this.

The batch file shows that the next application, WordPerfect, is executed by the command on line 31, WP. You want to copy lines 17 and 18 in front of line 31. The C command, below, uses three numbers to do this. The first represents the line number of the first line to copy, the second represents the last line to copy, and the third represents the location for the copied lines. For example, the command that would copy lines 17 through 18 to line 31 would be 17,18,31c. Enter

```
17,18,31c↵
```

To see the results of the command, enter

```
1↵
```

The screen will show the revised batch. Note that lines 31 and 32 are the copies of lines 18 and 19. The WP command has been moved to line 33.

```
*l
        20: cd\
        21: SET program = Lotus 1-2-3
        22: TM STOP "%program%" /C1/L/LOG>>timelog.txt
        23: TM STOP "%program%" /C2/L/N
        24: PAUSE
        25: menu
        26: :program2
        27: CLS
        28: ECHO ^[[5mLoading^[[0m WordPerfect
        29: ECHO Please Wait....................
        30: cd\wp
        31:*TM START /C1/N
        32: TM START /C2/N
        33: wp
        34: cd\
        35: menu
        36: :program3
        37: CLS
        38: ECHO ^[[5mLoading^[[0m dBASE III Plus
        39: ECHO Please Wait....................
        40: cd\db3
        41: dbase
        42: cd\
*
```

Figure 5-6

The next step is to copy the TM STOP command to follow WordPerfect. The ensuing command will copy lines 21 through 24 to line 35. Enter

```
21,24,35c↵
```

List the file again. Enter

```
l↵
```

Line 35 needs to be changed to read WordPerfect instead of Lotus. Enter

```
35↵
SET program=WordPerfect↵
```

You have now created a line log for both Lotus and WordPerfect.

> The SET command and the parameters it passes offer a shortcut method to identifying the application used in the time log. DOS automatically creates SET parameters for DOS operations. For example, when DOS boots, a parameter called COMSPEC is created, which is equal to the name of the command interpreter file from which the system was booted, for example, COMSPEC=C:\COMMAND.COM
>
> Another automatically created SET parameter is called PATH. PATH is always equal to the current drive and directory. PATH is updated each time a CD command is given.
>
> You can take a shortcut in creating the comment for the TM command by using %PATH% to insert the name of the directory that is currently active. You can usually tell what application was being run by the name of the directory that was being used. This would allow you to create a universal TM command that records the directory name. Example:
>
> ```
> TM STOP "%path%" /C1/L/LOG>>c:\timelog.txt
> TM STOP "%path%" /C2/L/N
> PAUSE
> CD\
> MENU
> ```
>
> Note that this time the TM commands should come before you change back to the root directory so that the current pathname is the directory from which the application was executed. Also note that the name of the time log file was extended to include the directory name, to make sure that you are not creating separate time log files in each application directory.

Repeat the steps shown above to create TM commands to log the use of dBASE III Plus.

The completed batch file should look like the illustration below. The line numbers are added for reference purposes only, they should not be entered. The arrows indicate the lines added to this batch:

Listing 5.2. Complete MENU.BAT file

```
ECHO OFF
CLS
TYPE menu.txt
ASK "Enter your choice ^[[5m►^[[0m^G", 123456E
IF errorlevel 7 GOTO program7
IF errorlevel 6 GOTO program6
IF errorlevel 5 GOTO program5
IF errorlevel 4 GOTO program4
IF errorlevel 3 GOTO program3
IF errorlevel 2 GOTO program2
IF errorlevel 1 GOTO program1
:program1
CLS
ECHO ^[[5mLoading^[[0m Lotus 1-2-3
ECHO Please Wait....................
cd\123
TM START /C1/N
TM START /C2/N
lotus
cd\
SET program=Lotus 1-2-3
TM STOP "%program%" /C1/L/LOG>>timelog.txt
TM STOP "%program%" /C2/L/N
PAUSE
menu
:program2
CLS
ECHO ^[[5mLoading^[[0m WordPerfect
ECHO Please Wait....................
cd\wp
TM START /C1/N
TM START /C2/N
wp
cd\
SET program=WordPerfect
TM STOP "%program%" /C1/L/LOG>>timelog.txt
TM STOP "%program%" /C2/L/N
PAUSE
menu
:program3
CLS
ECHO ^[[5mLoading^[[0m dBASE III Plus
ECHO Please Wait....................
```

(Continued)

Listing 5.2. Complete MENU.BAT file *(Continued)*

```
cd\db3
TM START /C1/N
TM START /C2/N
dbase
cd\
SET program=dBASE III Plus
TM STOP "%program%" /C1/L/LOG>>timelog.txt
TM STOP "%program%" /C2/L/N
PAUSE
menu
:program4
cd\
menu
:program5
cd\
menu
:program6
cd\
menu
:program7
cls
ECHO Menu Terminated - DOS now Active
```

Printing the Time Log

Before you save this batch file, include in the menu an option that would print a copy of the time log being accumulated on the disk. Use the DOS redirection command to TYPE the file to the printer. Example:

```
TYPE timelog.txt > PRN
```

This sends the text of the TIMELOG.TXT file, unformatted, to the printer. Unformatted output, typical of DOS commands, means that DOS does not take into consideration page breaks, page numbers, headers or footers, which help organize output onto pages of paper.

On the other hand, the Norton Utilities contain a program called LP.EXE (line printing) that is capable of printing text files in an organized format. LP is a formatted output program that takes into consideration useful formatting options. LP normally prints the text of the file and adds a header to each page, which includes the name of the file, the date and time of printing, and the page number.

The TIMELOG.TXT file is one that you may want to print out from time to time. Since program 4 in the batch file, which begins at line 55, is not being used, you can create a program to print the log, here. Enter

55i↵

The first command in this program will clear the screen. Enter

CLS↵

Blank Lines

With the screen cleared, enter some blank lines so that your message will not be placed at the top of the screen. Since the ECHO command is used to place text on the screen, it seems logical to print a blank line by simply using ECHO without text. Example:

ECHO

However, DOS does not accept that method. In DOS, ECHO used without text, prompts a display of the current status of the ECHO command. This means that if you place ECHO inside a batch it will print ECHO off instead of a blank line.

Entering blank spaces on the line seems logical, but it is incorrect. Spaces following the ECHO command are ignored, which is consistent with the way DOS treats spaces. For instance, in any ordinary DOS command, such as DIR, DOS ignores extra spaces entered after the command.

DIR [space][space][space]↵ is the same as **DIR↵**

You can solve the problem of how to create blank lines by entering a character following ECHO that acts like text but does not show on the screen. Many users simply use a period.

However, character 255 of the IBM character set suppresses the ECHO off message and appears on the screen as a blank. To enter this character use the [Alt/keypad] discussed earlier in this chapter.

To create a blank line, enter

ECHO
[space bar]

Next enter character 255.

[Alt/255]

Notice that the cursor moves to the right as if you typed a space. Remember that you must enter a space between ECHO and [Alt/255]. The space is a necessary delimiter between an ECHO command and its text. If you do not leave the space, DOS will not execute the command and print the **Bad command or filename** message.

Complete the line by entering

↵

To create more blanks, you can use the Copy command in EDLIN. Enter

```
[Ctrl/c]
56,56,57c↵
56,57,58c↵
```

You now have four blank lines. Test this by listing. Enter

l↵

Complete the printing program by entering

```
60i↵
ECHO Printing Time Log...↵
LP timelog.txt↵
```

Save the file by entering

```
[Ctrl/c]
e↵
```

Now that you have added another program to the MENU batch you should also add that program's name to the MENU.TXT file. Enter

edlin menu.txt↵

In this file, line 11 holds the name of program 4. Enter

11↵

The existing portion of line 11 should remain as it is. [F3] prompts EDLIN to retype the entry. Enter

[F3]

Add the name of the new program.

```
[space bar]
Print Time Log↵
```

Save the revised menu text.

```
e↵
```

Try your time log system at this time. Enter

```
menu↵
```

Run the applications from your menu. To view how the system creates a record of your usage, print the time log. When you are finished with the menu, exit the batch and return to DOS.

Submenus

The main hard disk menu that you created has one limitation: it can only hold a limited number of options. But the limitation is more apparent than real. The basic structure used for the MENU batch can be repeated to create as many submenus as possible. The menus can be tied together to form a system of menus that can include all of your basic system operations, such as formatting disks and backing up data. You can even create batch programs to send special instructions to your printer. As an example, a submenu batch file called UTILS will be created, which will contain examples of such operations.

The first step is to create copies of the two files that create the menu, MENU.BAT and MENU.TXT. Enter

```
COPY MENU.* UTIL.*↵
```

DOS will copy three files. The third file, MENU.BAK, is automatically created when you edit with EDLIN. It is not important and can be deleted from the disk.

Linking a Submenu

By using the copy command you have created duplicates of the menu batch files.

```
MENU.BAT copied to UTIL.BAT
MENU.TXT copied to UTIL.TXT
```

Before deciding what utility functions the submenu should contain, first address the problem of how to get one batch file, MENU, to call the other batch file, UTIL. This requires modifications to both program.

In MENU, a new command should be added that executes the UTIL batch. In UTIL, a program needs to be created that will return you to the MENU batch.

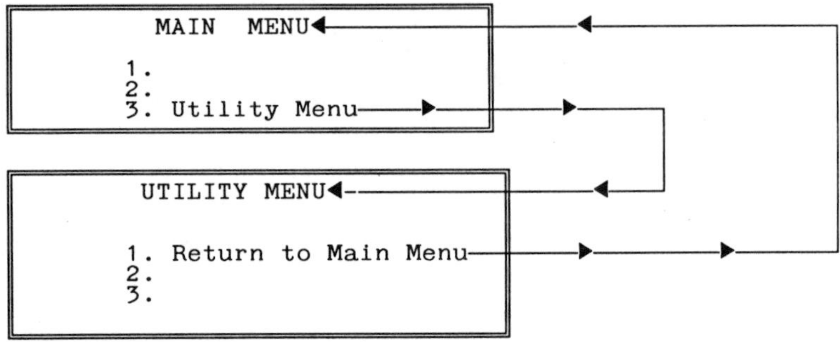

Begin with the MENU program. Currently, options 5 and 6 are unused. In this instance make option 6 the one that activates the submenu. Load the MENU.TXT file into the line editor by entering

```
edlin menu.txt↵
```

List the commands in this file.

```
l↵
```

Line 13 displays option 6. Change the line to indicate that option 6 will activate the submenu program. Enter

```
13↵
[F3]
[space bar]
Utility Menu↵
```

Save the modified file by entering

```
e↵
```

Next, change the commands in the MENU.BAT file for option 6, which is currently empty. Enter

```
edlin menu.bat↵
```

Locate the lines that control the program for option 6. The P(age) command will display consecutive screens. Enter

p↵ (3 times)

The screen should look like this:

```
*p
        47: dbase
        48: cd\
        49: SET program=dBASE III Plus
        50: TM STOP "%program%" /C1/L/LOG>>timelog.txt
        51: TM STOP "%program%" /C2/L/N
        52: PAUSE
        53: menu
        54: :program4
        55: CLS
        56: ECHO
        57: ECHO
        58: ECHO
        59: ECHO
        60: ECHO Printing Time Log...
        61: LP timelog.txt
        62: cd\
        63: menu
        64: :program5
        65: cd\
        66: menu
        67: :program6
        68: cd\
        69:*menu
*
```

Figure 5-7

Line 68 starts the program for option 6. To prompt this option to display another menu, simply enter the name of the menu batch file you want to display:

```
68i↵
util↵
```

You can now save the menu batch with this small but important modification. Enter

```
[Ctrl/c]
e↵
```

Preparing the Submenu

The next step is to change the UTIL batch to act as a submenu for the main menu program. The chief modification is to allow option 6 on the submenu to take you back to the main menu. Begin with the text in the UTIL.TXT file. Enter

```
edlin util.txt↵
1↵
```

The first change is in the title of the menu. Enter

```
5↵
UTILITY SUBMENU↵
```

Because this is a submenu, change the options to reflect the operations you want to carry out. In this example, the new options are shown in the file listing below. Change your file to emulate this one:

Listing 5.3. Submenu file UTIL.TXT (numbers added for reference)

```
1.
2.
3.
4.
5.    UTILITY SUBMENU
6.
7.
8.       [7m1.[0m Format a Floppy Disk
9.       [7m2.[0m Set Printer to Letter Quality
10.      [7m3.[0m Set Printer to Compressed Print
11.      [7m4.[0m Print Text Pattern
12.      [7m5.[0m
13.      [7m6.[0m Return to Main Menu
14.      [7mE.[0m Exit Menu - Activate DOS
15.
16.
17.
18.
19.
20.
```

When the modifications are complete, save the file.

The next step is to change the UTIL.BAT file. Delete the existing programs and create an option, 6, that will link this batch to the menu batch. Enter

```
edlin util.bat↵
```

Global Changes

As mentioned previously, EDLIN does not have the kind of editing features found in word processing programs or advanced program editors like the Norton Editor. However, it does have a method of performing search and replace operations, which is convenient for making the same change a number of times.

An example of a repetitive change occurs when creating a submenu from a copy of an existing menu. The commands that use MENU are to be changed to the submenu, UTIL, in this instance. You can avoid a lot of editing by entering a Replace (R) command. The command below searches all the lines specified, 1 to 100, and changes all occurrences of menu to util.

```
1,100Rmenu^zutil
```

The ^Z stands for [Ctrl/z], which is inserted by pressing [F6]. To carry out this action, enter

```
1,100r
menu
[F6]
util↵
```

EDLIN lists the lines in which the change has been made.

```
C:\>edlin util.bat
End of input file
*1,100rmenu^Zutil
          3: TYPE util.txt
         25: util
         39: util
         53: util
         63: util
         66: util
         69: util
*
```

Figure 5-8

Now add the commands for option 6. Because this file is an exact copy of the MENU.BAT you can insert the instruction for option 6 on the same line, 68. Enter

```
68i↵
menu↵
```

Save the file by entering

```
[Ctrl/c]
e↵
```

> Programs for formatting and setting the printer have not been created, but follow later in this chapter.

Start the main menu by entering

```
menu↵
```

The screen displays the menu. Choose option 6:

```
6
```

The submenu program appears on the screen. Return to the main menu by entering

```
6
```

You can create as many sub-levels of menus as you require using this system. Exit the menu by entering

```
e
```

Altering Existing Prompts

Suppose you intend to include in your batch program a section that formats a floppy disk. The simplest way to implement this operation is to enter the format command into your batch file. Example

```
FORMAT a:
```

When the batch executes, the format command enters an interactive mode in which it displays prompts and waits for user inputs. For example, format displays:

```
Insert new diskette for drive A:
  and strike ENTER when ready
```

While most experienced users take the meaning of this prompt for granted, it is not so for everyone who reads it. Some users get confused because they want to reformat an old disk, not a new one. And most PC and XT keyboards refer to a↵ key, not ENTER. While these points are very small, it raises the question about how much control you can have over DOS operations executed from batch files. Suppose you want to have a different type of interaction take place when formatting. What could you do, if anything, to change the way format operates?

It is possible to use DOS redirection commands to alter the interactive quality of various commands. This is an often overlooked feature of batch commands. It offers you a way to control, more precisely, what is displayed, and the type of responses required, even when using commands like format that have an interactive quality of their own. Because the Norton Utilities programs, ASK and BEEP, can be used to define your own prompts, you can create substitute dialogues that more closely support what you want to accomplish.

Before you actually create the UTIL menu and batch file explore the commands to get a feel for how they can be used.

Redirected Input

When formatting a floppy disk you enter,

```
Format a:↵
```

DOS asks you to press ENTER to begin. Then, when the formatting is complete, you enter N↵, to inform the system that no more disks are to be formatted.

It is possible to cut down the number of keystrokes needed to accomplish this task. You can also make the operation a single entry, rather than having to wait for the prompts to come up each time.

The DOS redirection command can be used to accomplish this and to automatically input your responses from keystrokes stored in a text file. In this example, the format command requires you to enter ↵ to start the formatting, then N↵ to end it. Create a text file called KEYS that contain these two keystrokes:

```
edlin keys↵
i↵
```

Enter the keystrokes into this file that you would normally use to answer the format prompts. Enter

↵

Save this file by entering

```
[Ctrl/c]
e↵
```

The < redirection command instructs DOS to read keystroke inputs from a specified file instead of waiting for you to enter the keystrokes at the keyboard. The concept is similar to the creation of keystroke macros in Lotus 1-2-3 in which text labels are used to automatically enter command keystrokes.

The command below executes FORMAT but instructs DOS to feed FORMAT the keystrokes stored in the file KEYS. KEYS contains your answers to the prompts FORMAT will display. The effect is that FORMAT becomes a non-interactive command. Make sure that you have a scratch disk in drive A to try this command. Enter

```
format a:<keys↵
```

The format command displays the prompts but does not wait for a response, because the response is entered from the file called KEYS. When the formatting is complete you are back at the DOS prompt.

Suppressing the Output

The redirection of the input from the keyboard to a text file is a way to circumvent prompts displayed by DOS programs. But the text of the prompts still appears on the screen. You can suppress the display of this text by using an output redirection command.

In this case, the output device will be called NUL. DOS recognizes the name NUL as a nonexistent device. Anything output to NUL is treated like it never existed; it does not appear on the screen, the printer, or a disk file. If the output of the format command is sent to the NUL device, you will not see any of the messages normally displayed in the format command.

Below is the same format command you just entered, but with its output suppressed. Notice that you must enter a space between <keys and >nul. Enter

```
format a:<keys >nul↵
```

The disk is formatted without any of the usual output or input. A reduction in keystrokes can be accomplished by putting the command into a batch file with a simple name. Enter

```
edlin f.bat↵
i↵
```

Enter the commands for this simple batch.

```
ECHO off↵
format a:<keys >nul↵
ECHO Disk Format Complete↵
```

Save the file.

```
[Ctrl/c]
i↵
```

Now execute that batch by entering

```
f↵
```

The formatting executes without any prompts or input.

A convenient variation on this idea can make formatting floppy disks on systems with a hard disk and two floppies much faster. Having two floppies does not make it easier to format two disks because the format command works with only one drive at a time. But if you have two drives installed, you can create a batch file that formats a disk in A, then formats a disk in B, with no pauses. Create a batch called FF.BAT (fast format). The file uses the KEYS text file that contains the keystrokes to answer the format prompts. The contents of FF.BAT are:

format a:<keys
format b:<keys

Enter FF↵ and the batch will format both disks.

A variation on the same theme will allow you to automatically copy data from drive A and B with a single command. This is useful when you are installing a new program and have to copy complete disks into the same directory. Create a batch file called MOVE.BAT with the following commands:

copy a:*.* \%1
copy b:*.* \%1

To use the command, enter MOVE followed by the directory into which you want the file copied. Example: MOVE 123. This will copy the contents of drive A and B into the 123 directory. The %1 is a command line parameter. This means that DOS interprets the first word following the batch file name as a SET parameter. DOS assigns these words parameter names %1, %2, %3, etc.

This means that entering MOVE 123 is roughly equal to two DOS commands, SET 1 = 123, then MOVE.

Audio Prompts

You have already seen that outputing the character [Ctrl/g] from your batch file prompts DOS to sound a beep. Norton Utilities provide a command called BEEP that enhances your ability to give audio prompts from your batch files. Used in it simplest form, the beep command duplicates the [Ctrl/g] by issuing a single tone. Enter

```
beep↵
```

But BEEP can go far beyond that simple tone. There are four parameters that you can specify for BEEP.

\F Frequency. This is a numeric value that corresponds to the frequency in Hz. Hz stands for Hertz, which is the unit of measurement used to count cycles per second. The greater the value the higher the pitch of the tone. For example, 262 Hz is approximately the same tone as middle C. 523 Hz is close to high C.

\D Duration. This value determines the tone. A value of 1 sets the tone to 1/18 or .0556 seconds. You can increase the duration of the tone by increasing the value of this parameter.

\R Repeat. Repeats the tone a specified number of times.

\W Wait. This option sets a time length between each repetition of the tone. A value of 1 sets the wait to 1/18 or .0556 seconds.

These parameters can be used to vary the type of sound created by BEEP. As an example, enter

```
beep /f880 /d4 /r10 /w2↵
```

The command sounded 10 tones, approximately A over high C(880Hz), for 1/5 of a second each, every 1/10 of a second.

BEEP also has the ability to read input parameters from a text file. This means you can enter parameters for several tones. You could actually play a tune using these concepts.

To create a file called TONE1.MUS, enter

```
edlin tone1.mus↵
i↵
```

Enter five short tones. Use the values 784 (G above high C), 880 (A), and 988 (B). To make a simple pattern you will move up and then down the scale with these tones. The duration will be the shortest possible length, 1. Enter

```
f784 d1↵
f880 d1↵
f988 d1↵
f880 d1↵
f784 d1↵
```

> When the parameters for the tones are entered into a separate file, it is not necessary to use the / characters. This is because when the values are stored in a file there is no need to distinguish them from other parameters. This is not so when the parameters are entered on a command line. For example, if you entered the command
>
> beep f220↵
>
> The command would tell BEEP to search for tones in a file called F220. In such a case the / would identify F220 as a parameter, not a filename.

Save the file by entering

```
[Ctrl/c]
e↵
```

To play the tones specified by the file, enter

```
beep tone1.mus↵
```

The tones are sounded according to the values stored in the text file. Make another tone file. Enter

```
edlin tone2.mus↵
i↵
```

This time the tones will come from the lower end of the scale, E(165) F(175) G(196) below middle C. Enter

```
f196 d1↵
f165 d1↵
f175 d1↵
f196 d1↵
f165 d1↵
f175 d1↵
```

Save the tone file by entering

```
[Ctrl/c]
e↵
```

Play this tone file by entering

```
beep tone2.mus↵
```

The beep command plays the tones listed in this file.

You have now created two unique audio prompts. Along with the other tools provided with DOS and Norton Utilities, you are ready to create batch programs that alter the appearance and user interface of some common DOS operations.

> The term user interface has come to refer to the dialogue of prompts and responses that take place between user and a program.

Screen Control in Batch Files

Because most screen output is unformatted, DOS places the prompt or echoed text on the next available line. The ANSI system also provides a means of placing text at specific locations on the screen display. You can use [Esc] codes, listed below, to move up and down lines, left or right columns and erase individual lines. The # stands for a number value, 1-24 for lines, or 1-80 for columns.

```
Cursor down 1 line              Esc[#B
Cursor up 1 line                Esc[#A
Cursor left 1 column            Esc[#D
Cursor right 1 column           Esc[#C
Cursor to line #, column#       Esc[#;#H
Erase current line              Esc[K
```

You can gain tighter control over the look of the screen display by adding these ANSI screen control commands to ECHO commands. For example, when text is placed on the screen during a batch file, the only way to erase the text is to clear the screen, CLS. With the ANSI screen commands you can move the cursor backward and selectively erase individual lines.

> In some systems, DOS command CLS is the same as the ANSI command [Esc][2J. If you enter CLS into a computer into which the ANSI system driver has not been installed the screen will not clear but the characters <-[2J will appear on the screen.

To see how this can be used, create a simple batch called SCREEN.BAT. Enter

```
edlin screen.bat↵
i↵
```

Begin the batch by clearing the screen and setting the ECHO off. Enter

```
ECHO off↵
CLS↵
```

Normally, an ECHO command specified next would print at the top of the screen display. But you can use an [Esc] command to place the cursor farther down on the screen. Move the cursor down seven lines, employing the [ESC][#B command. Enter

```
[Ctrl/v][[7B↵
```

Next, use ECHO to write two lines on the screen, then PAUSE the batch file. Enter

```
echo 1↵
echo 2↵
PAUSE↵
```

Erase the lines individually in this example. This can be done by moving the cursor up the screen and using the **[Esc][K** command to erase a line. You can place more than one **[Esc]** command in a single ECHO command. For example, below you will issue two ESC codes on the same line: one to move up and the second to erase a line. Enter

```
ECHO
[space bar]
[Ctrl/v][[3A[Ctrl/v][[K↵
```

The command will erase the first line, then proceed to erase the other two lines:

```
ECHO
[space bar]
[Ctrl/v][[K
[Ctrl/v][[1B
[Ctrl/v][[K↵
```

Save the file by entering

```
[Ctrl/c]
e↵
```

Execute the batch file by entering

```
screen↵
```

Notice that the lines of output from the batch appear in the center of the screen display, not at the very top. Respond to the prompt by entering

↵

The program moved the cursor back and erased the three lines. The use of [Esc] commands in batch files can lend your displays a more professional look.

An Alternate Formatting Program

The techniques just described can be assembled into an alternative form of format program. In this program you will make use of:

1. Redirection for input and output.
2. Screen display [Esc] codes.
3. The BEEP command to create audio prompts.

The name of the file will be NF.BAT (new format). Create the file by entering

```
edlin ff.bat↵
i↵
```

To use all the techniques described in the previous sections, enter the batch file as shown below. The line numbers are added for reference purposes only; you should not enter them. Note that ^[indicates the entry of an [Esc] code, [Ctrl/v][in EDLIN.

Listing 5.4. File NF.BAT

```
1.   ECHO OFF
2.   CLS
3.   echo ^[[7B
4.   ECHO You have selected to Format a Floppy Disk
5.   BEEP /f1000
```

(Continued)

Listing 5.4. File NF.BAT *(Continued)*

```
6.  ECHO ^[[7B
7.  PAUSE
8.  BEEP /f200
9.  CLS
10. ECHO ^[[7B
11. ECHO Place the disk to be formatted in Drive A
12. ECHO and close the disk drive door
13. BEEP /f1000
14. ECHO ^[[6B
15. PAUSE
16. BEEP /f200
17. CLS
18. ECHO ^[[7B
19. BEEP tone1.mus
20. ECHO The disk in drive A is being formatted.
21. ECHO Please wait .............
22. FORMAT a:<keys >nul
23. BEEP tone2.mus
24. ECHO ^[[2A^[[K^[[1B^[[K
25. BEEP tone2.mus
26. ECHO Disk Format Completed. Disk Statistics:
27. CHKDSK a:
28. ECHO ^[[2A^[[K^[[1B^[[K
29. ECHO ^[[3B
30. BEEP /f500 /r2
31. PAUSE
32. UTIL
```

On the FF.BAT file, lines 3, 7 and 10 use the [Esc][#B command to move the cursor down a set number of lines. This creates spacing on the screen without having to print blank lines.

The BEEP command is used in line 5 to issue a high pitch tone to draw the users attention to the screen. The command in line 8 issues a low pitched tone to confirm that the user wants to continue. The pattern is repeated in lines 13 and 16. Line 19 and 25 play the tones stored in files.

Line 22 executes the format command using the input and output redirection commands.

Lines 24 and 28 are used to erase part of the screen by moving the cursor up and erasing one line at a time. Line 28 is used to erase the part of the CHKDSK display that deals with internal memory size and is not related to disk formatting.

Line 32 is used to return to the UTIL batch program. The assumption is made that the FF.BAT will be executed from that menu.

When you finish entering the batch, save the file.

To test this program, make sure that you have a scratch disk in your floppy drive. Execute the command by entering

ff↵

The screen displays the first message and sounds the first audio prompt. The [Esc] commands achieve the spacing effect. Continue by entering

↵

The next series of audio and video prompts execute.

```
Place the disk to be formatted in Drive A
and close the disk drive door.



Strike a key when ready . . .
```

Figure 5-9

Begin the actual formatting by entering

↵

When the formatting is complete the screen will look like this:

```
Disk Format Completed. Disk Statistics:

   362496 bytes total disk space
   362496 bytes available on disk



Strike a key when ready . . .
```

Figure 5-10

Enter

↵

The program places you in the Utility menu. Exit the menu by entering

e↵

> Keep in mind that by suppressing the normal input and output operations of a program like FORMAT you will not see any error messages that might be generated by the program. The program discussed in this chapter is meant as an example of the kind of manipulation that is possible with batch files. The best use and organization of DOS operations depends on your own needs and desires.

Sending Printer Codes with DOS

Other convenient options to execute from a menu are commands that setup the printer for specific types of printing. Today, even the least expensive printers have different fonts, pitches and type styles. These features are selected by sending special codes to the printer that consist of control and escape characters combined with normal characters. When executed properly these codes do not print but change the printer's settings.

Printer codes are specific to each printer. However, because of the popularity of certain printers, their coding sequences are often duplicated by many manufacturers. For example, the command set used in the EPSON MX, FX and RX series printers is the same as the IBM graphics printer. You will find that many other printers share the same codes.

If your printer has a near letter quality mode it is common to use the codes sequence found on the IBM Proprinter series.

Check your printer's documentation to see if it emulates one of these printers.

In this chapter the codes entered will be the ones used with the IBM Proprinter series.

You can use batch files to send these codes to your printer and in that way control the style of printing from your batch file menu.

Understanding Printer Manuals

The first step in implementing printer operations from batch files is to understand the printer codes listed in your printer manual. It is your printer manual that lists the codes that affect your printer. However, the process of reading the manual can be confusing because of the way that the information is presented. Most printer manuals list the code for a particular print style in three ways. Below is an example of a typical entry:

```
ASCII                          DECIMAL
HEXADECIMAL
DC2(10 cpi)                    18              12
ESC : (12 cpi)                 27 58           1B 3A
SI (17.1cpi)                   15              0F
ESC I 1(near letter quality) 27 73 03
```

For more information about printer codes see the appendix at the end of this chapter.

To get a feel for how you can send these codes, create a batch called PRTTEST. Enter

```
prt.bat↵
i↵
```

The basic method is to use the ECHO command to redirect the output to the printer. Example:

```
ECHO printer codes >PRN
```

An alternative strategy is to store the codes in a text file, then use TYPE filename >PRN to print the text. This is similar to the way you stored the tone values in a file and output them by using the BEEP command with the filename.

For example, suppose that you want to enter compressed printing. You would need to execute the code for compressed printing, [Ctrl/o]. Enter

```
ECHO
[space bar]
[Ctrl/v]
O
[space bar]
>PRN↵
```

Now enter a line of text to demonstrate that the printer is set to compressed printing. Be sure that there is a space before the redirection command, >PRN. Enter

```
ECHO This is compressed printing. >PRN
```

Set the printing back to normal size by sending [Ctrl/r]. Enter

```
ECHO
[space bar]
[Ctrl/v]
R
[space bar]
>PRN↵
```

Enter a line to print at normal size.

```
ECHO This is normal printing. >PRN
```

Finally, add a command to feed the rest of the form. Enter

```
ECHO
[space bar]
[Ctrl/v]
L
[space bar]
>PRN↵
```

Save the file by entering

```
[Ctrl/c]
e↵
```

Execute the program by entering

```
prt↵
```

The two lines print with different size letters, and the form feeds the remainder of the form.

Up to this point You have worked out the principle by which you can implement printer settings from a batch file. The final step is to put the new techniques to work within the UTIL.BAT program.

The UTIL menu program has three printer options: set letter quality mode, set compressed printing, and print test pattern. Create two batch files to send the necessary codes to the printer, calling them NLQ.BAT (near letter quality), CMPRES.BAT (compressed print) and TSTPAT.BAT (test pattern). The files will set the printer into a specific print mode. The test pattern file will print some text and then feed a form.

Begin with the simplest of the three programs, the one that prints the test pattern. Enter

```
edlin tstpat.bat↵
i↵
```

Enter

```
ECHO off↵
ECHO Printing .....↵
ECHO ABCDEFGHIJKLMNOPQRSTUVWXYZ >PRN↵
ECHO abcdefghijklmnopqrstuvwxyz >PRN↵
```

The next command should feed the form in the printer. Most ASCII compatible printers recognize ASCII character 12, [Ctrl/L], as the form feed command. Enter

```
ECHO
[space bar]
[Ctrl/v]L
[space bar]
>PRN↵
util↵
```

> The UTIL command is added on the assumption that this batch file will be executed from the UTIL menu.

Save the file by entering

```
[Ctrl/c]
e↵
```

The next file is the one that sets the printer to compressed printing. Enter

```
edlin cmpres.bat↵
i↵
```

The code for compressed printing in the Proprinter is ASCII 15. In terms of control characters, ASCII 15 is [Ctrl/o]. Enter the following commands.

```
ECHO off↵
ECHO Setting Compressed Printing.....↵
ECHO
[space bar]
[Ctrl/v]O
[space bar]
>PRN↵
util↵
```

Save the file by entering

```
[Ctrl/c]
e↵
```

The final file is the one that sets letter quality printing. The Proprinter code for letter quality printing is [Esc]I3. In addition, letter quality printing is not possible when the compressed mode is active. It is therefore necessary to make sure that the print pitch is set for 10 before you attempt to set the letter quality. The code for 10 pitch print is ASCII 18, that is, [Ctrl/r]

> Printer effects are often mutually exclusive, such as the example of letter quality and compressed print. Others form special combinations. When you create batch files to set printer attributes keep in mind which attributes combine or exclude other features.
>
> Remember that you can set your printer back to its default settings by simply turning it off and then on again.

Create the NLQ batch. Enter

```
edlin nlq.bat↵
i↵
ECHO off↵
ECHO Setting Letter Quality Printing.....↵
```

Enter the code for normal (10 pitch) printing, then the code for letter quality printing.

```
ECHO
[space bar]
[Ctrl/v]R
[space bar]
>PRN↵
ECHO
[space bar]
[Ctrl/v][I3
[space bar]
>PRN↵
util↵
```

Save the file by entering

```
[Ctrl/c]
e↵
```

The final step is to integrate these commands into the UTIL.BAT file. Enter

```
edlin util.bat↵
```

Currently, the UTIL file contains copies of the programs originally entered into the MENU.BAT. Delete the commands in this menu that do not belong. For example, lines 14 through 25 should be deleted. Enter

```
14,25d↵
```

Continue deleting by entering

```
16,27d↵
18,29d↵
```

The programs that match the UTIL menu options are ready to be added. Enter the command for the NF (new format) batch.

```
14i↵
nf↵
[Ctrl/c]
```

Now add the three printing programs.

```
17i↵
nlq↵
[Ctrl/c]

19i↵
cmpres↵
[Ctrl/c]

22i↵
tstpat↵
```

Save the revised menu file by entering

```
[Ctrl/c]
e↵
```

Listing 5.5. UTIL.BAT (line numbers added for reference)

```
ECHO OFF
CLS
TYPE util.txt
ASK "Enter your choice ^V[[5m►^V[[0m^VP", 123456E
IF errorlevel 7 GOTO program7
IF errorlevel 6 GOTO program6
IF errorlevel 5 GOTO program5
IF errorlevel 4 GOTO program4
IF errorlevel 3 GOTO program3
IF errorlevel 2 GOTO program2
IF errorlevel 1 GOTO program1
```

(Continued)

Listing 5.5. UTIL.BAT (line numbers added for reference) *(Continued)*

```
:program1
CLS
nf
:program2
CLS
nlq
:program3
cmpres
CLS
:program4
tstpat
CLS
ECHO
ECHO
ECHO
ECHO
ECHO Printing Time Log...
LP timelog.txt
cd\
util
:program5
cd\
util
:program6
menu
cd\
util
:program7
cls
ECHO Menu Terminated - DOS now Active
```

At this point You can try your menu and submenu programs. Enter

menu↵

Experiment with the menu you have created. These batch files should help you create custom menu batches that will make it easier for you or others to use your computer and printer.

Summary

This chapter discussed the use of DOS batch files in combination with the Norton Utilities program designed to enhance batch file operations.

Norton Utilities Program

Main Program The main Norton Utilities program can be used to alter data stored in disk files by allowing you to modify parts of existing program files. Take care when making such modifications. It is very easy to damage a program making it inoperable due to changes produced by the Norton Utilities main program. Always make a copy of any file you are about to modify.

SA Screen attributes. This program is used to change the color of the screen display text.

ASK ASK allows you to create interactive batch files. The ASK command pauses the execution of a batch and allows the user to enter one of the specified characters.

Following the entry, ASK set the DOS errorlevel to correspond to the character entered by the user. You can use the DOS IF ERRORLEVEL-GOTO command to branch to a specified label in a batch file based on a user's entry

TM Time mark. This program allows you to create between 1 and 4 timers in memory. The timers can be used to calculate the elapsed time of activities. The values can be displayed on the screen or stored in a file. The file can serve as a time log.

BEEP BEEP creates tones that act as audio prompts for the user. You can set the pitch, duration, repetition, and pause length of a tone. You can play extended tone series by storing a list of tones in a text file and specifying that file as an argument of the Beep command.

Appendix

What You Find in the Printer Manual

The first step in the process of sending a command to the printer is to understand the kind of commands to which your printer will respond. There is section in your printer manual, sometimes several, that lists the special codes used to implement printer functions. These codes are often called Escape codes because the first character in their sequence is the Escape character.

The Escape character is used to signal the start of a direct printer command because it is a character that most word processing programs exclude from documents. When working with a word processor or EDLIN, pressing [Esc] does not place that character in your document. It is a signal to the program that you wish to carry out some command or operation.

Printers look for [Esc] characters as commands because they are almost never used as part of the text. The printer manual displays something like this:

```
ESC I           SELECT TYPE FONT
Function        This command selects type font.
Sequence        ESC I n (n= 1 to 7 in decimal or 01 to 07
                in hexadecimal)
Hexadecimal     1B 49 n
Decimal         27 73 n
                n=1, selects high speed font
                n=2, selects elite
                n=3, selects letter quality
                n= 4 or 5, selects downloadable font
                n= 6 or 7, selects optional font cartridge
```

A complete explanation of this display is beyond the scope of this book. In short, it is a statement of how the printer recognizes a command to change fonts. The two characters that signal the printer to change fonts are [Esc] followed by I. The I must be uppercase I, not lowercase i.

When the printer receives these codes, it then changes fonts according to number. Fonts numbered 1 through 3 are built-in. The other fonts, 4 through 7 are optional. The printer manual attempts to make things easy by showing you three different ways to discuss the same codes:

1. **Symbols.** In this style each character is shown as a character or mnemonic name. Example: ESC I

2. **Decimal value.** The ASCII (American Standard Code for Information Interchange) assigns a decimal number value to each of the characters in the

computer's character set. Oddly, character #1 is not the letter A, but the [Ctrl/a] combination. The letter A is assigned 65. The letter a (lowercase) is 97. The [Esc] key is assigned 27. In this way you can represent the characters as a sequence of numbers. ESC I become 27 73.

3. **Hexidecimal.** Hexadecimal values refer to a special type of numbering system used mainly by programmers. Hexadecimal is a system that uses 16, not 10 numbers. Following 9, the hexadecimal system uses A(10), B(11), C(12), D(13), E(14) and F(15). Example: ESC I, which is 27 73 in decimal, becomes 1B 49 in hexadecimal.

Why all three? The reason is that different programs require you to enter the codes in different ways. EDLIN allows you to insert code sequences directly into the body of the text by using [Ctrl/v][to represent the [Esc].

Control Codes

Some common printer codes do not make use of [Esc] as a way of signaling the printer that a command is coming. For example, the command to compress printing on Epson and IBM dot matrix printers is ASCII code 15. ASCII codes from 1 to 26 correspond tothe characters created with [Ctrl/a] (ASCII 1) through [Ctrl/z] (ASCII 26). The table below shows the ASCII values and the control codes. Some common printer codes are shown.

Table 5A.1. ASCII Values and Control Codes

ASCII Value	[Ctrl] Code
1	A
2	B
3	C
4	D
5	E
6	F
7	G(bell)
8	H
9	I(tab)
10	J(line feed)
11	K
12	L(form feed)
13	M(carriage return)
14	N(double width)
15	O(compressed)
16	P
17	Q
18	R(10 pitch)

(Continued)

Table 5.A1. ASCII Values and Control Codes *(Continued)*

ASCII Value	[Ctrl] Code
19	S
20	T(end double width)
21	U
22	V
23	W
24	X(clear buffer)
25	Y
26	Z

These values can be entered with EDLIN by using [Ctrl/v] followed an uppercase letter. Example

```
[Ctrl/o]=[Ctrl/v]O
```

The Norton Editor will also insert control and escape codes. The prefix in the Norton Editor is [Ctrl/p] instead of [Ctrl/v] used in EDLIN

Numeric Values

Some printer commands require the entry of numeric values. For example, the IBM/Epson code for **Esc C #**, sets the form length to # number of lines. The number value required is the ASCII decimal value of the character. Entering 84 would not convert directly to ASCII value. The following entry into EDLIN would be incorrect:

```
[Ctrl/v][C84
```

The correct entry is the character that corresponds to ASCII 84,T. For example, to set the form length at 84 lines you would enter:

```
[Ctrl/v][CT
```

Nul Values in Printer Codes

Almost all of the characters needed to implement printer controls can be handled with the control and Escape codes discussed previously. However, some printers still require you to enter an ASCII value of zero. This value is called a NUL. The character 0 has an ASCII value of 48. A NUL has no keyboard equivalent since the lowest value you can enter with a [Ctrl/] combination is 1, [Ctrl/a].

> [Alt/0] on the keypad will not work either.

The only way to create the NUL is to use the main Norton Utilities program to change the character in the file to a NUL value, 0 decimal and hex.

Suppose you have a batch file that consists of a single command whose purpose is to send [Esc]W0 to the printer. This latter code is used in the Epson system to turn off expanded printing. (Note that in older printers the 0 is an ASCII 0, not the character 0.) To produce this character you would enter the following into the batch file:

```
[Ctrl/v][W0
```

The 0 is used to hold the place where the NUL should be inserted in the file. Holding this position is important because the Norton Utilities program cannot insert characters into a file, only change the characters already there.

After entering the keystrokes you would use the Norton Utilities main program to display the file in the hex mode.

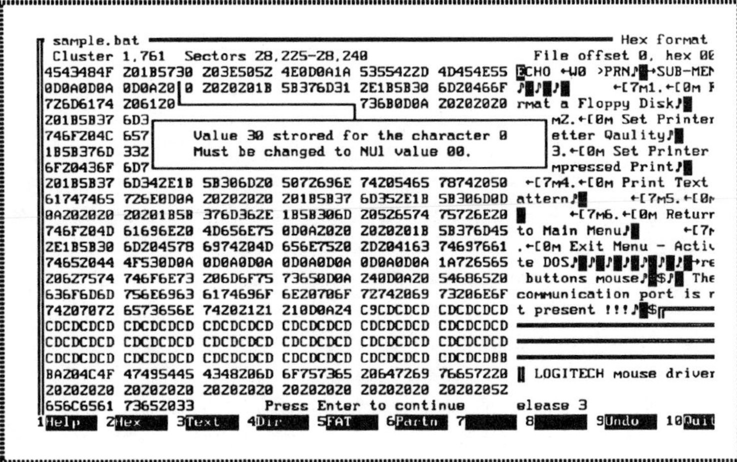

Figure 5-11

In the illustration, the eighth byte is 30, the value of the character 0. Change it to read 00, the value of a NUL.

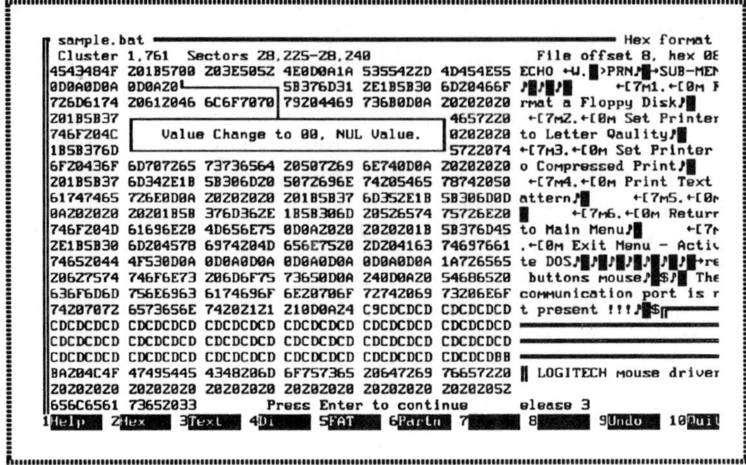

Figure 5-12

Save the file. The command will execute the NUL and control the printer properly.

> Many printers today avoid the problem of nuls by allowing you to enter the characters 0 and 1, ASCII values 48 and 49, instead of the ASCII value 0 and 1, NUL and [Ctrl/a]. This makes the procedure discussed in this section unnecessary.

Extra Returns

When creating batch files with EDLIN you may notice that two prompts appear when the batch file ends. The redundancy is caused because EDLIN automatically inserts CR/LF and [Ctrl/z] (end of file marker) characters at the end of a batch file. When the batch file is executed, DOS reacts to both the ↵ and the end of file marker characters by displaying a prompt for the ↵ and a prompt for the [Ctrl/z]. Hence, many batch files are followed by double prompts, not the single one that you would expect.

This can be eliminated by using the main Norton Utilities program. For instance, suppose you created a one line batch file with EDLIN called TEST.BAT. You would enter

```
edlin test.bat↵
i↵
dir↵
[Ctrl/c]
e↵
```

This is the simplest possible batch file. Execute the batch by entering

```
test↵
```

When the directory listing completes, you will notice that two prompts are generated. Use the main Norton Utilities program to load the file into the editing display and place it in the Hex display mode. Example:

```
nu text.bat↵
```

The display looks something like this:

```
test.bat ─────────────────────────────────────────── Hex format
Cluster 1,773   Sectors 28,417-28,432          File offset 0, hex 0E
4449520D 0A1A0000 00000000 00000000 00000000 00000000 DIR♪◙→...............
                          Enf of File, 1A  [Ctrl/z]
        Line Feed, 0D
                    Carriage Return, 0A
00000000 00000000          Press Enter to continue       ........
1Help  2Hex  3Text  4Dir  5FAT  6Partn  7  8  9Undo  10Quit
```

Figure 5-13

If you change the 0D to a 1A, end of file character, the batch file terminates without a CR/LF and only a single prompt is displayed.

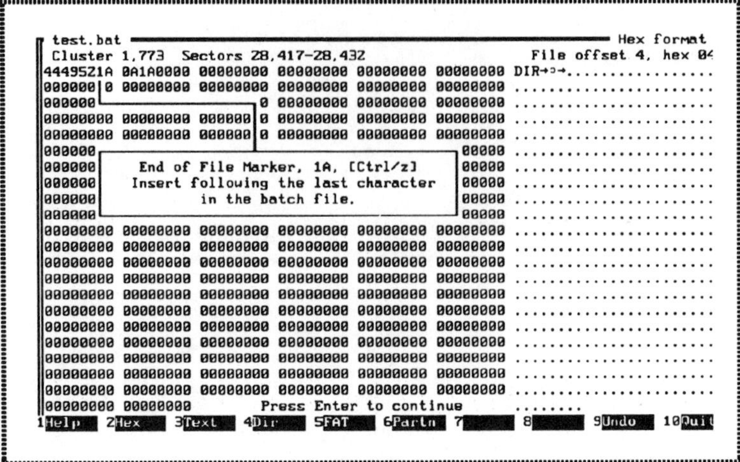

Figure 5-14

If you save this modification the batch file will end with a single prompt being displayed.

SECTION III
EVERYDAY TASKS

This section discusses typical computer tasks that are performed every day and describes how the Norton Utilities program can be used to execute those tasks faster, in a better way, and with more assurance. The Norton Utilities complement and enhance DOS operations in some cases, and in other cases bypass DOS procedures.

If you find that when executing any of the commands in this section, you see the message **Bad command or filename,** see Chapter 1 for how to setup the Norton Utilities programs.

6

LOCATING FILES AND INFORMATION

One of the most difficult problems to solve on a hard disk system is how to locate a file when you do not know what directory you stored it in. A few years ago this was particularly difficult because many of the popular applications, WordStar, dBASE II, and so on, did not take advantage of the DOS directory system. However, today, that situation has been resolved. Almost without exception, most programs allow you to enter a pathname, not just a filename, as a file specification. This advantage can become a nightmare, however, if you cannot remember where in the system you stored a particular file.

Why is this such a problem? The answer goes back to the way DOS commands are structured. The DIR, directory command, will list files from only one directory at a time. If you are not sure what directory a file has been stored in, the only solution is to change directories and enter DIR to get a listing. This tedious process usually nets poor results because when you're forced to do tedious work your attention level declines. After listing a few directories you may not catch the file, even if you are lucky enough to stumble on it.

The idea is, wherever possible, to get the computer to do the tedious work. Your job is to enter the correct command that will skillfully locate the information you require.

The key is to find a command that will search not just a specific directory but the entire disk. Both DOS and the Norton Utilities programs supply such a command. Before looking at the Norton Utilities program you might find it instructive to look at the DOS command first.

The command that searches the entire disk, or at least all the directories, is CHKDSK (check disk). The main purpose of CHKDSK is to check the file allocation table and the disk directories for consistency. In order to perform this function CHKDSK must look at the names of all of the files on the disk; thus CHKDSK has the power to view all the filenames. The CHKDSK command accepts a switch, **/V**, which stands for Verbose. The /V switch is a prompt to the CHKDSK command to display a list of the files it is examining. To see how this works, enter

```
chkdsk/v ↵
```

The program displays a long list of files on the screen. The list will greatly exceed the length of the screen so that the names of the files will scroll by too quickly for you to read. The end of the display will look like this:

```
        C:\OWP\BACKUP.EXE
        C:\OWP\RESTORE.EXE
        C:\OWP\DISKCOPY.COM
        C:\OWP\COMMON.DAT
        C:\OWP\CONTROL.DAT
        C:\OWP\MASTER.HLP
        C:\OWP.BAT
        C:\NB4-38.SCR
        C:\NB1A-01.SCR
        C:\NB1A-02.SCR
        C:\NB1A-03.SCR
        C:\NB1A-04.SCR
        C:\NB1A-05.SCR
        C:\NB1A-06.SCR

 21204992 bytes total disk space
    47104 bytes in 2 hidden files
    45056 bytes in 15 directories
 18388992 bytes in 768 user files
  2723840 bytes available on disk

   655360 bytes total memory
   462368 bytes free

[C:\]
```

Figure 6-1

The filenames listed with this command display the directory name as a prefix to the filename. You can create a printed copy of this list by entering

```
chkdsk/v>prn ↵
```

So far, you have only created a list of all the files. In theory this solves your problem, but in practice it is still difficult to find a file from these lists.

One possible solution is to employ another DOS command called FIND. FIND, a program supplied with MS-DOS as FIND.EXE or FIND.COM, was first introduced in version 2.0 of DOS and is not a program that can be used alone, like CHKDSK. It is called a “filter” because it isused to control the output of other programs. In theory, the FIND command can be used to filter the output of any command to include or exclude specific characters.

For example, suppose you want to list all the files on the hard disk that contain the characters DISK. The FIND filter is attached to a command by using the | (vertical line) character. FIND is then followed by the text string you want to locate. The command below combines CHKDSK/V with FIND to create a command that produces a list of items containing the letters DISK. Note that the text string, DISK, is entered in uppercase characters because DOS is sensitive to the case of the text string. Since DOS always prints filenames in uppercase your search string must also be entered in uppercase. Enter

```
chkdsk/v|find "DISK" ↵
```

The screen displays the following:

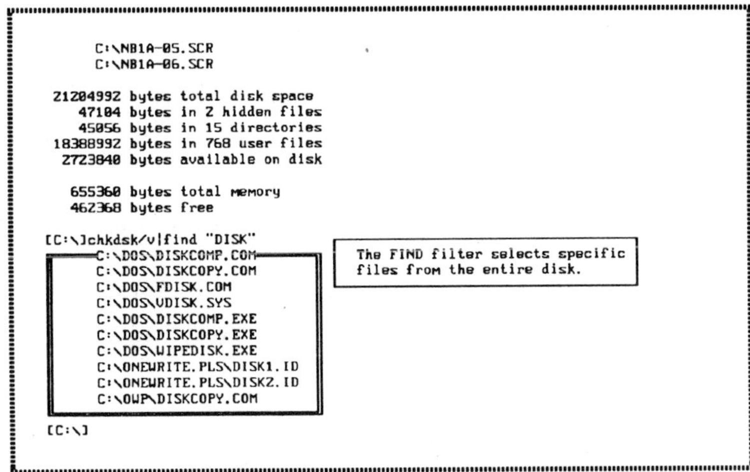

Figure 6-2

You may have noticed that for a long time the disk was being accessed but nothing was displayed on the screen. The reason has to do with the way a filter command like FIND operates.

The FIND command cannot interfere or change the normal operation of the CHKDSK command. Rather, it is meant to filter its output. The FIND command is used to select only those lines of output that contain the specified characters, DISK. But if Find cannot interfere with CHKDSK, how can the results of the command be altered?

The answer is that FIND allows CHKDSK to output its usual list of filenames. But instead of allowing the lines to appear on the screen they are captured in files called pipe files. In the DOS 2 level the filenames for the piping files are always %PIPE1.$$$ and %PIPE2.$$$. In DOS 3 level the names of the piping files are determined by the values in the date and time area of the memory. The filenames will vary each time you run a DOS filter program.

> The filenames created by piping in DOS 3 are eight-character names that usually contain numbers and letters. Examples: 001e2c22 or 001e2c01

The command then displays the contents of these files, selecting lines that contain the search string.

You might ask why you have never seen these filenames on any directory. The answer is that FIND erases the files as soon as the command is completed.

To prove that this is true you can use the Quick Unerase program to list some erased files. If you were using DOS 2 you could search for files that contain the word "pipe". In DOS 3 it becomes a bit trickier to accomplish because the filenames vary each time you run a filter command. But there is a strategy you can use. The pipe files in DOS 3 do not have file extensions. Thus, you can find the erased filenames by searching for files with three spaces as their extension. Depending on how you have been using your computer, you may also encounter some other erased files without extensions so that your results may vary a bit from this book.

Enter

```
qu *.↵
```

The Quick Unerase program displays the first erased file it encounters.

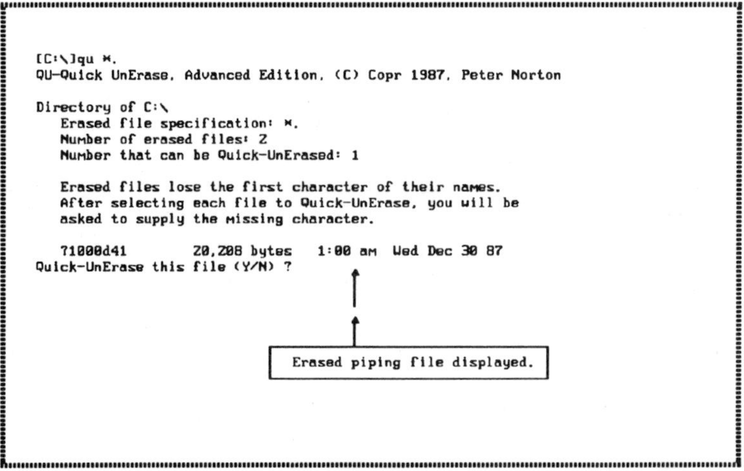

Figure 6-3

This file was used by the FIND command to store the normal output of the CHKDSK command. It then filtered that output selecting for the lines that contained "DISK".

> Because of differences, your computer may not display this file first. Enter N to skip to the next file until you encounter a filename characteristic of piping.

To display the next erased file, enter

```
n
```

The next filename is the second pipe file. DOS normally uses two files for piping operations.

> The QU (Quick Unerase) program is discussed in detail in Section IV.

Break execution of the program by entering

```
[Ctrl/c]
```

What does all this show? First it shows that a filtering command like CHKDSK is a very slow process because (1) the CHKDSK command must complete its usual operation and then (2) have its output written to a file which is then (3) filtered for a match of a specified string. Also, it does not allow you to match the text string against any specific part of text. For example, suppose that you had a directory on your disk called DISKUTILS. The FIND command would select the line c:\DISKUTILS\QU.EXE because the directory name contained the letters DISK, even though the filename did not.

The Norton Utilities program offers a better and faster solution to the problem of lost files, in the form of the FF (file find) command. File Find, like CHKDSK, searches the entire disk so that you can locate a file stored anywhere on the disk.

Search for a Specific File

To use File Find you search for a specific file. Suppose that you want to know if the file WIPEDISK.EXE is located on your hard disk. Enter

```
ff wipedisk.exe ↵
```

The program displays the file you are searching for. This program operates much more quickly than CHKDSK because it is concerned only with reading the names of the files and reporting the information back to you. CHKDSK needs to analyze the file allocation table for errors, which slows down its performance.

```
[C:\]ff wipedisk.exe
FF-File Find, Advanced Edition, (C) Copr 1987, Peter Norton

C:\DOS
        wipedisk.exe    10,338 bytes   4:00 pm  Sun Mar  1 87

1 file found

[C:\]
```

Figure 6-4

Notice that File Find displays the full directory entry for the file including time and date of creation and size of the file, as well as the name of the directory in which it is contained.

Search for Groups of Files

Another advantage that File Find has over CHKDSK is that you can enter a DOS wildcard as a file specification. In that way you can locate files that have similar but not identical names. The README or READ files commonly waste space on hard disks. README or READ are text files usually placed onto a program disk by the manufacturer and contain information garnered too late to be printed in the program's documentation. In many cases these files are copied onto the hard disk along with a new program. After a while you find that these files begin to accumulate on the disk. To find out if you have any such files, enter

```
ff read*.* ↵
```

The program displays all the files on your hard disk that begin with **README.** If you have README files, you might want to read them to see what new information they contain.

```
          readme.doc       1,792 bytes   3:20 am  Mon Dec 22 86
          readme.txt      10,496 bytes   8:51 am  Mon Jun 29 87
          readme.com      16,074 bytes  10:27 am  Fri Aug  2 85
          read-me.sk      13,458 bytes   6:17 pm  Mon Aug  5 85

C:\FONTS
          readme.doc       7,168 bytes   3:31 am  Thu May 14 87

C:\123
          read.me          3,446 bytes   1:39 pm  Wed Nov  4 87
          readme.prn       1,920 bytes  12:00 am  Wed Nov 25 87

C:\WORD
          readme.doc       6,638 bytes   2:14 pm  Fri Jan  4 80

C:\4
          readme.com       4,066 bytes   1:00 am  Tue Dec  1 87
          readme          23,307 bytes   1:00 am  Tue Dec  1 87

C:\OWP
          readme.doc       2,159 bytes  12:00 pm  Tue Nov 24 87

11 files found

[C:\]
```

Figure 6-5

One way to view the contents of these files is to use the DOS command TYPE. Because the contents of the READ or README file may exceed the length of the screen, you can use the DOS filter program, More, to pause the text after a screen has been filled. More will work with DOS commands but is particularly helpful when typing a text file onto the screen. For example, suppose the file READ.ME was found in the \DOS directory. To list the file you would enter:

```
type \dos\read.me-more ↵
```

The more filter pauses the display at the end of one full screen and displays the message **-- More --** at the bottom left corner of the screen. Pressing any key, with the exceptions of [Ctrl/c] and [Break], will cause the scrolling to continue another screen.

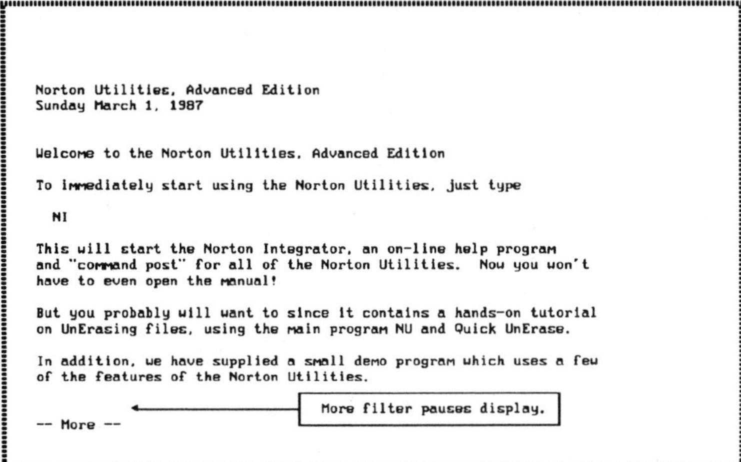
Norton Utilities, Advanced Edition
Sunday March 1, 1987

Welcome to the Norton Utilities, Advanced Edition

To immediately start using the Norton Utilities, just type

NI

This will start the Norton Integrator, an on-line help program
and "command post" for all of the Norton Utilities. Now you won't
have to even open the manual!

But you probably will want to since it contains a hands-on tutorial
on UnErasing files, using the main program NU and Quick UnErase.

In addition, we have supplied a small demo program which uses a few
of the features of the Norton Utilities.

-- More --

More filter pauses display.

Figure 6-6

Continue scrolling the file until the DOS prompt appears again, indicating you have seen the entire file.

You can print the file by using the LP command.

```
lp \dos\read.me ↵
```

The LP program allows you to specify an output device such as LPT1: or COM1:. You can use the LP program to send output to the screen by specifying the CON (console) device as the output destination. Enter

```
lp \dos\read.me CON ↵
```

This technique does not offer any advantages over TYPE since you cannot pause the LP display with the MORE filter the way you can with TYPE. Notice that LP adds formatting such as margins, headers, and footers to the display.

One possible reason for using LP is to count the number of lines in a file. The LP program accepts a switch, /N, which automatically numbers the lines as they are printed or displayed. Enter

```
lp \dos\read.me CON/n ↵
```

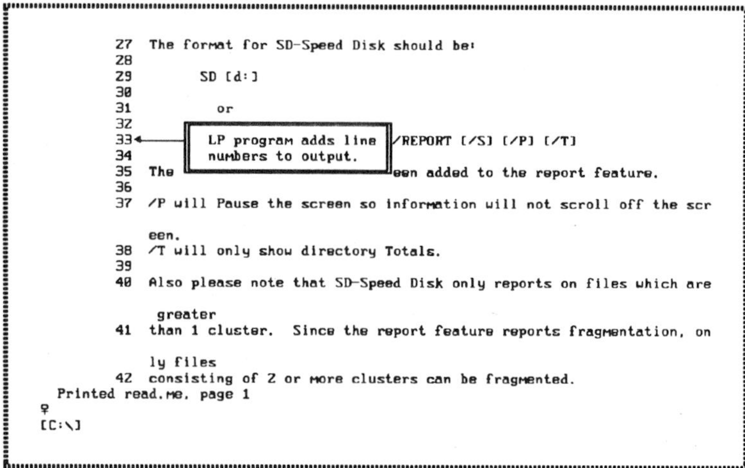

```
27  The format for SD-Speed Disk should be:
28
29          SD [d:]
30
31            or
32
33                                          /REPORT [/S] [/P] [/T]
34
35  The                                      een added to the report feature.
36
37  /P will Pause the screen so information will not scroll off the scr

    een.
38  /T will only show directory Totals.
39
40  Also please note that SD-Speed Disk only reports on files which are

     greater
41  than 1 cluster.  Since the report feature reports fragmentation, on

    ly files
42  consisting of 2 or more clusters can be fragmented.
 Printed read.me, page 1

[C:\]
```

LP program adds line numbers to output.

Figure 6-7

Another file that is commonly found in many directories is AUTOEXEC.BAT. This is because many floppy disk versions of programs contain an AUTOEXEC.BAT file, which is usually used to run an application when the computer boots. When the program is copied to the hard disk the AUTOEXEC.BAT is usually copied with it. Check your disk for AUTOEXEC.BAT files by entering

```
ff auto*.* ↵
```

> One common problem on hard disk systems occurs when an AUTOEXEC.BAT file is copied from a floppy into the root directory of the hard disk by mistake. The mistake has no effect on the computer at the moment it happens. Only later, when the computer is rebooted or turned on will the specious AUTOEXEC.BAT have an effect. The usual symptom is that the hard disk will boot directly into an application program.
>
> To correct the situation you must change the AUTOEXEC.BAT back to the correct series of commands. Unfortunately there is no sure way to recover the original AUTOEXEC.BAT.

When File Find is used without search criterion it will perform like **CHKDSK/V** and list all the files on the hard disk. If you are performing a list of all the files, you may want to pause the display from time to time to examine the listing. There are two ways to pause the File Find display.

1. Pressing the [space bar] will cause the program to suspend listing until you press the [space bar] a second time.

2. Using the **/P** switch causes the program to automatically pause after each full screen of files are listed.

For example, enter

```
ff/p ↵
```

The program automatically pauses after it has listed a full screen of files.

```
[C:\]ff/p
FF-File Find, Advanced Edition, (C) Copr 1987, Peter Norton

C:\
        io.sys          17,210 bytes   1:46 pm  Fri Dec 19 86
        msdos.sys       28,464 bytes  12:00 pm  Fri Mar 21 86
        command.com     23,612 bytes   3:20 am  Fri Nov 14 86
        DOS               <DIR>        8:36 pm  Mon Oct 26 87
        ask.exe          1,184 bytes   4:00 pm  Sun Mar  1 87
        FONTS             <DIR>        9:01 pm  Fri Dec 18 87
        ONEWRITE.PLS      <DIR>        1:09 am  Thu Dec 24 87
        autoexec.bat        73 bytes   2:58 am  Tue Dec 15 87
        menu.bat         1,971 bytes  12:54 am  Tue Dec 22 87
        nb1a-07.scr      8,128 bytes  12:44 am  Mon Dec 28 87
        nb1a-08.scr      8,128 bytes  10:46 pm  Mon Dec 28 87
        nb1a-09.scr      8,128 bytes  11:51 pm  Mon Dec 28 87
        menu.txt         1,584 bytes   9:38 pm
        sa.exe           4,506 bytes   4:00 pm
        nb1a-10.scr      8,128 bytes  12:36
        123               <DIR>        9:15 pm
        DB3               <DIR>       12:57 am
        autoexec.sav       126 bytes   8:40 am  Fri Dec  4 87
        JAV               <DIR>        8:51 am  Tue Oct 27 87
        WORD              <DIR>        9:25 am  Fri Oct 30 87
Program paused; press any key to continue..
```

/P causes Norton Utility programs to pause screen displays.

Figure 6-8

Once the display has been paused you have two ways of continuing the display.

1. Press ↵. Pressing ↵ advances the display one line each time the key is pressed. This allows you to examine the output one line at a time.

2. Press any other key. This will cause the program to display the next screen. Enter

↵

The display scrolls one line. Enter

```
[space bar]
```

The display scrolls one full screen. You can terminate the program when it is paused by using [Esc] as well as [Ctrl/c] and [Ctrl/Scroll Lock]. Enter

```
[Esc]
```

Search All Drives

The File Find program also contains an option that enables you to search all drives in the system with a single command. This is very valuable if you are running more than one hard disk, or you have a large capacity drive, greater than 32 megabytes, which is partitioned in several logical drives. The switch, /A, causes the File Find command to begin its search on the first drive in the system and continue the search through all the drives. Keep in mind that the program reads the drive table in the memory of the computer so that logical drives such as RAM drives will be included in the search.

Also note that in the case of floppy drives, the File Find program is prepared to handle empty drives. Unlike a DOS command that will display the Abort, Retry, Ignore message, File Find will simply proceed to the next available drive if there is no disk in the floppy drive. To see how this works, leave your A drive empty and enter

```
ff *.sys/a ↵
```

The red light on the A drive is lit indicating that File Find is searching for a disk. After a few moments (1.2 megabyte drives take longer than 360K drives) the program will display the message:

```
Unable to read from drive A
```

The program will then proceed to search the next drive in the system and so on until all the drives have been searched. The program produces a list of the SYS files on all of the disks in the system.

Documenting Your System

The File Find command is capable of providing a detailed summary of all the files stored on a hard disk, or with the /A parameter, all the files stored in a multi-drive system. Entering FF with no file specifications will cause the program to list all of the files on the disk. Keep in mind that hidden files are included in this list along with the files that normally appear in the directory listing.

There are two ways to produce a printed catalog of files: unformatted and formatted. The catalog can be useful in maintaining a computer system and for recovering erased files. (Section IV demonstrates how to recover erased files.) A list of filenames is useful, but not absolutely necessary, in trying to reconstruct the erased information.

Unformatted File Lists

An unformatted list is one in which no accommodation is made for page breaks, page numbers, margins or other formatting niceties. To produce an unformatted list, simply take advantage of the DOS redirection options and send the output of the File Find program to the printer. Since this printing can take some time, you may want to skip this command until you are ready to print the long list. The command is:

```
ff >prn ↵
```

As an example, you can produce a shorter list by selecting files. Enter

```
ff *.sys >prn ↵
```

Notice that unformatted printing does not advance the paper to the end of the page. It simply stops when there is no more data to print.

Formatted Output

If you intend to keep a catalog of disk files, it might be preferable to have a formatted printout with page numbers, page breaks, margins, and so on. This can be done by combining the operations of two Norton Utilities programs. The File Find command is used to generate the file information. Instead of putting the information on the screen or sending it to the printer, you can use the DOS redirection commands to create a text file. The LP (Line Print) program can then print the contents of the text file created by FF (File Find) and insert the desired formatting.

The first step is to create the text file. This is done by adding a redirection command, >, to the FF command and following it with the name of the text file you want to create. Enter

```
ff >catalog ↵
```

The program begins but no files appear on the screen. Instead, the data is being captured in a file on the disk called CATALOG. When the file is complete, the DOS prompt returns.

The file created by the command contains the same information that would normally appear on the screen or printer. This can be large for a text file. A listing of 800 files might take up 55K.

You can now use the LP command to print out the contents of the CATALOG file with page formatting. (Skip this command at this time if you wish.) You can stop the printing at any time by entering [Esc]. Enter

```
LP catalog ↵
```

> There is one file listed in the catalog whose information will be inaccurate, the CATALOG text file. It appears in the list but its file size will show 0 because DOS creates the filename in the directory before the FF program sends its information to the file. In that way FF includes the CATALOG entry in its list. However, because the file is still open while the writing is taking place, DOS has not yet written the file size into the directory. Of course, this minor defect won't have much practical effect.

The LP command will automatically number lines. This might be a convenient feature when you are printing out file lists. You can add line numbers with the /N switch. Example:

```
lp catalog/n ↵
```

The logic of redirection allows you to take advantage of the DOS Print command. PRINT.COM is a program provided with DOS that allows you to print a text file in the background while you proceed to other tasks. This means that you do not have to wait for the printing to complete before you can enter commands.

To take advantage of the PRINT command, you will create a second text file which is the output of the LP command. This produces a text file that contains the data produced by FF. The formatting added by LP. PRINT can then finally send the formatted text file to the printer in the background as you go on to other tasks.

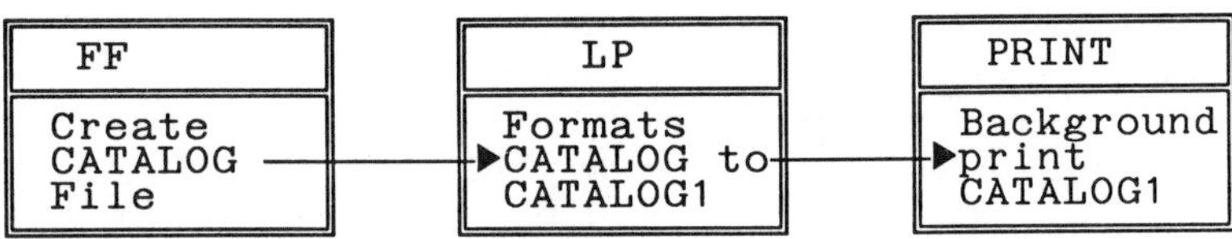

To create the formatted text file, **CATALOG1**, you need to run the LP command and specify a text file as the output, rather than the printer. This is easy to do. If you follow the LP command with a name, the program will create a text file with that name instead of sending the data to the printer. Remember that the filenames must be different. Enter

```
lp catalogl ↵
```

The LP program creates a file with the formatted contents of the CATALOG file, and displays the number of pages that the new file contains. The LP program will print 53 lines of data on each page. Remember that the File Find listing includes directories as well as files.

The final step is to use the DOS PRINT program to print this file in the background. Enter

```
print catalogl ↵
```

The DOS program will display a prompt:

```
Name of list device [PRN]:
```

This allows you to enter the name of an alternate print device. The default is PRN, the normal DOS print device. To begin the printing enter

↵

The printing begins. You can now enter commands while the printing is taking place. Enter

```
dir/w ↵
```

You may notice that while the disk is being read for the directory, the printing pauses. This is because DOS does not support true multitasking. As soon as the disk read operation is performed the print continues.

Cancelling a background print started with the DOS PRINT program is not quite as easy as stopping a foreground printing operation. Enter PRINT with a /T (terminate) switch that will stop the printing and clear the print queue. Enter

```
print/t ↵
```

> The queue refers to the ability of the PRINT program to create a queue of files to print. You can cancel the printing of a specific file in the queue by using the /C. Example:
>
> print catalog1/C
>
> This would cancel only the printing of CATALOG1 and leave any other files in the queue alone.

To simplify the process you can place all of the necessary commands into a batch file. Below is a sample of what that batch file might contain.

Listing 6.1. File CATALOG.BAT

```
ff>catalog
lp catalog catalog1
print catalog1
del catalog
```

When the printing is complete, you might want to delete the CATALOG1 file. Note that the command to delete the text file CATALOG is included in the batch, but the command to delete CATALOG1 is not. This is because the PRINT command will go back to the CATALOG1 file from time to time to get more text to print. Because the printing is taking place in the background, DOS will execute a command in the batch that follows the print command before the printing is complete. This means that when PRINT looks for the rest of the text file it will fail to find it because it is now erased. For that reason you must wait until the background printing is complete to delete the CATALOG1 file.

For more information about batch files, see Section II.

COM vs. EXE Files

DOS recognizes two types of executable files: COM and EXE. The difference between the two file types is rather technical and not very important to the user. Because the extensions are different, it is possible to have two files with the same name. For example, Version 3.0 of the Norton Utilities programs included files with the same names as many of the 4.0 utilities. However, the 3.0 files used the COM extension while the 4.0 Version uses EXE. Example: FF.COM, and FF.EXE. The same is true of DOS utility programs from level 2 to 3. Example: FORMAT.COM (DOS 2.10), FORMAT.EXE (DOS 3.10).

This change can cause a problem that at first seems quite bewildering. Suppose that you have just purchased an upgrade of the Norton Utilities program, Version 4.0, to replace the 3.0 Version you have been using. Your first step would be to copy the program files onto your hard disk, into the same directory in which you kept your previous version.

Normally this is all you would have to consider. If the new program has the same filenames, they would overwrite the outdated programs. If the new programs use different names then they would be added to the disk. However, in the case where the filenames are the same except that the extensions differ between COM and EXE, an odd state of affairs exists. Because the filenames are different, DOS writes both files. But what happens when you want to execute the new version of FF or LP?

When you enter FF, DOS gives priority to the COM version of the program, ignoring the EXE version. The only way to resolve the problem is to locate and delete the COM versions. FF can be very handy. Use FF to locate all the files with the same name but different extensions. Example:

```
ff diskcopy.* ↵
```

This will locate any copies of the file on the disk. The illustration shows that both a COM and EXE version of the program are present on this hard disk.

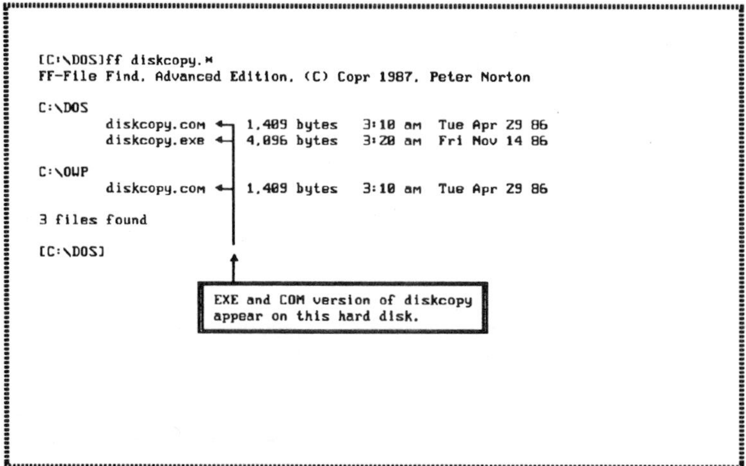
```
[C:\DOS]ff diskcopy.*
FF-File Find, Advanced Edition, (C) Copr 1987, Peter Norton

C:\DOS
        diskcopy.com    1,409 bytes   3:10 am  Tue Apr 29 86
        diskcopy.exe    4,096 bytes   3:20 am  Fri Nov 14 86

C:\OWP
        diskcopy.com    1,409 bytes   3:10 am  Tue Apr 29 86

3 files found

[C:\DOS]
```

EXE and COM version of diskcopy
appear on this hard disk.

Figure 6-9

See Chapter 1 for information about the difference between COM and EXE files.

Building Selected Lists

The previous procedure for creating a catalog of all the disk files can be modified to create a more selective list of files. Suppose you want to create a catalog of only the EXE and COM files on the disk. This could be done by using the FF command twice.

The tactic is to combine the output of both commands into a single file and print it out as a single catalog. This can be done by using a slightly modified redirection command. DOS recognizes >> as the command to append text onto an existing text file.

> If >> is used and the specified file does not already exist, DOS will simply create the file. Subsequent >> commands will append text to that file.

Begin by creating a text file with the file of all COM files. Enter

```
ff *.com>programs ↵
```

Next, append onto the PROGRAMS file the list of EXE files. The key to this command is the >> redirection command. Enter

```
ff *.exe>>programs ↵
```

You can now use LP to print the combined lists.

```
LP catalog
```

> Keep in mind that programs often require other files such as configuration and overlay files to support their operations. The COM and EXE programs listed probably do not represent a complete list of all the files needed to run all the programs on your hard disk.

You can see that having a distinctive file extension makes it easy to locate and catalog files. For example, Lotus 1-2-3 produces files that are automatically assigned file extensions beginning with WK to all the Lotus files on a hard disk. Enter

```
ff *.wk* ↵
```

The same is true of dBASE III Plus. The database and memo files have extensions that begin with DB. To list all the dBASE III files, enter

```
ff *.db* ↵
```

> dBASE III files keep data in DBF files with the exception of data entered into memo fields, which are stored in DBT files. If you copy a DBF file without the DBT that goes with it, dBASE will refuse to open the file.

Most word processing programs do not impose a file extension automatically. Microsoft Word and Multimate are exceptions to that rule because they add DOC extensions to their document file. WordPerfect and WordStar do not add extensions. If you use such programs you might want to adapt the habit of adding an extension that would identify the files as word processing files, for example, WP.

Text Search

The File Find command locates files based on their filenames. But the Norton Utilities programs provide a way to locate files based on the information they contain. The TS (Text Search) program performs this operation and it is one of the most helpful of all the very useful programs included with the Norton Utilities package.

While DOS has similar commands to FF (File Find), there is no method by which DOS can help you locate text stored within a file. The ability to search the contents of a file for specific information is important because you are more likely to remember the content of a file than you are the filename.

The TS program is designed to search the disk to find any instances of a specific group of characters. TS can operate from a command line or interactive mode. To see how TS works in an interactive mode, assume that you want to locate a file or files that contain a key word, **FATAL**. Start the TS program by entering

```
ts ↵
```

The first option that you need to select concerns the part of the disk you want to search.

```
[C:\]ts
TS-Text Search, Advanced Edition, (C) Copr 1987,
Peter Norton

Select search within FILES, all of DISK, or ERASED
file space
Press F, D, or E ...
```

The TS program has three options.

F **Files**. This option limits the search to data clusters currently marked as in use by active files. This is the most common way to search. The program will specify the file that contains the text you are looking for.

D **Disk.** This option searches all of the disk sectors. Included in this search are the boot sector, FAT and directory areas, file areas and data areas not currently in use by any data files. Note that if the text is found the program tells you its location in terms of disk sector rather than filename.

E **Erased.** This limits the search to space not in use by active files. This space may contain information that belongs to files that have been erased. Note that DOS does not remove data when a file is erased. If a match is found the program tells you the sector and cluster numbers.

In this case choose the file area. Keep in mind that the TS program will tell you the name of the file in which the text is found only if you select the F(ile) option. Selecting D(isk) or E(rase) will prove the text's location on the disk by disk sector or cluster numbers. Enter

```
f
```

The next prompt asks you to enter a wildcard or filename.

```
[C:\]ts
TS-Text Search, Advanced Edition, (C) Copr 1987,
Peter Norton

Select search within FILES, all of DISK, or ERASED
file space
Press F, D, or E ... F

Searching contents of files

Enter the file specification for the files to
search
  File:
```

The purpose of this option is to limit the search to a file or group of files. For example, if you were searching for a 1-2-3 worksheet you would enter *.wk* to limit the search to worksheet files. Entering ↵ automatically selects *.*, that is, all the files in the active directory. Enter

↵

The next prompt asks you to enter the text you want to search for.

```
TS-Text Search, Advanced Edition, (C) Copr 1987,
Peter Norton

Select search within FILES, all of DISK, or ERASED
file space
Press F, D, or E ... F

Searching contents of files

Enter the file specification for the files to
search
  File: *.* used.

Enter specific text to search for
Or press enter for any text
  Text:
```

You are also presented with the option to enter ↵ to search for any text. If you enter ↵, the TS program scans the selected area and files for any block of text. Remember that the program cannot use the same logical criterion used by a person to detect text. Instead, the program looks for a block of information that contains text characters. Data that contains control characters is automatically excluded.

Enter a word that you want to find. The TS program does not take into consideration differences in case when matching characters. Entering F or f will match F or f. In this example, you are looking for the word fatal. Enter

fatal ↵

When the program locates a match, the screen displays the name of the file, the location within the file where the match is found and the matched text along with its context.

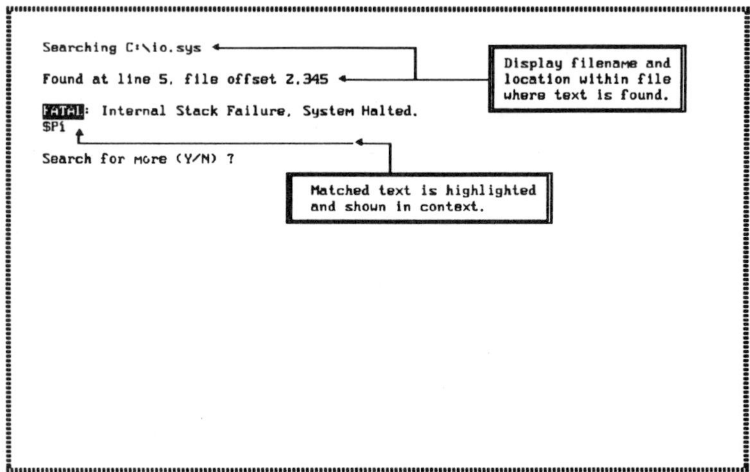
Searching C:\io.sys
Found at line 5, file offset 2,345
FATAL: Internal Stack Failure, System Halted.
$P1
Search for more (Y/N) ?
Display filename and location within file where text is found.
Matched text is highlighted and shown in context.

Figure 6-10

In this case, the text is located in the IO.SYS file. If you are using IBM DOS the filename will appear as IBMBIO.COM. The text matches part of a message used by the IO.SYS/IBMBIO.COM program, which is one of the hidden DOS files. The location of the text is shown in terms of lines or byte offset. The line number is useful if the file is a pure text file. If not, the byte offset can be used to locate the text using the main Norton Utilities program.

You can continue the search by entering

y

Depending on the files you have stored in the current directory you may or may not encounter another instance of the word fatal. If you have a copy of the Norton editor program, the word fatal appears several times in error messages. If you have such files, continue the search until the program has completed its exploration. It then presents a summary of what was found.

```
Searching C:\io.sys

Found at line 5, file offset 2,345

FATAL: Internal Stack Failure, System Halted.
$P1

Search for more (Y/N) ? Y

Searching C:\nb1a-06.scr

Search Complete

1 file found containing the text "FATAL"

1 occurrence of the text "FATAL"

[C:\]
```

Figure 6-11

The TS program can also be executed as a command line. For example, to perform the previous search from a single command entry you would enter the following:

```
ts *.* fatal ↵
```

ts	*.*	fatal
Program name	Files to search	Text to search for

The program locates the same occurrences of FATAL as it did in the interactive mode.

If you want to locate a phrase with several words you need to enclose the phrase in quotation marks. For example, suppose you wanted to locate the program that contained the message "Abort, Retry, Ignore", which DOS will display upon occasion. Enter

```
ts *.* "abort, retry, ignore" ↵
```

The text is located in the COMMAND.COM file.

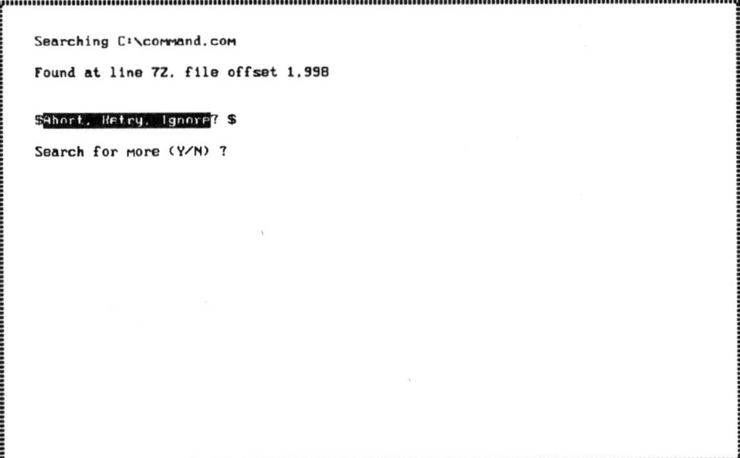

Figure 6-12

Terminate the search by entering

```
n
```

Broad or Narrow Searches

The TS program can be altered to perform broad or narrow searches. The /S switch will cause the program to search the files stored in all the subdirectories that branch from the current directory. If the current directory is the root directory, then the program will search all the files on the hard disk. Suppose that you wanted to see if any of the files on the hard disk contain the word **Norton Utilities**. If you are not sure what file or what directory the file might be stored in, you can use the TS in its broadest form. First, change to the root directory by entering

```
cd\ ↵
```

The assumption is made that you still have access to the TS.EXE file. This means that the file is stored in the root directory or that a path is open to the directory that contains the Norton Utilities programs.

The next step is to perform a search for the text using the /S switch. Enter

```
ts *.* "Norton Utilities"/s ↵
```

The TS program displays the names of the files as it searches. The time it takes to perform this search will vary with the number of files stored on the hard disk and the arrangement of the directories.

If you have copied all the files from both Norton Utilities disks you should encounter the date in at least one file, the file called READ.ME.

```
Searching C:\DOS\read.me

Found at line 4, file offset 47


Norton Utilities, Advanced Edition
Sunday March 1, 1987

Welcome to the Norton Utilities, Advanced Edition

To immediately start using the Norton Utilities, just type

  NI


Search for more (Y/N) ?
```

Figure 6-13

The text will occur a number of times. You can enter **y** to continue the search. You can stop the TS program while it is searching by entering

```
[Ctrl/Scroll Lock]
```

Logging the Results

So far, the TS command has been used in an interactive mode to locate specific text items within files. This means that the program performs assuming that someone is watching the progress of the search on the screen. The program displays the names of the files that are being searched, to inform the observer about the progress being made. When a match is found, the program comes to a halt, displays the information about the matched text, and awaits the entry of a Y or N for continuing the search.

The TS program has two switches that alter or suppress the interactive nature of the program. By combining these switches in different ways and using the DOS redirection commands you can obtain text files or printed reports about the text search, in contrast to simply reading the information as it comes up on the screen.

The two switches are:

/T **Total.** This switch changes the goal of the TS program. With /T active the program does not attempt to show you where or how many times the text occurs in a given file. Instead, it produces a list of the filenames that contain a match for the search text. No interaction on the part of the user is needed.

/LOG **Log Data.** With this mode active the program outputs information in a form suitable for printing or storing in a disk file. The parts of the normal display that would make sense only when someone is monitoring the screen are suppressed.

For example, suppose you want to know which files in the DOS directory contain the phrase **Incorrect DOS version**. Because you are interested only in filenames, not the location of the phrase Incorrect DOS version within them, you would use the /T option. Enter

```
ts \dos "incorrect dos version"/t ↵
```

In this case, the TS program produces a list of filenames that contain the selected phrase. There should be quite a few of these names since most DOS and Norton Utilities programs contain this message. Notice that the program does not stop for user input while it is working, and that entering the directory name, /DOS, was sufficient to search all the files in that directory.

At the bottom of the list a summary of the results is displayed.

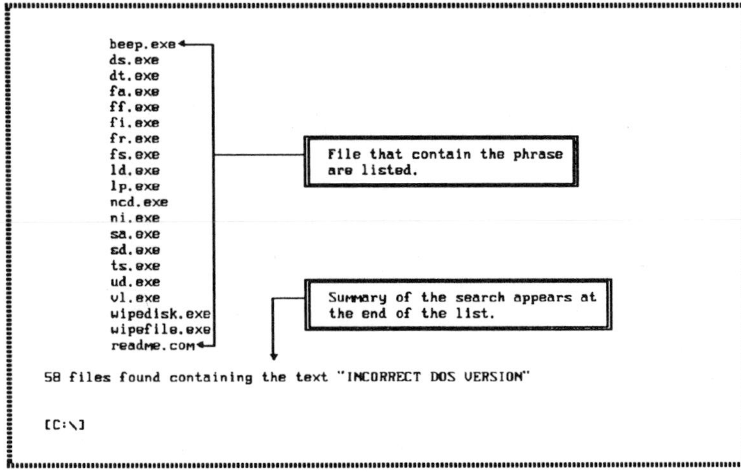

Figure 6-14

Suppose you wanted to print out this long list, instead of scrolling the screen. You would have to enter the same command, but add two items.

1. A DOS redirection command to send the output to the printer.

2. The /LOG option. Remember that TS displays the names of all the files that it searches as it is running. This output is designed for the screen where text can be printed over in the same position. Such output would not print correctly. The /LOG option suppresses this output and replaces it with a format appropriate for a printer. Enter

```
ts \dos "incorrect dos version"/t/log>prn ↵
```

The /LOG command can be used without the /T. If it is, the output lists both the files and the occurrences of the search text. As an example, search the DOS directory for the word COMSPEC in any of the files. Enter

```
ts \dos comspec/log ↵
```

> COMSPEC is a DOS term which refers to the drive and directory location of the COMMAND.COM. file. Some programs, like the Norton Commander program and Lotus 1-2-3, prompt DOS to reload the COMMAND.COM files after they have been terminated. The COMSPEC value stored in memory tells DOS where to look for the COMMAND.COM file. Usually, the COMSPEC is the drive and directory from which the computer booted, C:\. In some cases, usually when running programs with multiple disks on a floppy disk system, the COMSPEC is changed to a different drive other than the boot drive. Borland's Quatro running on a floppy drive system does this.

The program displays the data about each occurrence of COMSPEC. The /LOG also suppresses the pauses in the program because they would be inappropriate for a printed output.

```
Searching C:\DOS\nc.exe
Found at line 430, file offset 64,107
comspec

Searching C:\DOS\nc.exe
Found at line 431, file offset 64,829
comspec


Search Complete
6 files found containing the text "COMSPEC"
11 occurrences of the text "COMSPEC"
[C:\]
```

Figure 6-15

A summary appears at the bottom of the display. This summary lists the numbers of files and total number of occurrences of the search text.

Using the DOS redirection command you can obtain a printed copy of this information. Enter

```
ts \dos comspec/log >prn ↵
```

Notice that output from the TS program is not page formatted. To get a page formatted listing you can use the same method applied to the FF program. The first step is to capture the output into a text file. Then use LP to print the text with page formatting. Example:

```
ts \dos comspec/log >search.txt ↵
lp search.txt ↵
```

Another purpose in directing the output of the TS program to a text file is so that you can load that text file into a word processor or text editor. This enables you to examine at your own pace, the information returned by the TS program. Because a word processor allows you to move forward and backward in the text you can compare the items found by TS by skipping around in the file. When you run the TS program the information is displayed as it is found and you cannot go back to previous displays.

About Searching Files

The TS program is one of the most valuable of the utilities provided in the Norton Utilities package. The most common usage is to search word processor files for phrases or keywords. The TS program can quickly locate all the files that contain references to specific topics. Because TS displays the context in which the search text is found, you can quickly decide if this match is relevant to your needs. The filenames provided with the match make it simple to know which files to load and examine.

When searching for text, it is important to understand that the contents of the files created by various applications do not correspond directly to the data you see displayed on your screen. Most programs store additional information, usually in a non-text format, along with the data you enter.

For example, most word processing programs insert special characters or codes into the text you type to indicate formatting attributes. The most common attribute to enter is a line ending code. This code indicates where the word processor should wrap text to the next line. This code or character is significant when you search for a phrase. For example, if you look for the phrase **vagaries and vicissitudes**, TS would fail to make a match if the phrase was broken by a line wrap code. The illustration below shows the phrase in a WordPerfect document format. Notice that the phrase contains a character that did not appear on the WordPerfect display, a soft return.

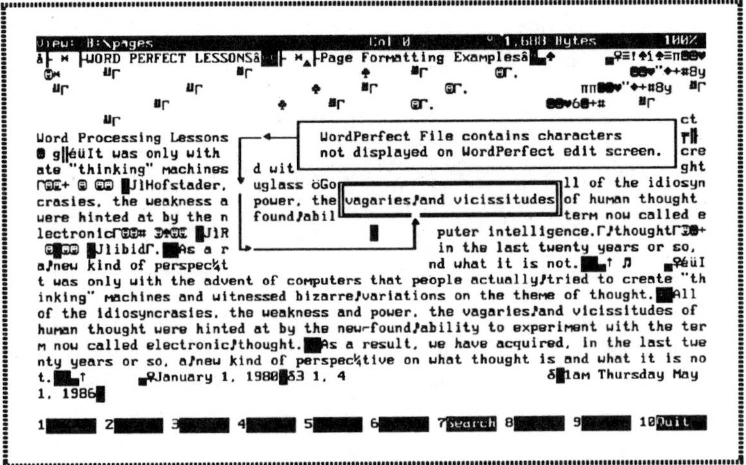

Figure 6-16

TS would fail to find this phrase because your search text would contain a space, not a [Ctrl/m] character (represented by the musical note symbol). For this reason it is better to search for individual words than phrases when searching through some file formats.

TS also tells you what line the text appears on. Most word processing programs do not count lines consecutively but restart the line counting on each page. The Norton Editor program is not page oriented and can locate text by line number. If you use WordStar, the non-document mode counts both consecutive lines and characters. For example, suppose you load a WordStar document with the D command and want to locate the 75th line in the file. The status line normally displays Page, Line and character. Entering the command **[Ctrl/o]p** will turn off the page break display. WordStar will display FL for file line and FC for file character, which count those values consecutively from the beginning of the file.

While on the subject of WordStar, it is important to mention that WordStar document files use a special system of coding that should be taken into consideration if you are searching these files with TS. When WordStar implements wrap-around typing, it changes some of the normal text characters by adding 128 to their ASCII character value. This technique is called changing the **high order bit**, referring to the change made in the binary number that represents the character. The diagram below shows how the a character is changed when its high order bit is manipulated.

		ASCII value
Character	a	97
Plus	+	128
Equals	ß	225

The text of a WordStar file will have many such changes. When you use WordStar, the text appears as normal because WordStar subtracts the high order bit when it displays the text. However, to programs like TS the document appears with the high order bit in place.

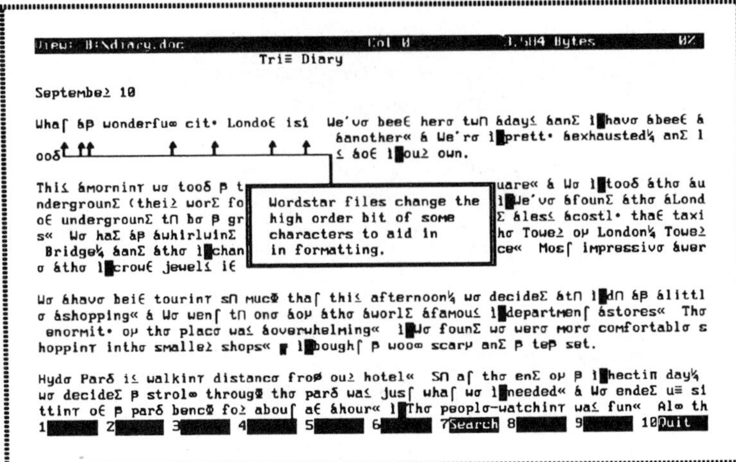

Figure 6-17

The TS program has a special option that should be used when searching WordStar or WordStar compatible files (for example, NewWord files). The switch, /WS, will tell TS to ignore the high order bits. For example, suppose you wanted to search WordStar files for the word London, you would enter a command that looks like this:

```
ts *.* london/ws ↵
```

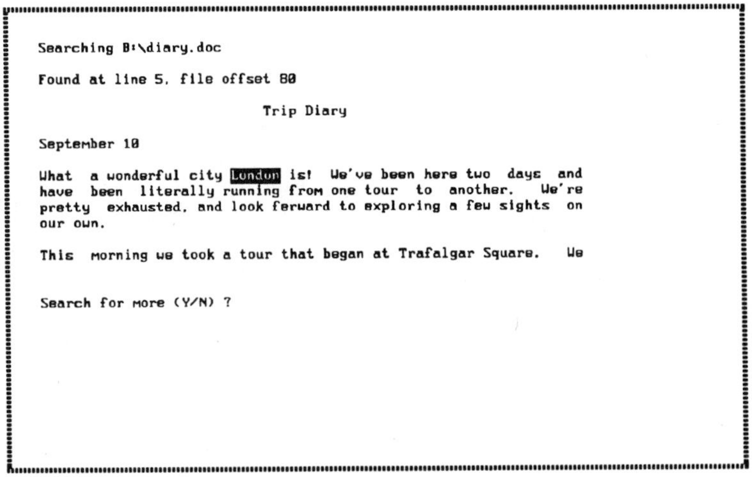

```
Searching B:\diary.doc

Found at line 5, file offset 80

                         Trip Diary

September 10

What  a wonderful city London is!  We've been here two  days  and
have  been  literally running from one tour  to  another.  We're
pretty  exhausted, and look forward to exploring a few sights  on
our own.

This  morning we took a tour that began at Trafalgar Square.   We


Search for more (Y/N) ?
```

Figure 6-18

This applies to WordStar Version 3 and 4. It does not apply to WordStar 2000 files, which do not use the high order bit technique. Also keep in mind that using the /WS on non-WordStar files will cause the TS program to match characters based on only the first 7 bits which is misleading. Limit /WS to WordStar or compatible document files.

Microsoft Word files are the closest to pure text files since most of the formatting codes are stored at the bottom of the file. This means that phrases that occur within paragraphs will not contain line ending codes. These files can be searched for phrases much more reliably than can WordPerfect, Multimate or WordStar.

dBASE III Plus files are executed in a way that work well with TS. dBASE DBF files begin with a file structure header that is not text. But the rest of the file, which contains the actual data, is a pure ASCII text file. dBASE does not insert any special codes to mark field or record endings, which might interfere with matching. An exception to this rule are dBASE date and logical fields. dBASE stores dates in a different format than they appear on the screen. For example, the date 01/05/87 would appear as 19870105 in the actual DBF file. Logical fields are **T** or **F**, even if they appear on the screen as **Y** or **N**.

dBASE DBT files, used to hold memos, are also text files. Note that the dBASE word processor will insert line ending character ASCII 141, (the same as WordStar) into the text of memos.

PFS Files, on the other hand, store data in a binary format that bears no resemblance to the text you type in.

Spreadsheet files also contain a great deal of binary coding. Numeric values and formulas are not stored as text and cannot be searched for. However, labels are stored as text and can be searched for.

EBCDIC Option

The TS program, along with the main Norton Utilities program and the LP program, provide an option for using the EBCDIC coding system.

EBCDIC stands for Extended Binary Coded Decimal Interchange Code and is commonly used on IBM and other mainframe computers. The system serves the same purpose as the ASCII coding system but assigns characters to different values than does ASCII.

The name EBCDIC implies that it is an enhanced coding system. The ASCII coding system was originally developed as a 7 bit system with a total of 128 (2 to the 7th power = 128) characters. The eighth bit was not used for characters and was reserved for parity checking, a technique commonly used in telecommunications to trap errors in long distance communications. EBCDIC code was considered extended because it used all 8 bits for characters, doubling the total number of characters in the coding (2 to the 8th power = 256).

Today, most MS-DOS computers treat ASCII as an extended character set with 256 characters. The additional character usually conforms to the extended set supplied on the original IBM PC. Before that time, computer manufacturers chose to provide or not to provide characters for the extended codes. The Osborne I computer supplied a set of graphics characters for the extended code values that were quite different from the one used by most MS-DOS computers.

> While most MS-DOS computers display the extended character set on the screen, the same cannot be said of most printers. Daisy wheel printers use 96 character wheels that do not support the extended characters. Even most dot matrix printers do not support the full character set. The term "IBM graphics compatible" is often used to express the fact that this printer will print the extended character set. The fonts used on most laser printers are usually limited to the standard 128 character ASCII set. To produce the full character set you will have to look for fonts that specifically support the full extended character set.

If you have text files, usually down loaded from a mainframe computer, stored in EBCDIC code, use the /EBCDIC switch with the TS, LP and NU programs so that the text will be interpreted correctly.

> In the main Norton Utilities program [Alt/F5] will toggle the character display from ASCII to EDCDIC, and then from EBCDIC to ASCII. You might try this just to see what happens when you change coding systems. Note that if you enter [Alt/F5] the program will not automatically re-draw the screen in EBCDIC. If you enter [Pg Dn], causing the program to re-draw the screen, the EBCDIC coding will be used for that and all subsequent screens. The word EBCDIC will appear at the top of the display to remind you that you have activated EBCDIC coding.

Searching for Non-Text Characters

The TS program is primarily designed to search for text files of normal keyboard characters. However, it is possible to search for characters in the extended character set. For example, one of the batch files supplied with the Norton Utilities program uses some of the non-keyboard characters to create graphics. One of the characters is character 219, █. Suppose that you wanted to use TS to determine which file contains this character. Begin by entering a normal TS command. Note, you need to type a space after bat. Enter

```
ts \dos\*.bat
 [space bar]
```

Use the [Alt/keypad] method to enter an extended character as the search text. Note that you should hold the [Alt] key down while you are typing each of the digits, and that you must type the digits on the numeric keypad. The numbers on the top row of the keyboard will not work. Enter

```
[Alt/219]
↵
```

If you have the NUDEMO.BAT file in the DOS directory the program will stop at line 8, offset 84. The word echo appears as the text, not the character you were looking for. This is because the character at offset 84 matches the [Alt/219] character. However, the TS program is designed to suppress display of these extended characters. The result is that you find the character, but see a blank space displayed in its place. Exit the search by entering

```
n
```

Searching with the Main Program

The previous example raises a point about the Norton Utilities programs. The TS program is not the only means by which you can search the disk. The main Norton Utilities program also contains a search facility. To clarify the differences between the two search facilities, load the main Norton Utilities program by entering

```
nu ↵
```

Choose the Explore Disk option by entering

```
e
```

The next menu lists the options for locating data on the disk. The fourth item on the list is a search option. Enter

```
s
```

Menu 1.4 is the search menu.

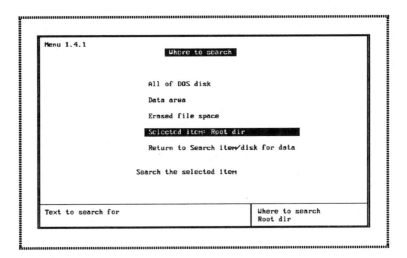

```
Menu 1.4
                    Search item/disk for data

                        Where to search

                        Text to search for

                        (start search)

                        (display found text)

                        (continue search)

                        Leave search

                     Specify the text to search for

Text to search for                          Where to search
                                            Root dir
```

Figure 6-19

The first task is to select the area to search. Enter

```
W
```

This display menu 1.4.1.

```
Menu 1.4.1
                      Where to search


                    All of DOS disk

                    Data area

                    Erased file space

                    Selected item: Root dir

                    Return to Search item/disk for data

                  Search the selected item

Text to search for                          Where to search
                                            Root dir
```

Figure 6-20

The menu offers options that are similar to TS.

All This option searches the entire disk, sector by sector.

Data This option searches all data clusters on the disk, including areas in use by files and data clusters not currently in use by files.

Erased This limits the search to data areas not in use by active files. This may include areas used by erased files or areas never used by any files.

Select This option allows you to select an item such as a directory, FAT, or file to search. The program automatically defaults to the root directory as the selected item. If you select another item anywhere else in the program, that item will appear as the selected item.

Choose the data area. Enter

```
d
```

You return to the search menu. The next step is to select the text to search for. Enter

```
t
```

The text entry menu appears.

```
Menu 1.4.2
                         Text to search for

              Search data, in character format:
              ____________________________________

             Tab switches between the character and hex windows

              Search data, in hexadecimal format:
              ____________________________________

                    0 characters in search string

Text to search for                            Where to search
                                              Data area
```

Figure 6-21

The text entry screen is divided into two windows. The top area allows you to enter text characters, while the bottom window allows you to enter hexadecimal values. You can move between the two windows with the [Tab] key. Whatever you enter in one window is automatically echoed in the other.

This display points up the major difference between the TS program and the text search facility of the main Norton Utilities program. The main Norton Utilities program allows you to search for non-text characters as well as text items.

In order to take advantage of this ability you need to have in mind some non-text items to search for. For example, Lotus 1-2-3, Version 2.01, worksheet files always begin with a specific sequence of hex values.

Lotus File Beginning

00	00	02	00	06	04	06	00

You can enter those hex values as the search key. Switch to the hex window. Enter

[Tab]

Enter the hex values.

```
00
00
02
00
06
04
06
00
```

The program automatically inserts space between the number pairs to make it easier to read. The other window displays the character symbol, if any, for the hex values as you enter them.

When you have completed the search key, enter

↵

The menu now shows the search key and the selected area at the bottom of the screen.

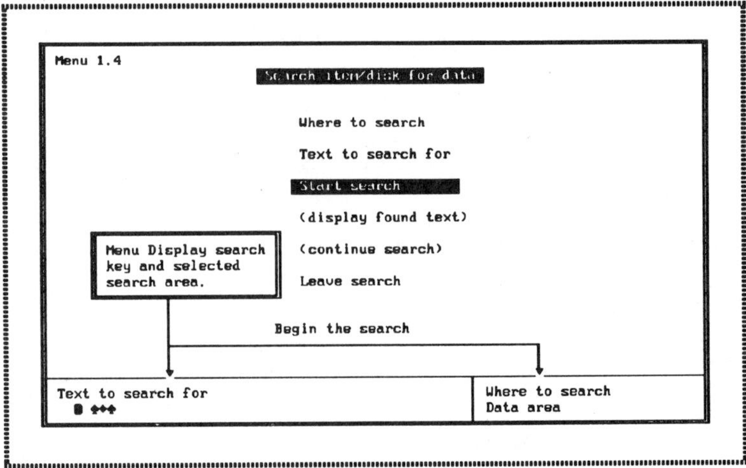

Figure 6-22

To start the actual search, enter

s

The program displays the cluster numbers as it searches. If it encounters a match, it stops the search and displays the cluster number. If you use 1-2-3 Release 2.01 the program should find a worksheet file.

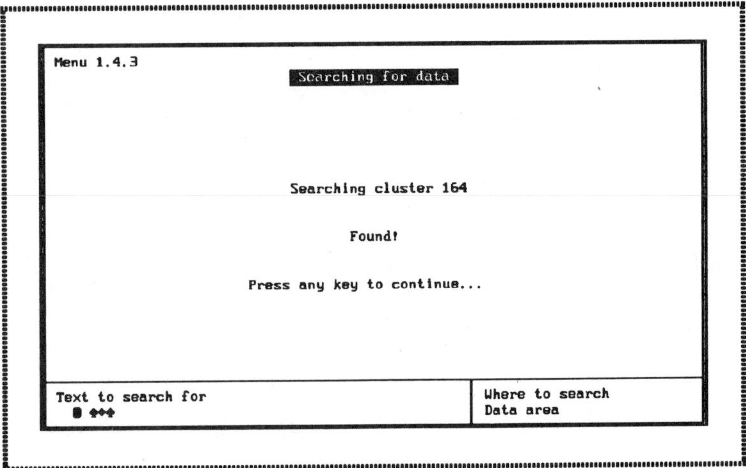

Figure 6-23

Once the search has located a match you can return to the search menu by entering

↵

The program now offers you additional options:

Display the data cluster where the match is found.

Continue searching for the next match.

Leave search menu.

In this case, display the data. Enter

d

Since 1-2-3 worksheets are not stored as text files, the program displays the contents of the sector in hex format.

There is one problem. The program tells you what data cluster you are looking at but not what file, if any, this cluster belongs to. This is another difference between the TS program and the text search in the main program.

One possible solution is to look at the information in the cluster and try to find text that you might use with TS. For example, **@isapp** and **@isaaf**, as well as the cell range **A11.A12**, also part of this cluster, are items that TS can look for.

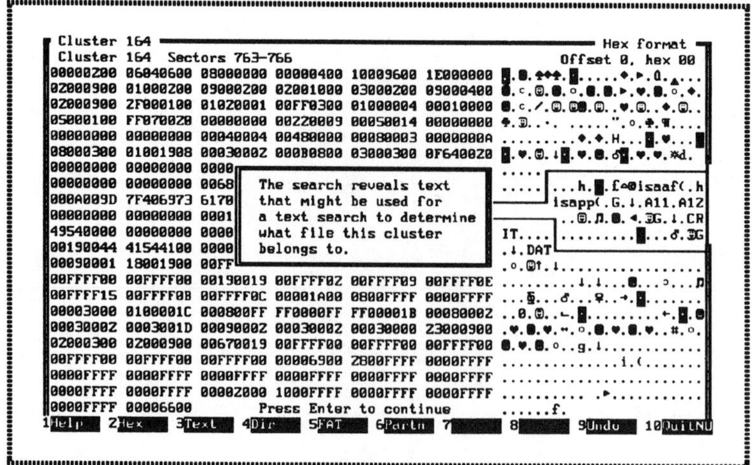

Figure 6-24

> The @isapp function indicates that this file was created using a Lotus add-in program. You can use the text to search worksheet files to find the ones that have information related to add-in products, as opposed to files that contain only normal 1-2-3 information. This is important if you want to share files with other users who may not have the same add-ins.

But there is a simpler method. Return to the search menu. Enter

↵

Leave the search menu by entering

`1`

You are now at menu 1, explore disk. You know that the search key is found in cluster 164. But what file, if any, is that? To find out, select I for information. Enter

`i`

The program analyzes the directory and FAT information and displays the file and directory related to that cluster.

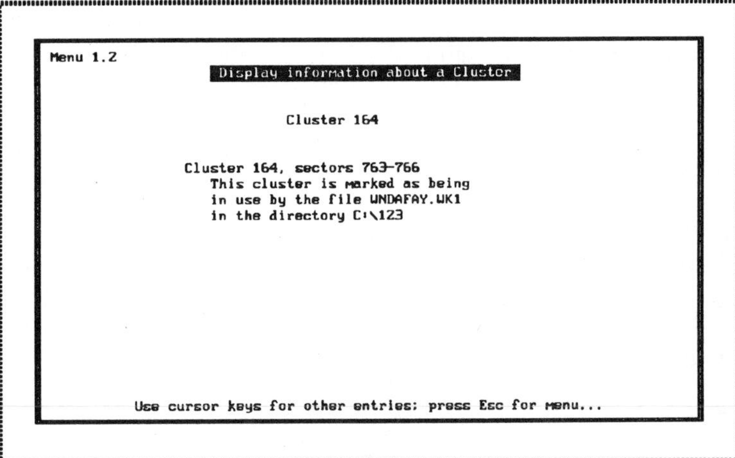

Figure 6-25

In this example the file is called WNDAFAY.WK1 in the \123 directory.
Return to the explore disk menu by entering

`[Esc]`

You can return to the search menu, exactly where you left it, by entering

```
s
```

The program has maintained the search options that you had selected earlier. You can continue the search or change some or all of the options.

If you wanted to check for erased worksheet files on the disk you could change your selection for where to search. Enter

```
w
e
s
```

The program would search for the search key in all of the unused sectors. The ability to search erased areas is advantageous because the Norton Utilities program provides a way to recover files, in some cases, after they have been erased. A full discussion of erased files and recover can be found in Section IV.

The program may encounter the data in an erased area or simply go until it has reached the end of disk. Exit the main program by entering

`[Esc]` (3 times)

The search facility of the main Norton Utilities program approaches the task of locating disk information in a slightly different way than the TS program.

1. The TS program is oriented towards text search while the main program can search for text and non-text sequences.

2. The TS program allows you to select groups of files to search using DOS wildcards. The main program searches one file at a time or the entire disk.

3. The TS program takes a complete search command and carries it out. The main program allows you to go back and forth, change text or location selection, continue, suspend or re-start a selected search.

Depending upon your needs you may find that one or both programs are necessary. The major factor in determining which program you use is the type of files you are searching. Files that contain non-text information, like worksheet files, will often require you to use the main program's search facility since you can include hex values as well as text.

The TS program's major advantage is that it can be aimed at a specific group of files, instead of checking all the disk clusters like the main program does. In either case, the search abilities form an invaluable aid in locating information. They also play a key role in recovering erased data, discussed in Section IV.

Searching in Non-File Areas

The TS program can also duplicate the sector by sector or erased cluster searches performed by the main Norton Utilities program. TS will accept two switches that change its orientation from files to clusters and sectors.

/D This option places TS into a full-disk scan. When this switch is used, any file wildcards included in the command line are ignored. TS searches the disk beginning with sector 0. You are prompted to enter the letter of the disk you want to search.

/E This option places TS into a mode in which all data clusters not assigned to a file in the FAT are searched for the specified text. When this switch is used, any file specifications are ignored by TS. The search begins with the first unused cluster on the disk.

/C# The /C switch is followed by a decimal number corresponding to the cluster number where you want the search to begin. Note that /C can only be used if /D or /E are also used. If you enter /C# without /E or /D on the command line, the /C# is ignored.

Using the TS program with the /E or /D options allows you to take advantage of a special option that will copy the data from any located data clusters to a new file. As you locate the clusters, TS will paste them together into a new file by copying clusters. This technique is usually related to recovering erased data but can be used with any disk cluster if desired.

> The copying feature of the TS program requires that the data to be copied should be stored on a different disk than the one being searched. This is done to avoid overwriting any data that is currently stored in unused clusters. As discussed in Chapter 4, data from erased files remains in the disk clusters until that cluster is used by another file to hold new data. By copying the cluster to a different disk, TS makes sure that you are not destroying any of the information you might be searching for.

For example, suppose that you wanted to see if the name Peter Norton was stored in any of the clusters on the disk. Enter

```
ts "peter norton"/d ↵
```

The program prompts you to enter the name of the disk to search. Enter

```
c
```

You are prompted for the name of a file into which you can copy the data from the located clusters. You must copy the data to a disk other than the one you are searching. TS will reject any entry that uses the search disk. Entering ↵ will skip this option. Enter

```
↵
```

The program should find a match in one of the Norton Utilities programs. The ASK.EXE file is probably the first Norton Utilities program copied to the hard disk and chances are that the program will stop at that file.

To stop the search, enter

```
[Ctrl/Scroll Lock]
```

To search only the unused clusters, you would substitute a /E for the /D switch. Example:

```
ts "peter norton"/e ↵
```

The /C option allows you to begin the search at a specific cluster number. Suppose that in a previous search you found a match in cluster 500. The next search should begin in the unused portions of the disk, starting at cluster 501. The following command would be used:

```
ts "peter norton"/e/c501 ↵
```

7

DIRECTORIES

Section I discusses the DOS concept of directories. Directories are essential to the efficient use of hard disks, but the DOS commands supplied to deal with directories are difficult and obtuse. Even if you understand the commands well, they are not easy to use because they require you to remember the organization of the disk's directories. The commands themselves provide no information about what directories are on the disk.

To simplify life with hard disks, the Norton Utilities provide two programs that address directory problems. The first program, LD, List Directories, is carried over from earlier versions of the Norton Utilities. The second, NCD, Norton Change Directory, is a new program supplied with Version 4.0. The NCD program is a visual, interactive program that combines the functions of all the DOS directory commands into an easy to operate format.

To learn more about these programs place a blank, formatted disk in drive A of your computer. This disk will allow you to experiment with directories without affecting your current hard disk.

Make sure that you have a path open to the directory that contains your Norton Utilities programs. Include the drive letter with that path to enable you to execute programs from drive C while you are working on drive A. To check the current path specification, enter

```
path ↵
```

If your Norton Utilities programs are stored in the \DOS directory, one of the paths should be **C:\DOS**;. If your path does not include the drive letter, change the path by entering a new path command. Example:

```
path c:\dos; ↵
```

Change the active drive to A by entering

```
a: ↵
```

Start by making some directories on the floppy disk using the standard DOS commands. Begin with three directories for the three most popular applications. Enter

```
md\dbase ↵
md\wp ↵
md lotus↵
```

Notice that the backslash (\) was left out of the last command. With the backslash inserted, DOS creates a new directory with the root directory as the parent. If a blank space is used instead of a backslash, DOS assumes that the parent of the new directory is the active directory. Since the root was the active directory the command **MD\LOTUS** and **MD LOTUS** have the same result. But if the active directory was something other than the root, then the two commands would have a different result. For example, suppose you wanted to make two directories under Lotus, one for 1-2-3 and one for Symphony. One way to accomplish this is to use the explicit name for that directory, that is, using the parent directory's name. Enter

```
md\lotus\123 ↵
```

The other method is to change to the parent directory and let DOS fill in the default directory in the MD command. Enter

```
cd lotus ↵
md symphony ↵
```

The new directory is **\lotus\symphony** because DOS automatically filled in the parent directory with the directory selected with the previous CD command.

The explicit form of the command has the advantage of not depending on any previous commands. For example, even though the active directory is \lotus, you can create subdirectories for **\wp**. Enter

```
md\wp\letters ↵
md\wp\memos ↵
```

For good measure, create a MEMOS directory under letters called PLANS. Enter

```
md\wp\memos\plans ↵
```

You now have plenty of directories to work with. Return to the root directory by entering

```
cd\
```

List Directories

The LD (list directories) program, a much simpler program than NCD, provides a list of the directories on the disk. The program displays the list on the screen but it is probably more useful to use the command to print the list or save the list in a text file for later use. The LD command can display directory information in two formats.

DOS Style This is the default style for the LD command. DOS style refers to a linear list of the directories. Subdirectories are listed after their parent directories showing their full path name. The relationship between directories is implied by the names of the directories. Example:

C:\LOTUS
C:\LOTUS\123
C:\LOTUS\SYMPHONY

Graphic The graphics style is selected by using the /G switch with the LD program. In this mode the relationship between directories is shown visually. Subdirectories are indented and lines are drawn between related items. Example:

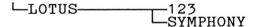

To see the difference between the two styles, enter

```
ld ↵
ld/g ↵
```

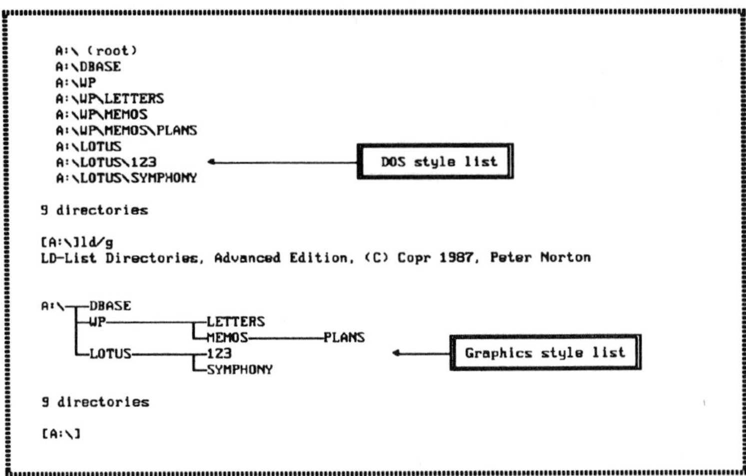

Figure 7-1

Note that both styles display a count of the number of directories at the bottom of the listing.

The main purpose of the LD command is to print the directory list. This is done by taking advantage of DOS redirection. Enter

```
ld >prn ↵
```

Printing the graphics display poses a question about the capabilities of your printer. As mentioned in the previous section on EDCDIC coding, not all printers are capable of supporting the full-extended character set that is used to display such graphics items as lines and boxes on the screen. In order to print the graphic display on printers that do not support the full IBM character set, the /N switch is provided. Used with /G, it tells LD to substitute normal characters in place of the graphic lines. Enter

```
ld/g/n ↵
```

To send that display to print, enter

```
ld/g/n >prn ↵
```

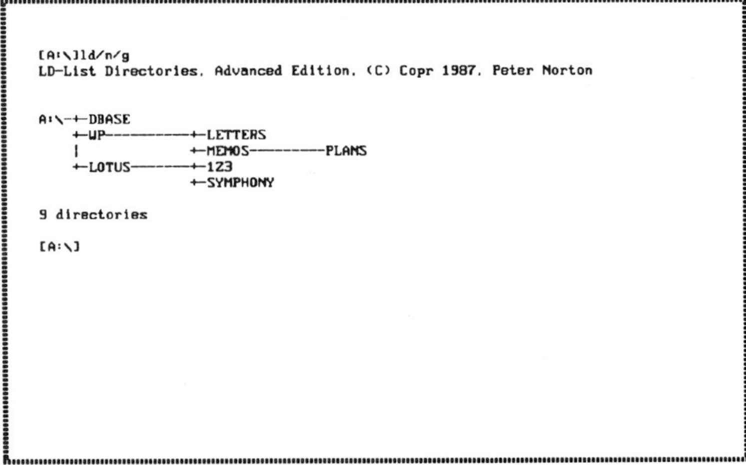

```
[A:\]ld/n/g
LD-List Directories, Advanced Edition, (C) Copr 1987, Peter Norton

A:\-+-DBASE
    +-WP----------+-LETTERS
    |             +-MEMOS---------PLANS
    +-LOTUS-------+-123
                  +-SYMPHONY

9 directories

[A:\]
```

Figure 7-2

LD also recognizes a /A switch that will list the directories on all the drives. Enter

```
ld/g/a ↵
```

Finally, the LD command accepts /T. /T enhances the list of directories by counting the number of files and the amount of disk space for each directory with a summary for the entire disk. The /T switch can help you get an idea of how much room a given directory is taking up. To see how much room the DOS directory in drive C takes up, enter

```
ld c:\dos/t ↵
```

The DOS pathname c:\dos is used to narrow the scope of the LD command. You can get a listing of the size of all the directories on a disk by entering

```
ld/t ↵
```

You can use the DOS redirection commands to store the results of an LD command to a text file, usually with the /T switch on. You can then get an idea of which directories are growing. If a directory gets too large you might want to divide its files into smaller directories.

Some of the LD switches are mutually exclusive. For example, /T will not operate if /G is used.

Norton Change Directories

The second program provided with the Norton Utilities to help with directory operation is the NCD (Norton Change Directory) program. This program is similar to the main Norton Utilities program in that it is a full-screen, interactive program. To see how it works, enter

`ncd ↵`

When the program loads for the first time, it creates a special file called TREEINFO.NCD, which contains a list of the directories on the disk. With this file in place, the NCD program can quickly display the diagram of the directories without having to read the entire disk each time it is loaded. The program now displays a graphics diagram of the directories on the disk.

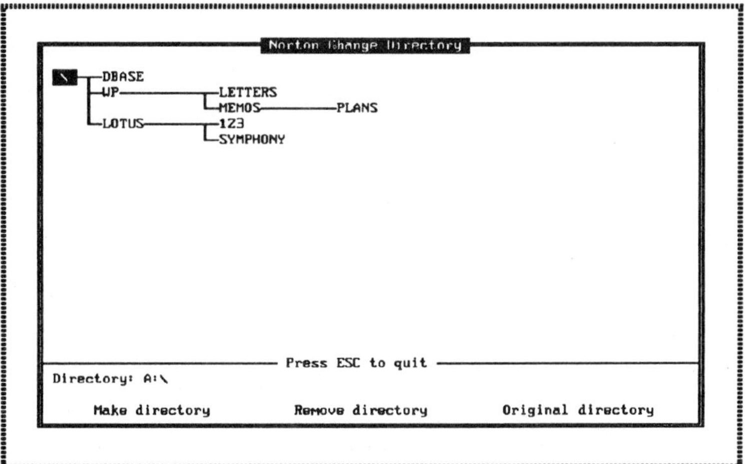

Figure 7-3

To change to a directory, all you need do is use the arrow keys to move the highlight to the part of the tree that represents the directory you want to activate. For example, suppose you wanted to change to the plans directory. Enter

`[right arrow]` (5 times)

To select this directory simply press ↵. Enter

↵

The program terminates. You are returned to DOS with the active directory \WP\MEMOS\PLANS. To change to a different directory, enter

`ncd`↵

Move the highlight to SYMPHONY. Notice that the original directory, **PLANS**, appears in bold to indicate that was the active directory when you loaded the program. To select SYMPHONY, enter

↵

SYMPHONY becomes the active directory. Enter

`ncd` ↵

In addition to the arrow keys, NCD will recognize:

[Home] Highlights the first directory on the list.

[End] Highlights the last directory on the list.

[Pg Dn] Displays the next page of the directory display. This command is used when the directory tree is too large to fit on a single screen.

[Pg Up] Displays the previous screen.

To jump to the first directory, the root of A, enter

`[Home]`

NCD will jump back to the original directory at any point by entering the letter O. Enter

`o`

The highlight moves back to SYMPHONY. The command in DOS to change to the root is CD\. To change to the root in NCD, enter

`[Home]` ↵

Quick Changes

The NCD program provides an even faster way of selecting a directory. You can follow the NCD command with the name or part of the name of the directory to which you want to change. The program will search the tree for a directory name that matches your specification and change to that directory. Suppose you wanted to change to the PLANS directory. The appropriate DOS command is **CD\WP\MEMOS\PLANS**. With NCD, you do not need to type that full pathname or even remember that WP\MEMOS is the parent directory for PLANS. Enter

ncd plans ↵

The NCD program finds that matching directory name and automatically performs the CD command for you.

```
[A:\]ncd plans
NCD-Norton Change Directory, Advanced Edition, (C)
Copr 1987, Peter Norton

Changing to A:\WP\MEMOS\PLANS

[A:\WP\MEMOS\PLANS]
```

The NCD command does not require you to enter the entire directory name. You need enter only as much of the directory name as will prompt the program to match a unique name. Enter

ncd sym ↵

The program finds SYMPHONY when only the first three letters are specified. To see what would happen if you entered a specification that was not unique, enter

ncd L ↵

The NCD program changes the directory to \WP\LETTERS because that was the first match in the directory tree for the letter L. If you wanted to find LOTUS you would have to enter

ncd lo ↵

Adding and Subtracting Directories

The NCD program allows you to create new directories and remove existing directories. There are two ways this can be accomplished.

1. You can perform directory operations from the graphics display using the M and R commands.

2. You can specify MD and RD as part of the command line. First, try the graphics method. Enter

```
ncd
```

Suppose that you want to create a directory of 123 called BUDGETS. Highlight 123 by entering

```
[right arrow]
```

To create a new directory, enter

```
m
```

The program creates a blank directory under 123.

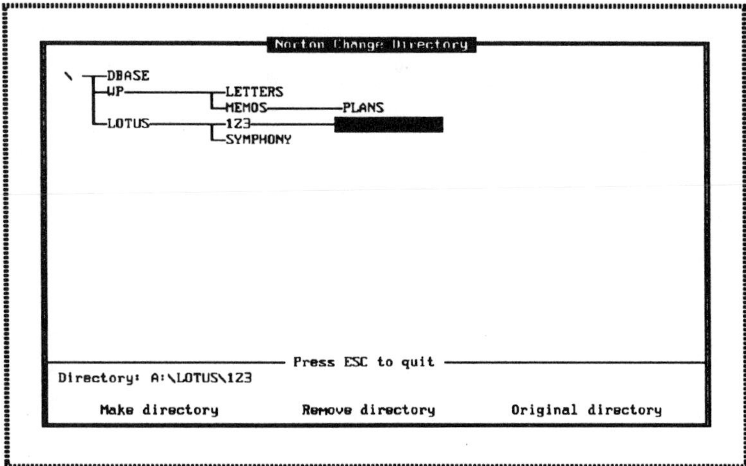

Figure 7-4

You can now fill in the name for that directory. Enter

```
budgets ↵
```

The directory is now added to the tree. Directories can be removed just as easily. Highlight the PLANS directory by entering

```
[up arrow]
```

To remove the directory, enter

```
r
```

The directory is removed and the highlight placed on the part directory.

> You cannot remove a directory unless all of the files in that directory have been deleted. The NCD program will display an error message if you attempt to remove a directory that is not empty.
>
> Keep in mind that a subdirectory represents an entry in a directory similar to a file. This means that even if you have deleted all the files from a directory, it is not empty if it serves as the parent directory for one or more directories. In this example, you could not remove LOTUS, even though it has no file, unless you first removed both of the subdirectories, 123 and SYMPHONY.

You can exit the NCD program without changing directories by entering

```
[Esc]
```

The second method of using NCD to create new directories is as a DOS line command. For example, to create an ACCOUNTS subdirectory of the DBASE directory, enter

```
ncd md \dbase\accounts ↵
```

Note that the space between MD and \DBASE is necessary. If you do not leave the space, the NCD program searches for a directory instead of creating one.

In looking at the previous command you may wonder what advantage there is in using NCD. Using DOS requires that you only enter

```
md\dbase\accounts ↵
```

Here, there is no apparent benefit to using NCD in terms of saving time or effort. However, since it is the TREEINFO.NCD file that the NCD program reads when you enter a command, if you create or remove a directory without allowing NCD to update that file, the NCD program will be out of synch with the actual structure of the disk. Thus the only reason to use the NCD command to make or remove a directory from a command line is to update the TREEINFO.NCD file.

What would happen if you used the DOS MD command to make a new directory? Is there any way to get NCD back in synch with the disk's structure? The problem can be solved by using the /R switch. Create a new directory with DOS. Enter

```
md\dbase\clients ↵
```

Load the NCD program.

```
ncd ↵
```

The display shows the ACCOUNTS directory but not the CLIENTS.

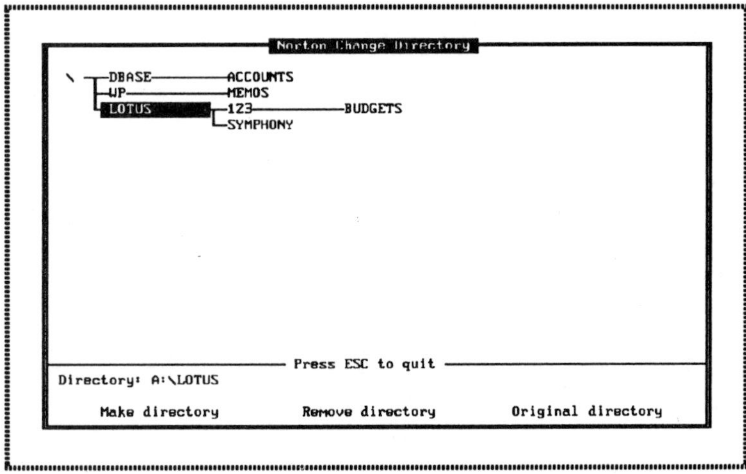

Figure 7-5

To update the display, exit the program and then run the /R switch. Enter

```
[Esc]
ncd/r ↵
```

The program starts by reading the disk information again and then displaying the updated tree.

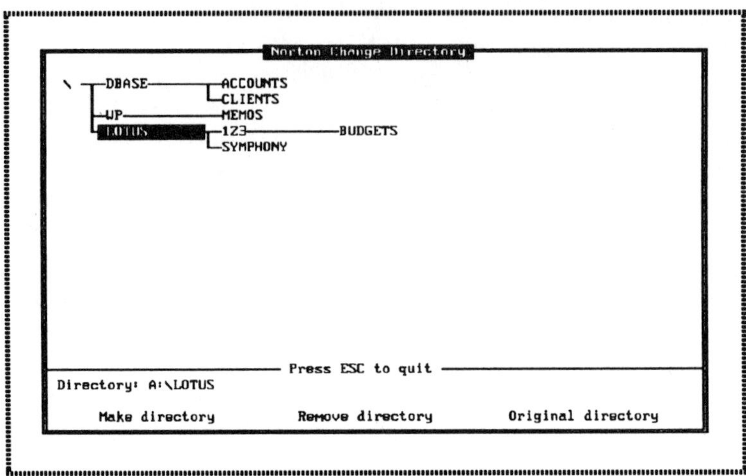

Figure 7-6

Exit the program and change to the root directory by entering

[Home] ↵

The NCD program has a number of advantages over DOS and some hard disk manager programs, such as the Norton Commander.

One advantage is that the program is designed for a limited but important purpose, to help you quickly access the correct directory. Since the program is not designed as a general purpose hard disk manager it does not have to read the entire disk each time it loads. The TREEINFO.NCD file can be quickly loaded or read to carry out the necessary operations.

Although you must make sure that the TREEINFO.NCD file is up to date, most users do not create or remove directories often, so that it is not a major inconvenience to update the tree file when necessary.

The NCD program is important for another reason. The DOS directory system offers the user convenient tools for organization. For example, by using directories to group together related files you can cut down on the time it takes to backup or copy files. You can avoid backing up the entire disk and only backup the directories that you have worked with on a particular day. In addition, the ease of locating directories with NCD should encourage users to make more directories and use more descriptive names.

If you are working without NCD, making a complicated network of directories is not practical. The entry of commands, CD, COPY, and so on, with long pathnames, for example, \LOTUS\123\BUDGETS, is too difficult and time consuming. The time wasted in typos alone is frustrating. But NCD resolves the entry problem quite nicely. You can then feel free to make as many directories as you need to help you get organized.

There is no need to use short names. If you are working strictly with DOS, it makes sense to choose short directory names to help in command entry. But with NCD you can use more descriptive names and not have to do any more typing when you change directories. Return to drive C by entering

```
c:
```

Counting Space

The LD program is capable of calculating the total amount of space used by the files in a given directory. But what about other groups of files? Norton Utilities provides a program called FS (File Size) that calculates the size of a file or group of files.

This very handy program (a personal favorite) provides some useful information that can be invaluable in managing a computer system.

The basic operation of FS could not be simpler-it functions like the DOS DIR command. For example, to list the files in the \DOS directory, enter

```
fs \dos ↵
```

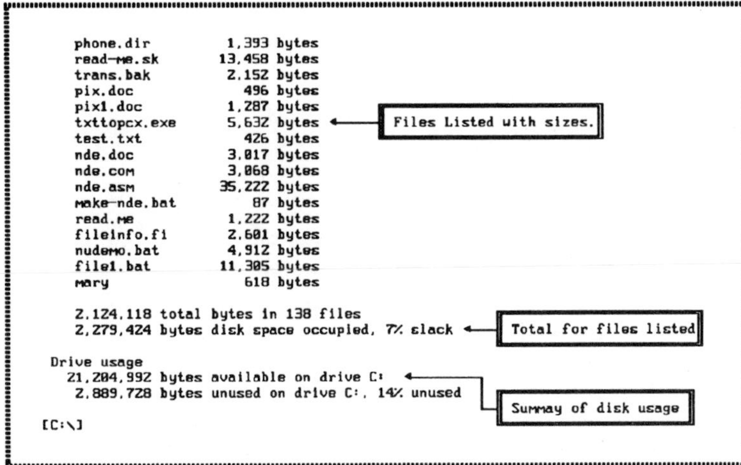

Figure 7-7

The command produces distinct pieces of information.

File List

The File List displays the size of all the selected files. This is the same information that the DIR command provides, except that the FL formats the numbers with commas to make them easier to read.

File Summary

At the bottom of the file list, FS displays a summary of the all the files listed. The first line contains a count of the files listed and the total size of all the files based on the size specification stored in the disk directory. The second line contains the total amount of disk space occupied by those files and an estimate of the amount of "slack" space.

Disk Summary

This occupies the last two lines of the display. It shows the total capacity of the disk. The amount still left for files is shown as a number of bytes and a percentage of the total disk space.

The important difference between the list of files produced with FS and a DIR command is that FS does not include directory names in its listing. You might well prefer to use FS to list only filenames in place of DIR which includes directories as well. This is particularly true when you are listing files in the root directory, which will contain a large number of directories.

The concept of slack space is discussed in Section I, but it might bear repeating since it is so closely related to the FS program.

The size of the file listed in the directory represents the logical size of the file. Logical size refers to the number of bytes from the beginning of a file until the end of the file information. But that is not necessarily the same as the a mount of disk space taken up by the file. The reason for the difference is that DOS assigns space to files using the data cluster as a minimum allocation unit. A minimum allocation is a familiar concept. When you go to the store you can't buy one aspirin or one egg. For efficient packaging, a minimum allocation unit, that is, a dozen eggs, is established.

> The file size listed in the directory may vary from the actual number of bytes stored in the file due to the way some programs read and write blocks of data. For example, if you use WordStar to create a file with only one word, for instance, Hello, the file size listed in the directory will show 128 not 5 or 6. This is because WordStar reads and writes data in blocks of 128 characters at a time. This difference has no practical significance.

The data cluster is the minimum allocation unit used by DOS. It is interesting to note that the size of the cluster will vary with the type of disk being used and the version of DOS used to format the disk. Below is a table that shows the cluster sizes of various disks and formats.

Table 7.1. Cluster Sizes

Disk Type	DOS Version	Cluster Size
360K	3 or 2	1024
1.2 Meg	3	512
20 Meg	2	8192
20 Meg	3	2048

Slack space is created by the very natural fact that files do not always end at the exact end of a cluster. For example, a file with 1025 characters would require two data clusters on a 360K floppy disk because it has one more character than would fit into a 1024 byte cluster. This causes 1023 bytes of slack space in the second cluster.

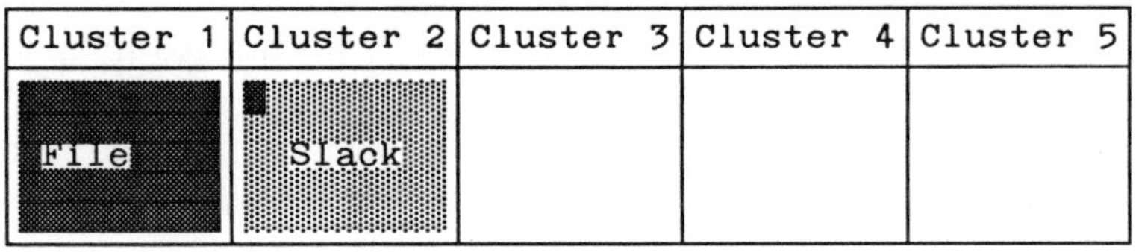

Cluster 1	Cluster 2	Cluster 3	Cluster 4	Cluster 5
File	Slack			

The next file to be added to the disk begins at the beginning of cluster 3. This means that the space at the end of the second cluster cannot be used by any other file. As chance will have it a certain amount of slack will occur whenever a file is written.

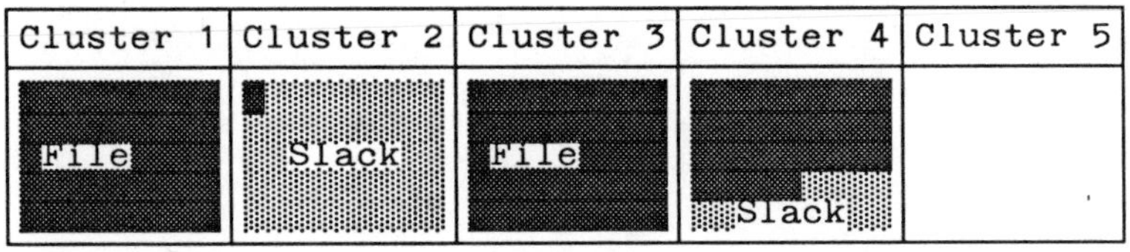

Cluster 1	Cluster 2	Cluster 3	Cluster 4	Cluster 5
File	Slack	File	Slack	

Keep in mind that should the file expand, the file will use up the remainder of the cluster before allocating a new cluster to that file.

The table below shows the amount of disk space used by a 200 byte file on different disk formats.

Table 7.2. Disk Space Used by a 200 Byte File

Disk Type	DOS Version	Cluster Size	200 byte file	% Slack
360K	3 or 2	1024	1024	80.5
1.2 Meg	3	512	512	60
20 Meg	2	8192	8192	98
20 Meg	3	2048	2048	90

The cluster size is always a trade off. If the cluster size is too small, the slack space is cut down, but the disk works slower because it has to keep track of so many more clusters. Performance improves with larger clusters but the amount of slack space rises.

> To find out the cluster size used on your hard disk, use the main Norton Utilities program, NU, and select Disk Information, D, then Technical information, T. The 5th line under logical dimension will tell you the number of sectors in each cluster. To find the cluster size in bytes multiply the number of sectors by 512, for instance, 4 * 512 = 2048.

If all you are interested in is the summary totals, you can suppress the display of the individual filenames by using the /T switch. Suppose you wanted to find the total amount of space occupied by EXE files in the DOS directory. Enter

```
fs \dos /t ↵
```

FS will also operate with a /S switch, which will prompt it to include subdirectories as well in its count. If you start with the root directory you can include the entire disk. Enter

```
fs \/s/t
```

The program will output a set of totals for each directory and the a summary for all the directories.

You can use DOS redirection to capture the data in a text file or send it directly to a printer. One handy listing is a summary of the space used on the hard disk. Since this listing might exceed a single page it would be best to capture the output in a text file and then use the LP program to make a page formatted print out. Example:

```
fs \ /t/s >catalog ↵
   lp catalogue
```

Estimating Room

One of the main reasons for using the FS program is to estimate if you have enough room on a destination disk to copy a group of files. You can determine this by running FS on the group of files you want to copy, then again on the disk that you want to copy to and comparing the amount of space the file takes up with the empty space on the destination disk. But that effort is unnecessary. By specifying the destination disk, FS will make the comparison for you.

Suppose that you wanted to copy all COM files in the DOS directory to the floppy disk in drive A. Using FS can avoid being surprised by an insufficient disk space message. Enter

```
fs \dos\*.com a:/t ↵
```

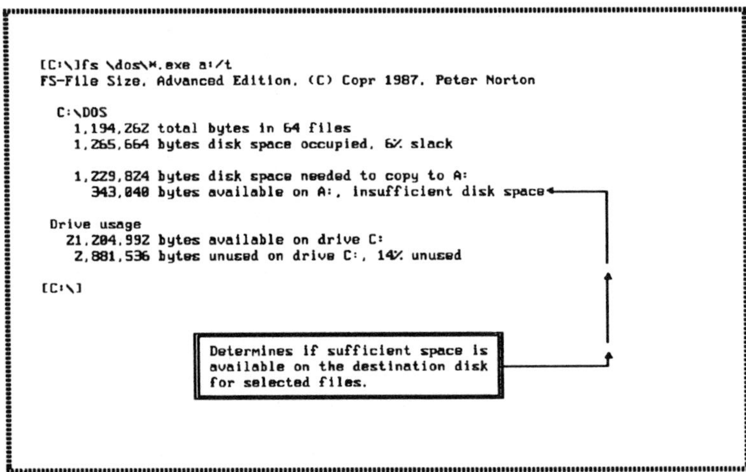

Figure 7-8

SECTION IV
ORGANIZATIONAL TASKS

8

PROTECTING FILES

The old expression "out of sight, out of mind" can be applied to files on the hard disk. In Chapter 1, the concept of hidden files was discussed in terms of the two system files, BIO and DOS, which are stored on the disk but hidden from display. Because the files are hidden they cannot be erased with the DEL or ERASE command and they do not clutter up the display when you list a directory.

As you work with your hard disk you may find that there are a number of files you want to treat like the two hidden files that DOS places on the disk. These are files you do not want to erase but you do not need to be reminded of every time you list the root directory.

It has always been a personal preference to try to keep the root directory as uncluttered as possible. Ideally, the root directory might simply consist of the list of directories.

There are, however, some files that absolutely must be placed in the root, such as COMMAND.COM, CONFIG.SYS, and AUTOEXEC.BAT. In addition, you may also have some batch files such as the MENU batches discussed in Section II, as well as some device drivers stored in the root directory. Taken all together, the root appears pretty cluttered before you even begin.

> It is not strictly necessary to place device driver files such as ANSI.SYS, or VDISK.SYS in the root directory. You can place these files in the any directory you like, for instance, DOS.
>
> The only file that must be in the root is CONFIG.SYS. The trick is to use the full pathname with the device driver in the CONFIG.SYS command.

For example, suppose you placed the ANSI.SYS file in the DOS directory. The line in the CONFIG.SYS file that device drive should read:

DEVICE=\DOS\ANSI.SYS

When the computer boots it will search the \DOS directory for the specified device driver. Remember that the CONFIG.SYS file is read after the IBMBIO.COM and IBMDOS.COM files have been loaded, which means the computer can search the drive for files.

With this change you can remove the device drivers from the root directory. This does not apply to CONFIG.SYS, which must remain in the root directory of the boot disk.

DOS provides an opportunity, and Norton Utilities the means, to protect files from accidental erasure or modification. DOS reserves a byte in the directory entry for file attributes of each file.

The concept of file attributes is borrowed from larger computers systems. In the latter computer system files, directories and drives have levels of security that permit only certain operators to gain access to certain programs and files. But DOS is designed to operate a personal computer and the file attributes are not very complex. There are two that are relevant to this purpose.

Read-Only

If a file is marked as read-only most of the commands issued by DOS or programs running under DOS will not erase or modify this file. If you attempt to copy a new file to a filename marked as read-only, DOS will display a file creation error and refuse to make the copy.

Read-only files appear in normal directory listing and can be loaded into most programs.

Hidden

A hidden file is one that does not appear in the directory. For that reason commands like DEL and ERASE will not remove them. However, a hidden file is accessible to programs and can be modified or overwritten. For example, if a file is hidden and you copy a new file to the same name, DOS will overwrite the hidden file with the new file.

If you modify a hidden file, DOS will write the modification to the disk. In the process, DOS also removes the hidden attribute and the file becomes visible again.

> There are two attributes available in DOS: archive and System. The archive attribute is assigned to all files when they are first written. Programs like BACKUP use this in backing up revised files. The SYSTEM attribute is not generally used.

Files can be Read-only, hidden, or both. You can use the attributes to hide or protect important files. The Norton Utilities program FA (file attributes) can be used to determine or modify the attributes of a file or group of files.

Begin by listing the files in the root directory. Instead of using DIR, use FS, which will list files, not directories and files. Enter

```
cd\ ↵
fs ↵
```

The listing shown in the illustration below is typical.

```
[C:\]fs
FS-File Size, Advanced Edition, (C) Copr 1987, Peter Norton

  C:\
    io.sys              17,210 bytes
    msdos.sys           28,464 bytes
    command.com         23,612 bytes
    ask.exe              1,184 bytes
    catalog             12,600 bytes
    autoexec.bat            73 bytes
    menu.bat             1,971 bytes
    treeinfo.ncd           283 bytes
    menu.txt             1,584 bytes
    config.sys              68 bytes
    catalog.bat             71 bytes
    oup.bat                490 bytes

      87,610 total bytes in 12 files
     102,400 bytes disk space occupied, 14% slack

 Drive usage
   21,204,992 bytes available on drive C:
    2,996,224 bytes unused on drive C:, 14% unused

[C:\]
```

Figure 8-1

The list contains the essential files, COMMAND.COM, CONFIG.SYS, AUTOEXEC.BAT and MENU.BAT, plus some miscellaneous files.

The FA command can be used to list the attributes of the files. Enter

```
fa ↵
```

```
Drive usage
  21,284,992 bytes available on drive C:
   2,996,224 bytes unused on drive C:, 14% unused

[C:\]fa
FA-File Attributes, Advanced Edition, (C) Copr 1987, Peter Norton

C:\
     io.sys         Archive Read-only Hidden System
     msdos.sys      Archive Read-only Hidden System
     command.com    Archive
     ask.exe        Archive
     catalog        Archive
     autoexec.bat   Archive
     menu.bat       Archive
     treeinfo.ncd   Archive
     menu.txt       Archive
     config.sys     Archive
     catalog.bat    Archive
     owp.bat        Archive

   12 files shown
   no files changed

[C:\]
```

Figure 8-2

You can see that the systems files, in this case IO.SYS and MS-DOS.SYS, are marked as both hidden and read-only. This means they will not be accidentally erased or overwritten by another file. The third of the MS-DOS files, COMMAND.COM, is marked only as an archive file because the MS-DOS designers intended it to be one of a variety of processors.

COMMAND.COM translates resident DOS commands such as DIR, COPY, TYPE, and so on, into operations. Many application programs, when run, remove COMMAND.COM from memory in order to use that space for the application. When the program is exited, DOS reloads the COMMAND.COM file automatically giving the illusion that the COMMAND.COM command interpreter is always present. The designers of DOS anticipated that designers of other software applications might engineer alternatives to COMMAND.COM that would replace commands like DIR and COPY.

Very few alternative command processors were developed, however. Most MS-DOS users employ COMMAND.COM as their exclusive command interpreter. In practice, COMMAND.COM is as much a part of the basic DOS system as the two hidden files. There is no reason that you cannot change the attributes of the COMMAND.COM file to match the other systems files. In doing so you accomplish two things.

1. You remove a file from the directory listing. Since seeing the filename is not necessary this will reduce some of the clutter in the root directory.

2. This will also protect the COMMAND.COM file from accidental overwriting or erasure.

The FA command uses the switches /HID and /R for the hidden and read-only attributes respectively. To add the attribute to a file follow the switch with a plus sign (+). To remove an attribute follow the switch with a minus sign (–). Here, add the hidden attribute to the COMMAND.COM file:

fa command.com/hid+ ↵

The program displays a message indicating that COMMAND.COM is now an archive and hidden file.

```
[C:\]fa command.com/hid+
FA-File Attributes, Advanced Edition, (C) Co

C:\
  command.com   Archive            Hidden

  1 file changed
```

To see if the file is really hidden use the DIR command to list all files that begin with the letter C. Enter

dir c*.* ↵

COMMAND.COM does not appear. The file is now protected from accidental erasure. To demonstrate this, try to erase COMMAND.COM by entering

del command.com ↵

DOS returns the message that the file cannot be found. The protection from erasure appears to work.

However, the protection is not complete. If you were to copy files from a disk or directory into the root directory, any file named COMMAND.COM would overwrite the hidden file. Because each different version of DOS uses its own version of COMMAND.COM you cannot use the COMMAND.COM file for DOS 3.1, with DOS 3.3, for instance. The next time DOS attempts to load the COMMAND.COM file it would cause an error. The only solution is to boot the computer from a DOS system floppy disk. You then must copy the correct version of COMMAND.COM from a floppy disk to the root directory.

This error, which seems to happen a lot now that there are several versions of DOS, can be avoided by taking the additional step of making COMMAND.COM read-only. Enter

fa command.com/r+ ↵

This change in the status of COMMAND.COM will not effect the use of the file. The file is listed in the disk directory just as are the other hidden files. DOS will be able to load the COMMAND.COM exactly as it would normally.

The same is true of the CONFIG.SYS file. The FA command can change more than one attribute at a time. Change CONFIG.SYS by entering

```
fa config.sys/r+/hid+ ↵
```

Keep in mind that unlike COMMAND.COM, CONFIG.SYS is a user defined file that you may need to modify from time to time. Right now, DOS will refuse to overwrite the file. For example, suppose you attempted to edit this file with EDLIN. Enter

```
edlin config.sys ↵
```

DOS displays the message File is READ-ONLY. Interestingly, DOS was able to locate the file even though it is set as a hidden file. If you wanted to edit the file you would have to remove the Read-Only attribute. Enter

```
fa config.sys/r- ↵
edlin config.sys ↵
```

This time EDLIN loads the file correctly. Note that CONFIG.SYS is still a hidden file. Return to DOS by entering

```
e ↵
```

You can perform the same changes on batch files like AUTOEXEC.BAT and MENU.BAT, as well. However, you should consider your purposes. If the goal is to remove the clutter and protect against deleting, the hidden attribute should be used. This assumes that you do not need to see the filenames in the DIR listing to operate your computer. It is not necessary to see the MENU.BAT file to know that your program is started by entering menu. You may prefer to have these files listed, but protected, by the read-only attribute. Depending upon what you want to achieve, you can manipulate the attributes to suit your desires.

> Another consideration is that most word processing programs will not load hidden files. If you use WordPerfect to edit your batch files you will have to make the files visible before you load them into WordPerfect.

In this example the goal is to make the root directory as clean as possible. You can change the attributes for groups of files by using a wildcard with the FA command. Enter

```
fa *.bat/hid+ ↵
```

List the root directory.

```
dir ↵
```

You have hidden all the batch files. To see if they will still work execute the autoexec by entering

```
autoexec ↵
```

The batch executes normally. The hidden attribute has no effect on its operation. To achieve a totally uncluttered look you might want to hide all the files in the root directory (as I do on my system) and leave only the directories to be displayed with the DIR.

> If you want to put the files back to their original attributes, simply reverse the attributes by entering FA commands. A summary of the operations is shown below:
>
> FA *.bat/hid-
> FS command.com/hid-/r-
> FS config.sys/hid-/r-

Note that if you use NCD the TREEINFO.NCD file will reappear in the directory after a NCD/R command. This is because DOS automatically assigns a normal attribute to a file that is rewritten. To hide the revised file you will need to execute another FA command.

Attributes in the Main Program

The main Norton Utilities program, NU, also allows you to change the attributes of a file. This is done by editing the directory. To demonstrate this, load the main program. Enter

```
nu ↵
```

Display the contents of the directory that contains the files you want to modify. In this case, select the root directory. Enter

↵ (4 times)

To edit the information, enter

e

The directory of the disk is displayed.

```
 Root dir                                              Directory format
 Sector 83 in root directory                           Offset 0, hex 00
                                                       Attributes
Filename Ext     Size      Date      Time    Cluster   Arc R/O Sys Hid Dir Vol

IO       SYS    17210  12/19/86   1:46 pm        2     Arc R/O Sys Hid
MSDOS    SYS    28464   3/21/86  12:00 pm       11     Arc R/O Sys Hid
COMMAND  COM    23612  11/14/86   3:20 am     6789     Arc R/O     Hid
DOS                    10/26/87   8:36 pm       34                     Dir
ASK      EXE     1184   3/01/87   4:00 pm      180     Arc
FONTS                  12/18/87   9:01 pm     5150                     Dir
ONEWRITE PLS           12/24/87   1:09 am      120                     Dir
CATALOG         12600  12/30/87   4:47 am     4968     Arc
AUTOEXEC BAT       73  12/15/87   2:58 am      551     Arc         Hid
MENU     BAT     1971  12/22/87  12:54 am     3689     Arc         Hid
USE      TXT      193  12/31/87  10:34 pm      126     Arc
CONFIG   SYS       68  12/31/87  11:30 pm      257     Arc
TREEINFO NCD      283  12/31/87   3:31 am     4865     Arc
σCR2     $SV     4128  12/31/87   8:57 am     5309     Arc
MENU     TXT     1584  12/18/87   9:38 pm     8957     Arc
σA       EXE     4506   3/01/87   4:00 pm      257     Arc

         Filenames beginning with 'σ' indicate erased entries
                      Press Enter to continue
1Help  2Hex  3Text  4Dir  5FAT  6Partn  7  8  9Undo  10QuitNU
```

Figure 8-3

Use the [Tab] key to move the highlight to the column that contains the attribute you want to change. For example, if you wanted to work with the hidden attribute, enter

`[Tab]` (13 times)

Here, the cursor is on the IO.SYS (IBMBIO.COM for IBM DOS). Because this file is hidden the letters hid appear to indicate the file's attribute.

To change the attribute, that is, to remove the hidden attribute, enter

`[space bar]`

The space becomes blank indicating that the hidden attribute will be reversed. To move to the next file in the directory, enter

`[down arrow]`

Changing the attributes on the screen has not changed the information written on the disk. Enter

[Esc]

The program asks you if you want to write the changes to the disk or discard the changes.

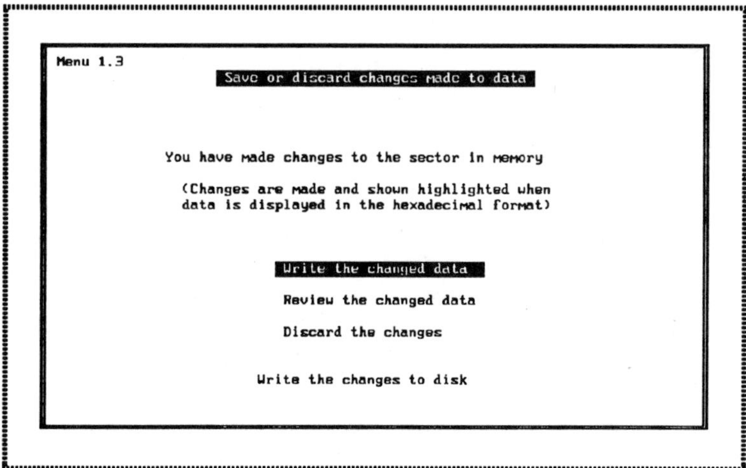
Menu 1.3
Save or discard changes made to data
You have made changes to the sector in memory
(Changes are made and shown highlighted when data is displayed in the hexadecimal format)
Write the changed data
Review the changed data
Discard the changes
Write the changes to disk

Figure 8-4

In this case, disregard the changes. Enter

d

Exit the main program by entering

[F10]

Sorting Directories

The order in which files appear in directory listings seems to vary as files are added and deleted. The reason is that DOS attempts to re-use empty spaces in the directory in order to save space. For example, if you copy four files, A,B,C, and D to a blank disk, DOS, logically enough, places them into the directory in the order in which they are copied.

1	FileA
2	FileB
3	FileC
4	FileD

But suppose you erase file B and copy a new file, E, to the disk. The new file will appear in the place in the directory left vacant by the erased file.

T

1	FileA
2	FileE
3	FileC
4	FileD

The directory now reads A, E, C, D. As you add new files and directories to the disk the order in which they appear will vary depending upon the open spaces created in the directory by deletions. Reusing the directory entries is efficient in terms of space but perplexing to read. New filenames pop-up all over the directory.

DOS offers a filter program called SORT to resolve the confusion. This filter program is not meant to solve the problem of directory order but to sort the output of the DIR command. It does not affect the actual information written in the disk directory. The Norton Utilities program DS (directory sort) will rewrite the directory information on the disk itself.

To experiment with DS, create a new directory called SORTTEST. Enter

```
ncd md \sorttest ↵
```

Activate the directory. Enter

```
ncd sort ↵
```

Copy all the COM files from \DOS directory to your new directory. Enter

```
copy \dos\*.com ↵
```

Now copy some additional files from DOS in order to get a variety of filenames. Enter

```
copy \dos\f*.exe ↵
copy \dos\*.sys ↵
```

You now have a mix of files in the test directory. The DS program will provide a means of organizing these files. There are two way to operate the DS program.

1. **Full Screen.** In this mode the directory sort program works the main Norton Utilities and NCD programs. The directory is displayed on the screen along with special commands that change the sequence of the filenames.

2. **Command Line.** The DS program can be implemented as a single command line from DOS without entering the interactive mode.

Begin with the interactive mode. Enter

```
ds ↵
```

The full screen display shows a list of the first 17 files in the directory and a set of commands for manipulating the files.

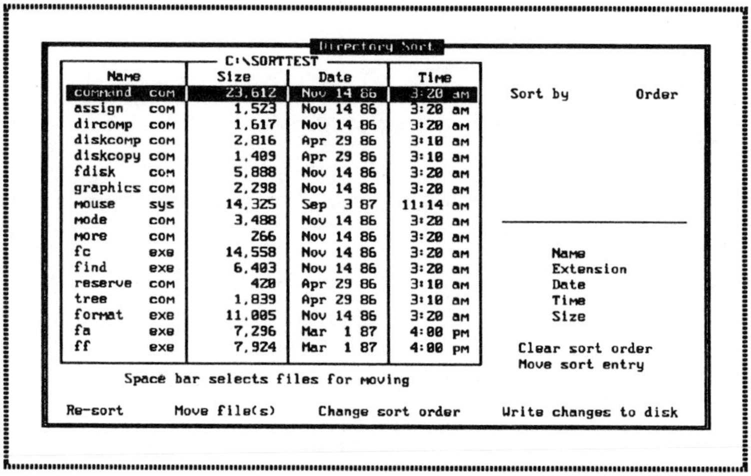

```
                              Directory Sort
                     C:\SORTTEST
   Name            Size      Date        Time
command   com    23,612   Nov 14 86    3:20 am      Sort by          Order
assign    com     1,523   Nov 14 86    3:20 am
dircomp   com     1,617   Nov 14 86    3:20 am
diskcomp  com     2,816   Apr 29 86    3:10 am
diskcopy  com     1,409   Apr 29 86    3:10 am
fdisk     com     5,888   Nov 14 86    3:20 am
graphics  com     2,298   Nov 14 86    3:20 am
mouse     sys    14,325   Sep  3 87   11:14 am
mode      com     3,488   Nov 14 86    3:20 am
more      com       266   Nov 14 86    3:20 am
fc        exe    14,558   Nov 14 86    3:20 am           Name
find      exe     6,403   Nov 14 86    3:20 am           Extension
reserve   com       420   Apr 29 86    3:10 am           Date
tree      com     1,839   Apr 29 86    3:10 am           Time
format    exe    11,005   Nov 14 86    3:20 am           Size
fa        exe     7,296   Mar  1 87    4:00 pm
ff        exe     7,924   Mar  1 87    4:00 pm      Clear sort order
                                                    Move sort entry
          Space bar selects files for moving

Re-sort     Move file(s)     Change sort order     Write changes to disk
```

Figure 8-5

The interactive program has two functions.

1. **Sort Files.** This function uses a logical criterion to rearrange all the filenames in a directory. The program can sort files according to one or more factors. They are name, extension, date, time and size. You can perform the same function using DS in the command line mode.

2. **Move Individual Files.** DS allows you to manually rearrange the order of files by moving one or more files at a time to a specific location in the file directory. This function can only be carried out in the interactive mode. It cannot be implemented through a command line.

Another benefit of the interactive mode is that the changes do not become permanent until you specifically write the changes to the disk. This gives you a chance to change your mind before the directory is rewritten.

To sort all the files in a directory select the sort criterion by placing the cursor in the Sort By column. Enter

`[Tab]`

Select the sort order by entering N, E, D, T or S, which correspond to name, extension, date, time or size. The most common order is by extension. Enter

`e`

Extension is added to the sort order list.

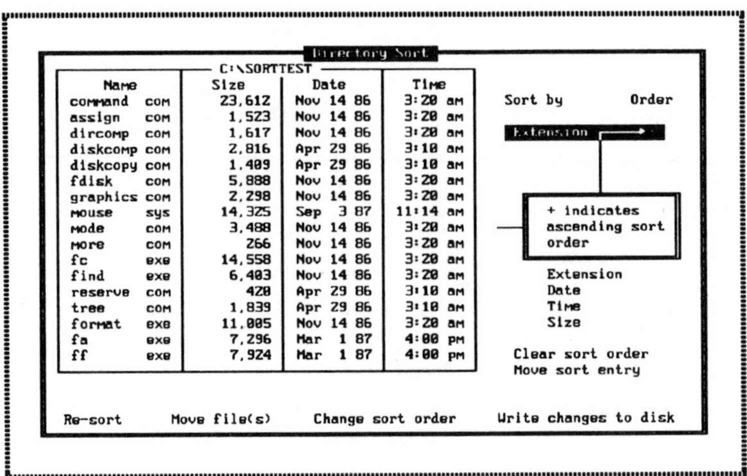

Figure 8-6

Notice that a plus appears next to Extension indicating that the sort is to be in ascending order. To change the order to a descending order, enter

`-`

To change it back to ascending order enter

+

You can add a second level of sort criteria. Suppose that you wanted files with the same extension, ranked within extension by name. Enter

n

Name is added to the sort order list. Note that the files have not been rearranged yet. To place the files in the order that you have specified, enter

r

The files are rearranged.

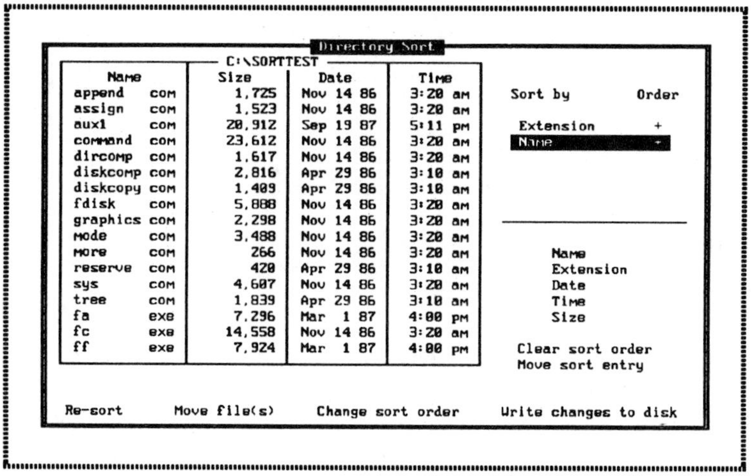

```
                         Directory Sort
            C:\SORTTEST
    Name            Size       Date        Time
append   com       1,725   Nov 14 86   3:20 am     Sort by        Order
assign   com       1,523   Nov 14 86   3:20 am
aux1     com      20,912   Sep 19 87   5:11 pm      Extension       +
command  com      23,612   Nov 14 86   3:20 am      Name            +
dircomp  com       1,617   Nov 14 86   3:20 am
diskcomp com       2,816   Apr 29 86   3:10 am
diskcopy com       1,409   Apr 29 86   3:10 am
fdisk    com       5,888   Nov 14 86   3:20 am
graphics com       2,298   Nov 14 86   3:20 am
mode     com       3,488   Nov 14 86   3:20 am
more     com         266   Nov 14 86   3:20 am          Name
reserve  com         420   Apr 29 86   3:10 am          Extension
sys      com       4,607   Nov 14 86   3:20 am          Date
tree     com       1,839   Apr 29 86   3:10 am          Time
fa       exe       7,296   Mar  1 87   4:00 pm          Size
fc       exe      14,558   Nov 14 86   3:20 am
ff       exe       7,924   Mar  1 87   4:00 pm      Clear sort order
                                                    Move sort entry

Re-sort       Move file(s)      Change sort order      Write changes to disk
```

Figure 8-7

Remember that these changes have not yet been written to the disk.

Another useful way to list files is by the date and time of creation. To start a new sequence, clear the existing sort order by entering

c

Sort by date and time by entering

```
d
t
r
```

This sorts the files so that the oldest files appear first. You might want to use date to place the newest files at the top. This requires a descending sort. Enter

```
d-
t-
r
```

The files are arranged so that the most recent files appear first.

```
                              Directory Sort
                 C:\SORTTEST
     Name           Size      Date        Time
auxl      com     20,912  Sep 19 87    5:11 pm      Sort by        Order
mouse     sys     14,325  Sep  3 87   11:14 am
ff        exe      7,924  Mar  1 87    4:00 pm       Date            -
fs        exe      8,536  Mar  1 87    4:00 pm       Time            -
fr        exe     12,610  Mar  1 87    4:00 pm
fa        exe      7,296  Mar  1 87    4:00 pm
fi        exe     14,668  Mar  1 87    4:00 pm
driver    sys      1,102  Nov 14 86    3:20 am
fc        exe     14,558  Nov 14 86    3:20 am
format    exe     11,005  Nov 14 86    3:20 am
vdisk     sys      2,976  Nov 14 86    3:20 am          Name
append    com      1,725  Nov 14 86    3:20 am          Extension
mode      com      3,488  Nov 14 86    3:20 am          Date
command   com     23,612  Nov 14 86    3:20 am          Time
assign    com      1,523  Nov 14 86    3:20 am          Size
graphics  com      2,298  Nov 14 86    3:20 am
config    sys         26  Nov 14 86    3:20 am       Clear sort order
                                                     Move sort entry

Re-sort      Move file(s)      Change sort order      Write changes to disk
```

Figure 8-8

Another feature of the interactive DS program is that you can manually change the location of any file or group of files that you like. Suppose that you wanted to place the first three files in this list, at the end of the directory rather than the beginning. Place the highlight into the file list frame by entering

```
[Tab]
```

To select a file for movement, enter

```
[space bar]
```

A ▸ marks the file as selected for movement. Mark the next two files in the list the same way. Enter

```
[down arrow]
[space bar]
[down arrow]
[space bar]
```

To change the position of the files, move the highlight to the position in the list where you want them to appear. To skip to end of the directory, enter

```
[End]
```

Move the files by entering

```
m
```

Notice that the files are inserted above the last file in the list. If you do not like the placement, enter [Esc] to undo the move, or ↵ to make the move permanent. Enter

↵

To write the new directory order to the disk, enter

```
w
```

The disk directory is updated. Exit the program by entering

`[Esc]` (2 times)

List the files with the DOS DIR command.

```
dir ↵
```

You can see that the files are listed in the same order as you selected in the DS program. You can execute sort, but not file movements, through command line operation. To place the directory into size order, enter

```
ds s ↵
dir ↵
```

The files are listed by size order from smallest to largest. You can perform multilevel sorts by using more than one letter. For example, to sort by name and extension enter

```
ds ne ↵
dir ↵
```

You can select descending sort order by adding – signs to the letters. Enter

```
ds n-e- ↵
dir ↵
```

The DS command will also accept a subdirectory switch. The effect of this is to have DS sort all subdirectories included in the beginning directory. If you start at the root, you will be able to sort all the files on the hard disk with a single command. The command below arranges all of the directories in order by extension and name. Observe that \ tells DS to begin at the root directory.

```
ds en \ /s ↵
```

The program follows the tree structure and sorts the files in all the directories.

```
[C:\SORTTEST]ds en \ /s
DS-Directory Sort, Advanced Edition, (C) Copr 1987, Peter
Norton

 C:\ ... reading, sorting, writing, done.
 C:\123 ... reading, sorting, writing, done.
 C:\4 ... reading, sorting, writing, done.
 C:\DB3 ... reading, sorting, writing, done.
 C:\DOS ... reading, sorting, writing, done.
 C:\FONTS ... reading, sorting, writing, done.
 C:\JAV ... reading, sorting, writing, done.
 C :\MOD ... reading, sorting, writing, done.
 C:\OWP ... reading, sorting, writing, done.
 C:\PUB ... reading, sorting, writing, done.
 C:\SCR ... reading, sorting, writing, done.
 C:\SIERRA ... reading, sorting, writing, done.
 C:\SORTTEST ... reading, sorting, writing, done.
 C:\WINDOWS ... reading, sorting, writing, done.
 C:\WORD ... reading, sorting, writing, done.
 C:\WP ... reading, sorting, writing, done.
 C:\ONEWRITE.PLS ... reading, sorting, writing, done.
```

File Info

The size of the filename used by DOS applications can be a source of frustration because it leaves so little room to identify the file. If the application you are working with reserves the extension, for instance, 1-2-3, you are left with 8 characters with which to designate the file's meaning.

The FI (file information) program provides a method of annotating files, and is used as an alternative way to list files. The FI program creates a special file in each directory in which it is used. FI allows you to enter comments about files and stores them in a file called FILEINFO.FI.

To get a list of files with comments, use FI as you would DIR. The first step in using FI is to create comments for files by using the /E switch. Suppose you want to add a comment to the file VDISK.SYS. Enter

```
fi vdisk.sys/e ↵
```

The program displays a box on the screen into which you can type the text of the comment for this file. The name and the directory of the file you are annotating are displayed for reference purposes.

When entering a comment you should remember that the FI listing can display up to 36 characters next to the file information. If you want to create longer comments you can do so, but you will have to use the /L switch to display the full text. Enter

```
Creates RAM drive - related to CONFIG.SYS ↵
```

The FI program has created a new file FILEINFO.FI and added the comment to it. To see the files with comments use FI to list files. In this case, restrict the list to SYS files. Enter

```
fi *.sys ↵
```

```
[C:\SORTTEST]fi *.sys
FI-File Info, Advanced Edition, (C) Copr 1987, Peter Norton

 Directory of C:\SORTTEST

ansi      sys      1,651  11-14-86   3:20a
config    sys         26  11-14-86   3:20a
driver    sys      1,102  11-14-86   3:20a
mouse     sys     14,325   9-03-87  11:14a
ramdrive  sys      6,462  11-14-86   3:20a
vdisk     sys      2,976  11-14-86   3:20a  Creates RAM drive - related to CONFI

  6 files found    2,703,360 bytes free

[C:\SORTTEST]
```

File comment turncated at 36 characters

Figure 8-9

The file comment appears next to the VDISK.SYS file. Note that the last part of the file comment was cut off. To see the entire comment, enter

```
fi *.sys/l ↵
```

You can also add a comment as a single command line. This is done by entering the FI command followed by the name of the file to annotate and the text of the comment. For example, to add a comment to the ANSI.SYS file, enter

```
fi ansi.sys Amer. Stand. device driver ↵
```

List the SYS file by entering

```
fi *.sys ↵
```

The FI program accepts a /C switch that lists only those files in the directory that have comments. Files without comments are ignored. Enter

```
fi/c ↵
```

```
[C:\SORTTEST]fi/c
FI-File Info, Advanced Edition, (C) Copr 1987, Peter Norton

 Directory of C:\SORTTEST

ansi     sys     1,651  11-14-86   3:20a  Amer. Stand. device driver
vdisk    sys     2,976  11-14-86   3:20a  Creates RAM drive - related to CONFI

  2 files found     2,695,168 bytes free

[C:\SORTTEST]
```

Figure 8-10

You can tag a group of files with the same comment by using a DOS wildcard. For example, to tag all of the COM files with the same comment, enter

```
fi *.com don't know what these do↵
```

The entire group is tagged with the same comment. List the commented files by entering

```
fi/c ↵
```

You can also enter comments interactively in groups. To change some of the comments you had placed on the COM files, enter

```
fi *.com/e ↵
```

The window appears and displays the first matching file along with its comment. To move to the next file in the group, enter

You can edit the comment. To clear the old comment enter

```
[Ctrl/y]
```

Enter

```
swaps drive designations ↵
```

Exit the interactive mode and return to DOS:

```
[Esc]
```

Like many of the other Norton Utilities programs you can perform a global search by using the /S switch, beginning at the root directory. For example, to list all the files on the hard disk that have comments, enter

```
fi \/s/c/l ↵
```

Note that the /L is used to allow the longer comments to show in full. The Norton Utilities program comes with a FILEINFO.FI for the Norton Utilities program files.

File information lists can be printed by using the DOS redirection commands. As an example, send the output of the FI program to the printer, enter

```
fi/c >prn ↵
```

For long lists of files, it would be better to create a text file from FI and use LP to print the list with page formatting. Example:

```
FI \ /s/c/l >catalog ↵
     LP catalog ↵
```

You can remove a comment by using the /D switch from a file or group of files. Enter

```
fi *.com/d ↵
   fi/c ↵
```

The comments have been removed from the COM files.

The FI program provides a very important feature that DOS and most DOS applications lack. It enables you to attach comments that identify files much more clearly than you can with filenames alone.

Keep in mind that when a file is copied by DOS the file's comment is not copied with it.

Printing Data

The LP (line print) program fills a significant gap left in system's operations by DOS. There are three basic ways to print from the operating system.

1. Use the PrtSc command to dump the screen text to the printer.

2. Use **[Ctrl/p]** to echo the information displayed on the screen to the printer. This means that whatever you type and whatever text the computer responds with, will be sent to the printer. A second [Ctrl/p] turns the printing off.

3. Use the redirection commands to send program output to the printer.

In all three of these cases page formatting is lacking. Page formatting refers to the process by which data is organized to print on pages of a specific size. This means that in addition to the raw text, margins, headers, footers, page numbers, and so on, are added to the output. Unformatted output pays no attention to page breaks and margins.

If you intend to work with lists of files it pays to print formatted information rather than unformatted text. The LP program is provided to make that possible. LP prints text files with page formatting and is set with a series of default values that define the way the text is placed on the page.

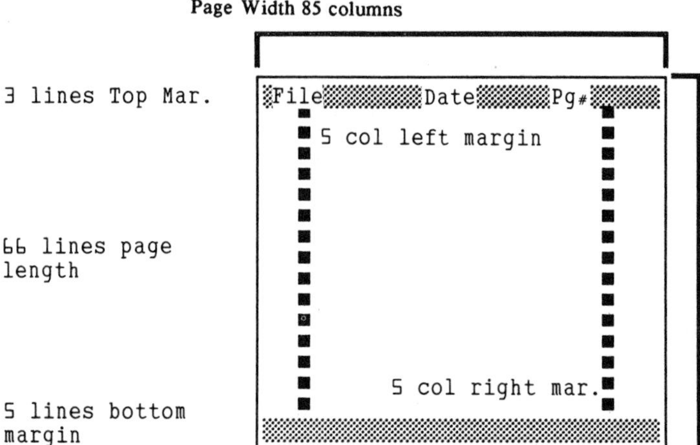

The program automatically prints a header line in the top margin that shows the name of the file being printed, the date of the printing and the page numbers.

The program uses a number of switches to alter the page format. The table below lists the switches that can be used to alter the page formatting. The # stands for a number value, e.g., /T10 for a ten line top margin.

Table 8.1. Switches Used to Alter Page Formatting

Top Margin	/T#
Bottom Margin	/B#
Left Margin	/L#
Right Margin	/R#
Page Length (height)	/H#
Page Width	/W#
Page with 80 columns (Epson FX width)	/80
Page with 132 columns (wide carriage)	/132
Line Spacing (1 = single, 2 = double)	/S#
Starting Page number	/P#
Automatic line numbering	/N
Header Format (0, 1 or 2)	/HEADER#

The LP program assumes that you are printing a standard text file. However, two switches are provided to accommodate other types of files.

/EBCDIC Use this to print files stored in Extended Binary Coded Decimal Interchange Code.

/EXT This switch tells LP to print the IBM PC extended character set, that is, characters with ASCII values 128 and higher. Normally LP ignores characters over 128 and prints their 7 bit equivalent. WordStar files can be printed with LP without the /EXT. Use EXT when you want to include the graphics and foreign characters in the extended character set.

Setup Codes

As a line printing program, LP is not designed to implement word processing features such as underlines or font changes. You can, however, send a printer setup string at the beginning of each printing. The setup string must be stored in a text file. LP accepts a /SET:filename switch in which the filename is the name of the file that contains the setup codes.

In Chapter 5, Advanced Batch procedures, the concepts of printer codes is discussed. The LP program allows you to create printer code files in two formats:

1. **Number Format.** This format is one in which each character in the code sequence is expressed as a three digit decimal number equal to the ASCII decimal value for the character. Each character is preceded by a \.

2. **Character Format.** The LP program will recognize combinations of text and control characters. The \ is used to mark a character as a control character.

You can create setup files by using EDLIN or any text editor. Below are examples of setup strings. They begin by using EDLIN to create a file called PRTSETUP.STR.

```
edlin prtsetup.str ↵
i
```

The most common use of setup strings is for compressed print. The IBM graphics and Epson printers can use:

\015 Number format or

\O Character format for [Ctrl/o]

If you are using an HP laser Jet printer the setup string is much more complex.

\027E\027&l0O\027&k2S Number Format

\[E\[&l0O\[&k2S Character Format

Conclude the entry of the setup string with

```
↵
[Ctrl/c]
e ↵
```

\027 is the decimal value of [Esc]. [Esc] can also be implemented by a control code [Ctrl/[] expressed in Norton notation as \[.

The final step is to use the setup string with LP. For example, suppose you wanted to print a file TEST.TXT using compressed printing to enable you to increase the line width to 132 characters. Enter

```
lp test.txt/132/set:prtsetup.str ↵
```

If you use LP with a laser printer set for proportionally-spaced font you will find that the text column will not line up. LP can only print in monospaced fonts in which all characters are allocated the same horizontal width value.

Norton Integrator

The NI (Norton Integrator) program is designed to provide a program to coordinate the operations of all of the Norton Utilities programs. The NI program is a good way to learn about and experiment with the individual Norton Utilities programs that it coordinates. The NI program does not provide any additional functionality but it does display a help screen that furnishes information about each of the Norton Utilities programs. The NI program allows you to implement Norton Utilities commands directly from the program without having to return to DOS.

If you have worked through Section II on batch files you will see that the NI program ties together all of the individual parts of the Norton Utilities package into a single menu operation.

Eventually you will find it easier to use the Norton Utilities programs without the NI menu display. However, it is very helpful when your are learning how to use the programs, or when you want to use a program that you do not work with very often.

To start the Integrator, enter

```
ni ↵
```

The program divides the screen into three parts.

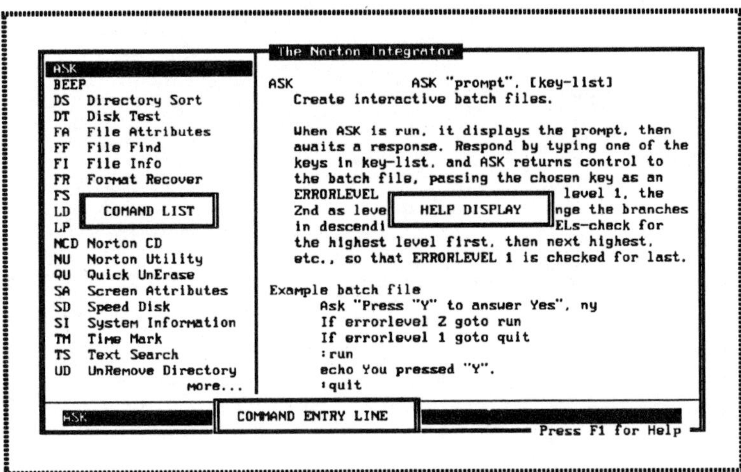

Figure 8-11

The left side of the display lists all the programs in the Norton Utilities package. The right panel is a help screen that displays a summary of information about the program that is currently being highlighted. The bottom windows allow you to enter a command.

You can change the active command by using the up and down arrow keys to move the highlight to another command. Enter

```
[down arrow]
```

The BEEP command is highlighted. Note that the help screen changes to display information about BEEP and the command on the command line now reads BEEP.

The NI program features a speed search. If you want to move to the FI program, enter

```
[Tab]
```

The command line changes to a search line. Enter

```
f
```

The highlight jumps to the first program that beings with F, FA. Enter

i

The highlight moves to FI. If you want to execute the command, enter

↵

The NI runs the FI, file information, program. The program pauses after it completes. Enter

↵

You return to the NI menu. You can run any of the commands discussed in this section from the NI menu system. To exit the NI program enter

[F10]

Summary

Sections III and IV deal with tasks that are performed on a day to day basis with the Norton Utilities programs. The Norton Utilities programs enhance the ways in which you organize and maintain the information stored in your computer system. Some of the programs amplify already existing DOS functions while other programs provide new capabilities that compensate for limitations in DOS. The techniques discussed are:

File Search

The FF (File Find) program performs global disk searches that can locate files or groups of files. The DIR command in DOS is limited to a single directory. FF will search one disk, or all the disks in the system.

Text Search

The Norton Utilities programs, TS and NU, provide the ability to search the contents of the disk to locate specific key words, phrase or hexadecimal sequences. The searches can locate information by file, data cluster number or sector number. You can search for data stored in existing files or in disk space not currently allocated to existing files. Searching unused space is useful when attempting to recover erased files.

Directories

The Norton Utilities LD command produces a listing of disk directories. The list can include a summary of spaces used for files stored in the directories. NCD is a program designed to replace the DOS commands CD, MD and RD. NCD maintains a list of disk directories in the root directory of each drive. You can use NCD to locate directories without having to enter the full pathnames.

Disk Usage

The FS (File Size) program provides a full range of statistics about the use of disk space. The program computes the amount of slack space.

File Protection

The FA (File Attributes) and NU programs can be used to change the attributes of files. Files can be protected by assigning hidden or read-only attributes to those files.

Sort

The DS (Directory Sort) program sorts the file listing in disk directories according to name, extension, date, time or file size.

File Comments

FI (File Information) allows you to create an annotated list for files. Comments are stored in a file called FILEINFO.FI in each directory.

Printing

The LP (Line Print) program produces page formatted output from ASCII text files.

Redirection

Many of the programs discussed in these sections produce lists of information that you may want to print. You can use the DOS redirection commands to produce these lists.

To create an unformatted output, simply use >PRN to redirect the program's output to the printer. Example:

```
FS >prn ↵
```

To create a page formatted printing, construct a text file from the program output and use the LP program to print the text file. Example:

```
FS >OUTPUT.TXT ↵
LP OUTPUT.TXT ↵
```

SECTION V
SURVIVAL SKILLS

The purpose of this section is to explain in detail some of the skills you will need from time to time in working with a computer system. The majority of this section is dedicated to the procedures for recovering erased data. Protecting against accidental hard disk formats, what to do when you encounter **Error reading drive C** and how to maximize the performance of your hard disk are also covered.

The subject of this section concerns the programs provided in the Norton Utilities package that are used to overcome common problems occurring in MS-DOS systems. Some of the problems are caused by glitches in your computer system while others are caused by user error.

If you are new to computers, or simply live a charmed life, you may be unfamiliar with the problems discussed here. Familiarizing yourself with this section, however, will prepare you for when these problems come up.

Because the topics in this section involve errors and mistakes, not all of the procedures can be discussed in the hands-on manner used throughout this book. For example, unformatting a hard disk is something that most people cannot practice since they don't have extra computers upon which they can experiment.

But there is no substitute for such firsthand experience when dealing with unexpected problems. This section will attempt, as best as possible, to give you the background information that will aid in dealing with the small and large computer disasters that may arise. Whenever possible the chapter will use a hands-on approach so that you can re-create the operations on your own computer.

9

PERFORMANCE INFORMATION

One of the best known Norton Utilities program is the SI (System's Information) program. The SI program has three functions.

1. Displays the logical DOS environment. This refers to the setting that DOS reads from your hardware, such as the number of disks and ports operating in the computer.

2. Memory Map. This map details the installed memory in the computer, including the hex locations.

3. Performance Test. SI tests your computer's performance against the standard IBM XT.

SI can be run in two ways.

1. SI. Internal Text Only.

2. SD d: Test designated hard disk.

The illustration below shows the output from a typical AT compatible computer.

```
        Computer Name:  IBM/PC-AT
     Operating System:  DOS 3.30
   Built-in BIOS dated:  Thursday, April 30, 1987
       Main Processor:  Intel 80286                Serial Ports:  1
         Co-Processor:  None                     Parallel Ports:  0
 Video Display Adapter:  Color/Graphics
    Current Video Mode:  Text, 80 x 25 Color
 Available Disk Drives:  4, A: - D:

DOS reports 640 K-bytes of memory:
   145 K-bytes used by DOS and resident programs
   495 K-bytes available for application programs
A search for active memory finds:
   640 K-bytes main memory      (at hex 00000-0A000)
    16 K-bytes display memory   (at hex 0A800-0AC00)
    16 K-bytes display memory   (at hex 0B800-0BC00)
   896 K-bytes extended memory  (at hex 10000-1E000)
   128 K-bytes expanded memory

  Computing Index (CI), relative to IBM/XT: 11.2
       Disk Index (DI), relative to IBM/XT: 2.5

Performance Index (PI), relative to IBM/XT: 8.3

C:\>
```

Figure 9-1

Below is a more detailed breakdown of the information contained within this display.

Computer Name: IBM/PC-AT

This is the name of the computer stored in the system's ROM memory. Some systems will show a name while others will show a copyright.

Operating System: DOS 3.30

The is the version of DOS running in the computer at the time the SI test is performed.

Built-in BIOS dated: Thursday, April 30, 1987

The BIOS, **B**asic **I**nput **O**utput **S**ystem, is a ROM chip that contains the hardware portion of the operating system. The BIOS is a very important part of the computer because it is the link between software, including DOS, and the basic hardware. The BIOS contains a date to identify when it was manufactured.

Because the MS-DOS program is available from IBM and other manufacturers, it is the BIOS built into the computer that determines how compatible one PC is with another. It also determines the limitations of the hardware. For example, old IBM PC computers with BIOS dates earlier than 10/27/82 will not accept a hard disk drive. Since the BIOS is a ROM chip it cannot be altered. It can be replaced in some cases, with an updated ROM, which will increase the capabilities. Obtaining the BIOS date is important if you suspect that your computer may be incompatible with a specific device.

```
Main Processor:  Intel 80286
```

The main processor refers to the microprocessor in your computer. The microprocessor is the brain of the computer that decodes the instructions stored in program files and turns them into actual computer operations. The most common microprocessor in PC/XT and compatible machines is the 8088 chip made by Intel. It still comes as a surprise to some people that IBM or Compaq do not make this main component of the computer. For example, the 8088 processor has a set of about 150 instruction codes that it will recognize. All of the programs on the IBM PC and XT are constructed, at base, of these 150 basic instructions.

The PC/AT and compatible machines use the Intel 80286 microprocessor. The 80286 can translate all of the codes used for the 8088 but contain additional features. Because the 80286 is compatible with the instruction set of the 8088 processor, PC programs can run on AT machines. The AT class machines will run the program faster than the 8088 machine. As of the writing of this book, (Winter, 1988) there are very few programs that take advantage of these additional features. This should change with the introduction of the OS/2 operating system for 80286 computers in the beginning of 1988.

```
Co-Processor:  None
```

The PC/XT and AT type machines provide room on their circuit board for an additional processor called a co-processor. The co-processor is usually used to help speed up programs that perform intensive mathematical calculations. Engineering and spreadsheet programs will often benefit from a math co-processor. Word processing programs that do not do a lot of math calculations would not benefit from a co-processor. Keep in mind that programs must be specifically designed to take advantage of the co-processor. Just inserting a co-processor into the computer will have no effect if the programs are not designed to use it. For example, Lotus 1-2-3 Version 1A does not support a co-processor while 1-2-3 Release 2.01 does.

The co-processor used with the Intel 8088 is the Intel 8087, which costs about two hundred dollars. Intel makes an 80287 as a co-processor for the 80286 microprocessor.

```
Parallel Ports:  1
```

```
Serial Ports:  1
```

These items report the number of parallel and serial interfaces installed in the computer. Parallel interfaces are usually used for printers. Serial interfaces are used for printers, modems, mice and some types of networks.

The difference between parallel and serial interfaces is the sequence in which they transmit data. Each character sent to a printer usually requires one byte of information. The byte is composed of 8 individual signals called bits. (For an in-depth explanation see Chapter 1) A parallel interface sends all eight signals over a multiwire at one time. A serial interface sends one bit at a time until all eight have been transmitted. The parallel interface is generally faster than the serial. But traditionally, the reliability of parallel transmission declines the longer the transmission distance. The longest parallel cables are between 6 and 12 feet long. Serial transmission of data is the preferred means of transmission over longer distances. This includes printers in remote locations, other computers on a network, or telecommunications via modems.

Another advantage of serial communication is that serial interfaces can be programmed to transmit at different rates of speed and can add special error checking information to the transmitted data. Error checking can be accomplished by adding extra data bits to the transmitted information. For example, the sending computer might add an extra bit with a value of 1 following each character. If the receiving computer encountered a 0 in the position where the 1 should be, it would assume that some error has taken place during transmission and inform the user.

Current versions of DOS are limited in the number of interfaces that can be used. DOS currently supports only 2 serial interfaces with the exception of DOS 3.3 which can support 4 serial ports.

```
Video Display Adapter:  Color/Graphics
```

```
Current Video Mode:  Text, 80 x 25 Color
```

This information describes the type of display monitor attached to the computer. It also tells you the display mode the computer is operating in at the time of the system's check. For example, the Color/Graphics Adapter (CGA) can run in 80 x 25 or 40 x 25 modes.

```
Available Disk Drives:  4, A: - D:
```

This line tells you the number of logical disks available in the system. Note that a logical drive can be a RAM disk, which is really part of the computer's memory emulating a disk, not a physical disk drive.

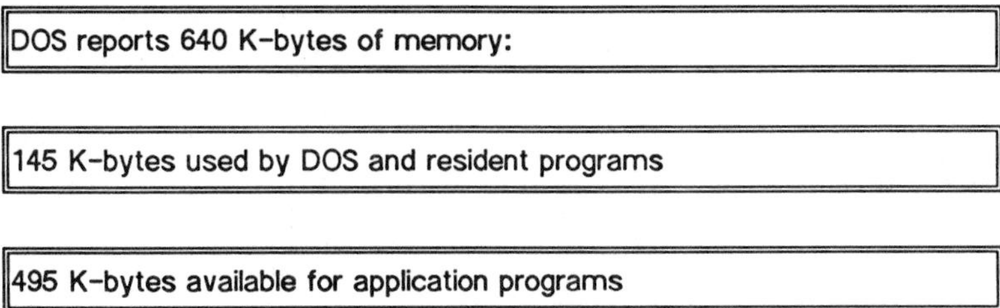
DOS reports 640 K-bytes of memory:

145 K-bytes used by DOS and resident programs

495 K-bytes available for application programs

This display is a summary of the same information seen at the bottom of the CHKDSK. It tells you the total amount of memory available to DOS, the amount already in use by resident programs that include DOS and TSR (Terminate and Stay Resident) programs like Sidekick, and the amount available for programs to use. Note that DOS will not directly support additional memory installed in the computer for program usage. Below you will see how that memory is reported.

A search for active memory finds:

640 K-bytes main memory (at hex 00000-0A000)

16 K-bytes display memory (at hex 0A800-0AC00)

16 K-bytes display memory (at hex 0B800-0BC00)

This section displays the information found when the SI program actually reads the memory of the computer. This is different from the previous display, which reports what DOS sees as the memory capacity of the computer. Note that because DOS has a fixed limit on memory, 640K, which it can use, it does not report on additional types of memory that might be installed in the computer.

This section of the SI display provides a more detailed description of the memory usage in the computer. The memory items are listed with the size of the blocks they occupy and the starting and ending addresses. Address refers to the scheme by which the computer organizes memory. The scheme assigns each byte of memory a specific address. The address numbers in the PC, referred to as conventional, can vary from 0 to 1,048,575 (FFFFF in hex notation). Not all 1,048,576 bytes of conventional memory are available for user programs. The conventional memory is divided into blocks, and each block assigned a specific purpose.

For the average user, the most significant block is the one numbered from 0 to 655,360 (A0000 in hex format). It is this block of memory that is used for user programs. When people rate computers by the amount of memory they contain, it is this specific block of memory they are usually referring to. The 640K limit refers to the largest possible block of conventional memory used for programs in today's MS-DOS computers.

In the memory report illustration above, the first block of memory is shown as a block of 640K from 00000-0A000, expressed in hex notation. This means that this PC contains the maximum amount of conventional memory.

> The actual address of memory locations in the IBM PC and compatibles is a complicated method in which each address is composed of two portions. The addresses here have an assumed segment of F000 hex and an offset of 0.

The display also shows the locations used for display memory. For example, a color graphics adapter will use a block of 16K located at B800. A monochrome adapter uses a 4K block located at B000. Note that this scheme allows you to have both a monochrome and a color graphics adapter. EGA adapters use a block of memory, usually 64K, located at A800.

On PC and XT systems SI will report an extension to the BIOS at C800 used for hard disks. AT systems have the hard disk support built into the normal BIOS and do not need the extension. The locating of display memory is usually not very important. It is useful to know when you are installing new hardware expansion such as extended boards.

> When you install an extended memory board, the software requests the type of monitor you are using, for example, Monochrome, Color graphics or EGA. This may seem an odd question to ask when you are adding memory, but the reason for the request is that the software used with the memory card is attempting to avoid a conflict in addressing between the display adapter and the extended memory card.
>
> The install software will create a special device driver command based on your monitor type. The AST Rampage board uses a driver called REMM.SYS. For example, the AST Rampage Board software will automatically exclude the block of memory from B800-BFFF if you select color graphics, or B000-BFFF for a Hercules graphics card.
>
> DEVICE=REMM.SYS /X=B800-BFFF (color/graphics)
>
> DEVICE=REMM.SYS /X=B000-BFFF (Hercules)
>
> The /X stands for EXCLUDE. Note that the Hercules card requires more memory than the color graphics adapter.

> I use a special monitor on my computer that maps display memory in two locations, 0A800-0AC00 and 0B800-0BC00. The SI program helped me figure out which blocks to exclude when I installed an extended memory card. Example:
>
> device = remm.sys /x = A800-AFFF /x = B800-BFFF

```
896 K-bytes extended memory (at hex 10000-1E000)
```

```
128 K-bytes expanded memory
```

The next two values will be displayed if your computer has additional user memory installed beyond the 640K limit. Although DOS cannot use this memory directly for applications, it can be used in one of two special ways.

Extended Memory

Extended memory refers to memory added following the first 1,048,576 bytes of memory address in the standard PC. The extended memory is addressed consecutively starting with the ending address of conventional memory, 10000 hex. While this memory cannot be used by applications like spreadsheets, it can be used for creating performance enhancements such as RAM drives, disk caching or print buffers.

Expanded Memory

Expanded memory refers to blocks of memory, 16K each, that are not allocated as part of the DOS memory scheme. Rather, these blocks are addressed by a special programming technique called LIM (Lotus-Intel-Microsoft) expanded memory specification. This programming technique requires that special boards, designed for LIM compatibility, be used in conjunction with programs that are specifically programmed to use LIM memory. Examples of such programs are Lotus 1-2-3 Release 2, Microsoft Excel and Ashton-Tate's Framework.

Many memory boards can be configured as either expanded or extended. In fact, you can usually allocate part of the board as extended and part expanded. In the example shown, a 1 megabyte expansion board is divided into 896K of extended memory and 128K of expanded memory. The 896K is used as a RAM drive, while the expanded memory supplies 128K of additional memory for specific applications such as 1-2-3 and Excel.

```
Computing Index (CI), relative to IBM/XT: 11.2
```

```
Disk Index (DI), relative to IBM/XT: 2.5
```

```
Performance Index (PI), relative to IBM/XT: 8.3
```

The final section of the SI display shows the results of the three performance index texts.

The CI (Computing Index) tests the speed of the processor and memory. The DI (Disk Index) tests the speed of hard disks. The PI (Performance Index) is a combined score reflecting the results of the CI and DI.

The index uses the speed of the IBM XT as 1.0 for both the CI and DI. In this example, the CI is 11.2, which means that the processor is more than 11 times faster than the processing speed of the original XT. The DI test shows that the hard disk is running at 2.5 times faster than the 10 megabyte disk on the XT. The combined PI is 8.3.

> The test was performed on a Dynatron AT compatible computer running at 10 MHz with a Seagate 4038 30 megabyte hard disk using a Western Digital A1 controller.

The Performance tests are very handy for evaluating the speed of various computers and configurations. It is important to understand that no one number can be reified into a total evaluation of the worth of a given computer. The way the hardware is used by specific software programs will affect the final performance.

The SI is a quick way to get a detailed description of the internal setup of a computer. If you are working on an unfamiliar machine, the SI will provide a fast summary of the hardware.

Erased Files

The Norton Utilities programs are probably best known for their ability to recover erased files. This ability is not the result of any special magic possessed by the programs, but is based on the way DOS goes about storing data on the disk and how operations like erasing are carried out.

Erase may have a certain meaning in the English language, but what happens when a file is erased from a disk can be quite different than the term seems to imply. Erased files are not automatically obliterated. Given the right circumstances and the right tools (the Norton Utilities programs) it is possible to recover or unerase files.

In order to learn more about erasing and unerasing, create a floppy disk that you can experiment with. As an example, this chapter uses a copy of the Norton Utilities, Advanced Edition, disk 1. If you have that program, you can follow the operations in this chapter exactly.

10

RECOVERING ERASED FILES

In order to perform the operations discussed in this chapter you will need access to the following files:

Table 10.1. DOS Programs

FORMAT.EXE(DOS 3) or FORMAT.COM(DOS 2)
CHKDSK.EXE(DOS 3) or CHKDSK.COM(DOS 2)

Table 10.2. Norton Utility Programs

DT.EXE (Disk Test)
FR.EXE (Format Recover)
NU.EXE (Norton Utilities Main Program)
QU.EXE (Quick Unerase)
TS.EXE (Text Search)
UD.EXE (Unremove Directory)
WIPEDISK.EXE
WIPEFILE.EXE

If you followed the instructions in Chapter One you should have all these files copied to a directory called \DOS on your hard disk. In order to get access to these files you must make sure that a PATH has been opened to this directory.

You also need a copy of the Norton Utilities Disk 1 of 2. **DO NOT USE THE ORIGINAL DISK.** You will be erasing and formatting this disk and you will destroy the information on it.

You can make a copy of a disk, even if you only have one floppy disk drive by using the DISKCOPY command. The first step is to format a disk. DOS 3 requires that you format the destination disk, the one that you are going to copy information onto, before you make the copy. This can be done by using the FORMAT command. Examples:

```
FORMAT a:        (360K disk drives)
FORMAT a:/4      (1.2 Megabyte disk drives)
```

> IF you are using DOS 2 level, the DISKCOPY command will automatically format the target disk as it copies. This saves you the step of formatting a disk before you make the copy.
>
> DOS 3 is designed to support 360K and 1.2 megabyte disk drives. Because of this added consideration, DOS 3 users are required to format the disk before the DISKCOPY command is used.

When the disk is formatted, use the DISKCOPY command to make a duplicate of the Norton Utilities Disk 1. Example:

```
DISKCOPY A: A:        (single disk systems)
```

The DISKCOPY command prompts you to enter the source (the original disk) and the target (the new copy) disks. When you have created the copy of the disk, you are ready to get started.

The key to understanding the Norton Utilities recover procedures is to understand how disks are organized and what happens when you delete a file or format a disk. The deleting and formatting process changes some, but not always all, of the information on the disk. The Norton Utilities programs provide you with a relatively easy way to fill in some or all of the missing information and thereby undo some of the damage done by deleting and formatting.

However, it is not always possible to undo the damage done by formatting or deleting. As you learn more about the process you will understand the limitations of the Norton Utilities recovery programs and how best to apply them.

Disk Directories

As discussed in Chapter 1, DOS functions as a kind of librarian for your disk system, along with its other responsibilities. In order to accomplish its task of keeping track of the information stored on a disk, DOS requires the division of the disk in several distinct parts. Each part plays a role in storing and deleting data from the disk.

For details about disk organization, see Chapter 1.

The disk directory is a special area on the disk that DOS uses to store information about the files on that disk. The directory can be displayed by using the DOS command DIR. For example, to list the directory information for the disk in drive A you would enter

```
dir a: ↵
```

In this example, DOS lists 28 files currently stored on the disk in drive A.

To get a better understanding of what a directory actually consists of you can use the main Norton Utilities program to explore the disk. Enter

```
nu a:↵
```

To get a look at how the disk is organized, enter

```
ecs
```

This displays the Select Sector menu.

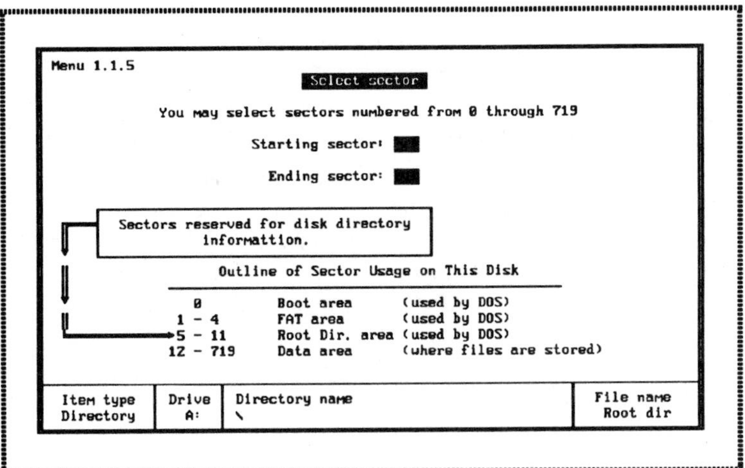

Figure 10-1

The outline at the bottom of the screen shows you the sections of the disk.

Boot Area This area is the first sector on the disk. It holds information about the way the disk was formatted, how it is organized and its capacity.

FAT Area The File Allocation Table (FAT), is used to link disk sectors to filenames. The FAT is designed to allow files to expand and contract.

Root Directory The root directory area is established when the disk is formatted. This is the place where DOS stores information about the files stored on the disk.

Data Area This area consists of all of the sectors not assigned one of the previous special functions. The majority of the disk space falls into this category. It is in these sectors that the actual information is stored.

To take a look at the directory of this disk, enter the number of the first sector in the directory, sector 5. Enter

You are back at the explore disk menu. Note that the number of the selected sector appears at the bottom of the screen.

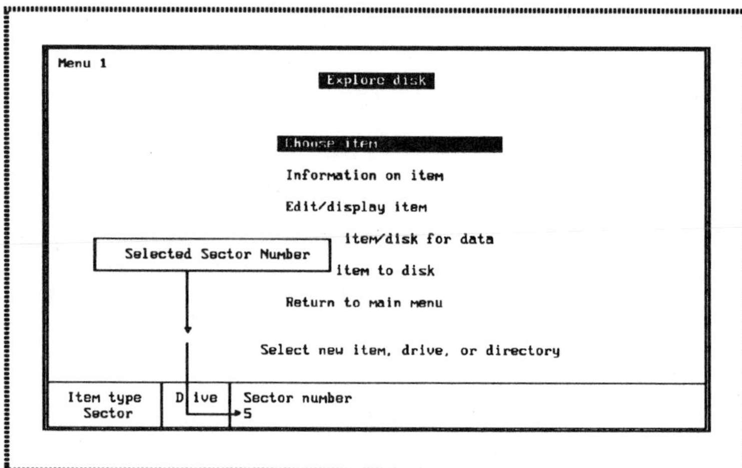

Figure 10-2

You can display the directory information by entering

e

Because the data in this sector is organized as a directory, the Norton Utilities program automatically displays the information in the Directory Format. The words Directory Format appear in the upper-right corner of the screen.

```
Sector 5                                                Directory format
Sector 5 in root directory                              Offset 0, hex 00
                                                        Attributes
Filename Ext    Size    Date      Time     Cluster  Arc R/O Sys Hid Dir Vol

NU Adv I d 1            2/20/87   6:56 am                               Vol
READ     ME     1222    3/01/87   4:00 pm        2  Arc R/O
ASK      EXE    1184    3/01/87   4:00 pm        4  Arc R/O
BEEP     EXE    5324    3/01/87   4:00 pm        6  Arc R/O
DS       EXE   25638    3/01/87   4:00 pm       12  Arc R/O
DT       EXE   17910    3/01/87   4:00 pm       38  Arc R/O
FA       EXE    7296    3/01/87   4:00 pm       56  Arc R/O
FF       EXE    7924    3/01/87   4:00 pm       64  Arc R/O
FI       EXE   14668    3/01/87   4:00 pm       72  Arc R/O
FR       EXE   12610    3/01/87   4:00 pm       87  Arc R/O
FS       EXE    8536    3/01/87   4:00 pm      100  Arc R/O
LD       EXE    7652    3/01/87   4:00 pm      109  Arc R/O
LP       EXE   11616    3/01/87   4:00 pm      117  Arc R/O
NCD      EXE   19496    3/01/87   4:00 pm      129  Arc R/O
NI       EXE   31963    3/01/87   4:00 pm      149  Arc R/O
SA       EXE    4506    3/01/87   4:00 pm      181  Arc R/O

                      Press Enter to continue
1Help  2Hex  3Text  4Dir  5FAT  6Partn  7  8  9Undo  10QuitNU
```

Figure 10-3

The information displayed is in part the same information DOS displays when the DIR command is used. The Norton Utilities display other information about the files:

Cluster This is the number of the first data cluster on the disk occupied by data from this file. (For information about data clusters, see Chapter 1).

Arc **Archive.** The Arc stands for archive status. Arc indicates that a file needs to be backed up. This status marker is used by some DOS commands, e.g., BACKUP and RESTORE, to determine if the file has been backed up since it was last revised.

R/O **Read Only.** Files marked as R/O will be ignored by DOS commands such as DEL and EDLIN that are used to erase or change a file's contents. The R/O attribute can be used to protect important files from accidental deletion.

Sys **System.** This attribute actually has no specific purpose in MS-DOS. It refers to a feature in CP/M that designated certain files as system files. Some DOS commands, such as DIR, DEL and COPY will ignore files with a sys attribute. The system attribute has about the same function as the hidden attribute, below.

Hid **Hidden.** This attribute is used to exclude certain files from DOS operations. For example, files marked as hidden will be ignored by commands such as DIR, DEL and COPY. Other commands, e.g., CHKDSK and BACKUP, will operate on hidden files. The Norton Utilities file programs, FA(file attribute), FF(file find), and FS(file size) ignore the hidden attribute and include hidden files in their operations.

> The system and hidden attributes function exactly alike. DOS commands that hide files, such as FORMAT /S, use hidden attributes and system. The system attribute is redundant but is probably maintained in new versions of DOS for compatibility purposes with older versions.

Dir **Directory.** This attribute indicates whether an entry is a subdirectory as opposed to a file entry. All directories other than the root will be indicated by this attribute.

Vol **Volume.** This attribute should appear only one time. It is the volume name for the disk and it is always stored in the root directory. Other than that it serves no purpose.

You can move the highlight down the list of files. In this example, highlight the ASK.EXE file by entering

```
[down arrow]
[down arrow]
```

The display on the screen is really an approximation of the actual directory entries. To see the actual way the directory information is stored, change to the Hex display. Enter

```
[F2]
```

The screen displays the bytes that make up a directory entry.

```
Sector 5 ──────────────────────────────────────────────── Hex format
Sector 5 in root directory                              Offset 64, hex 40
4E552041 64762045 64203108 00000000 00000000 00000137 NU Adv Ed 1...........37
540E0000 00000000 52454144 20202020 4D452021 00000000 T......READ    ME !....
00000000 00000080 610E0200 C6040000 41534B20 20202020 .......Ça.....ASK
45584521 00000000 00000000 00000080 610E0400 A0040000 EXE!...........Ça...á..
42454550 20202020 45584521 00000000 00000000 00000080 BEEP    EXE!...........Ç
610E0600 CC140000 44532020 20202020 45584521 00000000 a.....DS        EXE!....
00000000 00000080 610E0C00 26640000 44542020 20202020 .......Ça..&d..DT
45584521 00000000 00000000 00000080 610E2600 F6450000 EXE!...........Ça..÷E..
46412020 20202020 45584521 00000000 00000000 00000080 FA      EXE!...........Ç
610E3800 801C0000 46462020 20202020 45584521 00000000 a..Ç...FF        EXE!....
00000000 00000080 610E4000 F41E0000 46492020 20202020 .......Ça.....FI
45584521 00000000 00000000 00000080 610E4800 4C390000 EXE!...........Ça.H.L9..
46522020 20202020 45584521 00000000 00000000 00000080 FR      EXE!...........Ç
610E5700 42310000 46532020 20202020 45584521 00000000 a..B1..FS        EXE!....
00000000 00000080 610E6400 58210000 4C442020 20202020 .......Ça.d.X!..LD
45584521 00000000 00000000 00000080 610E6D00 E41D0000 EXE!...........Ça.m.Σ...
4C502020 20202020 45584521 00000000 00000000 00000080 LP      EXE!...........Ç
610E7500 602D0000 4E434420 20202020 45584521 00000000 a.u.`-..NCD      EXE!....
00000000 00000080 610E8100 284C0000 4E492020 20202020 .......Ça.ü.(L..NI
45584521 00000000 00000000 00000080 610E9500 DB7C0000 EXE!...........Ça.ò..|..
53412020 20202020 45584521 00000000 00000000 00000080 SA      EXE!...........Ç
610EB500 9A110000          Press Enter to continue      a...Ü◄..
1Help 2Hex 3Text 4Dir 5FAT 6Partn 7 8 9Undo 10QuitNU
```

Figure 10-4

As you can see, the display looks very different. The cursor is currently located on byte 64. The value at that point is the hex number 41, which stands for the letter A. This is the first byte of the directory entry for ASK.EXE.

In a DOS directory, each file record takes up 32 bytes. The first 11 bytes store the filename(8) and the extension(3).

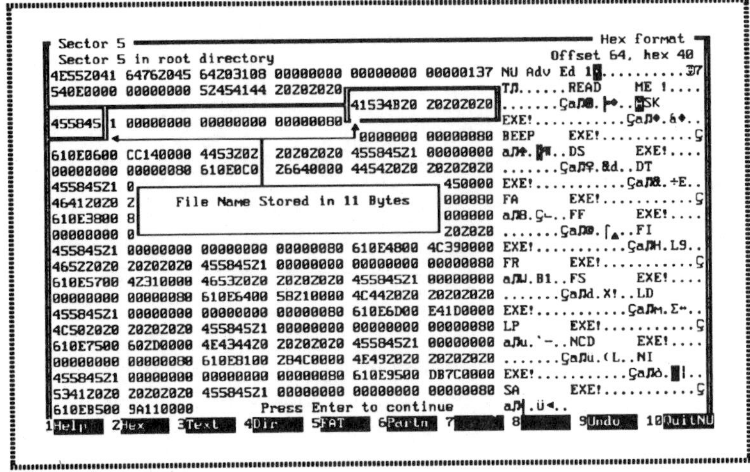

Figure 10-5

The twelfth byte, the one immediately following the filename, contains a number value that indicates what types of attributes the file should have. In this illustration, the value that follows ASK.EXE is 21.

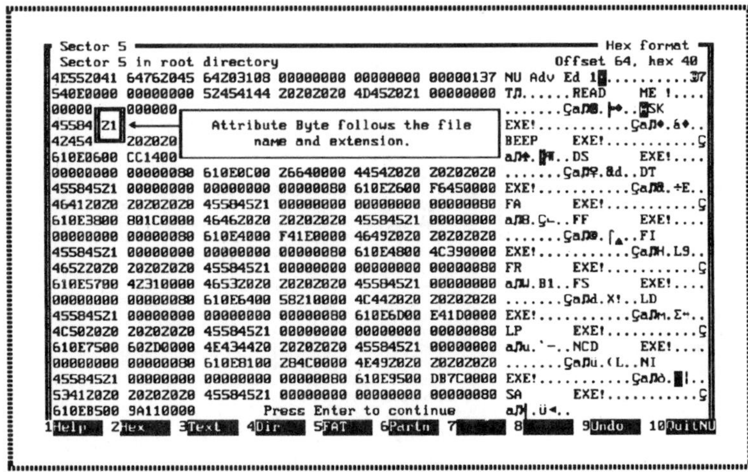

Figure 10-6

DOS assigns a value for each attribute that a file can possess.

> The values correspond to the values of the individual bits in the byte used for attributes.

Table 10.3. Individual Bits and the Values Assigned to Each Attribute

Bit #	Attribute	Decimal	Hex
Bit 0	Read-only	1	1
Bit 1	Hidden	2	2
Bit 2	System	4	4
Bit 3	Volume	8	8
Bit 4	Sub-Directory	16	10
Bit 5	Archive	32	20
Bit 6 and 7 are not used.			

For example, the ASK.EXE file is marked as a read only file, 1, and a archive file, 20, making the value of its attribute byte 21.

> The right side of the display shows the character that is displayed for hex 21, the exclamation point (!).

Another example is the first entry in this sector. That entry contains the volume label **NU Adv ED 1**. The label is followed by a value of 8. If you look back at the table, 8 indicates a volume label.

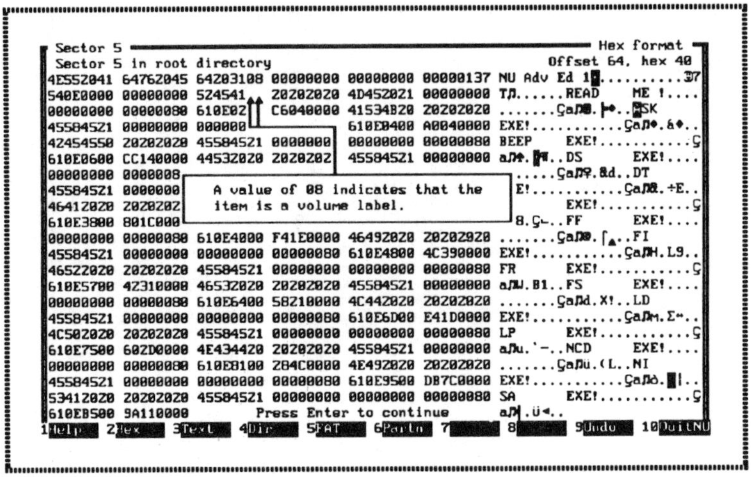

```
 Sector 5 ───────────────────────────────────────────────────── Hex format ─
 Sector 5 in root directory                                 Offset 64, hex 40
4E552041 64762045 64203108 00000000 00000000 00000137 NU Adv Ed 1▮..........╕7
540E0000 00000000 524541   20202020 4D452021 00000000 T♫......READ    ME !....
00000000 00000080 610E02   C6040000 41534B20 20202020 .......Ça♫●.├♦..▮SK
45584521 00000000 000000            610E8400 A0040000 EXE!...........Ça♫♦.á♦..
42454550 20202020 45584521 0000000  00000000 00000080 BEEP    EXE!...........Ç
610E0600 CC140000 44532020 2020202  45584521 00000000 a♫♠.▮╠..DS      EXE!....
00000000 0000008                                      .....Ça♫♀.&d..DT
45584521 0000000    A value of 08 indicates that the  E!...........Ça♫8.÷E..
46412020 202020Z    item is a volume label.                   EXE!...........Ç
610E3800 801C000                                      8.Ç∟..FF        EXE!....
00000000 00000080 610E4000 F41E0000 46492020 20202020 .......Ça♫@.⌠▲..FI
45584521 00000000 00000000 00000080 610E4800 4C390000 EXE!...........Ça♫H.L9..
46522020 20202020 45584521 00000000 00000000 00000080 FR      EXE!...........Ç
610E5700 42310000 46532020 20202020 45584521 00000000 a♫W.B1..FS      EXE!....
00000000 00000080 610E6400 58210000 4C442020 20202020 .......Ça♫d.X!..LD
45584521 00000000 00000000 00000080 610E6D00 E41D0000 EXE!...........Ça♫m.Σ↔..
4C502020 20202020 45584521 00000000 00000000 00000080 LP      EXE!...........Ç
610E7500 602D0000 4E434420 20202020 45584521 00000000 a♫u.`-..NCD     EXE!....
00000000 00000080 610E8100 284C0000 4E492020 20202020 .......Ça♫ü.(L..NI
45584521 00000000 00000000 00000080 610E9500 DB7C0000 EXE!...........Ça♫ò.█|..
53412020 20202020 45584521 00000000 00000000 00000080 SA      EXE!...........Ç
610EB500 9A110000        Press Enter to continue      a♫╡.Ü◄..
1Help  2Hex  3Text  4Dir  5FAT  6Partn  7      8      9Undo  10QuitNU
```

Figure 10-7

Because the Norton Utilities program allows you to edit as well as display data, you can change the attributes of files by altering the value of the byte that follows the filename. Use the [right arrow] key to move the cursor to offset 75, which is the attribute byte for ASK.EXE.

Suppose you wanted to change this file from a read-only file to a normal file. You would have to subtract the read-only value, 1, from the existing value, that is, $21 - 1 = 20$. Enter the new value.

```
20
```

> The Norton Utilities program displays the new entry in bold characters so that you can see which bytes have been modified.

If you look at the right display panel you will see that the exclamation point (!) has changed to a space character. The space is the character used to represent the hex value of 20.

To create a hidden file out of a file you would add 2 to its value. The next file in the directory listing is BEEP.EXE. Use the [right arrow] key to move the cursor to offset 107, which is the attribute byte for BEEP.EXE. To add the hidden attribute(2) to the existing attributes(21), enter

```
23
```

The BEEP.EXE file is now marked as read-only(1), hidden(2), and archive(20) for a total value of 23.

To see if the alteration in values actually changed the way DOS looks at the files, return to the directory format display by entering

```
[F4]
```

You can see that your numeric changes on the byte level register on this display as changes in the file's attributes. The ASK.EXE file is no longer read-only, while the BEEP.EXE file is marked as hidden.

```
 Sector 5                                                Directory format
 Sector 5 in root directory                             Offset 107, hex 6B
                                                            Attributes
Filename Ext     Size     Date       Time    Cluster  Arc R/O Sys Hid Dir Vol

NU Adv E d 1            2/20/87   6:56 am                                Vol
READ     ME      1222   3/01/87   4:00 pm        2    Arc R/O
ASK      EXE     1184   3/01/87   4:00 pm        4    Arc
BEEP     EXE     5324   3/01/87   4:00 pm        6    Arc R/O     Hid
DS       EXE    25638   3/01/87   4:00 pm       12    Arc R/O
DT       E                                              c R/O
FA       E    Read Only Attribute removed from ASK.EXE
FF       E                                              c R/O
FI       EXE     Hidden Attribute set for BEEP.EXE
FR       EXE                                          Arc R/O
FS       EXE     8536   3/01/87   4:00 pm      100    Arc R/O
LD       EXE     7652   3/01/87   4:00 pm      109    Arc R/O
LP       EXE    11616   3/01/87   4:00 pm      117    Arc R/O
NCD      EXE    19496   3/01/87   4:00 pm      129    Arc R/O
NI       EXE    31963   3/01/87   4:00 pm      149    Arc R/O
SA       EXE     4506   3/01/87   4:00 pm      181    Arc R/O

                       Press Enter to continue
1Help  2Hex  3Text  4Dir  5FAT  6Partn  7  8  9Undo  10QuitNU
```

Figure 10-8

> You can make changes to a directory in the directory display mode. For example, you can remove an R/O attribute by using the [right arrow] key to move the highlight to the R/O column. Pressing [space bar] toggles an attribute on or off.
>
> In this example, changing the hexadecimal value of the attribute byte was done to show how the values are used by DOS. If you want to make changes in a directory you will probably find it simpler to edit the directory display, rather than the Hex display.

You can make these changes permanent by writing the new bytes onto the disk. Enter

```
[Esc]
w
```

You have now changed the file attributes of two of the files on the sample disk. Exit the Norton Utilities program by entering

`[Esc]` (twice)

Use DOS commands to confirm the changes you have made to the disk's directory. For example, if you have changed BEEP.EXE to a hidden file, it will not appear in a directory listing. Enter

```
dir a:/w ↵
```

The commands list only 27 files, one less than before. The BEEP.EXE file is the missing one. To be sure that the missing file is only hidden and not erased, use a command that does not employ the hidden attribute, the DOS command CHKDSK. Enter

```
chkdsk a: ↵
```

Although CHKDSK reports that there are two hidden files, it does not absolutely confirm that BEEP.EXE is one because it does not list the names.

You may wonder why are there two files listed as hidden, not one. The answer is that CHKDSK reports volume labels (attribute 8) along with hidden files (attribute 2). This makes sense because neither entry appears as part of the file listing, although the disk label does appear at the head of the report.

> The number of hidden files on a system disk is usually two. These are the BIOS (basic input/output system) and BDOS (basic disk operating system) files placed on the disk at the time of formatting. If you also add a volume label, CHKDSK reports the third hidden file.

To make certain that BEEP is a hidden file you can use the Norton Utilities program FA(file attribute). Enter

```
fa a:/p ↵
```

The screen displays all of the files, including the hidden one.

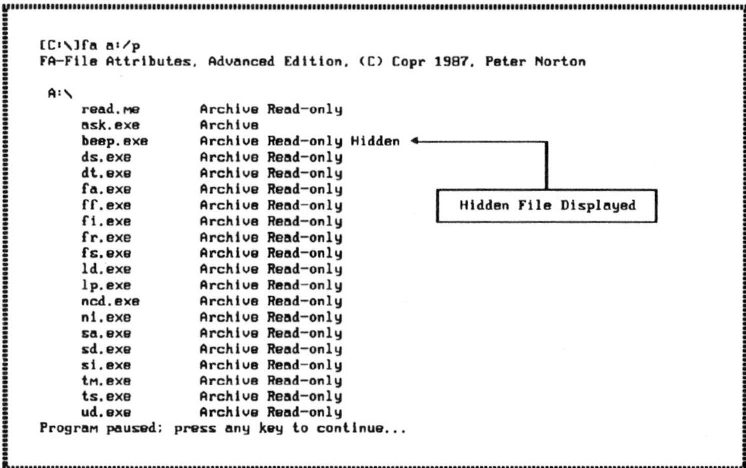

Figure 10-9

Press any key to complete the display.

Changing File Attributes

In the previous section you learned one way to change file attributes. The Norton Utilities program provides a simpler and more direct means of altering the attributes of a file or a group of files.

The FA (File Attribute) command is used to display the attributes of files. But the command also allows you to change the value of the attribute byte of a file or group of files without having to edit the directory. The FA command will accept five switches that effect specific bits of the attribute bytes.

Table 10.4. Switches Accepted by the File Attribute Command

Switch	Attribute	Bit Affected
/R+/-	Read-only	0
/HID+/-	Hidden	1
/SYS+/-	System	2
/A+/-	Archive	5
/CLEAR	Remove all attributes	0–7

The program allows you to specify for each attribute, except CLEAR, whether you want to add, +, or remove, −, that attribute from the file's attribute byte. If a switch is used without a + or −, it acts like a DOS wildcard to select only those files that match that attribute. For example, suppose you wanted to list all of the hidden files on drive A. Enter

```
fa a:/hid ↵
```

The program lists the BEEP.EXE file and displays a count of the number of files listed, 1, and the number of files changed, 0.

Check your hard disk for hidden files by entering the following command. Because a hard disk is likely to contain a number of directories, the FA command recognizes a /S switch, which includes subdirectories in the search. Enter

```
fa /hid/s ↵
```

You will find at least two hidden files, the BIO and the DOS system files. You may also find other unexpected hidden files. These are often the result of installation of copy protected programs such as Lotus products and 1.0 Versions of Framework and dBASE III.

> The names of the systems files will vary with the version of DOS used in your computer. IBM users will find the names of the hidden files as IBMDOS.COM and IBMBIO.COM. If you are using a compatible computer your hidden files may have different names, for example, IO.SYS (input/output system) and MSDOS.SYS (Microsoft disk operating system). The files serve the same purpose.

For example, you have set the BEEP.EXE file as a hidden file. If you wish to remove the hidden value from its attribute byte you can do so with the FA command and avoid having to edit the directory. Enter

```
fa a:beep.exe/hid- ↵
```

The program displays the file and shows that it now has only the Read-only and Archive attributes. To make sure that the file is no longer hidden, enter

```
dir a:/w ↵
```

The BEEP.EXE file appears in the directory once again.

You can affect more than one file at a time by selecting groups of files. The FA command allows you to select files in two ways.

1. You can use DOS file wildcards, * and ?, to select groups of files as you would with any DOS command.

2. You can use file attribute switches to locate files that contain specific attributes.

Using a + can add an attribute to a file or group of files. Suppose you wanted to hide the two files that begin with the word WIPE, WIPEFILE.EXE and WIPEDISK.EXE. You could use a DOS wildcard to select those files. Enter

```
fa a:wipe*.*/hid+ ↵
```

The two files are marked as hidden.

If you wanted to remove the archive attribute from all the hidden files, you would use the **/HID** to locate the hidden files and **/A-** to remove the archive attribute. Enter

```
fa a:/hid/a- ↵
```

In order to experiment with deleting and undeleting files, clear all the attributes from all the files on drive A. Enter

```
fa a:/clear ↵
```

All of the files are cleared of attributes, and the attribute byte is set to 0.

What Happens When You Delete Files?

To understand the unerase process it is necessary to understand what happens when a file is erased. The NUDEMO.BAT file supplied on the Norton Utilities Advanced Edition Disk 1 of 2 is used as an example because it is a text file and contains text information that is visually identifiable.

> Program files are affected by erasing just as text files are. However, since programs are stored in binary codes, they don't make much sense when you look at them as they are stored on the disk. To analyze the meaning of a program you must know assembly language quite well and use programs like debug to assemble the binary codes into assembly language.

Display the first part of the batch file by entering

```
type a:nudemo.bat|more ↵
```

The screen will display:

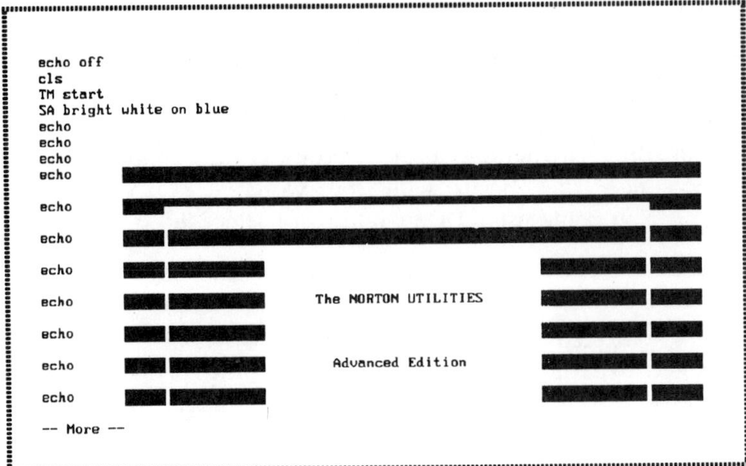

Figure 10-10

You can see the first part of the batch file displayed. Press any key to display the next screen. Continue until you have reached the final portion of the file. Notice the file begins with command batch file commands, **echo off, cls,** and so on. In addition, there is a rather striking display that announces the Norton Utilities program. Your screen should look like this:

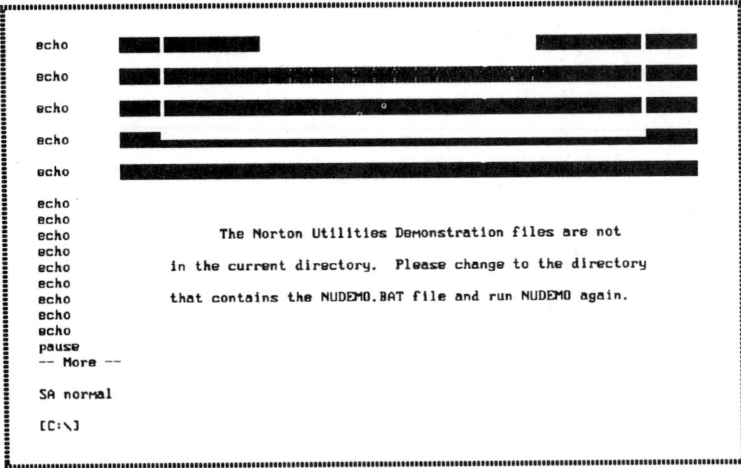

Figure 10-11

Note that the file ends with the command **SA normal**.

The reason for displaying the contents of the file is to allow you some familiarity with its substance. Because you have to recognize the data that belongs to that file, this is important.

You have seen the contents of the file displayed on the screen, but with normal DOS commands there is no way to obtain information about where a file is physically stored. With the Norton Utilities program however, you can get a lot of information about the file. Enter

nu a:nudemo.bat ↵

> The main Norton Utilities program can be loaded with a selected file specified as a parameter. This means that the program will load and automatically select the specified file for Norton Utilities operations.

The program displays the contents of the file and it shows you the location of the file on the disk. In this case the file begins at data cluster 311, which is located in disk sectors 630–631. Now move to the end of the file by entering

[End]

The final section of the file, the one that contains the SA normal command, is located in cluster 315 in disk sectors 638–639. Change the display to the data map. Enter

[Esc]
i

The screen shows a map of the disk. The F's mark the clusters used for the NUDEMO.BAT file.

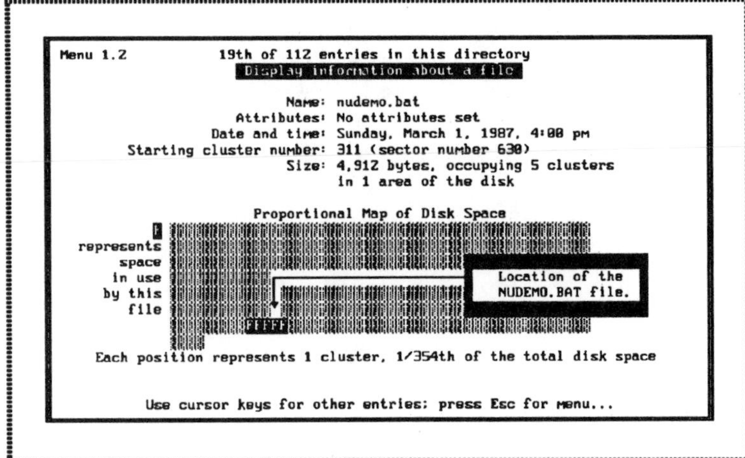

Figure 10-12

Seeing the location of the file is important because you want to see what happens to these exact areas when you erase the file. Return to DOS to erase the file. Enter

[Esc] (three times)

Erase that file from the disk. Enter

```
del a:nudemo.bat ↵
```

Display the directory of the disk. Enter

```
dir a:/w ↵
```

This time 27 files are listed, excluding the NUDEMO.BAT file. What actually happened to that file? When the file is erased is it really gone, and is the information contained within that file also gone?

You can use the TS command to search the disk for text. For example, the first command in the file was echo off. Search the disk to see if that text is still there. Enter

```
ts ↵
```

To search the entire disk, enter

```
d
```

In this case the disk is A. Enter

```
a ↵
```

Next, enter the text you want to search for.

```
echo off ↵
```

The program will examine all the sectors on the disk in drive A, looking for the specified text, echo off.

In a few minutes the screen will display:

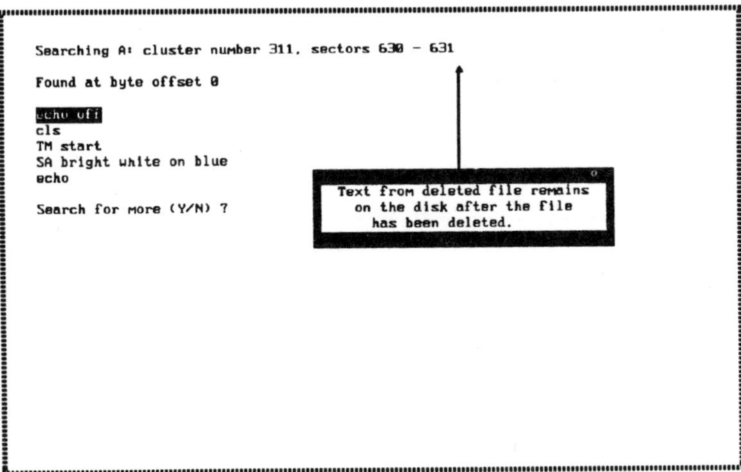

Figure 10-13

You can see that the text of the batch file is still stored on the disk in the same location, cluster 311 in sectors 630–631. The delete command did not affect the contents of the file. But what did it affect? To get the answer, stop the search and load the main Norton Utilities program. Enter

```
n
nu a: ↵
```

Display the disk directory. Enter

↵ (4 times)
e

The screen displays the first part of the disk directory. Enter

```
[Pg Dn]
```

This screen reveals what actually took place when the file was erased.

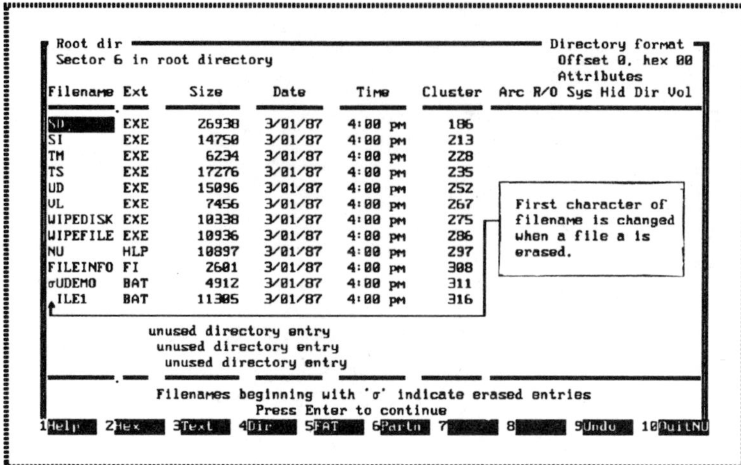

Figure 10-14

The first character of the filename is changed to a special symbol. Notice that all the other information about the file, the rest of the name, the date, time, size, and so on, is still intact.

> Alterations to the FAT (File Allocation Table) also takes place during file erasure. The FAT is used to keep track of the additional clusters used by a file following the first cluster recorded in the directory. Since a thorough discussion of the FAT is beyond the scope of this book, I recommend reading INSIDE THE IBM PC, by Peter Norton, published by Brady books.

Move the cursor down until it highlights the σUDEMO.

Change to the Hex display by entering

[F2]

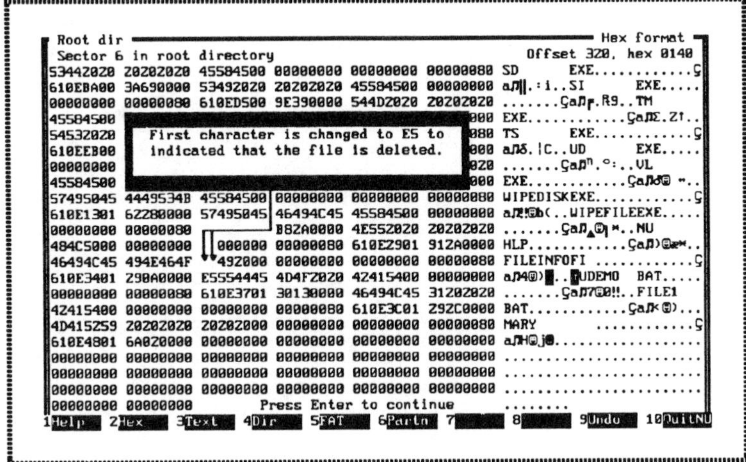

Figure 10-15

You can see that the DOS procedure for deleting a file does not actually wipe out the contents of the erased file. Rather, it alters the directory to indicate that the file is to be treated as a deleted file. This means that when new information is added to the disk, the space that was reserved for the contents of the deleted file, in this example, NUDEMO.BAT, can be used for the new data. It is this fact that allows the Norton Utilities program to recover some deleted files. But that ability is limited by the conditions on the disk.

Immediately after an erasure is made the information about the erased file is almost completely intact. But to see what happens if you continue to use the disk, exit the program and return to DOS.

[Esc] (3 times)

What Happens When New Files Are Added

In the previous section you saw how deleting a file affected only part of the information about that file. The actual contents of that file were left intact. But what will DOS do when new information is stored on the disk?

To produce that situation, use the COPY command to create a duplicate of the file called **MARY** on the Norton Utilities disk.

> MARY is a text file that contains parameters for the BEEP command which plays a tune, MARY Had a Little Lamb. The parameters contain the frequency of the notes and their duration. Example: /F330 /D1 plays E above middle C for .06 of a second.

Enter

```
copy a:mary a:newfile
```

Use the Norton Utilities program to display the disk directory again. Enter

```
nu a: ↵
↵ (4 times)
e
[Pg Dn]
```

The display shows that a new filename, NEWFILE, is stored in the position in the directory that used to be occupied by the NUDEMO.BAT file.

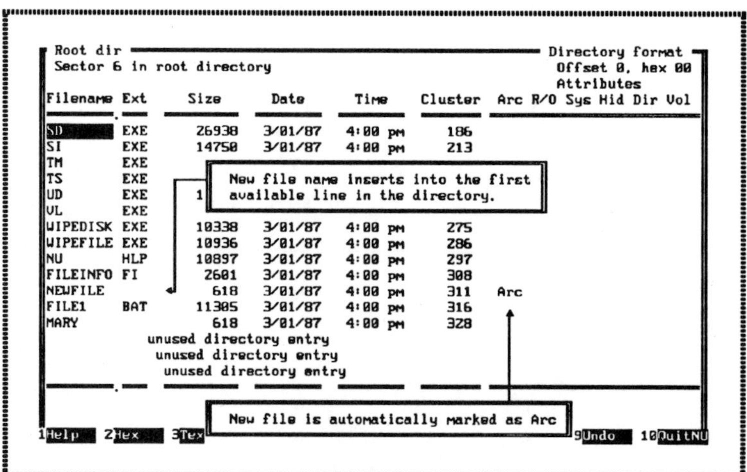

Figure 10-16

You can see that DOS uses the first available directory line for the new filename; thus the reason the name of a new file appears in the middle of a directory instead of the end. DOS also automatically places the **Arc** attribute **on** for this file. The purpose of this is to indicate that the new file needs to be backed up. The BACKUP command will turn off the attribute as part of the backup process.

Display the data area on the disk used by NUDEMO.BAT by entering

```
[Esc]
c
1
```

Because NUDEMO.BAT began in cluster 311, enter

```
311
↵ (2 times)
e
```

The display shows that the information in 311 is no longer the NUDEMO.BAT file but a copy of the contents of the MARY file.

```
Cluster 311 ───────────────────────────────────── Text format
Cluster 311  Sectors 630-631                     Offset 0, hex 00

 ►:──────────────────────────────────────────────◄
 ►:  Title: Mary had a Little Lamb  :◄
 ►:  Date:  March 1, 1987     :◄
 ►:────────────────────────────────────────────:◄
 ►◄
 ►/F330 /D1  : Mar-◄
 ►/F294 /D1  : -y◄
 ►/F262 /D1  : had◄
 ►/F294 /D1  : a◄
 ►/R2 /F330 /D1  : little◄
 ►/F330 /D2  : lamb◄
 ►:◄
 ►/R2 /F294 /D1  : little◄
 ►/F294 /D2  : lamb◄
 ►:◄
 ►/F330 /D1  : lit-◄
 ►/F392 /D1  : -tle◄
 ►/F392 /D2  : lamb◄
 ►:◄
  ...more
                        Press Enter to continue
1Help  2Hex  3Text  4Dir  5FAT  6Partn  7  8  9Undo  10QuitNU
```

Figure 10-17

Writing new information to the disk is what actually destroys the directory and file information. When it comes to data recovery the best time to recover a file is immediately after an erasure. As the disk is used, the space formerly occupied by the old files is used for new files. When that happens the old data can NO LONGER BE RECOVERED.

Partial Recovery

Whether or not NEWFILE destroyed all of NUDEMO.BAT depends upon the relative size of the two files. If NEWFILE is a smaller file than NUDEMO.BAT, DOS would overwrite as many sectors of NUDEMO.BAT as needed to complete the NEWFILE

file. If NEWFILE is larger, then it is more probable that all of the clusters used by NUDEMO.BAT will be used up by NEWFILE.

Examine the next sector of the NEWFILE file by entering

[Pg Dn]

You can see that there is an END OF FILE marker, indicating the end of the NEWFILE.

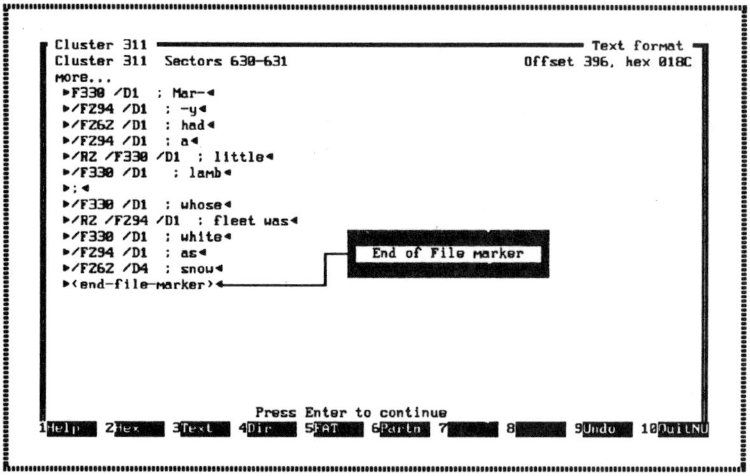

```
Cluster 311                                              Text format
Cluster 311  Sectors 630-631                       Offset 396, hex 018C
more...
 ►F330 /D1  : Mar-◄
 ►/F294 /D1  : -y◄
 ►/F262 /D1  : had◄
 ►/F294 /D1  : a◄
 ►/RZ /F330 /D1  : little◄
 ►/F330 /D1   : lamb◄
 ►:◄
 ►/F330 /D1  : whose◄
 ►/RZ /F294 /D1  : fleet was◄
 ►/F330 /D1  : white◄
 ►/F294 /D1  : as◄                      End of File marker
 ►/F262 /D4  : snow◄
 ►<end-file-marker>◄

                     Press Enter to continue
1Help  2Hex  3Text  4Dir  5FAT  6Partn  7  8  9Undo  10QuitNU
```

Figure 10-18

Remember that NUDEMO.BAT used clusters 311 through 315. The marker indicates that NEWFILE ends in 311. This means that at this moment the data in clusters 312 through 315 still contain data that formerly made up part of NUDEMO.BAT. It is possible to recover at least part of erased file NUDEMO.BAT at this point. But the problems of doing this are much greater than they would have been if the file had been recovered before new data was written.

1. The directory information about the file has been overwritten.

2. In this example, you knew the cluster numbers and the sequence in which they were used in the erased file. In normal operation, you would have no idea what clusters make up what files, or the order in which those clusters should be placed.

> File fragmentation is an important factor in attempting to recover a partially overwritten file. As files are deleted and added to a disk, hard or floppy, DOS will store the data in the next available location. If the entire file cannot fit, DOS skips over other files to locate the next open space. This can result in files that are stored in clusters that are not consecutive in number. On large disks, it is not unusual for files to use clusters in any pattern based on the shortest path for the disk drive to move.
>
> This complicates the job of recovering partial files since consecutive clusters may contain information from different files.

3. If the data you are recovering is part of a program, partial recovery, if possible, will not enable you to know what parts of the program are missing. Therefore, partial file recovery makes sense only with text files in which you can visually determine if the text belongs to the file you are trying to recover.

Exit the Norton Utilities program and return to DOS.

```
[F10]
```

You have now obtained some first-hand information about the process by which disk files are erased and replaced with new data. You are now ready to use the specialized tools provided by the Norton Utilities programs to recover erased information from a disk.

Quick Unerase

The simplest way to remove erased files is with the QU (Quick Unerase) program. The QU program is designed to recover files that do not appear to have been overwritten with new information.

When recovering erased files, start with QU. If QU fails to recover the file, attempt recovery with the Unerase function of the main Norton Utilities program, described later in this section.

To learn about the abilities and limitations of QU, begin by erasing some of the files on the disk in drive A. Enter

```
del a:*.exe ↵
```

Display the directory of the files that remain. Enter

```
dir a: ↵
```

There are only 6 files left on the disk. Because you have just erased the files this is an ideal time to try to recover some or all of the files, before they get written over.

The Quick Unerase program has several options.

Interactive

In this mode, the Quick Unerase program attempts to unerase as many files in the current directory as possible. Each file that is potentially recoverable is displayed. You are asked if you want to recover that file or not. If you do, you are asked to enter the first letter of the filename.

> Remember that the first letter of the filename is overwritten when a file is erased.

Files

The Quick Unerase command allows you to select a file or group of files for recovery. This option allows you to concentrate on a file or files to recover when there are a large number of erased entries in a directory.

> You cannot use a wildcard that selects by the first letter of a filename, e.g., m*.*, because the first letter of the erased file is overwritten when the file is erased.

Automatic

When set for automatic operation, the Quick Unerase command automatically fills in the missing letter of the filename with the letter A. If a name conflict occurs with an existing file, the program changes the first letter to B, C, D, etc., until it creates a unique filename.

The advantage of the automatic operation is that it is not necessary for you to approve each unerasure. You can later use the Rename command or the Norton Commander to alter the filenames that are not appropriate.

Suppose that you wanted to unerase some of the files you just erased from drive A. To begin, use the Quick Unerase command in the interactive mode. Enter

qu a: ↵

The program reads the disk directory, displays a summary of what is found and displays the first filename for recovery. In this case the ?SK.EXE.

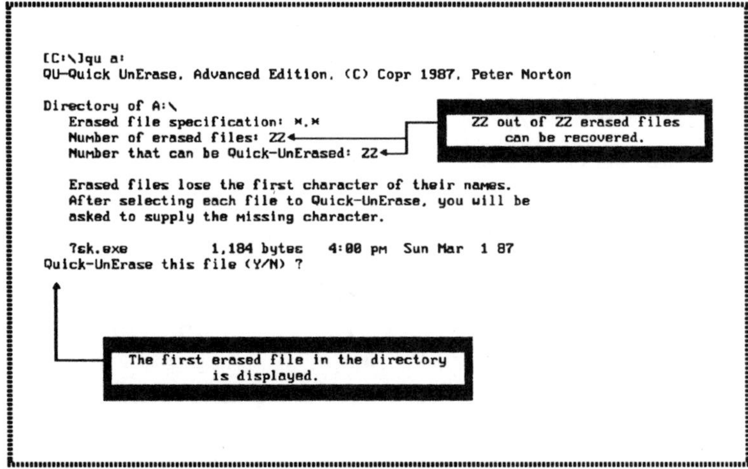

Figure 10-19

You can decide to unerase this file, Y, or leave it alone, N. Enter

y

The prompt asks you to enter the first character of the filename. In this example, the missing letter is A for the file ASK.EXE. Enter

a

The file is unerased restoring the entry in the directory (and the file allocation table) to its previous content. The file can be used just as it had been used before.

The program then displays the next filename found in the directory.

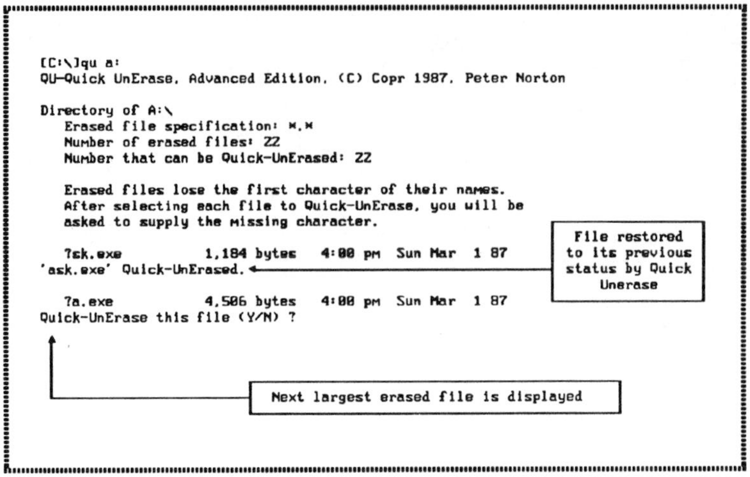

```
[C:\]qu a:
QU-Quick UnErase, Advanced Edition, (C) Copr 1987, Peter Norton

Directory of A:\
   Erased file specification: *.*
   Number of erased files: 22
   Number that can be Quick-UnErased: 22

   Erased files lose the first character of their names.
   After selecting each file to Quick-UnErase, you will be
   asked to supply the missing character.

   ?sk.exe          1,184 bytes   4:00 pm  Sun Mar  1 87
'ask.exe' Quick-UnErased.

   ?a.exe           4,586 bytes   4:00 pm  Sun Mar  1 87
Quick-UnErase this file (Y/N) ?
```

File restored to its previous status by Quick Unerase
Next largest erased file is displayed

Figure 10-20

This filename is difficult to decipher because it is not a common word like ASK. Even if you remember the names of the erased Norton Utilities files you still do not know if the file is FA.EXE (File Attribute) or SA.EXE (System's Attribute).

QU always begins with the smallest erased files and works through the list of erased files to the largest. This method is employed because the smaller files have a greater chance of being correctly recovered than do larger files.

Your choices involve skipping this file or making a guess. If you want to recover the file, whether it turns out to be FA or SA, it is a good idea to make a guess rather than skip it. If you skip the file, you might accidentally overwrite some of its data at a later point. By making a guess you preserve the data in the data clusters assigned to that filename. In EXAMINING A FILE, which comes later in this chapter, you will learn about other Norton Utilities programs used to discover what the real name of this file should be. For now, enter

```
y
x
```

The next file is probably BEEP.EXE. Enter

```
y
b
```

You can halt the program by entering the break command.

```
[Ctrl/c]
```

Most of the Norton Utilities programs recognize the break command with some exceptions. Use [Esc] to exit these programs.

Table 10.5. Commands That Do Not Recognize BREAK

FR	Format Recover
NCD	Norton Change Directory
NU	Main Program
SD	Speed Disk

> Traditionally, the break command is the one inherited from the ASCII code, [Ctrl/c]. The IBM PC keyboard offers an alternative for break, [Ctrl/Scroll Lock]. This redundancy also occurs in the **printer on** and **stop scroll** commands. ASCII uses [Ctrl/p] and [Ctrl/s] respectively. The IBM (and most compatibles) offer [Ctrl/PrtSc] and [Ctrl/Num Lock] which duplicate those functions in DOS.
>
> Keep in mind that the break combination will not affect most applications because those programs disable the break combination as soon as they load into memory.
>
> [Ctrl/c] or [Ctrl/Scroll Lock] will halt the execution of most DOS programs as well as the Norton Utilities programs.

The program terminates and returns you to DOS. Note that the files you recovered were not affected by breaking the program. The break simply stopped the program from continuing on to new files. Enter

```
dir a:
```

You can see that there are now nine files, six plus the three you recovered.

The BREAK command selects the number of times DOS checks to see if a break request has been entered. The normal setting for BREAK is off. This means that DOS checks for breaks only at specific points in its operation, such as when it completes an input or output operation to the disk.

With BREAK set on, DOS scans the keyboard more often. This allows you to stop operations that would normally have to complete before a break would be recognized. With BREAK ON, DOS will scan the keyboard during a disk input or output operations such as loading a file.

For example, suppose you have just entered a command to load Lotus 1-2-3. Since this is a large program it takes a few seconds to load before it executes. When BREAK is off, entering [Ctrl/c] will not halt the loading. If BREAK is on, [Ctrl/c] will halt the loading and return you to DOS. Keep in mind that you have to be quick to stop the loading since the time it takes varies depending upon the overall speed of your computer. Also note that once 1-2-3 has loaded, the [Ctrl/c] combination is disabled.

BREAK can be turned on or off by entering BREAK ON or BREAK OFF at DOS. You can also turn on BREAK by entering a command in your CONFIG.SYS file that reads BREAK=ON.

Examining a File

In the previous Quick Unerase operation you recovered file XA.EXE, whose name you were unsure of. The file could be either SA.EXE or FA.EXE, but was probably SA.EXE because it is a smaller file than FA. It is rare, however, that you would know or remember that.

There is another way to discover which of the two possible names go with this file: use the Norton Utilities program to display the file contents. Many programs include a message that identifies the program, such as that placed in the file to assert a programmer's copyrights. That copyright message can be used as a clue to ascertaining the correct name of a file.

Suppose you searched the file for the word "copyright." Enter

```
ts a:xa.exe "copyright" ↵
```

The program locates the copyright message.

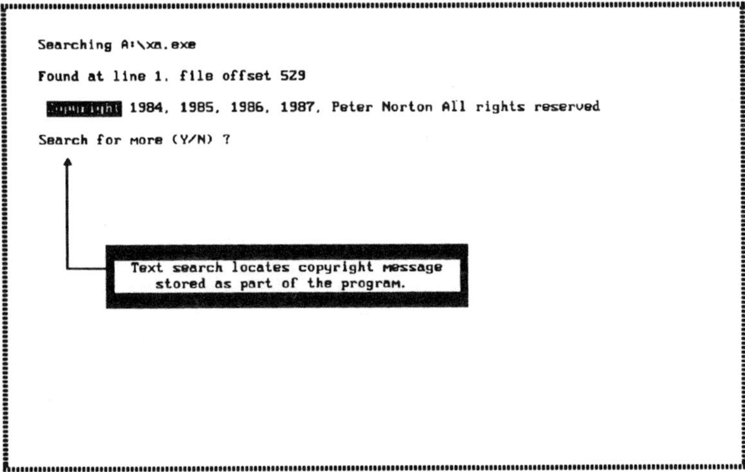

Searching A:\xa.exe
Found at line 1, file offset 529
Copyright 1984, 1985, 1986, 1987, Peter Norton All rights reserved
Search for more (Y/N) ?
Text search locates copyright message stored as part of the program.

Figure 10-21

The message establishes that this program belongs to the Norton Utilities collection but the name of the file is not included. Continue the search by entering

y

No other clues are found. Another alternative is to use the main Norton Utilities to browse the program for other messages that might give you a hint as to its original name. Enter

```
nu a:xa.exe ↵
```

The first screen displays mostly zeros.

```
 xa.exe                                                      Hex format
 Cluster 181   Sectors 370-371                          File offset 0, hex 00
4D5A9A01 09000200 2000FC00 FFFFB000 A00F182E 54000000 MZÜ☺.☻. .ⁿ...√.ô*↑.T...
1E000000 01005400 B7005500 00000000 00000000 00000000 ▲...☺.T.╖.U............
00000000 00000000 00000000 00000000 00000000 00000000 ........................
00000000 00000000 00000000 00000000 00000000 00000000 ........................
00000000 00000000 00000000 00000000 00000000 00000000 ........................
00000000 00000000 00000000 00000000 00000000 00000000 ........................
00000000 00000000 00000000 00000000 00000000 00000000 ........................
00000000 00000000 00000000 00000000 00000000 00000000 ........................
00000000 00000000 00000000 00000000 00000000 00000000 ........................
00000000 00000000 00000000 00000000 00000000 00000000 ........................
00000000 00000000 00000000 00000000 00000000 00000000 ........................
00000000 00000000 00000000 00000000 00000000 00000000 ........................
00000000 00000000 00000000 00000000 00000000 00000000 ........................
00000000 00000000 00000000 00000000 00000000 00000000 ........................
00000000 00000000 00000000 00000000 00000000 00000000 ........................
00000000 00000000 00000000 00000000 00000000 00000000 ........................
00000000 00000000 00000000 00000000 00000000 00000000 ........................
00000000 00000000 00000000 00000000 00000000 00000000 ........................
00000000 00000000 00000000 00000000 00000000 00000000 ........................
00000000 00000000 00000000 00000000 00000000 00000000 ........................
00000000 00000000 00000000 00000000 00000000 00000000 ........................
00000000 00000000          Press Enter to continue      ........
1Help  2Hex  3Text  4Dir  5FAT  6Partn  7  8  9Undo  10QuitNU
```

Figure 10-22

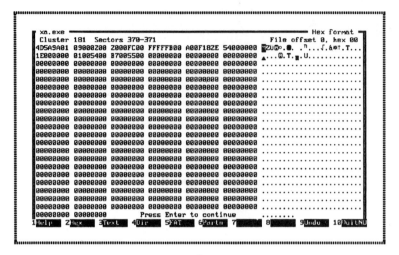

You can now use the [Pg Dn] key to display more of the file. You will have to enter seven [Pg Dn] commands before you see the message that gives you a clue as to the correct name of this file(file offset 3,584). The screen will display:

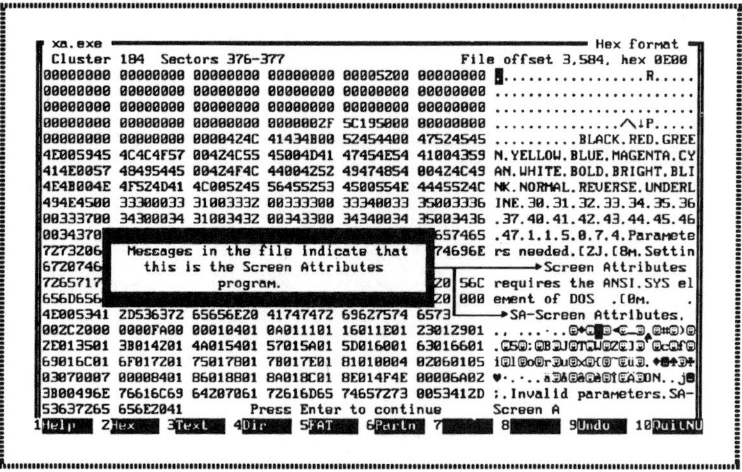

Figure 10-23

You can see that these messages refer to the SA, Screen Attributes program. Therefore the correct name for this file should be SA.EXE. The first guess that the file was FA.EXE because it was listed before SA.EXE in the directory was wrong. You can now rename the file. Exit the Norton Utilities program.

```
[10]
```

Use DOS to rename the file. Enter

```
rename a:sa.exe
```

The Norton Utilities programs do not provide a fool-proof method of undoing mistakes. But they do provide a set of useful tools that can help you make intelligent, educated guesses. The process of recovering a file often requires you to take several steps, using several different Norton Utilities programs, in order to gather the information you need to make a decision. The Norton Utilities programs work best when you take the time to question and analyze all of the information that is available to you just beneath the surface of DOS.

In a broader sense, these operations show the trade offs of a system like DOS. On the one hand, DOS is hard to understand and requires a good deal of effort to master. Its open nature, however, allows programmers like those at Norton Computing to create tools that address the needs of many users. These tools allow you to peer beneath the surface of the DOS interface and reveal what is really there.

Unerasing Groups

The Quick Unerase command allows you to unerase files from a selected group by using a DOS wildcard to select files. Because unerased files have the first character missing, the Quick Unerase performs differently when a wildcard contains a character in the first position than when it does not.

As a first example, now that you have located the SA.EXE file and unerased it, find the other file with a similar name, FA.EXE, and unerase it. To avoid having to look at all the unerased names in the directory you can use a file specification to select only files that have an A as the second character. Enter

```
qu a:?a.* ↵
```

The program locates the only filename that meets your criterion.

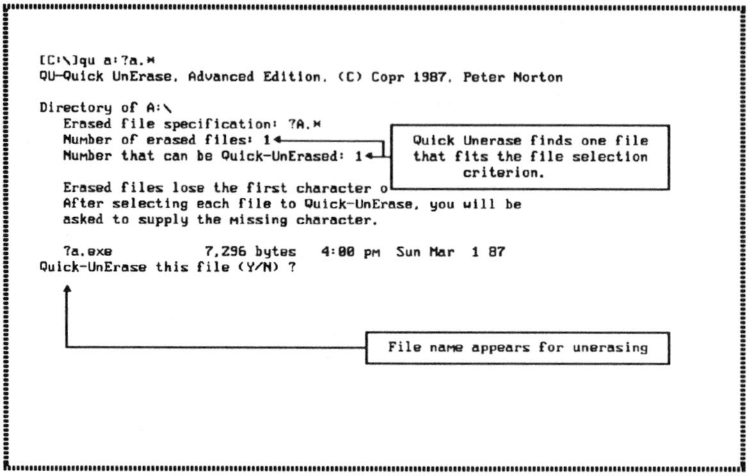

```
[C:\]qu a:?a.*
QU-Quick UnErase, Advanced Edition, (C) Copr 1987, Peter Norton

Directory of A:\
   Erased file specification: ?A.*
   Number of erased files: 1
   Number that can be Quick-UnErased: 1

   Erased files lose the first character o
   After selecting each file to Quick-UnErase, you will be
   asked to supply the missing character.

   ?a.exe          7,296 bytes   4:00 pm  Sun Mar  1 87
Quick-UnErase this file (Y/N) ?
```

Quick Unerase finds one file that fits the file selection criterion.

File name appears for unerasing

Figure 10-24

This file should be recovered as FA.EXE. Enter

```
y
f
```

The program terminates because there are no other files that meet the specifications.

It is important to keep in mind that including a first character in your file specification changes the way Quick Unerase functions, quite dramatically. Remember that two of the files in the Norton Utilities set begin with the letters **WIPE, WIPEDISK.EXE** and **WIPEFILE.EXE.** If you enter a file specification that looks for a file that begins with WIPE, Quick Unerase automatically enters an automatic recovery mode in which it assigns a first letter to the files. Enter

```
qu a:wipe*.* ↵
```

The program automatically inserts the W to complete the WIPE in both filenames.

The /A switch causes Quick Unerase to insert the first letter for the filenames of all the selected files. Automatic file naming is convenient when you have a number of files to recover. You can then look at the filenames as they are automatically generated and use the RENAME command to change the names as necessary. To automatically recover all of the files on disk A, use the Quick Unerase command with the /A switch. Enter

```
qu a:/a ↵
```

This time Quick Unerase does not stop at each file but automatically assigns a first letter, A, to the filename. If a second file with the same name occurs, Quick

Unerase moves to the next letter B, C, and so on. List the recovered files by entering

```
dir a:*.exe ↵
```

The list shows that the filenames were assigned first letters by the program. For example, three files have the same names, **?I.EXE,** which is what occurred when the first letters of NI.EXE, FI.EXE and SI.EXE were erased. The Quick Unerase program filled in the first letters of those files with **A, B** and **C** creating **AI.EXE, BI.EXE** and **CI.EXE.**

```
ASK      EXE     1184  3-01-87   4:00p
BEEP     EXE     5324  3-01-87   4:00p
CS       EXE    25638  3-01-87   4:00p
AT       EXE    17910  3-01-87   4:00p
FA       EXE     7296  3-01-87   4:00p
AF       EXE     7924  3-01-87   4:00p
AI
AR       EXE    12610  3-01-87   4:00p
AS       EXE     8536  3-01-87   4:00p
AD       EXE     7652  3-01-87   4:00p
AP       EXE    11616  3-01-87   4:00p
ACD      EXE    19496  3-01-87   4:00p
CI
XA       EXE     4506  3-01-87   4:00p
CD       EXE    26938  3-01-87   4:00p
BI
AM       EXE     6234  3-01-87   4:00p
BS       EXE    17276  3-01-87   4:00p
BD       EXE    15096  3-01-87   4:00p
AL       EXE     7456  3-01-87   4:00p
WIPEDISK EXE    10330  3-01-87   4:00p
WIPEFILE EXE    10936  3-01-87   4:00p
        22 File(s)   31744 bytes free

[C:\]
```

Quick Unerase assigns consecutive letters to file that have the same characters in the remainder of their file names.

Figure 10-25

Limits of Quick Unerase

The Quick Unerase will only attempt to recover files that are still intact. If the file has been partially overwritten, then Quick Unerase will not attempt to recover the information. You can explore what happens when erased files are overwritten by erasing some files from A and then adding new files to the disk. Enter the following commands that erase specific files from the disk in drive A. These files were selected because, as text files, partial recovery is possible with the main Norton Utilities program. Enter

```
del a:newfile ↵
del a:file1.bat ↵
del a:mary ↵
del a:read.me ↵
```

As you have learned, deleting of these files has not actually removed the information contained within them. However, if you begin to add information to the disk, some of the spaces used by the erased files will be overwritten, making it impossible to recover that file intact, or even in part.

To create this situation, make a copy of the FILEINFO.FI file. Enter

```
copy a:fileinfo.fi a:dup.fi ↵
```

Now run Quick Unerase and see what happens. Enter

```
qu a:↵
```

The first erased file found by Quick Unerase is **?ARY**. The statistics displayed about the disk show that there are three erased files in the directory, of which two can be completely recovered.

```
[C:\]qu a:
QU-Quick UnErase, Advanced Edition, (C) Copr 1987, Peter Norton

Directory of A:\                              Directory shows 3 erased files
   Erased file specification: *.*
   Number of erased files: 3
   Number that can be Quick-UnErased: 2
                                               Only 2 files can be
   Erased files lose the first character of th recovered completely.
   After selecting each file to Quick-UnErase,
   asked to supply the missing character.

   ?ary               618 bytes   4:00 pm  Sun Mar  1 87
Quick-UnErase this file (Y/N) ?
```

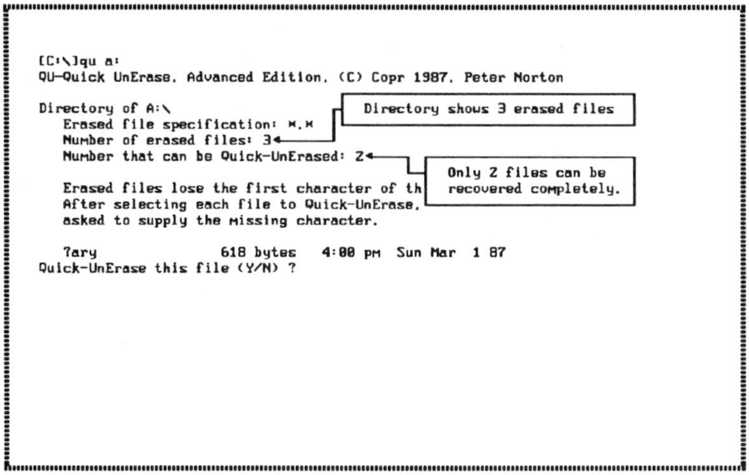

Figure 10-26

Comparing the statistics to the fact that you have just deleted four files tells you something about what happens to disks as files are added and deleted.

Immediately following the deletion of the four files, the disk's directory held four erased entries. When you added the new file, DOS used the first erased entry in the directory for the new file. This is why Quick Unerase found only three erased files. But why are only two files recoverable? The answer must be that the new file added to the disk was larger than the file that had previously been stored in the same position in the directory. The new file stored data in the area previously used by two erased files. Conversely, only two of the four files erased can be completely recovered.

This demonstration introduces the topic of unerasing with the main Norton Utilities program. Because this program contains more sophisticated commands and options it can recover entire or partial files. Terminate the Quick Unerase program by entering

[Ctrl/c]

Unerasing with the Main Program

The main Norton Utilities program has many uses. One of its major functions is to provide a means by which data can be recovered from erased sections of the disk. If the file is an erased file that has been left untouched by new files, the main Norton Utilities program will duplicate the operation of the Quick Unerase program. However, the main Norton Utilities program can go far beyond Quick Unerase to help locate and recover all types of data and files. Load the main program by entering

nu a: ↵

Select the Unerase menu by entering

u

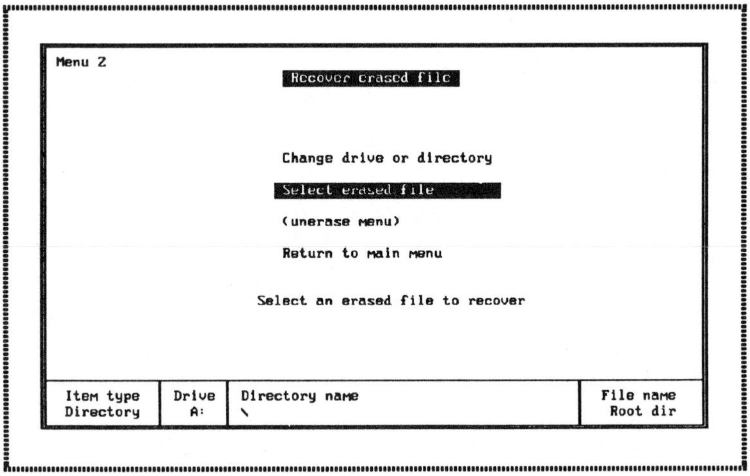

```
Menu 2
                    Recover erased file

                    Change drive or directory
                    Select erased file
                    (unerase menu)
                    Return to main menu

                 Select an erased file to recover

Item type | Drive | Directory name          | File name
Directory |  A:   | \                       | Root dir
```

Figure 10-27

When unerasing with the main program the first step is to select a filename. Enter

s

The main program lists all of the erased filenames in the current directory. You have two options.

1. Select an erased filename. You can select one of the filenames that appear. Naturally, the first letter of the filename is missing because they are erased files.

2. Create a new File. This option allows you to create a new file as part of the unerase process. This important option was missing in earlier versions of the Norton Utilities programs.

Since the goal of unerasing is to recover data that was once part of a file, to create a new file might seem strange. However, the ability to create a new file as part of the unerase process makes it easy to gather clusters of data together when performing partial file recoveries.

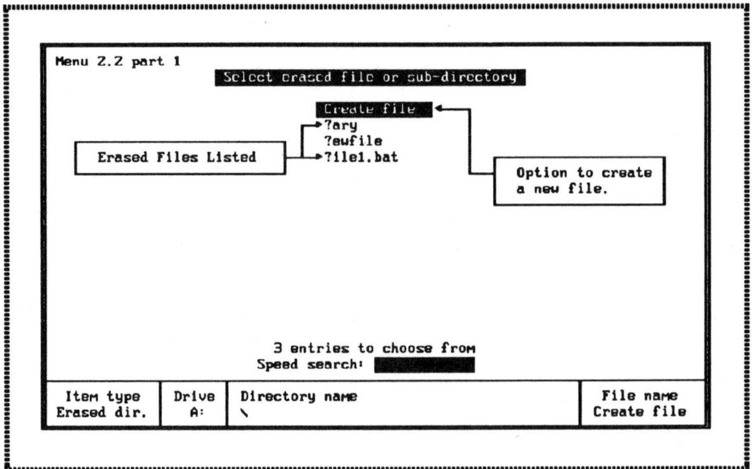

Figure 10-28

Select the ?ARY filename. Enter

a

The Norton Utilities speed search feature automatically positions your cursor at the first file that matches the letter you typed, a. Select that filename by entering

↵

The next screen displays the information that the Norton Utilities program can provide about the selected file.

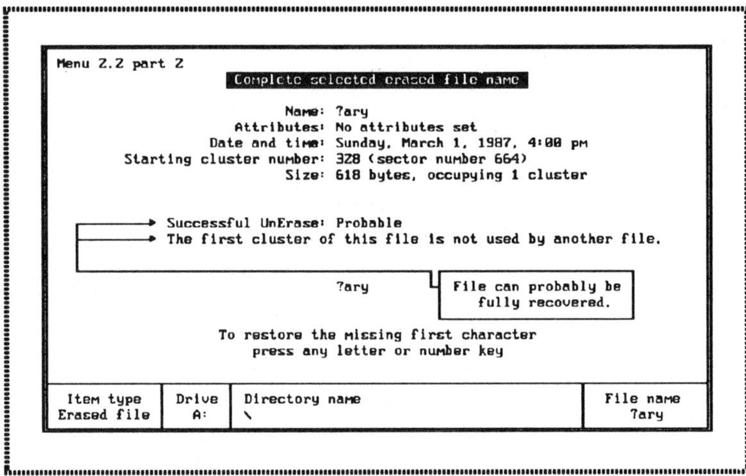

Figure 10-29

The screen displays the information found in the directory entry for that filename. It also indicates that you can probably recover the file in its entirety.

> The use of the word probably indicates the delicate nature of the unerase process. The Norton Utilities tests to see if the data cluster that was assigned to the beginning of the erased file is in use by another file. Doing so helps to indicate if the file has been overwritten by new data, but it is not absolutely certain.
>
> Imagine this scenario. A file, MARY, is erased. Then other files are added, and also erased. When you try to recover MARY, Norton Utilities finds that the cluster that begins MARY is not in use by another file. However, the file that was added and erased after MARY may have overwritten that cluster before it was erased. In that way the cluster is not attached to a file but no longer contains the data that it did when MARY was an active file.
>
> Keep in mind that there are no certainties in unerasing, only probabilities.

This is the simplest type of file to recover. Proceed to recover the file by entering a character for the first letter of the filename.

m ↵

You are now returned to the first unerase menu. There is one change: the option Unerase menu is added to the display. Notice that the name of the file you want to recover is listed at the bottom of the screen in the right corner.

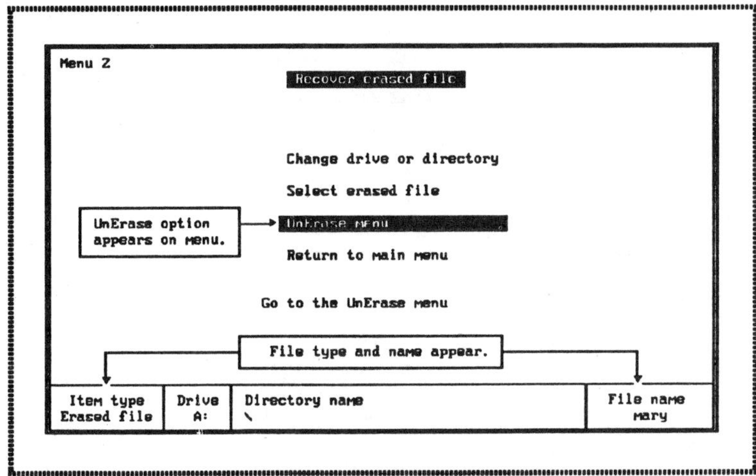

Figure 10-30

Activate the Unerase menu by entering

↵

The Unerase menu appears.

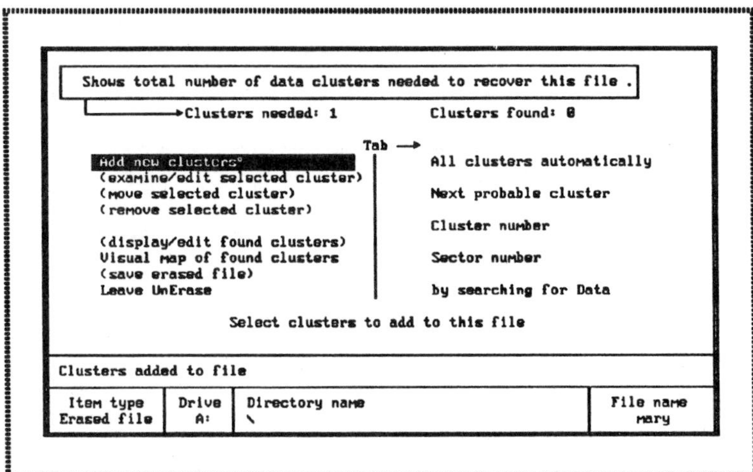

Figure 10-31

The menu consists of several parts. The first part appears at the top of the display. It shows the number of data clusters that originally belonged to this file. In this case the file was the minimum size, 1 cluster. The larger the file the larger the number of clusters that will have to be recovered. Directly to the right of that is the part of the menu showing the number of clusters recovered for that file, 0, since no clusters have been selected for the MARY file.

You can see by these items that the name of the game in unerasing files is selecting data clusters. The bottom portion of the menu is divided into two columns that list a variety of operations. They all have one thing in common: They are designed to help you find and select the data clusters needed to recover the file.

The two-column display is a bit misleading. All of the main commands are listed in the left column. The right column consists of a series of subcommands related to the first option in the left column, **Add new** clusters.

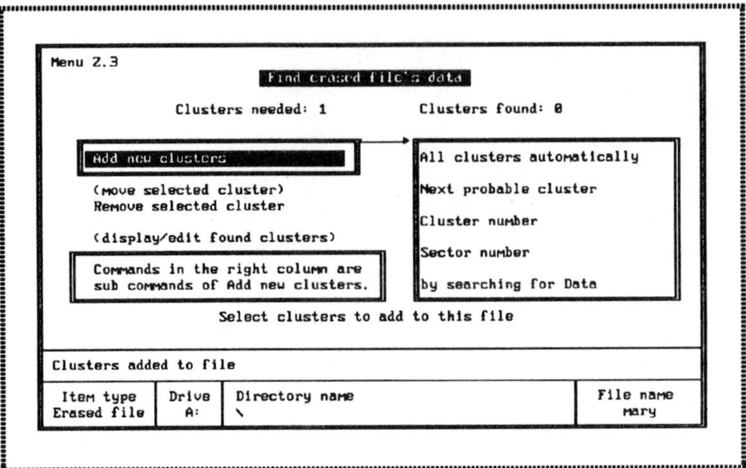

Figure 10-32

Below is a summary of the commands available on this menu:

1. **Add new clusters.** This option consists of a series of subcommands, each of which is designed to select data clusters to be added to the file you are trying to recover.

   i. **All clusters automatically.** This option allows the Norton Utilities program to automatically select the clusters that appear to belong with this file. The method used is the same as that used with the Quick Unerase command.

   ii. **Next probable cluster.** This option is used when you suspect that the files may be, in part, overwritten. This option selects one cluster at a time. The assumption is that you will then inspect the contents of this cluster to decide if it really belongs with the file you are trying to recover.

   iii. **Cluster number.** This command selects a specific data cluster by the specific cluster number. To use this option you must know the cluster number that you want to add. You would normally use this option to add a cluster located by a search of the disk with the TS(Text Search) program.

   iv. **Sector Number.** This option adds the cluster that contains the specific sector you request. Like the cluster number option, you need to know the exact sector number that you want to add. Note that sector selection still adds the contents of the entire cluster. Clusters on a floppy disk usually contain two sectors, while a hard disk will have between 4 and 16 sectors per cluster.

v. **Searching for Data.** This method locates clusters by searching for specific characters or hex values.

2. **Examine/edit selected cluster.** This command displays the contents of a selected cluster. This option is used when you want to visually inspect the data to determine if it is really part of the file you want to recover.

3. **Move selected sector.** This option is used to change the order in which the clusters selected for a file are arranged. In a simple case where there is only one cluster, you don't have to be concerned with sequence. But if you are assembling lost data, cluster by cluster, you may need to change the sequence of the data clusters to assemble the file correctly.

4. **Remove selected cluster.** This option allows you to change your mind about clusters you have selected. If you don't want this cluster to be included with the file, it can be removed before the file is saved.

5. **Display/edit found clusters.** This option can be used to change the data in the selected clusters as well as display it.

6. **Visual map of found clusters.** The map shows you visually where on the disk the selected cluster are located.

7. **Save erased file.** This step saves all the selected clusters as the recovered file.

8. **Leave Unerase.** Exits Unerase. Note that the selections will remain the same until you make a different selection.

When no clusters have been selected, as is the case at this point, examine, move, display and save are shown in parentheses to indicate that they are not available. After you have selected one or more clusters you will be able to use these commands. The first step is to select clusters. Enter

a

The highlight jumps to the right side of the screen to select All clusters.

Since the Norton Utilities program indicates that this file is probably intact, you can use the automatic selection feature to locate the file's clusters. Enter

a

Norton Utilities automatically selects cluster 328. If you recall, cluster 328 was the one that was displayed when the program showed the information stored in the directory. Since MARY was only one cluster in size, you can be pretty sure that you have recovered this file.

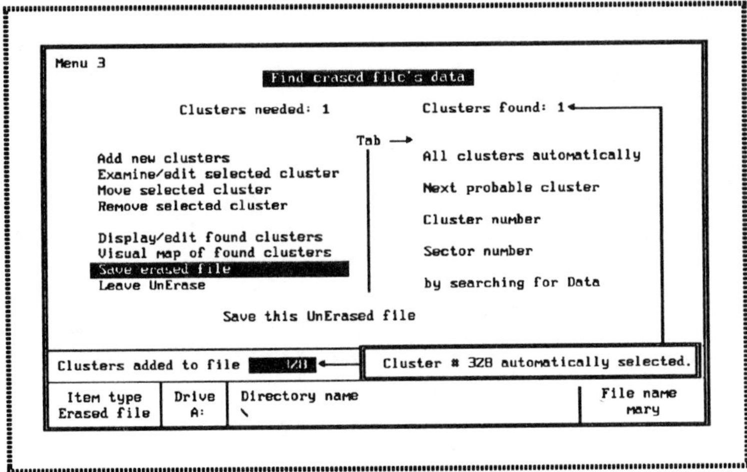

Figure 10-33

The highlight has automatically jumped to Save. However, inspect the contents of the selected file before you decide to save it. Enter

d

The next screen display shows the contents of the selected disk sector. Remember that a cluster will usually have more than one sector. The Norton Utilities program will display one sector, 512 bytes, at a time. At the bottom of the screen **...more** appears. This indicates that there is more data in this cluster than appears on the screen. At the top of the display you see the cluster and sector numbers. How do you know that this data belongs to the MARY file? A good indication is that the programmer left a note in the file to indicate what the file is and when it was made. Notes such as this are often included in source code files for computer

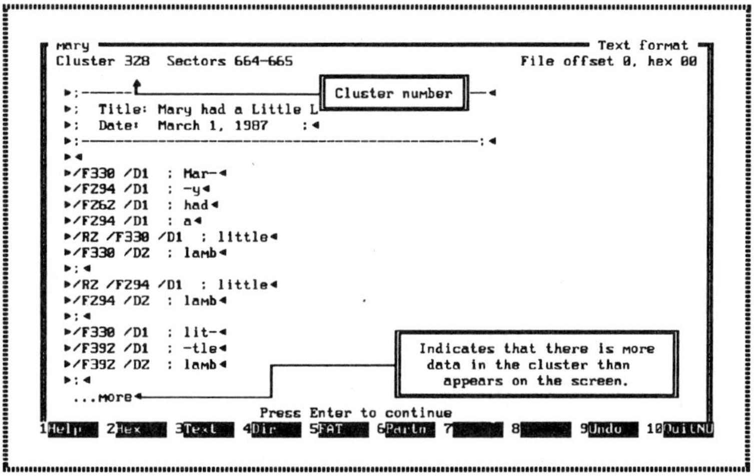

```
mary                                                        Text format
Cluster 328  Sectors 664-665                          File offset 0, hex 00

 ►:-------                                   ---◄
 ►:  Title: Mary had a Little L
 ►:  Date:  March 1, 1987      :◄
 ►:-----------------------------------------------:◄
 ►◄
 ►/F330 /D1   : Mar-◄
 ►/F294 /D1   : -y◄
 ►/F262 /D1   : had◄
 ►/F294 /D1   : a◄
 ►/R2 /F330 /D1   : little◄
 ►/F330 /D2   : lamb◄
 ►:◄
 ►/R2 /F294 /D1   : little◄
 ►/F294 /D2   : lamb◄
 ►:◄
 ►/F330 /D1   : lit-◄
 ►/F392 /D1   : -tle◄
 ►/F392 /D2   : lamb◄
 ►:◄
  ...more◄
                        Press Enter to continue
1Help  2Hex  3Text  4Dir  5FAT  6Partn  7      8      9Undo  10QuitNU
```

Cluster number

Indicates that there is more data in the cluster than appears on the screen.

Figure 10-34

programs, and in batch files. They help users understand the purpose and structure of the program. In this case the note helped confirm that this data belongs to the MARY file.

To see the next sector of data, enter

[Pg Dn]

The next sector is displayed. This sector contains an <end of file> marker, another clue indicating that you have recovered all the data that once belonged to MARY.

Now that you have inspected the contents of the file, you can return to the UnErase menu. Enter

↵

It is now time to save the file. Select the save command by entering

s

The Norton Utilities program writes the information necessary to recover the file, to the disk. When a file is recovered, all the information written to the disk is a modification to the directory and the file allocation table that reestablishes the selected clusters as a file. The contents of the clusters are not affected because they are already written to the disk.

It has taken you a few minutes to recover this file using UnErase. The steps that you have taken manually are the same ones that Quick Unerase does automatically. It is a good rule of thumb to always use Quick Unerase to recover files that have not been overwritten since it is faster and simpler. The Norton Utilities UnErase is needed when files have been partially overwritten.

Recovery of partially overwritten files is the next objective. Return to the UnErase menu by entering

↵

Exit the Norton Utilities program by entering

```
[F10]
```

Partial File Recovery

Partial recovery of files requires that you have some idea of the information that was stored in that file. If you have no idea what the information in the file was, you have no basis upon which to reconstruct the file. Partial recovery means that you are looking for specific information that was part of an erased file.

UnErase gives you a chance to search and look at the data clusters on the disk that are not presently in use by another file. If you are lucky, you may be able to find some of the missing data and recover it.

The file slated for recovery, FILE1.BAT, a file erased from the disk earlier, is one of several batch files used by the Norton Utilities demo programs. To create this situation you will partially overwrite FILE1.BAT.

To duplicate what would happen in normal use of a disk after files have been erased, use the EDLIN program to create some very simple text files. Remember that each file you create, no matter how small in actual content, will cause DOS to allocate an entire disk cluster. Create the first file by entering

```
edlin a:file0001.tst ↵
i ↵
This is a sample file. ↵
[Ctrl/c]
e ↵
```

Take a shortcut in making the next file by simply copying the last one you make. Enter

```
copy a:file0001.tst a:file0002.tst ↵
```

Make another file with EDLIN this time. Enter

```
edlin a:file0003.tst ↵
i ↵
This text might overwrite erased data. ↵
[Ctrl/c]
e ↵
```

Now make a copy of that file. Enter

```
copy a:file0003.tst a:file0004.tst ↵
```

The new files have used up some of the disk space formerly occupied by the erased files in the disk in drive A. But how much? Is there any part of the erased files left? The first step is to use Quick Unerase to see if the file is still intact. Enter

```
qu a: ↵
```

The Quick Unerase reports that none of the erased files on A can be unerased. This means that your only hope of recovering some of the data that was part of FILE1.BAT is to use the main Norton Utilities program. It is possible that the new files you have placed on the disk since the erasure, FILE0001.TST, and so on, have not overwritten the data that used to belong to FILE1.BAT. Remember that writing to the disk changes both the directory and the data clusters. When you add new files to a disk, the directory begins overwriting the erased filenames with the new filenames. Keep in mind that the name of an erased file remains in the directory with only the first letter removed until a new filenames is added.

You cannot jump to the conclusion that because there are no filenames listed for unerasing that some or all of the data that once belonged to those files are also overwritten. The differences in size between files may lead to a number of different situations. If large files are erased and small files added, some or all of the data of the erased files may still be intact. If the data you are looking for is valuable, it may be worth your while to determine if the data is really gone or simply lost because the directory and file allocation table have lost track of the data.

In this example your goal is to see if some or all of the information that was once in the **FILE1.BAT** file can be restored. To do this you must have a knowledge of the contents of that file. The entire contents of FILE1.BAT is several pages long. Below are two sections of that file from the beginning and the end, respectively.

Listing 10.1. Beginning FILE1.BAT

```
echo off
    cls
    if "%1" == "/bw" goto START
    if "%2" == "/bw" goto START
    SA bright yellow on blue
:START
    echo
    echo
    echo
    echo
    echo
    echo
    echo
    echo
    echo
    echo
    echo
    echo
    echo
    echo
    echo
    echo
    echo
    echo
    echo
    echo
    echo
    echo
    echo
    echo
    BEEP /f294 /d5
    pause
    BEEP /f440 /d2 /r2
    if "%1" == "/bw" goto SI
    if "%2" == "/bw" goto SI
    SA bright cyan on black
```

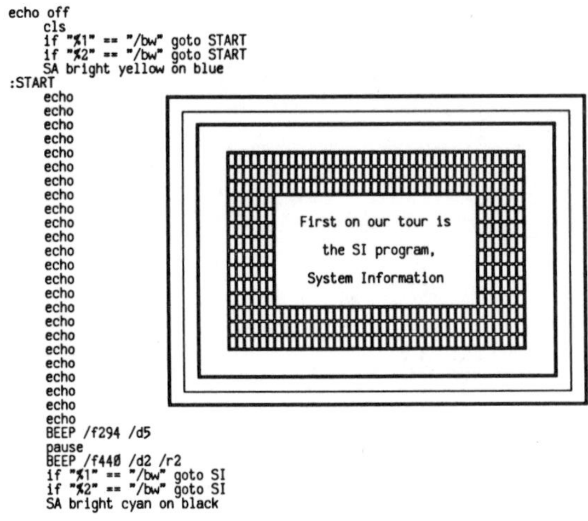
First on our tour is
the SI program,
System Information

Listing 10.2. End FILE1.BAT

```
:END
echo off
cls
SA bright white on blue
echo
echo
echo
echo
echo
echo
echo
echo
echo
echo
echo
echo
echo
echo
TM stop /n
echo
echo
echo
echo
echo
echo
echo
echo
echo
echo
ASK "  ",
SA normal
cls
```

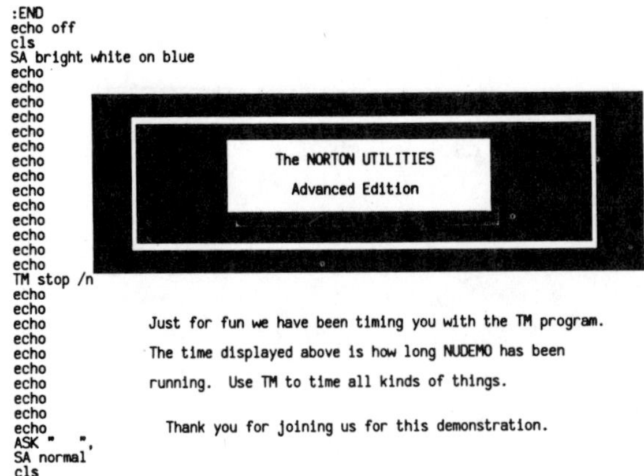
The NORTON UTILITIES
Advanced Edition

Just for fun we have been timing you with the TM program.
The time displayed above is how long NUDEMO has been
running. Use TM to time all kinds of things.

Thank you for joining us for this demonstration.

> You can get the full listing of this batch by placing the Norton Utilities Disk 1 in drive A and entering the command TYPE A:FILE1.BAT>PRN.
>
> Remember to replace the disk with the one you are using for this exercise after you print the file.

You will not always have a printed copy of the file and may only remember certain key words or phrases. In attempting partial recoveries you must use whatever clues you have to try to locate data. If you can locate a key word or phrase, you will probably recognize the rest of the data when you see it.

At this point, you face a decision. Should you attempt to recover whatever may be left of the file? The answer is based on two factors.

1. How important is the data in this file?

2. Do you know enough about the file to search for and recognize its contents? The only way to judge if data belongs to the file is if you inspect the data clusters and can identify the information visually.

> Because knowledge of the information contained in the file is crucial, it is very hard to recover files you know nothing about.

Activate the Norton Utilities program. Enter

nu a:↵

The next step is to select a file to unerase. Enter

us

Unfortunately there are no names of files to unerase.

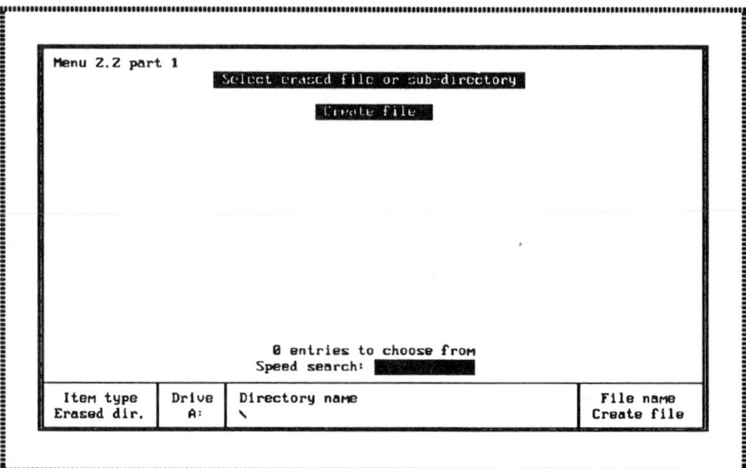

Figure 10-35

This does not mean all of the data is unrecoverable. But it does place you at an additional disadvantage because the directory entry for the file that you want to recover has been overwritten. This means information about the starting cluster and size of the file you are looking for is gone.

The starting cluster and file size are significant clues. The UnErase program uses these values to make a logical guess as to what clusters belong to that file. The assumption is made that a file was probably written in consecutive clusters when possible. If the starting cluster was 1000, and the file was 8 clusters in size, you would guess that the data in 1000 through 1007 make up the file. If you found that those clusters were free, that is, not in use by another file, you might assume that you can unerase the file based on that information. This is a simplified description of what happens in the QU (Quick Unerase) program.

To proceed you must create a new file, the currently highlighted option. Enter

↵

Enter the name of the new file, choosing one that does not conflict with any existing filenames. Enter

`recover1.tst ↵`

You are now ready to use the commands on the Unerase menu to locate and recover what, if any, is left of the batch file you want to restore. Enter

`u`

The UnErase menu appears. Note that because this is a new file, the program cannot estimate the number of clusters needed for recovery.

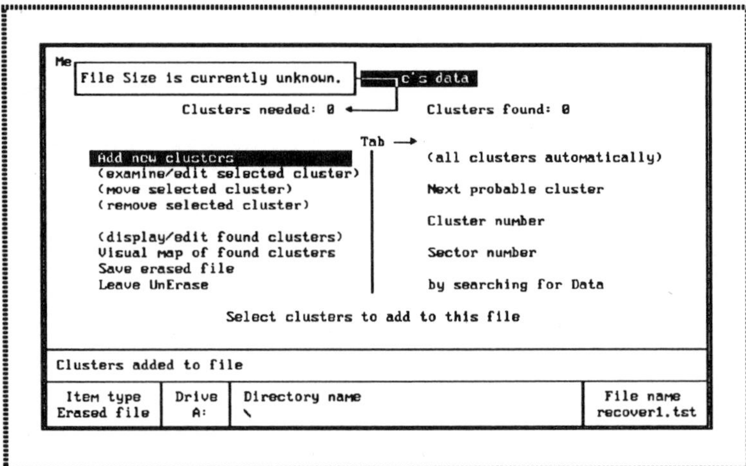

Figure 10-36

Your next task is to locate clusters that might have belonged to the file. Select the Add clusters command by entering

a

The first option, automatic select, is not available because the directory information that it uses to make the best guess is overwritten. You have three other options.

Next

Selecting next displays the next unused cluster on the disk. In this case it would automatically default to the first cluster shown in the FAT not in use by any other file. If you were without a clue as to how to proceed, and desperate to recover the data, you might simply begin by browsing the unused data clusters looking for something that you recognize. This is a course of last resort. Remember a 20 megabyte hard disk has over 10,000 data clusters.

Cluster/Sector

These two options display a specific cluster- or sector-based number. These options only make sense if you have some way of knowing what cluster or sector number the data might be stored in. For example, suppose you created two files FILE1.BAT and FILE2.BAT, one right after the other. By mistake you erased FILE1.BAT when you meant to erase FILE2.BAT. Where would you start to look for the erased data?

One guess would be in any open clusters on the disk that come directly before the cluster that begins FILE2.BAT. Using the Norton Utilities program to look at the file directory you could find the starting cluster number of FILE2.BAT, for instance, 290. You might guess that cluster 289 was the last part of FILE1.BAT. In that case you might enter 289 and display the cluster to see if your guess was correct. If so, you would then select 288, 287 and so on, until you ran out of data. You can see that file recovery is detective work as much as it is computer work.

Search

This option, the one you are most likely to start with, allows you to locate a specific key set of characters or values.

To begin a search, enter

d

The search menu appears.

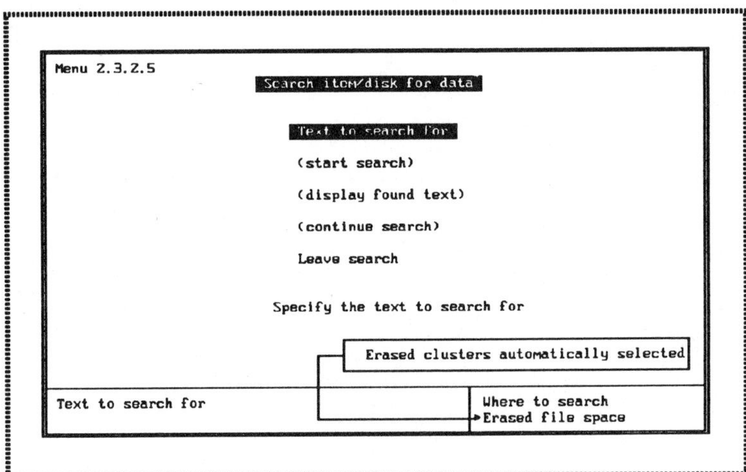

Figure 10-37

Because you selected search from the UnErase menu, the program automatically selected to search only the erased file space. The next step is to tell the program what you are looking for. Enter

↵

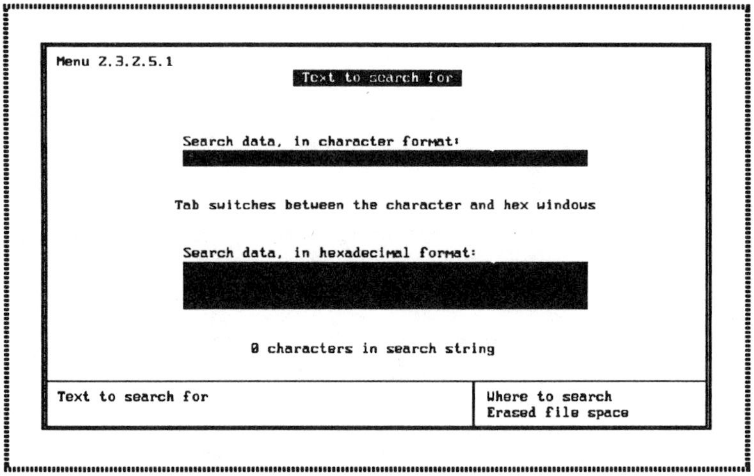

```
Menu 2.3.2.5.1
                    Text to search for

        Search data, in character format:


      Tab switches between the character and hex windows

        Search data, in hexadecimal format:



               0 characters in search string

Text to search for                        Where to search
                                          Erased file space
```

Figure 10-38

The search key can be entered in two forms: (1) **Text,** Normal keyboard characters, appropriate for search text files; and (2) **Hex Values,** an option that allows you to enter a sequence of hex bytes. You can use this to match any type of data sequence.

You can move between the two entry windows with [Tab]. Note that entries made in either window will be echoed in the other, meaning that you can enter a search key as part text and part hex values if necessary. This enables you to search for control or graphics characters that might be embedded in a text file.

In this case you have the contents of the FILE1.BAT file to use as a search key. The file begins with:

```
echo off
cls 3
if "%1" == "bw" goto START
if "%2" == "bw" goto START
SA bright yellow on blue
```

The **echo off** and **cls** commands are very common. But the next line, **if "%1" = = "/bw" goto START** is probably unique. To see if that line still exists on the disk, enter it as the search key. To save time, enter only the most unique section of the line, **"%1"= = "/bw"**.

"% 1" = = "/bw" represents a logical criterion used with the DOS batch command IF. The IF/GOTO part of the line is common because it is a standard DOS command. However, the specific criterion "% 1" = = "/bw" is probably unique to this program. Thus the reason it is selected as the search key.

Enter the characters to search for. Note that in this kind of search the keys must be entered exactly as they are in the actual file. Difference in case are not significant, but space characters are. Enter

"%1"   "/bw"

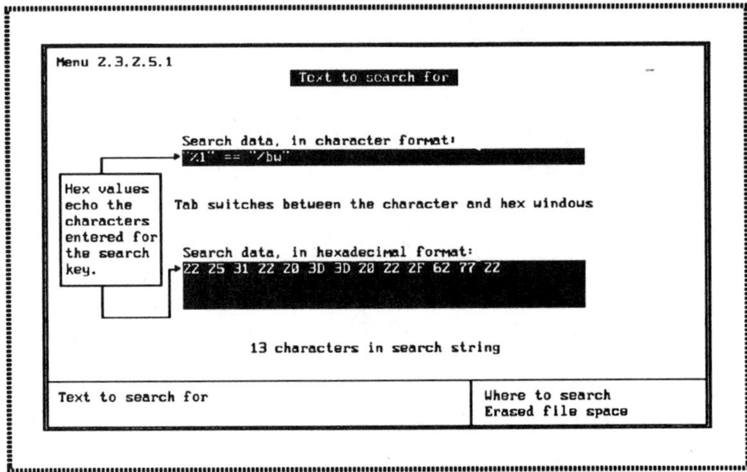

Figure 10-39

To complete the key, enter

You return to the search menu. Note that the key value now appears at the bottom of the screen.

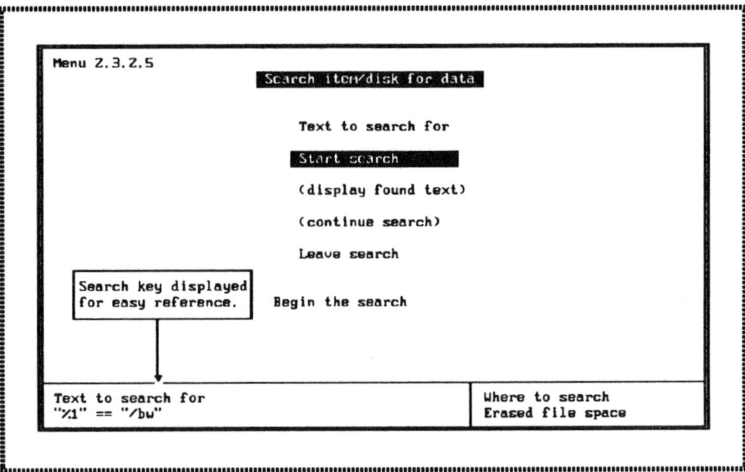

Figure 10-40

Begin the search by entering

S

The program will start with the first erased cluster, 313, and stop when it finds a match.

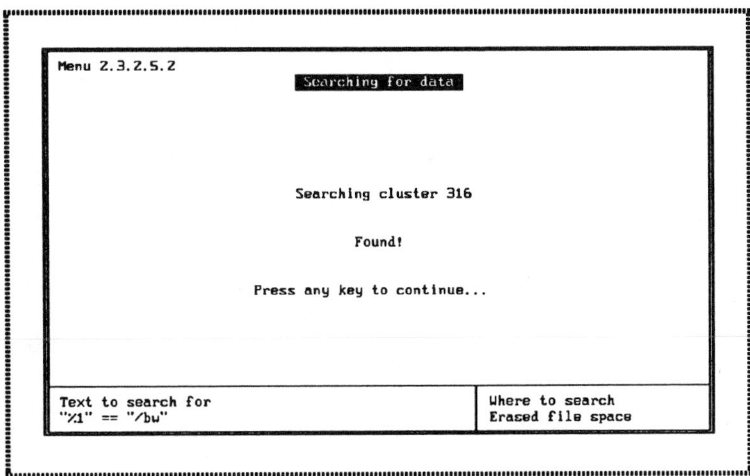

Figure 10-41

To continue, enter

↵

The program now displays three options.

Display the contents of the cluster.

Add the cluster to a list of clusters for the recovered file.

Skip this cluster, do not add it to the new file.

The first step is to display the cluster to see if it is really the one you were looking for. Enter

d

The program displays the contents of the cluster in hex format.

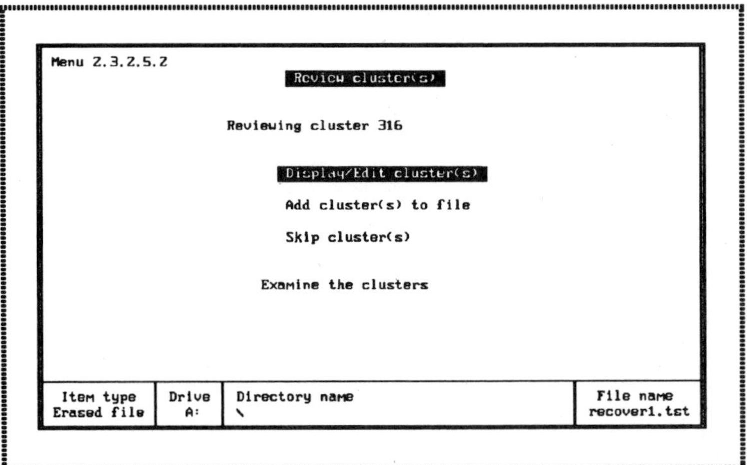

Figure 10-42

Since this is a batch file, character content, you might find the Text format easier to read. Enter

[F3]

```
recover1.tst                                         Text format
Cluster 316   Sectors 640-641                     Offset 0, hex 00

echo off                              Search key highlighted
cls
if "%1" == "/bw" goto START
if "%2" == "/bw" goto START
SA bright yellow on blue
:START
echo
echo
echo
echo
echo
echo
echo
echo
echo
echo          .......  First on our tour is  .......
echo
echo          .......     the SI program.    .......
...more
                 Press Enter to continue
1Help 2Hex 3Text 4Dir 5FAT 6Partn 7 8 9Undo 10QuitNU
```

Figure 10-43

This is the beginning of the file you are looking for. It would have been easier to identify it had the programmer placed a REM statement in the file.

To see the Review Cluster menu, enter

↵

To add the cluster, enter

a

Return to the search menu. The first cluster has been located and you can assume that the rest of the file is on the disk.

> As with any of these assumptions, you might be wrong. One factor that may produce a false sense of accomplishment is if the FILE1.BAT had been created on the disk. In writing a program, it is likely that the file was written and revised a great number of times. Programs always need revisions. Editing a file over and over again will cause the editing or word processing program to write and rewrite the file a number of times. The beginning of a file may end up written in a number of erased clusters depending on how many times it was revised. In this circumstance you may be faced with a number of erased clusters that have similar or identical information, each one having been the beginning of one of the versions of the file that was revised many times. In such a case, I generally assume that the last version (highest cluster number) or the largest version (most clusters) is the correct one. Of course, that assumption can be mistaken but it may be the best guess you can make at the time.

> In this example, since the file was part of a purchased program, it was probably copied to the disk rather than actually edited on that disk. When you are working on your own hard disk the opposite may be true. In that circumstance, you would probably continue to search for the first key to see if there were additional erased copies on the disk before you concluded that you had the beginning cluster of the file.

With the beginning of the file located, the next step is to find that last cluster. In this instance you would then assume that all the unused clusters in between belong to that file, and add them all to the recovery file. This is not absolutely the correct course but it is the most logical one to follow when you find both the first and last clusters intact.

To find the last cluster you need to select a unique looking item from the end of the file. To specify a new search key, enter

```
t
```

The end of the FILE1.BAT looks like this:

```
echo                Thank you for joining us for this demonstration.
ASK "   ",
SA normal
cls
```

The words **Thank you** are pretty unusual in computer programs. Enter

```
Thank you ↵
```

Start the search again by entering

```
s
```

This time a match is found in cluster 326. Display the information by entering

```
↵
d
[F3]
```

```
recover1.tst                                              Text format
Cluster 326  Sectors 660-661                        Offset 512, hex 0200
more...
 ►............... ◄
 ►echo      ...........................................................
  ...... ◄
 ►echo      ...........................................................
  ...... ◄
 ►TM stop /n◄
 ►echo .◄
 ►echo .◄
 ►echo            Just for fun we have been timing you with the TM program
  .◄
 ►echo .◄
 ►echo            The time displayed above is how long NUDEMO has been  ◄
 ►echo .◄
 ►echo            running.  Use TM to time all kinds of things.◄
 ►echo .◄
 ►echo .◄
 ►echo              Thank you for joining us for this demo


                          Press Enter to continue
1Help  2Hex  3Text  4Dir  5FAT  6Partn  7      8      9Undo  10QuitNU
```

Figure 10-44

You have found the end of the file, cluster 326. But take a closer look at the end. The word **demonstration** is cut off. It seems that the last few characters of the file lie in the next cluster, 327. Your best estimate tells you that you should use clusters 316 through 327 as the data for your recovered file. The search has located the cluster; you must now select them as part of the file.

> It is a good sign that the ending cluster is a higher number than the beginning cluster. If it was not, it would have caused you to re-examine your assumption that the file was in consecutive, ascending clusters. The implication would be that the file's recovery was going to be much more complex then finding the beginning and end points.
>
> It might also be a clue that there were multiple versions of the same file on the disk with that or different names. Remember that many programs create backup files when working. This means that there may be erased sectors that once belonged to a backup file on the same disk with the data that once belonged to the file you are looking for.
>
> File recovery is neither easy nor clear cut.

Leave the search menus by entering

s

1

You are now back at the UnErase menu. Note that the starting cluster number for your file appears at the bottom of the screen and the tally of 1 cluster is registered at the top.

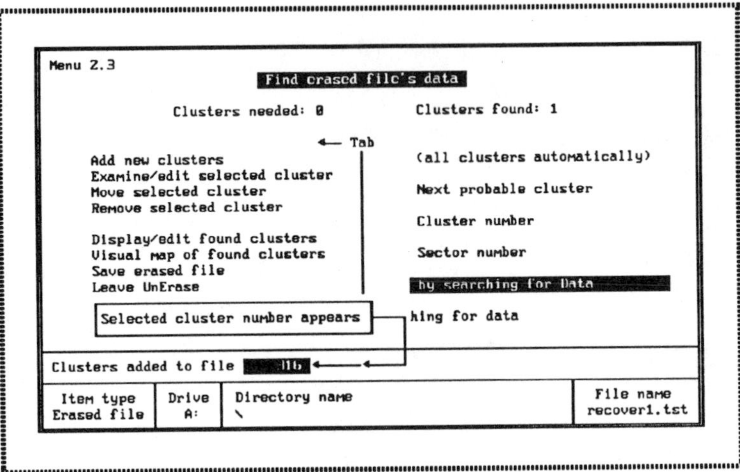

Figure 10-45

Because you know the numbers of the clusters you want to recover, use the Cluster option to enter those values.

C

The cluster selection menu appears and you can enter a starting and ending cluster value.

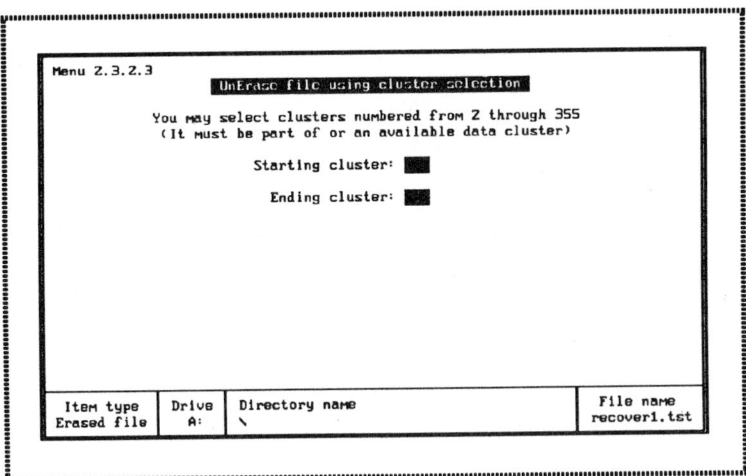

Figure 10-46

Enter the cluster numbers for the beginning and the end of the file. Keep in mind that 316 has already been selected for this file. Entering it again would prompt the program to think there was a conflict. Begin the cluster selection with 317. Enter

317 ↵
327 ↵

The program displays a message that clusters between 317 and 327 are selected for review.

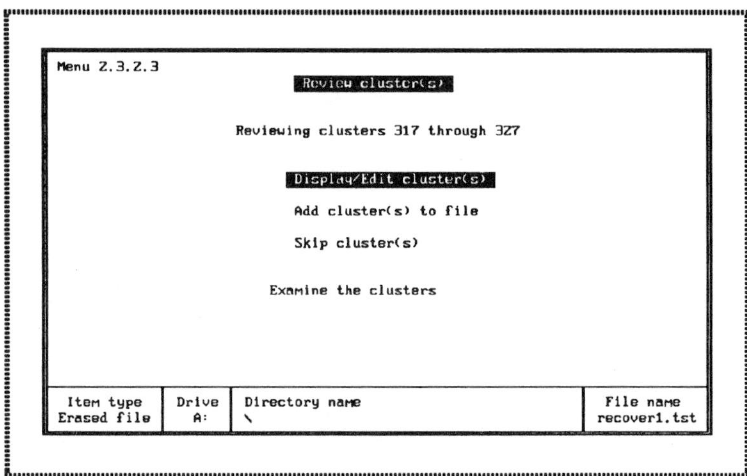

Figure 10-47

You can display the clusters one by one, or assume that you are correct and add them all. To save time, enter

a

The program displays the UnErase menu again. This time, note that 12 clusters have been selected. The bottom of the screen shows the clusters in the order in which they have been selected. The highlight is on the last cluster added, 327.

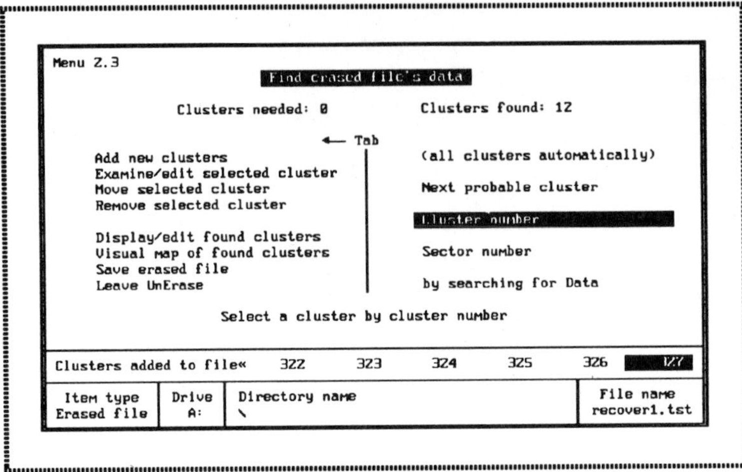

Figure 10-48

Now that you have selected the clusters, you can move to the left side of the UnErase menu by entering

[Tab]

The left side of the menu provides options for removing, moving and displaying the selected clusters. For example, cluster 327 was selected as a guess that it contained the last lines of the file. You might want to check that assumption before you save the recovered file.

Notice that the highlight at the bottom of the screen, located on 327, can be used to select different cluster numbers by using the left and right arrow keys. Enter

e

The cluster's contents show that it contains the rest of the word **demonstration**, and the end of the file.

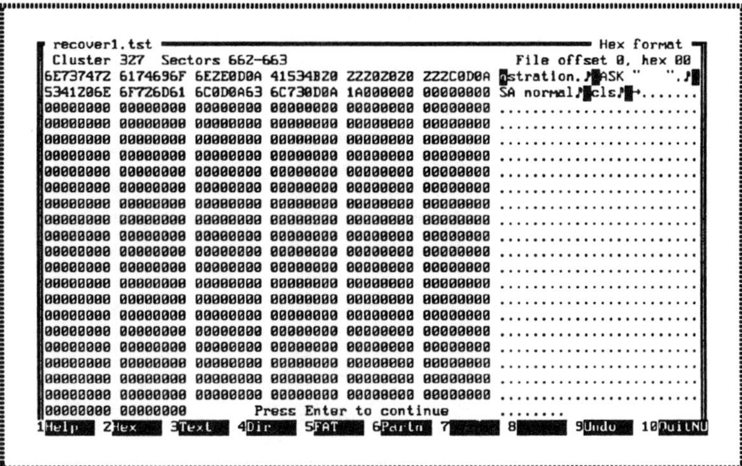

Figure 10-49

Return to the menu by entering

↵

To save the selected clusters as a file, enter

s

The Save UnErase file menu appears. Because you have selected more clusters than the directory entry showed (a new file will always have zero), you are asked if you want the file size adjusted. This is important since DOS uses the file size to determine how much of the disk to read. Enter

a

The file is recovered.

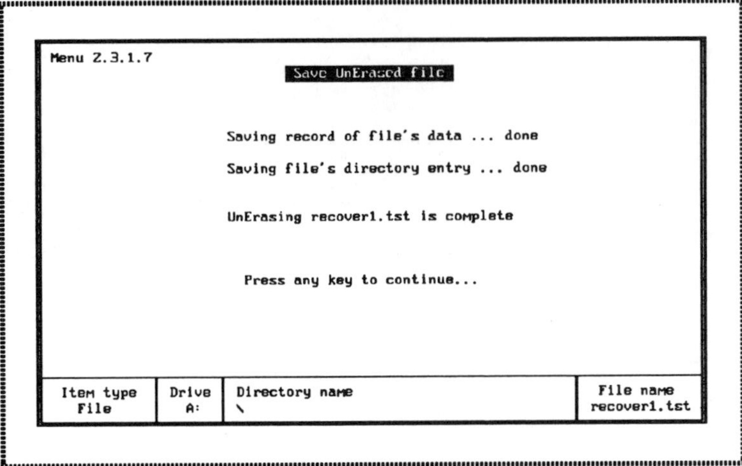

Figure 10-50

Exit the program by entering

[F10]

The process of file recovery is as complex as the system of file storage at times. To recover a file you need to be part detective and part programmer. But the process is interesting, and when needed, a lifesaver.

The key to locating files is to have some salient character in mind that will identify the data in an erased cluster as belonging to a particular file. If the file is a text file the contents of the file can be used as they were in the previous illustration. Text files are easy to recover because their contents are visually identifiable and recovering even part of a document is useful. The file can usually be loaded into a word processor and the missing information can be re-entered.

Other types of files are more difficult. Spreadsheet files are usually very hard to recover because they are not stored in text format. In Section III, under searching, the file header used for a 1-2-3 Release 2 worksheet was shown to be the hex sequence 0000020006040600. This is important since 1-2-3 will not load a partial file if the beginning sector is missing. If you can locate the beginning of a worksheet, 1-2-3 will load the file. If the correct file ending is missing, an error will be produced but the portion of the file recovered will appear on the spreadsheet. If you save the file under a new name, 1-2-3 will place the correct end of file information into the new file.

The same problem exists with dBASE III files. If the header section is missing the data portion of the file will not load. Since dBASE III files are mostly ASCII text files, you might be able to load them into a word processor. Not all word processing programs will allow this because the ASCII portion of a dBASE III file does not contain LF/CR characters after each record. WordStar will only load a portion of such a file. Microsoft Word and the Norton Editor will load as much of the file as will fit into memory.

Once you have loaded the file you can recover the data through a rather laborious process. First, edit the file by placing a ↵ at the end of each record. Count the exact number of characters, including spaces, that make up each field. Then create a new structure for the text in dBASE III Plus that matches the exact character count for each field in the text file. Finally, use the APPEND FROM filename SDF to load the text into a new dBASE III structure.

The main Norton Utilities program provides a means of examining the patterns of the file structure produced by various programs. By looking at correctly written files you may find a clue as to the type of patterns that would identify the lost data.

One of the most common types of recovery that requires the use of the main Norton Utilities program, rather than QU, is a program crash during a file save. In a floppy disk system this is caused often by disk-full problems. I have also seen this same problem in many applications. When saving a file, the program appears to be working, the disk light goes on indicating writing is taking place, but the program crashes before the saving is complete.

The usual symptom is a file with zero bytes showing in the directory. This entry is caused by a problem that has taken place as a file is being updated. In most cases, part or all of the affected file is still on the disk. The zero bytes size shows that the program crashed before the new file size could be written into the directory. Naturally, writing the size of the file is the last part of the file saving process. It may well be that all the data has been safely stored in clusters before the crash.

The key is to find the first cluster of that file by searching for data or header information. When you find that header, make a best guess, as shown in the previous section, to allocate consecutive data clusters to the file. Most programs will recover from bad file endings if the file begins correctly.

The Norton Utilities programs provide a means by which you can make at least a valiant attempt to recover from a disaster. If nothing else you can learn a lot about your computer in the attempt.

Unerasing Directories

File recovery can sometimes involve the recovery of the directory, if the directory that contained the files has been removed. The DOS command RD or the NCD program are capable of removing a directory from the disk.

In file recovery it may be necessary to recover a directory that has been removed in order to recover a file that was contained within that directory. The

Norton Utilities package contains a program, UD (Unremove Directory), which will accomplish this.

To illustrate the use of the UD program, create a directory on the disk in drive A of some files, and then delete the files and the directory.

Create a directory on A by entering

```
md a:\testdir ↵
```

Copy some files into that directory. Enter

```
copy a:file*.* a:\testdir ↵
```

Use the NCD (Norton Change directory) program to display the tree structure of the disk in drive A. Enter

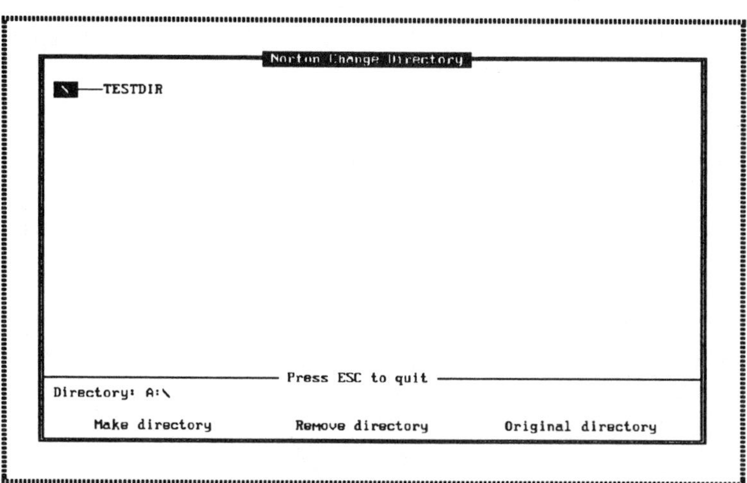

Figure 10-51

The display reveals the new directory. Exit the NCD program by entering

Now reverse the process and delete the files and the directory. Enter

```
del a:\testdir\*.* ↵
y ↵
```

Remove the directory by entering

```
rd a:\testdir ↵
```

Suppose that you want to recover one of the files that was located in the TESTDIR directory. Enter

```
qu a: ↵
```

The QU (Quick Unerase) cannot find the names of the erased files. This is because the names of the files are listed in the directory TESTDIR, not the root directory. Before the files can be recovered, you must re-establish the directory that contain those files.

Keep in mind the directory entry is listed as a file entry in its parent directory. In this case the parent directory is the root directory of drive A.

To confirm this, use the main Norton Utilities program to list the root directory of drive A. Enter

```
nu a: ↵
↵ (4 times)
e
[Pg Dn]
```

The display shows the entry for the TESTDIR directory with the first letter removed. DOS handles directory removal in the same way that it does file erasing. The same technique used to unerase a file works with a directory. The directory is really a data entry in cluster 313, which contains the directory information for the files that were part of the TESTDIR directory.

```
Root dir                                                  Directory format
Sector 6 in root directory                                 Offset 0, hex 00
                                                           Attributes
Filename Ext     Size      Date       Time     Cluster  Arc R/O Sys Hid Dir Vol

ED       EXE    26938    3/01/87   4:00 pm      186
BI       EXE    14750    3/01/87   4:00 pm      213
AM       EXE     6234    3/01/87   4:00 pm      228
BS       EXE    17276    3/01/87   4:00 pm      235
BD       EXE    15096    3/01/87   4:00 pm      252
AL       EXE     7456    3/01/87   4:00 pm      267
WIPEDISK EXE    10338    3/01/87   4:00 pm      275
WIPEFILE EXE    10936    3/01/87   4:00 pm      286
NU       HLP    10897    3/01/87   4:00 pm      297   Removed directory
                                                     appears as a deleted
 ILE0002 TST       25    1/03/88   6:30 am        3  A file.
 ILE0003 TST       41    1/03/88   6:32 am      311  A
 ILE0004 TST       41    1/03/88   6:32 am      312  Arc
 ECOVER1 TST    12288    1/04/88   1:08 am      316  Arc
σESTDIR                  1/05/88   1:33 am      313                 Dir
TREEINFO NCD       43    1/05/88   1:43 am      333  Arc

              Filenames beginning with 'σ' indicate erased entries
                          Press Enter to continue
1Help  2Hex  3Text  4Dir  5FAT  6Partn  7  8  9Undo  10QuitNU
```

Figure 10-52

Exit the program by entering

[F10]

The UD program requires that you know the exact pathname of the directory you want to recover. Enter

ud a:\testdir ↵

The program responds by locating and unremoving the directory. In addition the program lists the filenames of the erased files that are listed in the recovered directory.

```
Goodbye from The Norton Utilities, active for 7 seconds

[C:\]ud a:\testdir
UD-UnRemove Directory, Advanced Edition, (C) Copr 1987, Peter Norton

Directory of A:\
   Removed directory specification: TESTDIR.*
   Number of removed directories: 1
   Number that can be UnRemoved: 1

   ?ESTDIR            <DIR>         1:33 am  Tue Jan  5 88
Enter the first character of the filename: T

   ?ile0001.tst          25 bytes   6:30 am  Sun Jan  3 88
   ?ileinfo.fi        2,601 bytes   4:00 pm  Sun Mar  1 87
   ?ile0002.tst          25 bytes   6:30 am  Sun Jan  3 88
   ?ile0003.tst          41 bytes   6:32 am  Sun Jan  3 88
   ?ile0004.tst          41 bytes   6:32 am  Sun Jan  3 88

Files included in A:\TESTDIR

'TESTDIR' UnRemoved

[C:\]
```

Figure 10-53

Now that the directory is established, the path is open to recovery of the files that were part of that directory. Apply the QU program to files in the TESTDIR directory.

> Note that by using f*.* with the QU program, you are telling the program to use the F as the first letter of all the files recovered. The *.* following the F tells QU to unerase all recoverable files. Because of the nature of the QU program the file specification is treated differently than it would be with any other program.

```
qu a:\testdir\f*.* ↵
```

```
[C:\]qu a:\testdir\f*.*
QU-Quick UnErase, Advanced Edition, (C) Copr 1987, Peter Norton

Directory of A:\TESTDIR
   Erased file specification: F*.*
   Number of erased files: 5
   Number that can be Quick-UnErased: 5

   ?ile0001.tst        25 bytes   6:30 am  Sun Jan  3 88
'file0001.tst' Quick-UnErased.

   ?ile0002.tst        25 bytes   6:30 am  Sun Jan  3 88
'file0002.tst' Quick-UnErased.

   ?ile0003.tst        41 bytes   6:32 am  Sun Jan  3 88
'file0003.tst' Quick-UnErased.

   ?ile0004.tst        41 bytes   6:32 am  Sun Jan  3 88
'file0004.tst' Quick-UnErased.

   ?ileinfo.fi      2,601 bytes   4:00 pm  Sun Mar  1 87
'fileinfo.fi' Quick-UnErased.

[C:\]
```

Figure 10-54

11

DISK ERRORS, UNFORMAT, AND OTHER SKILLS

Wiping Data Clean

Much has been made of the fact that DOS takes a short cut when files are erased, making unerasing possible. Suppose you wanted to make sure that data was completely expunged from a file or an entire disk. The DOS DEL command would not accomplish this. The Norton Utilities program provides two programs, WIPEFILE and WIPEDISK that actually write entire new sectors containing all zero values to the disk. These commands eradicate the previous data by writing new information that replaces the old information. This type of operation is used where security requires that erased information not be recovered by unauthorized personnel.

To eradicate, not simply erase a file, the WIPEFILE command is used. As an example, eradicate the RECOVER1.TST file that you worked so hard to recover. This file is selected because you know that it is stored in clusters 316–327. It will then be easy for you to verify that the clusters have been wiped clean of data by examining those clusters specifically.

The WIPEFILE and WIPEDISK programs place a value of 0 in each byte. Note that the value is the hex value 0 called a nul value, not the ASCII character zero, which has a hex value of 30 and a decimal value 48. You can select a different value by using the /V switch with the decimal value you want to use. For example, /V65 would fill the data areas with A.

You can also specify a number of repetitions for the wiping. This adds to the security factor by recording information several times in the same spot.

> Since disk information is recorded magnetically it is, in theory, possible to use special electronic equipment to try to construct the faint magnetic image of the value that had previously been placed on the disk. Remember the recovery effort made on the 16 minute gap in the Watergate tapes!

Enter

```
wipefile a:recover1.tst/v65/r3 ↵
```

The program displays the selected options, **filename, operation, wipe count,** and **character**.

```
[C:\]wipefile a:recover1.tst/v65/r3
WF-Wipe Files, Advanced Edition, (C) Copr 1987, Peter Norton

Action:        Wipe the file
Filename:      RECOVER1.TST
Wipe count:    3
Wipe value:    65

Directory: A:\
    recover1.tst - Do you wish to Wipe this file (Y/N) ?
```

Figure 11-1

Confirm the operation by entering

```
y
```

If the wiping was successful, then clusters 316 through 327 should display all A's if you load their contents with the main Norton Utilities program. Enter

```
nu a: ↵
e
c
l
```

Enter the cluster numbers.

```
316 ↵
327 ↵
```

Display the information, enter

```
e
```

The screen shows all A characters.

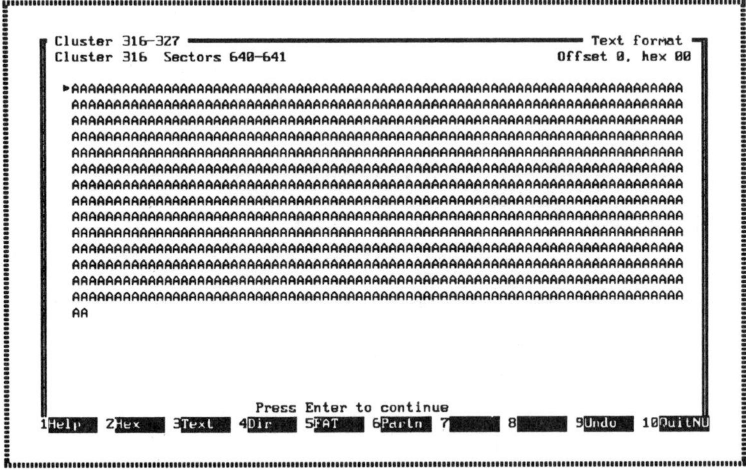

Figure 11-2

Use [Pg Dn] to look at the remaining clusters. When you are finished, exit the program by entering

```
[F10]
```

The /G switch is used to perform a disk wipe in accordance with government security standards set by the Department of Defense. The WIPEFILE and WIPEDISK commands also accept the standard switches, /S for subdirectory search, and /LOG to create a printer acceptable output. For example, if you wanted to wipe all the

BAK files on a hard disk, and record the dialogue on your printer, you would begin by opening a channel to the printer with

```
[Ctrl/p]
```

Then enter the command

```
wipefile \*.bak/s/log ↵
```

Turn off the printer by entering

```
[Ctrl/p]
```

> You can take a shortcut by using the DOS redirection command >PRN to redirect the output to the printer. Example:
>
> wipefile *.bak/s/log>prn

Another use of the WIPEFILE program is to delete files globally from a disk by using the /N switch. The /N switch tells the WIPEFILE program to perform the equivalent of the DOS DEL command and simply mark files as erased instead of wiping their contents clear. At first this might seem like a useless facility because DEL will do the same thing. However, there is one convenient difference. The WIPEFILE program can be made to search an entire disk by using /S from the root. This means that you can delete all the files, or the files that match a specific specification, in all directories, with a single command. This cannot be done with the DOS DEL command, which will operate on only one directory at a time. The /N (non-wipe) switch saves time by not wiping the disk contents, but just marking the directory entries as DOS does.

For example, suppose you wanted to delete all the BAK files from your hard disk. You would enter

```
wipefile \*.bak/s/n ↵
```

To delete all the files from a disk you would enter

```
wipefile \*.*/s/n ↵
```

Remember to take great care in using these programs since data removed in this way is not subject to unerasure.

Error Reading Drive

The most dreaded message that DOS can display about your hard disk is **Error reading drive C.** This error indicates that DOS has been unable to read the data stored in one of the sectors on the hard disk. The media on hard disks and floppy disks alike are vulnerable to failure, that is, the recording surface can contain a flaw which prevents the computer from reading the data contained in that sector. Since the coating of a disk is a magnetic medium, minute variations in the density of the coating can cause fluctuations in the intensity of the magnetic signals placed there by the disk drive. A flaw may be such that the computer can read the sector sometimes, and not others.

When such an error is encountered, DOS displays three alternatives:

A **Abort.** This cancels the command or the program that caused DOS to attempt the disk operation. Choosing abort may result in the loss of the data you were trying to save, since most programs are not prepared to deal with this type of error.

R **Retry.** This tells DOS to attempt the disk operation again. Sometimes, when the flaw is marginal, retrying will be successful. If it works you should quit the application as soon as possible and make a copy of the file. You should always Retry at least once. If it doesn't work you are no worse off then you were.

I **Ignore.** This option tells DOS to simply skip over that sector and continue with the next step in its operation. This will often allow you to complete the operation. But remember that the file you have just read or written may still contain the flawed sector. The next time you use the file, the same problem may arise.

DOS attempts to prevent this type of error by blocking out bad clusters that contain bad sectors when the disk is formatted. It is not unusual to have some bad sectors on a hard disk.

> Bad sectors are usually blocked out during the low level format of the hard disk. If any new problems arise while the high level formatting takes place, FORMAT C:, DOS marks those clusters as bad and reports the number of characters lost to bad sectors at the end of the formatting.

Disk Test

The DT (Disk Test) program is designed to help you handle problems that arise on your disks. DT cannot solve all the problems but it is a valuable tool. DT has three uses.

1. **Analysis.** The DT program performs tests on the disk data that will report to you the condition of the disk clusters and files.

2. **Recovery.** The DT program can be used to recover files corrupted by disk errors.

3. **Prevention.** Running DT can help to locate and isolate bad sectors before they corrupt files.

Disk Test can be run on either hard or floppy disks. The test performed by DT is different from that done by CHKDSK. In CHKDSK the test is one in which the data in the directory and the file allocation table are cross-correlated to locate any inconsistencies. The DT program actually attempts to read the information stored on the disk. For that reason the DT program takes much longer to operate.

The DT program can be run in one of two modes.

File In the file mode the DT program tests only the space currently shown to be used by files. This test is generally shorter than a full-disk test because it skips the root directory and File Allocation Table and any clusters not currently assigned to files.

An important aspect of the file test is that it will report the names of the files that contain problem sectors. By reading the name you can decide if you need to try to recover this file. For example, if the NU.EXE program reported an error you would probably not be concerned since you would have a copy of the program on the original floppy disk.

On the other hand, if the error was reported from a document or data file you would face the prospect of a loss of unique data if the file had not been copied or backed up.

Disk In the Disk Test mode, all of the sectors on the disk including the boot, root directory, file allocation table, and unused clusters are tested. The primary advantage of this mode is to locate potential problems before they are allocated to a file. When you locate a bad cluster the program reports if the cluster is in use by a file or not.

The DT program also provides an option in which both tests, disk then file, are performed consecutively. It is a good idea to run a DT at least once a month or more. Peter Norton Computing recommends that you perform the disk test every day. To perform both tests, enter

```
dt/b ↵
```

The DT program first tests the entire disk, sector by sector. It displays the number of clusters checked as it works through the disk. Remember, these tests take some time. A 20 megabyte hard disk has 10,355 clusters to check.

```
[C:\]dt/b
DT-Disk Test, Advanced Edition, (C) Copr 1987, Peter Norton

During the scan of the disk, you may press
BREAK (Control-C) to interrupt Disk Test

Test reading the entire disk C:, system area and data area
  The system area consists of boot, FAT, and directory
    No errors reading system area

  The data area consists of clusters numbered 2 - 10,355
    272
```

Figure 11-3

After the overall disk test the program then follows the directory tree and tests all the files on the hard disk. The test proceeds, directory by directory, displaying each filename as it does so. This part of the test should be shorter than the entire disk test but not always. The disk test proceeds in a straight path through all the sectors. The file test must jump around and test the clusters in the order in which they are used by the files, which is slower than going straight through the disk.

```
[C:\]dt/b
DT-Disk Test, Advanced Edition, (C) Copr 1987, Peter Norton

During the scan of the disk, you may press
BREAK (Control-C) to interrupt Disk Test

Test reading the entire disk C:, system area and data area
  The system area consists of boot, FAT, and directory
    No errors reading system area

  The data area consists of clusters numbered 2 - 10,355
    No errors reading data area

Test reading files
  Directory C:\
    File menu.og.bat
```

Figure 11-4

You can stop the test at any time by entering [Ctrl/c] or [Ctrl/Scroll Lock].

If you are lucky, the only messages from DT that you will see are the ones illustrated above. Below is an illustration of the type of messages that would be reported if errors were encountered during a total disk test. The command used for this test would be

```
dt/d ↵
```

```
    No errors reading system area

  The data area consists of clusters numbered 2 - 355
    130th cluster read error: in use by a file -- DANGER NOW
    134th cluster read error: in use by a file -- DANGER NOW
    139th cluster read error: in use by a file -- DANGER NOW
    143rd cluster read error: in use by a file -- DANGER NOW
    148th cluster read error: in use by a file -- DANGER NOW
    152nd cluster read error: in use by a file -- DANGER NOW
    157th cluster read error: in use by a file -- DANGER NOW
    161st cluster read error: in use by a file -- DANGER NOW
    166th cluster read error: in use by a file -- DANGER NOW
    170th cluster read error: in use by a file -- DANGER NOW
    175th cluster read error: in use by a file -- DANGER NOW
    179th cluster read error: in use by a file -- DANGER NOW
    184th cluster read error: in use by a file -- DANGER NOW
    188th cluster read error: in use by a file -- DANGER NOW
    193rd cluster read error: in use by a file -- DANGER NOW
    197th cluster read error: in use by a file -- DANGER NOW
    202nd cluster read error: in use by a file -- DANGER NOW
    206th cluster read error: in use by a file -- DANGER NOW
    211th cluster read error: in use by a file -- DANGER NOW
    215th cluster read error: in use by a file -- DANGER NOW
    220th cluster read error: in use by a file -- DANGER NOW
    221
```

DT reports errors in clusters already allocated to files.

Figure 11-5

Note that because the clusters are allocated to files, the DT program warns that there is **DANGER NOW!** The program is telling you that part or all of the data in the cluster is not readable. The disk test does not display the names of the files to which the clusters are allocated. That information can be found by running a File Test, the results of which are shown below. Example:

```
dt/f ↵
```

```
The data area consists of clusters numbered 2 - 355
  130th cluster read error: in use by a file -- DANGER NOW
  139th cluster read error: in use by a file -- DANGER NOW
  143rd cluster read error: in use by a file -- DANGER NOW
  148th cluster read error: in use by a file -- DANGER NOW
  152nd cluster read error: in use by a file -- DANGER NOW
  157th cluster read error: in use by a file -- DANGER NOW
  161st cluster read error: not currently in use — DANGER
  166th cluster read error: not currently in use — DANGER TO COME
  170th cluster read error: not currently in use — DANGER TO COME
  175th cluster read error: not currently in use — DANGER TO COME
  179th cluster read error: not currently in use — DANGER TO COME
  184th cluster read error: not currently in use — DANGER TO COME
  188th cluster read error: not currently in use — DANGER TO COME
  193rd cluster read error: not currently in use — DANGER TO COME
  197th cluster read error: not currently in use — DANGER TO COME
  202nd cluster read error: not currently in use — DANGER TO COME
  206th cluster read error: in use by a file -- DANGER NOW
  211th cluster read error: not currently in use — DANGER TO COME
  215th cluster read error: not currently in use — DANGER TO COME
  220th cluster read error: not currently in use — DANGER TO COME
  224th cluster read error: not currently in use — DANGER TO COME
  229th cluster read error: not currently in use — DANGER TO COME
  238th cluster read error: not currently in use — DANGER TO COME
  239
```

Bad Clusters not allocated to existing files.

Figure 11-6

This test lists the names of the files that contain the flawed clusters. Note that if you perform a disk test, sector by sector, and a bad sector is encountered, the program will automatically perform a file by file test to determine which file is in danger.

Once you have established where the bad clusters are, there are two ways to handle the problems.

1. If the files are ones for which you have duplicates you are not concerned with recovering the files. The files can simply be deleted. Remember that to delete a file, DOS does not have to read its contents, only the entries in the directory and the File Allocation Table.

   However, you will want to make sure that no new files are placed into the bad clusters. In this case, you will use DT to mark those clusters as unusable.

2. If the files represent valuable data, you will want to attempt to recover the files as well as block out those areas for future use. The DT program has an option that attempts to move the data to a usable cluster area.

Look at what both operations would consist of. Begin with the files you don't want to recover. For example, on the sample test shown above, some of the files were EXE, program files. Suppose you have copies of these programs on another disk, such as the original program disks supplied by the manufacturer. There is no point in wasting effort trying to recover the programs.

The first step would be to delete the programs from the disk. Keep in mind that deleting simply removes the allocation for these clusters from the directory and the FAT. The commands below are samples of how you would delete the files you have copies of.

```
del mergeprd.exe ↵
del word_dca.exe ↵
```

Once the files have been removed from the directory you would run the DT program again for the disk space. Specify the disk, not the files so that you can locate the bad clusters that used to belong to those deleted files. At this point you do not know which of the bad clusters belonged to **mergeprd.exe** and **word_dca.exe.** Enter

```
dt/d ↵
```

This time when the program encounters the bad clusters, some of them are shown as DANGER TO COME. This means that you have the opportunity of marking these clusters as unusable in order to prevent DOS from attempting to write data into these clusters. Once blocked out, these clusters will no longer pose a danger.

```
148th cluster read error: in use by a file -- DANGER NOW
152nd cluster read error: in use by a file -- DANGER NOW
157th cluster read error: in use by a file -- DANGER NOW
161st cluster read error: not currently in use — DANGER TO COME
166th cluster read error: not currently in use — DANGER TO COME
170th cluster read error: not currently in use — DANGER TO COME
175th cluster read error: not currently in use — DANGER TO COME
179th cluster read error: not currently in use — DANGER TO COME
184th cluster read error: not currently in use — DANGER TO COME
188th cluster read error: not currently in use — DANGER TO COME
193rd cluster read error: not currently in use — DANGER TO COME
197th cluster read error: not currently in use — DANGER TO COME
202nd cluster read error: not currently in use — DANGER TO COME
206th cluster read error: in use by a file -- DANGER NOW
211th cluster read error: not currently in use — DANGER TO COME
215th cluster read error: not currently in use — DANGER TO COME
220th cluster read error: not currently in use — DANGER TO COME
224th cluster read error: not currently in use — DANGER TO COME
229th cluster read error: not currently in use — DANGER TO COME
238th cluster read error: not currently in use — DANGER TO COME

During this operation, do not press
BREAK (Control-C) to interrupt Disk Test
Errors found in disk areas not currently in use
Mark them as bad sectors, to prevent use (Y/N) ?
```

Program will mark ba clusters.

Figure 11-7

Once the entire disk is tested, the program asks if you want to mark the bad sectors and the clusters which contain them. Enter

y

Because the DT program found errors in the file area it automatically displays the name of the files that still are in danger after it has marked the DANGER TO COME clusters as unusable.

How should you handle the files that you do want to recover? For example, the file SEMI.STY on the sample disk might represent a user-file for which there is no duplicate. The DT program recognizes a /M switch. /M is used to tell DT to attempt to move the data contained in the file with the bad sector to another location on the disk. You can use DT/M to recover all of the files, or select a specific file by entering its name, or group of files by using a DOS wildcard. In this case, the command is aimed at a specific file that you want to recover. Enter

`dt semi.sty/m` ↵

The DT program attempts to read the file and place its contents into a new area of the disk. If successful it will display a message indicating that the file is safely moved.

```
During this operation, do not press
BREAK (Control-C) to interrupt Disk Test
Errors found in disk areas not currently in use
Mark them as bad sectors, to prevent use (Y/N) ? Y

Disk errors found in data area: now checking files

You may again press BREAK (Control-C) to interrupt Disk Test
  Directory B:\
    File mw.hlp: error reading file in the used area -- DANGER NOW
    File hyph.dat: error reading file in the used area — DANGER NOW
    File semi.sty: error reading file in the used area — DANGER NOW

[C:\]dt b:semi.sty/m
DT-Disk Test, Advanced Edition, (C) Copr 1987, Peter Norton

During the scan of the disk, you may press
BREAK (Control-C) to interrupt Disk Test          File moved to new location

Test reading files

    File semi.sty: error reading file. Moved to safe area.

[C:\]
```

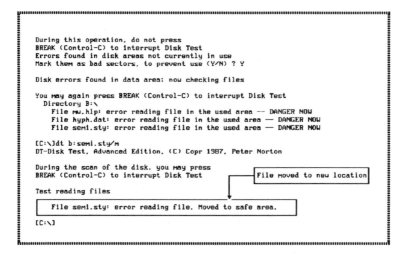

Figure 11-8

You can enter a general form of DT to attempt to move any file that appears to be in danger. Enter

`dt/m/f` ↵

The program automatically attempts to recover any endangered files it encounters.

```
    238th cluster read error: already marked as bad: no danger

Disk errors found in data area: now checking files
  Directory B:\
    File mw.hlp: error reading file in the used area -- DANGER NOW
    File hyph.dat: error reading file in the used area — DANGER NOW

[C:\]dt b:/m
DT-Disk Test, Advanced Edition, (C) Copr 1987, Peter Norton

Select DISK test, FILE test, or BOTH
Press D, F, or B ...

[C:\]dt b:/m/f
DT-Disk Test, Advanced Edition, (C) Copr 1987, Peter Norton

During the scan of the disk, you may press
BREAK (Control-C) to interrupt Disk Test

Test reading files

    File mw.hlp: error reading file. Moved to safe area.
    File hyph.dat: error reading file. Moved to safe area.

[C:\]
```

Figure 11-9

If you perform a DT on the disk, the program reports the bad clusters that have been marked.

dt/d↵

```
    130th cluster read error: already marked as bad: no danger
    139th cluster read error: already marked as bad: no danger
    148th cluster read error: already marked as bad: no danger
    152nd cluster read error: already marked as bad: no danger
    157th cluster read error: already marked as bad: no danger
    161st cluster read error: already marked as bad: no danger
    166th cluster read error: already marked as bad: no danger
    170th cluster read error: already marked as bad: no danger
    175th cluster read error: already marked as bad: no danger
    179th cluster read error: already marked as bad: no danger
    184th cluster read error: already marked as bad: no danger
    188th cluster read error: already marked as bad: no danger
    193rd cluster read error: already marked as bad: no danger
    197th cluster read error: already marked as bad: no danger
    202nd cluster read error: already marked as bad: no danger
    206th cluster read error: already marked as bad: no danger
    211th cluster read error: already marked as bad: no danger
    215th cluster read error: already marked as bad: no danger
    220th cluster read error: already marked as bad: no danger
    224th cluster read error: already marked as bad: no danger
    229th cluster read error: already marked as bad: no danger
    238th cluster read error: already marked as bad: no danger

[C:\]
```

Figure 11-10

If you were to display a map of the disk usage with the main Norton Utilities program, the bad clusters would appear marked with **B**. Example:

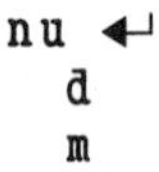

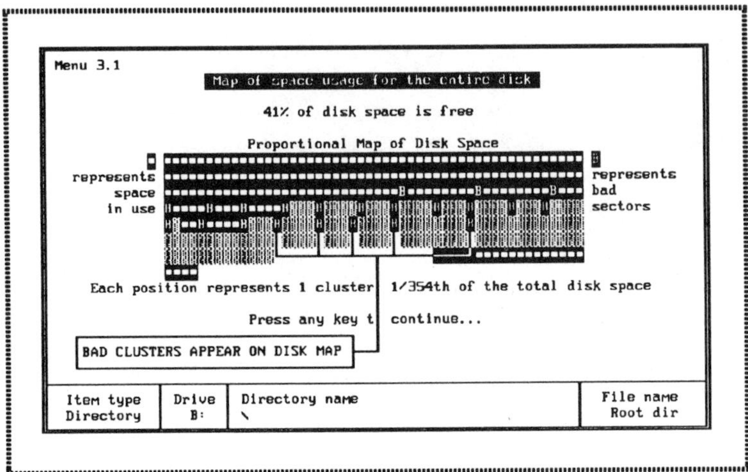

Figure 11-11

On a large disk you may want to print the output of the DT program rather than simply have it displayed on the screen. The usual DOS redirection technique can be applied to the DT command. Note that you should use the /LOG switch to suppress the portions of the display that are not appropriate for printer output. Below is an example of a page formatted report on disk integrity.

```
dt /b/log >diskstat↵
    lp diskstat↵
```

You might want to create a batch file for this operation and perform it on a regular basis.

> If bad sectors are encountered as part of the DT command when the redirection is set to redirect the output to a file, the program will appear to hang-up. The reason is that the program has paused to ask you if you want to mark the bad clusters. But because you have redirected the output to the disk, the question does not appear on the screen. If this happens, break the program with [Ctrl/c] and run the test again with the output displayed on the screen.
>
> Note that the /LOG switch, which is normally used to suppress interactive dialogue in a program, does not work in this case.

Manual Marking of Bad Clusters

The DT program has a facility for marking or unmarking specific data clusters. This feature is employed when you have a reason to suspect that a cluster should not be used. Suppose that you want to mark cluster 555 as bad. You would enter

```
dt/c555 ↵
```

The mark could be removed by entering

```
dt/c555- ↵
```

Speed Disk

The system used by MS-DOS to allocate space for files has been described in some detail. The key element to this system is the use of the directory and file allocation table to assign data clusters to specific filenames. The major advantage of this system is its ability to use all available disk space for files currently in use. When a file is erased, the clusters that were occupied by that file are now free to be used for other files. These can be existing files that are expanded or entirely new files.

One result of this type of system is that the clusters allocated to a given file are not necessarily consecutive. In fact, the allocation chain of clusters may jump back and forth between lower and higher cluster numbers. Remember that DOS seeks to use up all the unallocated clusters on the disk to maximize your storage space. When files consist of scattered groups of clusters they are called **fragmented files.** Fragmented files generally take longer to read and write because the disk drive must move back and forth around the disk to locate the clusters.

Depending upon the amount of deleting and adding of files that has been performed on a disk, a certain degree of file fragmentation will exist. The fragmentation will decrease the overall speed of your hard disk. If your hard disk is very full and you delete old files to make room for new ones you probably have noticed a decrease in performance.

The solution to this problem is to give DOS an opportunity to rearrange the clusters so that the logical groupings, the files themselves, match up with the physical groups, the list of clusters allocated to that file.

> Fragmentation can occur on hard or floppy disks. While the concern for performance is usually related to hard disks only, you can unfragment floppy disks.

One way to do this is to backup your entire hard disk, reformat the disk and then restore the files. The Norton Utilities program provides a much simpler and safer method of eliminating the fragmentation from a disk. The **SD** (**Speed Disk**) program can both analyze and correct fragmentation on a hard or floppy disk. SD works by analyzing the fragmentation on the disk as reflected in the file allocation table. It can then correct the fragmentation by reading cluster data into the memory and rewriting it into contiguous clusters. In addition, the SD performs other organizational operations such as placing all the directory information at the beginning of the disk. Remember that directories, other than the root, are stored in data clusters like files and are therefore subject to problems with fragmentation also.

SD also collects all the empty clusters on the disk and places them into a single block at the end of the existing files. This helps new files to be written in contiguous blocks and so cuts down on fragmenting of new files and increasing the time period before another SD is necessary.

The SD program takes some time to run because it needs to read and rewrite the information on the entire disk. It is important to remember that programs like SD can be potentially dangerous because they are changing the data on the hard disk. If the SD program is interrupted by a reboot, disk error, power failure, etc., permanent loss of information is possible. Before you perform an SD you should perform a CHKDSK/F and a DT (Disk Test) to eliminate any existing problems on the disk.

In addition, because SD actually rewrites the data on the disk, it will probably make unerasing of files impossible. If you need to recover data in the unused areas of the disk, do not perform an SD until you have completed your unerase operations.

You can interrupt the SD program once it has begun by pressing [Esc]. Remember that when you enter [Esc], the SD program will not stop immediately. Instead it completes the operation it was performing when you entered [Esc] and stops at the next safe point.

SD has two functions:

1. **Report.** This function is used to report on the current state of fragmentation on the disk. The report can be displayed in several ways. The simplest report is a total of the percentage of fragmentation on the disk. You can list the fragmentation for individual directories or groups of files.

2. **Unfragment.** This operation is the one that actually changes the disk by condensing the files into contiguous cluster groups.

The report function is useful in determining when it is necessary to condense the hard disk. To analyze the overall fragmentation, enter

```
sd/report ↵
```

The program will display a single line of information.

```
Total of the entire disk: 95% unfragmented
```

This tells you that only 5 percent of the files on the disk are stored in noncontiguous chains of clusters.

The report function can display the status of individual files or groups of files. For example, suppose you wanted to know the degree of fragmentation that exists among the EXE file in the DOS directory. Enter

```
sd \dos\*.exe /report ↵
```

```
[C:\]sd \dos\*.exe/report
SD-Speed Disk, Advanced Edition, (C) Copr 1987, Peter Norton

C:\DOS
attrib.exe     60%   backup.exe    100%   beep.exe      100%   chkdsk.exe     80%
cvrt.exe      100%   dbase.exe     100%   debug.exe     100%   diskcomp.exe  100%
diskcopy.exe   50%   ds.exe        100%   dt.exe        100%   duet.exe       81%
edlin.exe     100%   exe2bin.exe   100%   fa.exe        100%   fc.exe         75%
ff.exe        100%   fi.exe        100%   find.exe      100%   format.exe    100%
fr.exe        100%   fs.exe        100%   grab.exe      100%   graftabl.exe   80%
hs.exe         80%   hsinstal.exe  100%   id.exe        100%   join.exe       80%
label.exe     100%   ld.exe        100%   ll.exe         90%   lp.exe        100%
nc.exe         90%   ncd.exe       100%   ncdemo.exe    100%   ncsmall.exe   100%
ni.exe         93%   nu.exe         98%   print.exe     100%   qu.exe        100%
recover.exe    66%   replace.exe   100%   restore.exe   100%   sa.exe        100%
saver.exe     100%   sd.exe        100%   share.exe     100%   si.exe        100%
subst.exe     100%   sys.exe       100%   tm.exe        100%   tree.exe       80%
ts.exe        100%   txttopcx.exe  100%   ud.exe        100%   vl.exe        100%
wingrab.exe   100%   wipedisk.exe  100%   wipefile.exe  100%   xcopy.exe     100%
xtree.exe      86%

Directory Total: 94% unfragmented

[C:\]
```

Figure 11-12

The command displays a list of all of the specified files and shows the degree of fragmentation expressed as a percentage.

CHKDSK can be used to produce a similar list of file fragmentation. If the CHKDSK command is followed by a file specification, DOS will list any files that are noncontiguous. Enter

```
chkdsk \dos\*.exe ↵
```

```
   Contains 8 non-contiguous blocks.
C:\DOS\FC.EXE
   Contains 3 non-contiguous blocks.
C:\DOS\GRAFTABL.EXE
   Contains 2 non-contiguous blocks.
C:\DOS\HS.EXE
   Contains 5 non-contiguous blocks.
C:\DOS\JOIN.EXE
   Contains 2 non-contiguous blocks.
C:\DOS\LL.EXE
   Contains 4 non-contiguous blocks.
C:\DOS\NC.EXE
   Contains 4 non-contiguous blocks.
C:\DOS\NI.EXE
   Contains 2 non-contiguous blocks.
C:\DOS\NU.EXE
   Contains 2 non-contiguous blocks.
C:\DOS\RECOVER.EXE
   Contains 2 non-contiguous blocks.
C:\DOS\TREE.EXE
   Contains 2 non-contiguous blocks.
C:\DOS\XTREE.EXE
   Contains 4 non-contiguous blocks.

[C:\]
```

Figure 11-13

Notice that DOS simply reports the number of blocks, that is, groups of clusters of which a file is composed. The SD report is a bit more compact and shows a percentage of fragmentation. SD reports on all files showing the contiguous files as 100 percent unfragmented.

To produce a list of the fragmentation status of all of the files on a disk, you can use the /S switch and start the search at the root directory. Enter

```
sd \ /s/report ↵
```

This report produces a list of all the files grouped by directory with a value for each file, a total for each directory and a grand total for the entire disk.

To create a printed copy of that report you can use the DOS redirection command to create a text file and use LP to print a page formatted report. Example:

```
sd \ /s/report>fragrpt ↵
lp fragrpt ↵
```

To perform the condensing of the disk, enter SD by itself or with the drive letter, if you want to condense a disk other than the active one. Enter

```
sd ↵
```

The program displays a screen which gives you an opportunity to change the disk or exit the program before the condensing starts.

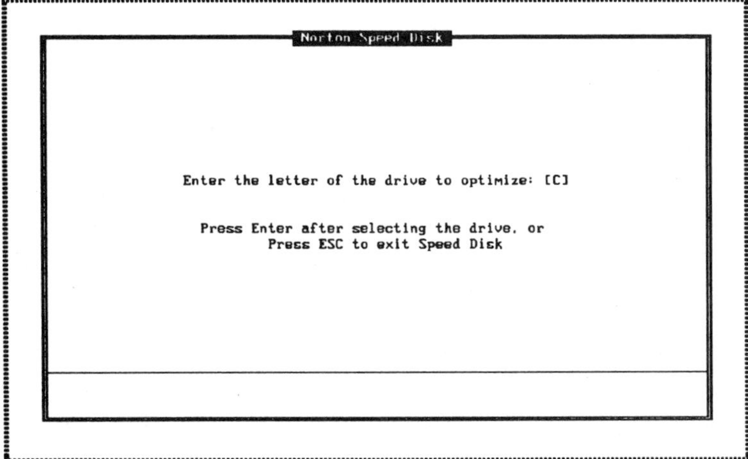

Figure 11-14

To begin the condensing enter

↵

The program then displays a map of the current state of space usage on the disk.

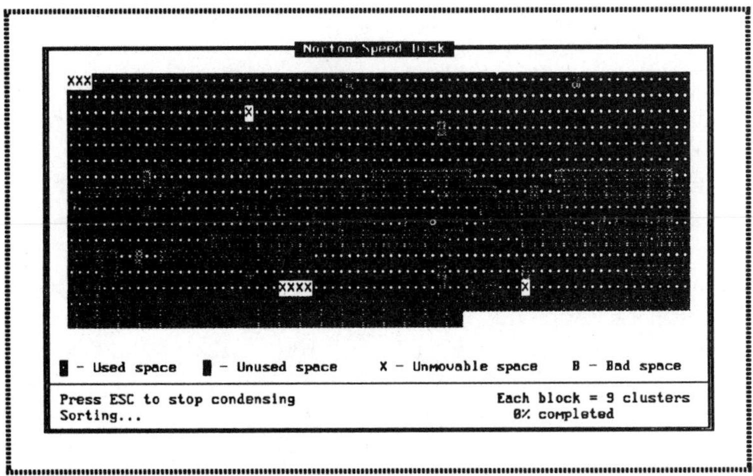

Figure 11-15

The map displays special symbols to indicate the status or the space. There are four areas shown.

1. **Used.** This is space that is used by normal files.

2. **Unused.** These are clusters not currently allocated to files. Note that because these clusters are moved as part of the condensing operation, unerasing of files is probably not possible following an SD condensing.

3. **Position Sensitive Files.** Certain files on the disk may be position sensitive. This means that the exact locations of these files may be significant to certain programs. The most common example of this type of file include the DOS system files IO.SYS (IBMBIO.COM) and MSDOS.SYS (IBMDOS.COM). Other position sensitive files are placed on the disk as part of copy protection schemes implemented by some programs. The SD program attempts to avoid rewriting such files because this could prevent your copy protected programs from running.

   In addition, the SD program treats as position sensitive any files or directories with a hidden or system attribute. If you have marked files as hidden they will not be unfragmented.

4. **Bad Clusters.** These are areas marked by DOS at the time of formatting as unusable. They can also include clusters marked as bad by the DT (Disk Test) program.

As the condensing proceeds the map will be updated to show how the space allocations are being changed. As each area of the disk is read and rewritten the blank clusters begin to be pushed to the end of the disk creating a solid block of contiguous files at the beginning of the disk. The program displays the amount of condensing accomplished in the lower right-hand corner of the display.

You can stop the condensing by pressing [Esc] and waiting for the program to stop. Keep in mind that it may take a minute or two for the program to reach a safe point at which it can stop condensing.

If you stop the condensing, you can return to the condensing procedure at the same point at which you stopped by entering SD again. For example, if you stop at 50 percent and restart SD, it will begin at 50 percent, not the beginning of the disk. If you write or update files after you halt condensing, SD must begin its condensing from the beginning of the disk all over again.

When the condensing is complete the screen will display a graphic map that looks like this:

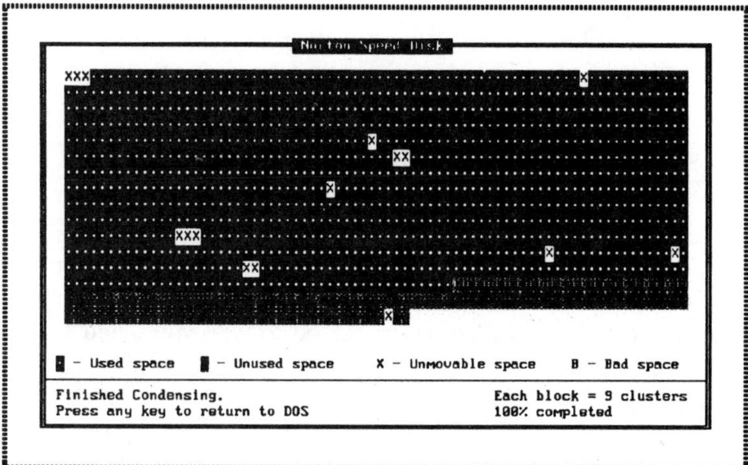

Figure 11-16

Exit the SD program by entering

↵

SD is a program that you should run on a regular basis. Most users will run the program every month or so. If you load and unload large numbers of files (a book or programming project) you may want to perform SD weekly.

It is not recommended that you perform SD from a batch file. Because SD will change the location of files on the disk, DOS will get hung-up after the SD is completed and you attempt to return to DOS.

Remember that while copy protected programs are becoming more rare, it is impossible to know if SD is 100 percent compatible with the myriad of copy protection schemes that were developed during the heyday of protection in the mid-80s. If you are using a major product from Lotus or Ashton-Tate you are safe. If you are using a less well known program, usually a vertical market software, consult the manufacturer before running SD.

Unformatting

Formatting a hard disk drive accidentally is a disaster that happens from time to time, often when people are in a hurry to complete an important task. The Norton Utilities program provides a mean by which recovery of some or all of the data on the hard disk can be achieved.

Formatting a hard disk is usually the result of forgetting to specify the floppy drive A or B when you enter a format command.

```
Format ↵   Formats current disk, C if hard drive.
Format a:   ↵           Formats floppy disk.
```

This mistake was quite easy to make with DOS 2. That version of DOS displayed no special warning that you were about to format a hard disk rather than a floppy disk. In DOS 3, three new protections are added to help you avoid this mistake.

1. **Disk Specification.** The format command will not run unless a drive letter is specified. For example, entering FORMAT ↵, will cause DOS to display **Drive letter must be specified** and cancel the format command.

2. **Volume Label Identification.** The optional volume label that can be added to the disk at the time of formatting or with the Norton Utilities VL program is used to verify hard disk formatting. When a hard disk is selected for formatting you must enter the correct volume label or the format command will terminate. Used in this way, the volume label is a sort of "password" that tries to catch accidental hard disk formatting.

3. **Warning Message.** If the first two options fail to stop you, DOS will then display **WARNING: ALL DATA ON NON-REMOVABLE DISK DRIVE C: WILL BE LOST! Proceed with Format (Y/N)?.** You must enter Y ↵ to format. Entering ↵ by itself will cause the format command to terminate.

If you have DOS 3.0 or higher, you can use the VL program to take advantage of protection scheme 2. The volume label protection is one that many people fail to take advantage of because they do not use the /V switch when formatting their hard drive. Most hard drives are formatted by the computer store personnel before you get the computer and they usually won't bother to put a volume label on the disk.

The VL (Volume Label) allows you to insert a label at any time. Enter

```
vl ↵
```

The VL program displays:

```
[C:\]vl
VL-Volume Label, Advanced Edition, (C) Copr 1987, Peter Norton

There currently is no volume label in drive C

  Press Enter to leave old label unchanged, or
  Press Delete to remove old label, or
  Enter new label: -----------
```

Figure 11-17

The volume label can be 1 to 11 characters in length. A volume label can contain the same characters as a filename, with the exception of spaces which are allowed in volume labels but not in filenames. As an example, enter

`password ↵`

The program will confirm the new volume label. If you are running level 3 DOS you can see how the volume label will prevent an accidental format.

> If you are not using level 3 DOS do not attempt the next step. To check your DOS version simply type in VER ↵ at the DOS prompt.

Enter

`format c:↵`

The program displays:

```
Enter current Volume Label for drive C:
```

Enter

↵

Because you did not enter the correct volume label password, DOS rejects your attempt to format the disk and displays **Invalid Volume ID, Format failure.**

How is it possible to recover a hard disk after it has been formatted, should you be so unlucky as to circumvent these protections? The key is the fact that hard disks, unlike floppy disks, are formatted on two different levels by two different programs. (See Chapter 1 for details about formatting hard disks). When the DOS format program is used on a hard disk (non-removable is a more accurate term), DOS performs only one part of the formatting, the high level format. This high level or logical format does not actually overwrite all the information on the disk, with the exception of the boot sector, directory and File Allocation Table. If you have a copy of that information, it would be possible to place all of the data on the disk back into the correct files and directories.

The Norton Utilities package includes a program, FR (Format Recover) that copies the directory and FAT data into a special file called FRECOVER.DAT.

To create this file, enter

```
fr/save ↵
```

This creates the file FRECOVER.DAT. If you should accidentally format the hard disk, you will need to locate a copy of the FR.EXE program on a floppy disk because FR.EXE has just been wiped off your hard disk when it was formatted. Place the disk, your original Norton Utilities program disk 1, into the floppy drive, for instance, drive A, and enter

```
a:fr ↵
```

You will be asked if you want to recover the hard disk information.

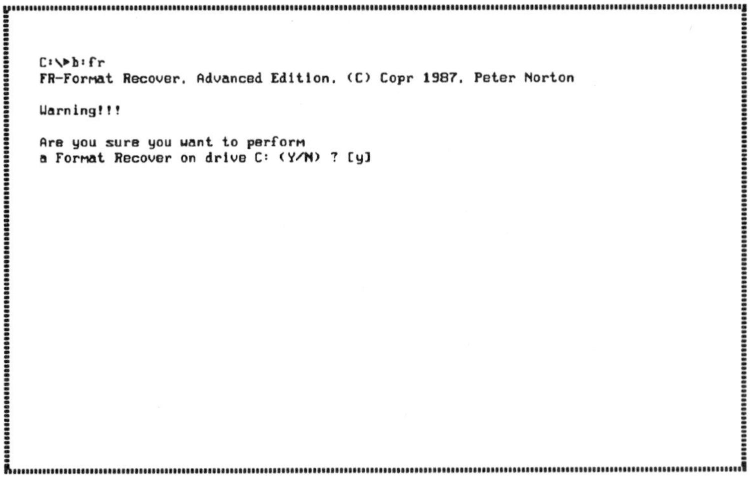

```
C:\>b:fr
FR-Format Recover, Advanced Edition, (C) Copr 1987, Peter Norton

Warning!!!

Are you sure you want to perform
a Format Recover on drive C: (Y/N) ? [y]
```

Figure 11-18

If you enter

y ↵

The program will proceed to restore the hard disk to the way it was when the **FR/SAVE** command was last used.

```
C:\>b:fr
FR-Format Recover, Advanced Edition, (C) Copr 1987, Peter Norton

Warning!!!

Are you sure you want to perform
a Format Recover on drive C: (Y/N) ? [y]

Searching for system information in sectors 41 through 10,312
Finished searching for the system information

Finished checking data integrity

The disk has been recovered by Format Recover

The information used by Format Recover was
recorded on Thursday January 1, 1988 at  2:11 pm

C:\>
```

Figure 11-19

This is possible even though FRECOVER.DAT file is erased when the hard disk is formatted because the contents of the file stay intact. For example, suppose you formatted a hard disk that was full of information.

The directory and file allocation table have been wiped clean. But that data is still stored in the data clusters. The cluster that contained the file FRECOVER.DAT begins with a special sequence of characters, PNCIFRID (Peter Norton Computing Inc Format Recovery ID). You could use the main Norton Utilities program to search for those characters.

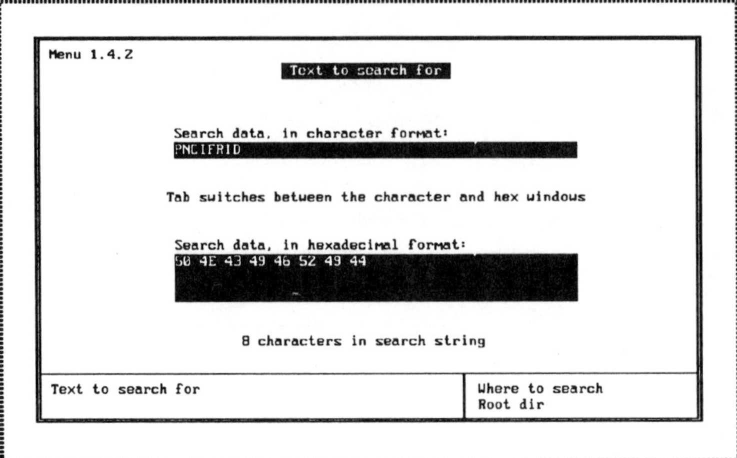

Figure 11-20

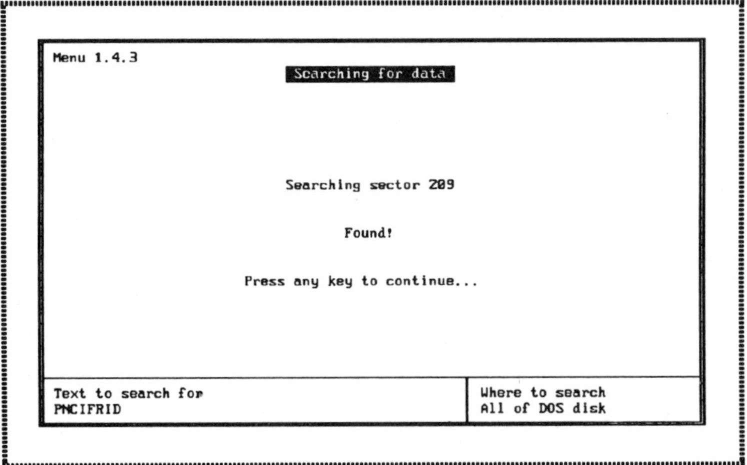

Figure 11-21

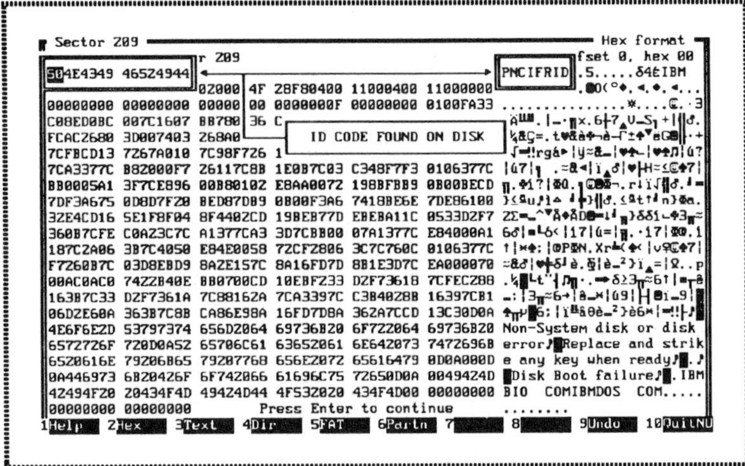

Figure 11-22

Because the data in the clusters is intact, the program will locate the data that once belonged to the FRECOVER.DAT file. Thus it is possible to locate the information necessary for recovering a formatted hard disk if the FRECOVER.DAT file had existed prior to the formatting.

You can see that the FR program uses some of the same concepts as the UnErase programs. This also implies that it is subject to the same types of limitations. FR is not magic. Keep the following points in mind.

1. The recovery of the formatted disk depends on the accuracy of the information stored in the FRECOVER.DAT file. Ideally, this file should be updated each time a change is made to the hard disk, but that is probably not practical. One suggestion is to place the command **FR/SAVE** into the AUTOEXEC.BAT. This will ensure that the file FRECOVER.DAT file is updated each time the computer is rebooted.

   A more extreme measure would be to add the command FR/SAVE to the your MENU.BAT program so that after each application has been run the FRECOVER.DAT is updated. This will provide a much greater measure of protection but it will cause a delay each time the application is run from the menu. It all depends on how paranoid you are about formatting the hard disk accidentally.

2. If you recover a hard disk when the FRECOVER.DAT is not up to date with all of the changes, the result may prove to be less than 100 percent accurate. If files have been deleted and new files added, it is possible that the recovery will assign data to files that are no longer valid. The exact limitations of the

recovery depends upon how much the actual disk information is at variance with the last data stored in the FRECOVER.DAT.

3. If you format the hard disk and begin to place new data on the disk, that is, replacing erased programs with the original from the floppy disks, you are overwriting information that will make it impossible to create a 100 percent recovery of the hard disk. If you have overwritten the clusters that contain the FRECOVER.DAT information, FR will not be able to function at all.

The FR program can be a lifesaver but it would be much better all around if you never needed to use it. If you are concerned about accidental formatting you may want to take the trouble to make frequent updates of the FRECOVER.DAT.

> Certain formatting programs provided by computer manufacturers perform both a high and low level format with a single command. The format command supplied with certain Compaq computers, for example, DOS 3.1 version, will alter disk data making unformatting impossible.

Summary

The Norton Utilities program provides solutions to many of the problems that you will encounter from time to time on your computer system.

Testing. The SI program will display information about the computer, its memory usage and its performance capabilities.

Unerase files. The Norton Utilities programs NU and QU provide a means by which information stored in erased files can be fully or partially recovered. QU will operate on files that have not been overwritten by new information. the main Norton Utilities program can be used for recovery or partial recovery of files that are beyond the capacity of QU to recover. The UD program will recover directories that have removed with the RD command. This enables you to attempt file recovery on files previously contained in the directory.

Wipe files and disk. The Norton Utilities programs WIPEFILE and WIPEDISK are used to eradicate data from a disk or file for security purposes.

Disk tests. The DT program can be used to recover data from files that contain disk errors. DT can also be used to prevent problems by marking bad sectors before they are used by files.

Consolidation of files. The SD program is used to increase disk performance by condensing fragmented files.

Unformatting. The FR/SAVE program will create a file that can be used by the FR program to restore a hard disk after it has been formatted. Note that the FR/SAVE must be done before the disk is formatted. If not used, FR cannot recover a formatted hard disk.

SECTION VI
OTHER PROGRAMS

12

THE NORTON COMMANDER

The Norton Commander is a program designed to make operation of your MS-DOS computer faster, simpler and more effective. The Commander seeks to replace or extend the DOS command language with a menu and a selection-oriented interface. What makes the Norton Commander exceptional is that it seeks to enhance DOS without replacing it. When you work with the Norton Commander, you can select and access any entry of normal DOS commands, without having to leave the Commander.

In this chapter you will learn about the features and abilities of the Norton Commander program, including how to build a system of user menus that allow people unfamiliar with either DOS or the Norton Commander to run programs and perform maintenance operations.

Load the Norton Commander program by entering

nc↵

Normal Display

When the Norton Commander is first loaded it displays two boxes called **panels**. The boxes are designed to display information about the disk with which you are working. The left panel displays the first eleven files or directories listed in the current directory. The right panel displays summary information about the entire disk. At the bottom of the screen a list of the Commander function key commands is displayed.

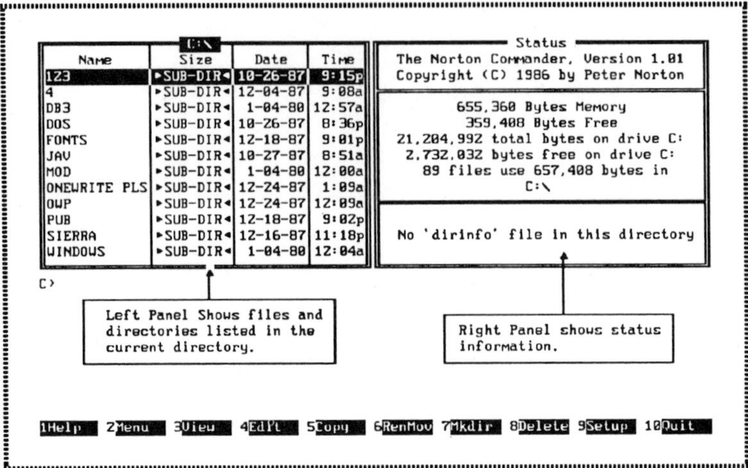

Figure 12-1

What makes the Norton Commander different from most hard disk management programs is that the panels do not take up the entire screen display. The bottom half shows a DOS prompt.

> The prompt is controlled by the Commander settings. If you have used a PROMPT command, for example, in the AUTOEXEC batch to change the prompt style, it will not affect the style of prompt displayed in the Commander program.

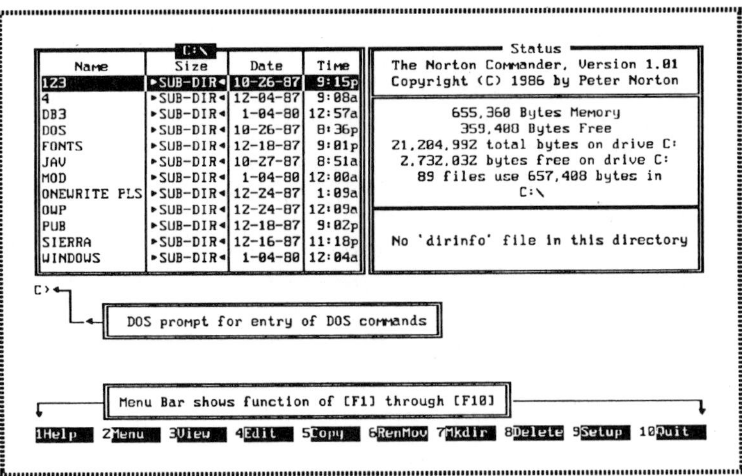

Figure 12-2

The design of the Norton Commander by John Socha, includes a number of innovative features. The most interesting theme is that the Norton Commander blends whatever knowledge you have of DOS, little or great, with its own methods of handling basic operational tasks. Unlike other hard disk manager programs, the Norton Commander will be used differently by almost everyone who uses it based on how comfortable they are with existing DOS procedures. If you are just learning about DOS and system management, then the Norton Commander operations will simplify your tasks. If you are experienced, try the Norton Commander operations anyway. You may find that you will want to break some old habits.

Change, Make, and Delete Directories

The Commander provides an easy way to navigate through the directories on your hard disk. The Commander displays the directories marked with a SUB DIR at the top of the display window.

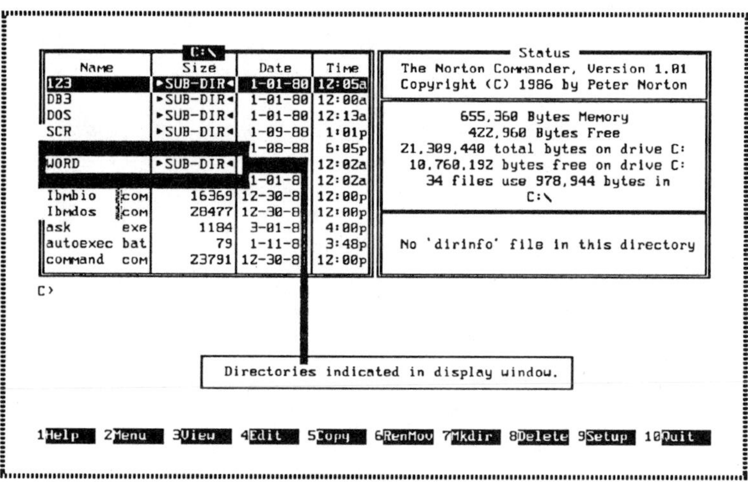

Figure 12-3

To change to the highlighted directory, enter

↵

If the directory displayed has a parent directory, the parent is indicated by an **UP DIR**.

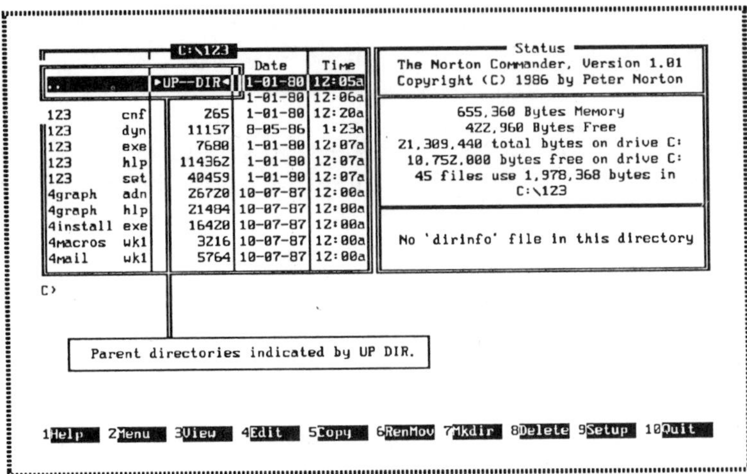

Figure 12-4

There are two ways to move back up the directory tree.

1. **Highlight.** Highlight the **UP DIR** at the top of the file window display and press ↵.

2. **[Ctrl/Pg Up].** This command will move you to the parent directory, no matter what file the highlight is positioned on.

You can return to the root directory at any time by entering a combination of [Ctrl] and [backslash], [**Ctrl**]/\].

You can create additional directories by using the [F7], MKDIR, command. The directory you make will branch off the current directory as indicated at the top of the file windows. When you enter [F7] the Commander displays a window into which you can enter the name of the new directory.

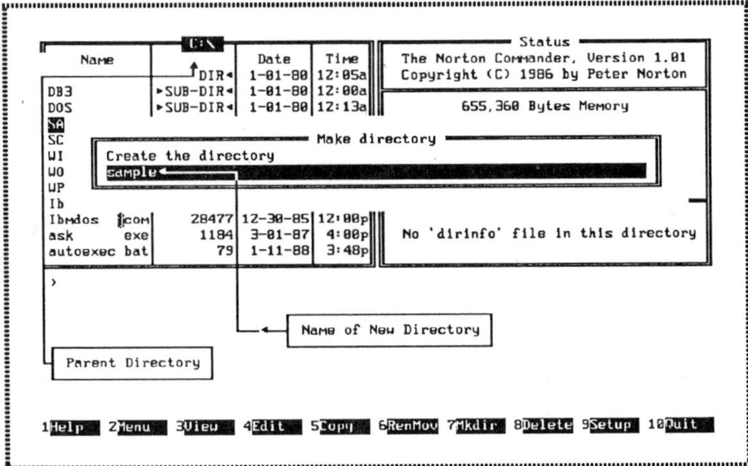

Figure 12-5

A directory can be deleted, assuming that it contains no active files, by using the [F8], delete, command. Highlight the directory that you want to remove. Enter

[F8]

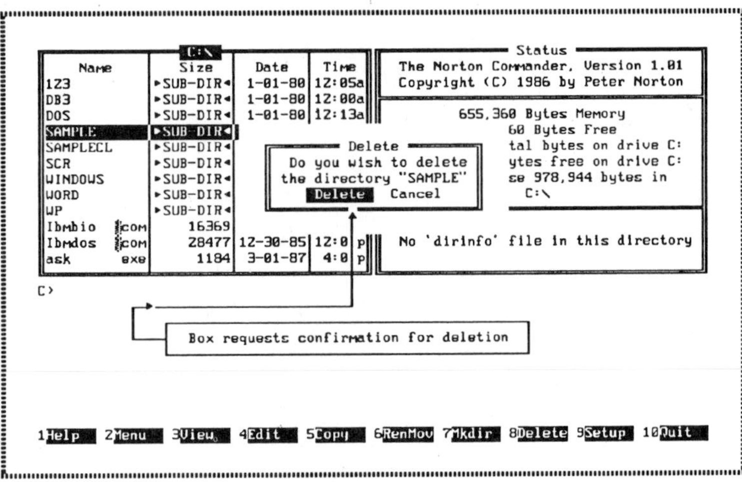

Figure 12-6

The Commander displays a box that asks you to confirm your intention to remove the directory. Throughout the Commander, you will be asked to confirm deletions or commands that overwrite files.

Note that the rename command, [F6] can be used to change the name of an existing directory. This is an operation that cannot be done with DOS or with the Norton Utilities programs.

File Operations

The most obvious advantage of the Norton Commander over using DOS alone is that the Commander displays a list of names, files, and directories, that would normally be displayed only if you use the DIR command. Not only are these displayed but they are interactively displayed, which means you can select files and directories by pointing the highlight rather than typing the name.

A second benefit of the Commander is that it creates an object-oriented environment. Most DOS commands require you to begin with the name of the command (the verb) you want to use. The Commander allows you to point at the file or directories and the commands are issued by pressing the appropriate function keys.

The two most common operations performed on files are deleting and copying. Both of these operations can be performed in the Commander point mode. When a file is highlighted, enter

```
[F5]
```

The Commander displays a box in the center of the screen with a blank line for the name of the new file.

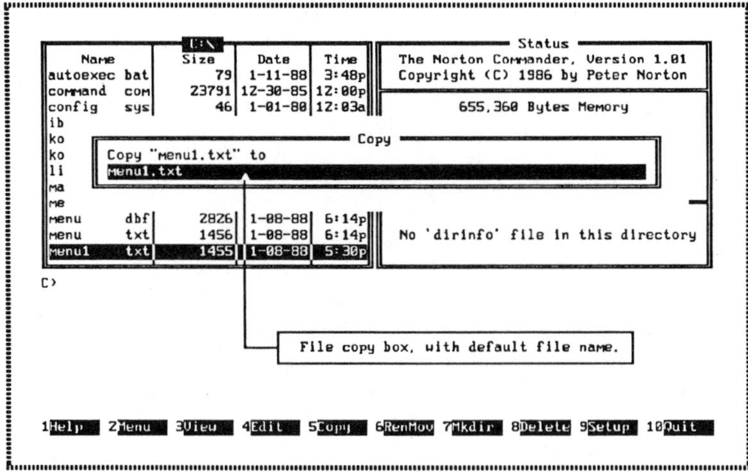

Figure 12-7

The default name disappears as soon as you begin to enter the destination for the copy. You should enter the destination as you would in DOS, that is, a disk, directory or filename. The Commander will warn you if the destination file already exists. You can delete files in a similar manner by using the [F8] command. Highlight a file and enter

[F8]

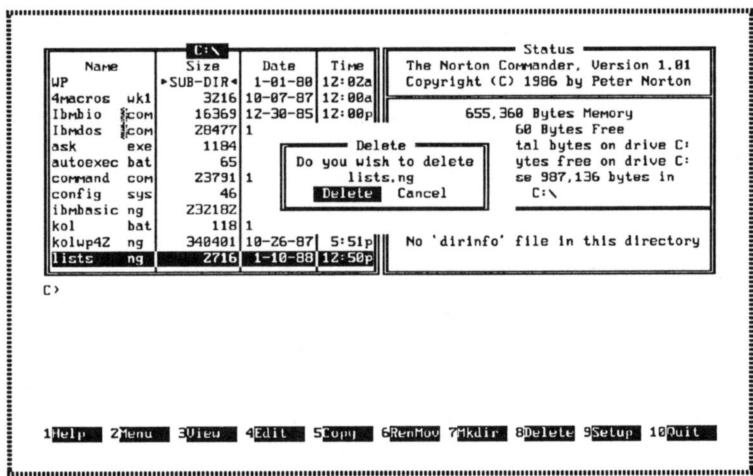

Figure 12-8

Notice that you are warned about the deletion. You can confirm the deletion or cancel it with [Esc]. Enter

[Esc]

If you want to enter a copy command and specify both the source and destination you can use [Shift/F5]. This displays a box with two lines for entry.

Moving Files

The [F6] key has two functions, depending upon what you enter. The command can be used for renaming or moving a file. When you enter [F6] the filename is displayed in the edit box.

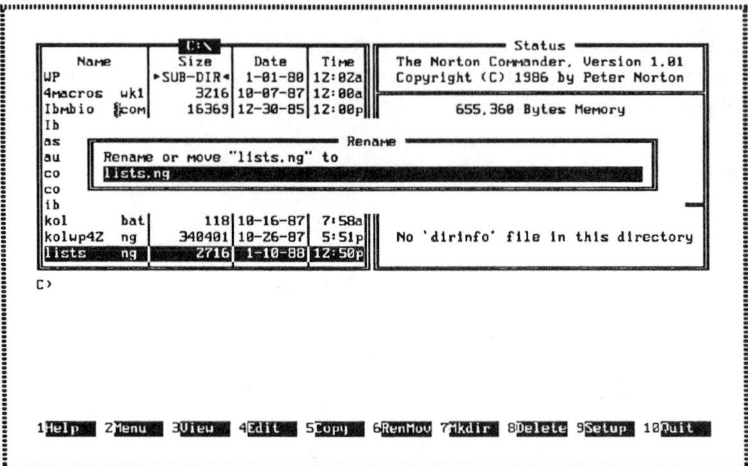

Figure 12-9

You can enter a new filename or use the editing keys to alter the existing name. If you create a filename that conflicts with an existing filename you will be asked if you intend to overwrite that file. In effect, the rename command will function like a copy command.

If you enter a directory instead of a filename, the rename command becomes the move command. A move command is different from a copy command in that it is removed from the current directory and placed in the specified directory. Moving a file is faster than copying it because the file itself is not duplicated. Only the entry for that file remains in the directory. This also saves file space because you do not create a duplicate file, which then must be removed with delete.

If the directory you are moving to contains a file with the same name you will be warned about the conflict. Files can only be moved to different directories on the same disk. To place a a file on a different disk you must use copy.

Group Operations

The copy, delete, rename, and move commands can be executed on groups of files as well as individual files. File groups can be established in two ways:

1. **Marking Files.** You can mark individual files as part of a group by moving the highlight to the filename and entering [Ins]. the filename is highlighted to indicate it is part of the marked group. If you enter [Ins] a second time the marking is removed.

2. **Wildcard.** You can use a wildcard specification to mark all of the files in the current directory that fall under the specification. To select files by wildcard press the gray [+] sign on the numeric keypad. A box appears on the screen. You can enter a wildcard in the same format as a DOS wildcard. The default is *.*.

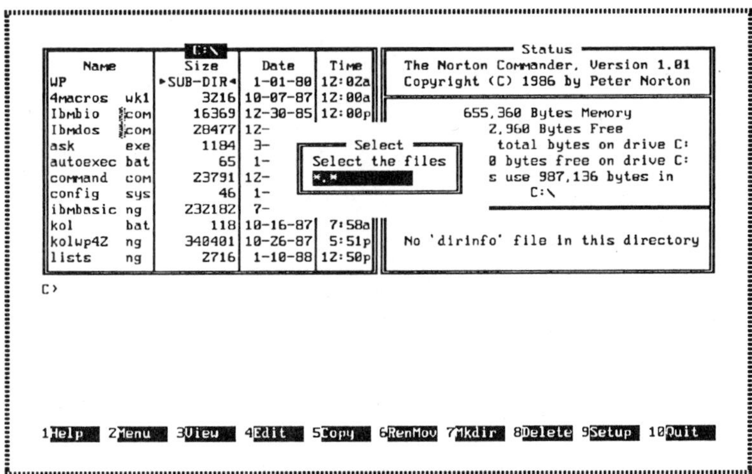

Figure 12-10

Once a group has been marked, entering a copy, move or delete command will affect all of the selected files. Marking and wildcard selection is cumulative. For example, if you used the wildcard to mark all the BAT files, *.BAT, and then used another wildcard to select all the EXE files, *.EXE, both groups would be marked. The marked files will stay marked until they are unmarked or you change to another directory. The gray [-] key can be used to unmark files with wildcard specifications.

Speed Search

The Commander will speed search a list of files. To search for a specific filename, enter the letters of the name with the [Alt] key held down. Example:

```
[Alt/f]
```

The highlight will jump to the first file that begins with F. If there are several files that begin with F, you can enter as many letters as you need to locate the unique filename. Example:

[Alt/fd]

Find the first file the begins FD, for instance, FDISK.COM.

Directory Information

The Commander allows you to create notes that describe each directory. The notes will appear in the directory information box in the Status panel.

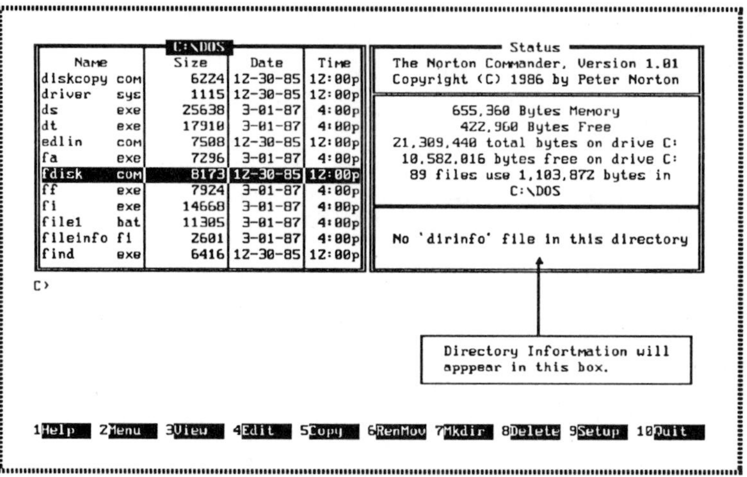

Figure 12-11

Because you must create these files before they can appear, the Commander shows a default message when no directory file is present. To create a directory information file you must activate the right panel. Enter

[Tab]

The highlight jumps to the word **Status** at the top of the right panel.

To add a comment, use the **Edit** command, [F4]. Enter

[F4]

The cursor moves to the directory information box. The box scrolls up and down and to the right, and you can enter as much information as you like in it. But for practical purposes you should keep your entry to three lines of text, no longer than 30 characters per line. To create a second or third line, enter ↵. The text will not automatically wrap.

When you have completed your entry, save the text by entering

[F2]
[F10]

This procedure creates a file called DIRINFO in the current directory.

> You can create a DIRINFO file with any text editor. The text will be displayed by the Commander so long as the file is given the name DIRINFO.

The Commander displays the text in the DIRINFO file in the box in the status window. Deleting this file from the disk will remove the directory information displays. You can have a DIRINFO for each directory on your disk.

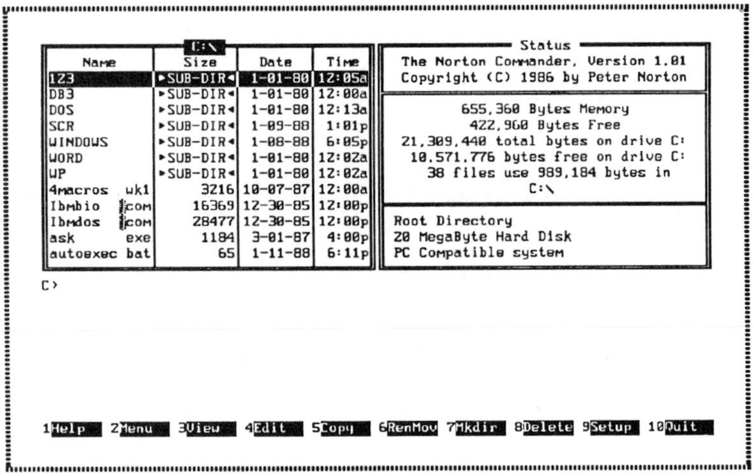

```
                          C:\                                      Status
Name            Size        Date      Time    The Norton Commander, Version 1.01
123          ►SUB-DIR◄   1-01-80  12:05a    Copyright (C) 1986 by Peter Norton
DB3          ►SUB-DIR◄   1-01-80  12:00a
DOS          ►SUB-DIR◄   1-01-80  12:13a          655,360 Bytes Memory
SCR          ►SUB-DIR◄   1-09-88   1:01p           422,960 Bytes Free
WINDOWS      ►SUB-DIR◄   1-08-88   6:05p    21,309,440 total bytes on drive C:
WORD         ►SUB-DIR◄   1-01-80  12:02a     10,571,776 bytes free on drive C:
WP           ►SUB-DIR◄   1-01-80  12:02a      38 files use 989,184 bytes in
4macros  wk1      3216  10-07-87  12:00a                 C:\
Ibmbio   com     16369  12-30-85  12:00p
Ibmdos   com     28477  12-30-85  12:00p    Root Directory
ask      exe      1184   3-01-87   4:00p    20 MegaByte Hard Disk
autoexec bat        65   1-11-88   6:11p    PC Compatible system
C>

1Help 2Menu 3View 4Edit 5Copy 6RenMov 7Mkdir 8Delete 9Setup 10Quit
```

Figure 12-12

Place the cursor back in the left panel by entering

[Tab]

Panel Options

The normal display of the panels in the Commander is that the left panel shows a list of the files in the current directory and the right panel shows the hard disk status summary.

The left panel displays:

1. **File and directory names.** Files are displayed in name order with directories, followed by filenames. Files with a hidden attribute will have ▮ displayed in the filename, and the first letter of the filename will be capitalized. By capitalizing the first letter, hidden files will be at the top of the file list. However, files that begin with numbers will be sequenced before hidden files. This is due to the collating sequence in the ASCII system in which numbers precede letters. Directory names appear in uppercase letters.

2. **Size.** This shows the file size in bytes as recorded in the directory. Directories show either SUB DIR for sub-directories or UP DIR for parent directories. Note that a directory uses one data cluster, usually 2048 bytes.

3. **Date.**

4. **Time.**

The right panel shows:

1. **Memory Status.** The total memory available to DOS and the current amount of memory free.

2. **Disk Usage.** Summary of disk space used.

3. **Directory Summary.** Total of files and spaces used for current directory.

4. **Directory Information.** Contents of the DIRINFO file, if any.

Movement between the panels is accomplished by using the [Tab] key. Enter

```
[Tab]
```

The cursor highlights the word **Status** on the top of the right panel. To return, enter

[Tab]

You can suppress the display of the unselected panel, in this case the right panel, by using the [Ctrl/p] command. Enter

[Ctrl/p]

```
                     C:\
Name          Size       Date      Time
123        ►SUB-DIR◄   1-01-80  12:05a
DB3        ►SUB-DIR◄   1-01-80  12:00a
DOS        ►SUB-DIR◄   1-01-80  12:13a
SCR        ►SUB-DIR◄   1-09-88   1:01p
WINDOWS    ►SUB-DIR◄   1-08-88   6:05p
WORD       ►SUB-DIR◄   1-01-80  12:02a
WP         ►SUB-DIR◄   1-01-80  12:02a
4macros  wk1    3216  10-07-87  12:00a
Command  com   23791  12-30-85  12:00p
Ibmbio   com   16369  12-30-85  12:00p
Ibmdos   com   28477  12-30-85  12:00p
ask      exe    1184   3-01-87   4:00p
C>

1Help  2Menu  3View  4Edit  5Copy  6RenMov  7Mkdir  8Delete  9Setup  10Quit
```

Figure 12-13

A second [Ctrl/p] will redisplay the panel. Enter

[Ctrl/p]

You can turn off both panels by entering

[Ctrl/o]

Like [Ctrl/p], [Ctrl/o] is a toggle. Turn the panels back on by entering

[Ctrl/o]

The function key bar at the bottom of the screen is controlled by [Ctrl/b]. Turn the bar off by entering

[Ctrl/b]

Return the bar to the bottom of the screen by entering a second [Ctrl/b].

[Ctrl/b]

The panels can be exchanged by using [Ctrl/u]. Enter

[Ctrl/u]

The panels switch functions with the left panel showing status and the right, now active, displaying files.

```
            Status                                  C:\
 The Norton Commander, Version 1.01      Name        Size      Date     Time
 Copyright (C) 1986 by Peter Norton     123       ►SUB-DIR◄  1-01-80  12:05a
                                        DB3       ►SUB-DIR◄  1-01-80  12:00a
        655,360 Bytes Memory            DOS       ►SUB-DIR◄  1-01-80  12:13a
        426,480 Bytes Free              SCR       ►SUB-DIR◄  1-09-88   1:01p
 21,309,440 total bytes on drive C:     WINDOWS   ►SUB-DIR◄  1-08-88   6:05p
  10,563,584 bytes free on drive C:     WORD      ►SUB-DIR◄  1-01-80  12:02a
    38 files use 989,184 bytes in       WP        ►SUB-DIR◄  1-01-80  12:02a
              C:\                       4macros  wk1    3216 10-07-87 12:00a
                                        Command  com   23791 12-30-85 12:00p
 Root Directory                         Ibmbio   com   16369 12-30-85 12:00p
 20 MegaByte Hard Disk                  Ibmdos   com   28477 12-30-85 12:00p
 PC Compatible system                   ask      exe    1184  3-01-87  4:00p
C>

1Help 2Menu 3View 4Edit 5Copy 6RenMov 7Mkdir 8Delete 9Setup 10Quit
```

Figure 12-14

You can toggle the menu back to the original positions by entering

[Ctrl/u]

Displaying Two Directories

In addition to the previous panel commands there is another command, [Ctrl/L], which has a more practical use. [Ctrl/L] will toggle the display type of the unselected panel. In this case, the right panel is the unselected panel, that is, without the highlight. Enter

[Ctrl/L]

The right panel now shows a directory display. But what good does that do? The answer is that only the selected panel, the one with the highlight, will change when a new disk or directory is selected. In this way you can get the Commander to display two different directories in each panel. As an example, change the directory to DOS by entering

`cd\dos ↵`

```
              C:\DOS                                              C:\
Name              Size       Date      Time    Name              Size       Date      Time
..              ►UP--DIR◄  1-01-80   12:13a   123              ►SUB-DIR◄  1-01-80   12:05a
Command  com       23791  12-30-85   12:00p   DB3              ►SUB-DIR◄  1-01-80   12:00a
_file_0  dbd       48712   3-01-87    4:00p   DOS              ►SUB-DIR◄  1-01-80   12:13a
ansi     sys        1651  12-30-85   12:00p   SCR              ►SUB-DIR◄  1-09-88    1:01p
ask      exe        1184   3-01-87    4:00p   WINDOWS          ►SUB-DIR◄  1-08-88    6:05p
assign   com        1536  12-30-85   12:00p   WORD             ►SUB-DIR◄  1-01-80   12:02a
attrib   exe        8247  12-30-85   12:00p   WP               ►SUB-DIR◄  1-01-80   12:02a
backup   com        6234  12-30-85   12:00p   4macros  wk1          3216  10-07-87   12:00a
basica   exe       78864   7-07-86   12:00p   Command  com         23791  12-30-85   12:00p
beep     exe        5324   3-01-87    4:00p   Ibmbio   com         16369  12-30-85   12:00p
catalog             3025   1-01-80   12:06a   Ibmdos   com         28477  12-30-85   12:00p
chkdsk   com        9832  12-30-85   12:00p   ask      exe          1184   3-01-87    4:00p

C>a:

A>c:

C>cd\dos          Left Panel shows new directory
                  while right panel still shows
C>                the root directory.

1Help  2Menu  3View  4Edit  5Copy  6RenMov  7Mkdir  8Delete  9Setup  10Quit
```

Figure 12-15

When two panels are displayed, the Commander will use the unselected panel as the default destination for copy and move commands. With the panels set up as they are, you can copy or move files from the DOS directory (the selected panel) to the root directory (the unselected panel). As an example, highlight the FDISK.COM file by entering

`[Alt/fd]`

Enter the move command.

`[F6]`

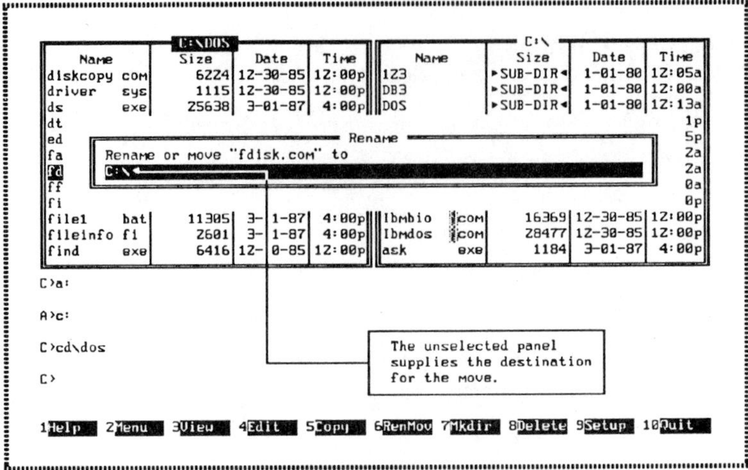

Figure 12-16

To move the file, enter

↵

You can reverse source and destination drives by switching panels, thereby making the right panel (the root directory) the source and the left (\DOS) the destination. Enter

`[Tab]`

Locate the FDISK.COM file again. Enter

`[Alt/fd]`

You can move it back to the \DOS directory by entering

`[F6]`
↵

By using the two panels as source and destination you can speed the copying or moving process between directories or different disks. For example, if you have a disk in drive A you would enter

`a:` ↵

The selected panel would then select drive A as the source.

Panel Display Options

The directory display in the panels can be altered by selecting options from the setup menu. To change the display modes, enter

[F9]

The Commander displays the setup menu.

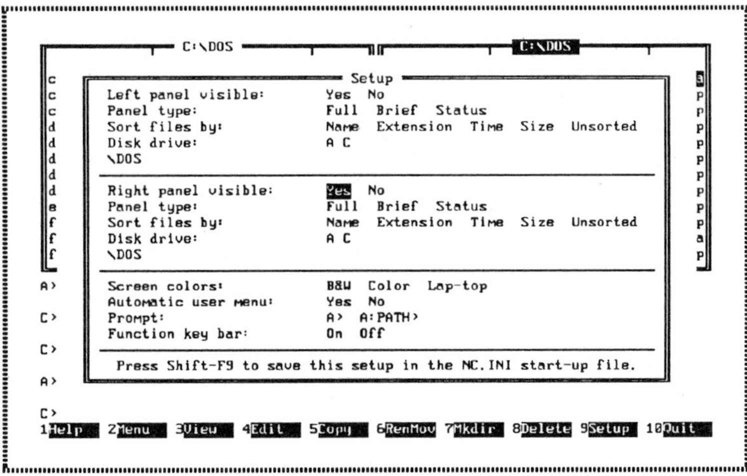

Figure 12-17

The menu displays three sections. The top two sections are identical and they control the left and right panel displays. The bottom section of the menu controls the display options that apply to other aspects of the Commander.

The active options are highlighted. The panel options are:

1. **Visible.** Whether the panel should be displayed or not.

2. **Type.** The panels can be displayed in three ways. **Full** refers to the directory display. **Brief** is a modified directory display in which only the filenames appear, and the size, date and time are omitted. The **brief** display shows more files, four columns full, than the **full** display. **Status** refers to the disk status display.

3. **Sort order.** You can select to have the file displayed by name, extension, time and date, or size. You can also select an unsorted display. Unsorted displays

the files as they are written in the disk directory. The sort order refers to the panel displays; it does not affect the actual order in which files are written in the disk directory. You can use the Norton Utilities program DS (directory sort) to actually rewrite the disk directory.

4. **Drive and Directory**. You can enter the directory and drive for each panel.

Most of the options on this menu can be implemented by [Ctrl] commands during the panel display. The exceptions are selecting the sort order of the directory and selecting a brief file type display.

The status of the setup menu will always reflect the current status of the Commander. For example, if the right panel is highlighted, the cursor on the menu display will appear in the right panel section of the menu.

You can change the display options of the panel by moving the cursor to the item you want to change and typing the letter of the option. For example, to change the right panel to brief display sorted by extension, enter

```
[down arrow]
     b
[down arrow]
     e
```

To see the change in the panels, enter

↵

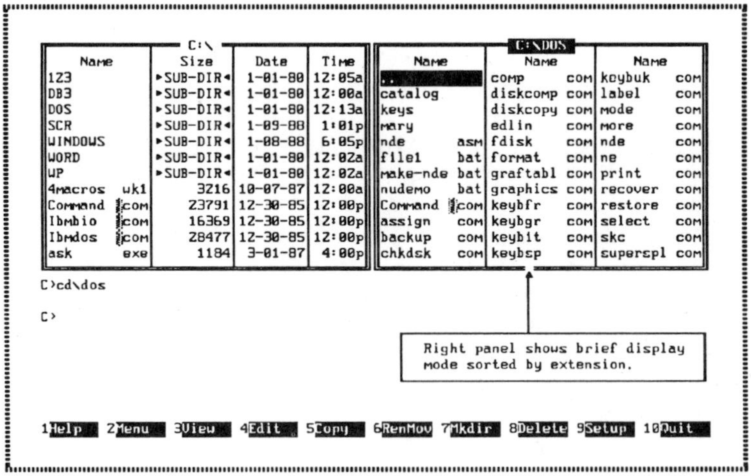

```
                     C:\                                          C:\DOS
     Name             Size      Date      Time      Name        Name             Name
123                ►SUB-DIR◄  1-01-80   12:05a   ..          comp      com   keybuk    com
DB3                ►SUB-DIR◄  1-01-80   12:00a   catalog     diskcomp  com   label     com
DOS                ►SUB-DIR◄  1-01-80   12:13a   keys        diskcopy  com   mode      com
SCR                ►SUB-DIR◄  1-09-88    1:01p   mary        edlin     com   more      com
WINDOWS            ►SUB-DIR◄  1-08-88    6:05p   nde     asm fdisk     com   nde       com
WORD               ►SUB-DIR◄  1-01-80   12:02a   file1   bat format    com   ne        com
WP                 ►SUB-DIR◄  1-01-80   12:02a   make-nde bat graftabl com   print     com
4macros    wk1          3216 10-07-87   12:00a   nudemo  bat graphics  com   recover   com
Command    com         23791 12-30-85   12:00p   Command com keybfr    com   restore   com
Ibmbio     com         16369 12-30-85   12:00p   assign  com keybgr    com   select    com
Ibmdos     com         28477 12-30-85   12:00p   backup  com keybit    com   skc       com
ask        exe          1184  3-01-87    4:00p   chkdsk  com keybsp    com   superspl  com
C>cd\dos

C>

                                   Right panel shows brief display
                                   mode sorted by extension.

1Help  2Menu  3View  4Edit  5Copy  6RenMov  7Mkdir  8Delete  9Setup  10Quit
```

Figure 12-18

Setting Defaults

The options displayed on the setup menu can be stored in a file called NC.INI, (Norton Commander Initialization). This file is used to store user selected default settings. This initialization feature allows you to customize the commander to fit your needs.

The **[Shift/F9]** command will write the current settings to the NC.INI file. You do not have to display the settings menu, **[F9]**, in order to save the settings. You can enter [Shift/F9] when the panels are displayed, as well as when the setup menu is displayed.

Typical Tasks

The Commander is a superb tool for people who need to make changes on their computers. While there are many people whose systems remain largely the same year in and year out, the majority of computer users are finding that there are almost always changes that need to be made because of new programs, program upgrades and new ideas about how to use their systems more effectively.

As an example, suppose you just received a new copy of the Norton Utilities programs. You can use the Commander to install the programs and make any other changes needed for accommodations. You will see how the Commander improves the operation.

Begin by placing both windows into the root directory. Enter

```
[Ctrl \ ]
  [Tab]
[Ctrl \ ]
```

Create a new directory for the Norton Utilities programs.

```
[F7]
nu ↵
```

> Normally, I like to place these programs in the DOS directory but for the sake of this example I will break my own rule.

Place the Norton Utilities program disk 1 in Drive A. You can now setup the panels as source and destination for copying files. Since the new directory is automatically highlighted, enter

↵

You have now set this panel as the destination. Move to the other panel by entering

[Tab]

Change disks by entering the command at DOS. The Commander's ability to access DOS at the same time that the Commander is running makes the line between the Commander and DOS transparent. Enter

a: ↵

You are now set to copy files from **A** to **C:\NU**.

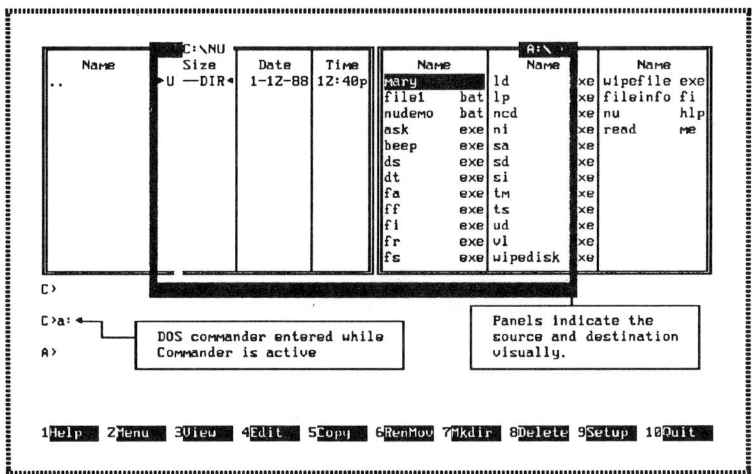

Figure 12-19

To select all the files on A, use the wildcard command. Remember that [+] refers to the gray plus sign on the number keypad. Enter

[+] ↵
[F5] ↵

All of the files from the disk are copied to the destination on the hard disk.

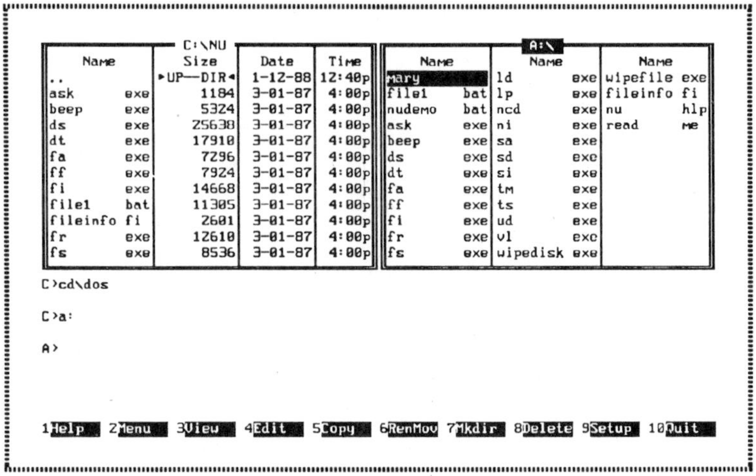

```
                    C:\NU                                        A:\
     Name          Size      Date     Time       Name           Name            Name
..             ►UP—DIR◄  1-12-88  12:40p   mary           ld        exe   wipefile exe
ask       exe      1184  3-01-87   4:00p   file1     bat  lp        exe   fileinfo fi
beep      exe      5324  3-01-87   4:00p   nudemo    bat  ncd       exe   nu       hlp
ds        exe     25638  3-01-87   4:00p   ask       exe  ni        exe   read     me
dt        exe     17910  3-01-87   4:00p   beep      exe  sa        exe
fa        exe      7296  3-01-87   4:00p   ds        exe  sd        exe
ff        exe      7924  3-01-87   4:00p   dt        exe  si        exe
fi        exe     14668  3-01-87   4:00p   fa        exe  tm        exe
file1     bat     11305  3-01-87   4:00p   ff        exe  ts        exe
fileinfo  fi       2601  3-01-87   4:00p   fi        exe  ud        exe
fr        exe     12610  3-01-87   4:00p   fr        exe  vl        exe
fs        exe      8536  3-01-87   4:00p   fs        exe  wipedisk  exe

C>cd\dos

C>a:

A>

1Help  2Menu  3View  4Edit  5Copy  6RenMov  7Mkdir  8Delete  9Setup  10Quit
```

Figure 12-20

Since there are two disks in the Norton Utilities set, place the second disk in drive A. Note that the panel for drive A still shows the directory listing for the previous disk. To get the Commander to update the display, enter

[Ctrl/r]

The program reads the disk again and displays the correct list of files. Copy the files from this second disk by entering

[+] ↵
[F5] ↵

When the program reaches the file NU.HLP, a message box is displayed because there is already a file with the same name on the disk.

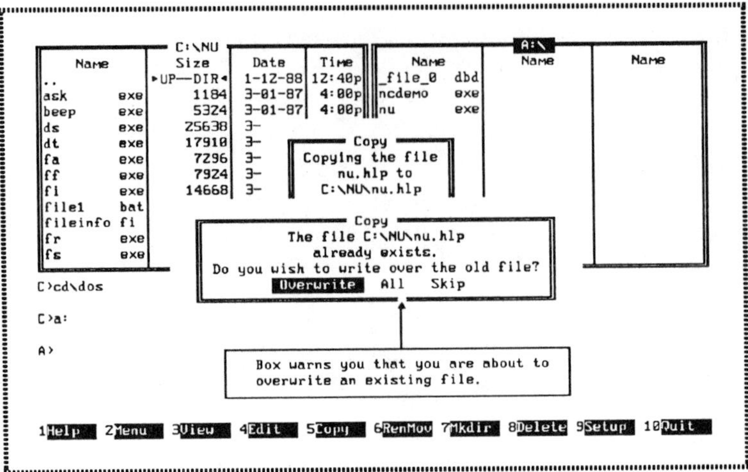

Figure 12-21

For now, skip the file. Options for this are explained under Pointing with DOS Commands, below. Enter

s

The copying continues until all the files on A, with the exception of the one skipped, have been copied to C.

Pointing with DOS Commands

What about the duplicate file, NU.HLP? It appears that the Norton Utilities program came with two copies of the same file. However, you cannot be sure that the files are exactly the same. DOS provides a program called FC (file compare), which checks two files to see if they are identical.

> In the DOS 2 version, the COMP program is used for this purpose. The DOS 3 version is usually supplied with FC in place of COMP.

To use the FC program you must enter a command that tells the program what to files to test. Example:

```
FC a:nu.hlp c:nu.hlp
```

However, it is not required that you enter the filenames with the Commander. Instead, you can simply point at them. You can use the Commander in combination with DOS to make entry of DOS commands simpler and avoid typing mistakes.

> This operation assumes that you have a PATH open to the directory on drive C that contains the FC program, C:\DOS. If you do not have this path open you can enter a PATH command like this:
>
> path c:\dos; ↵

Begin by entering the DOS command.

```
fc
[space bar]
```

Instead of typing in the name of the file, use the arrow keys to point at the name NU.HLP. When the filename is highlighted, you can transfer the filename to the DOS command line by entering

```
[Ctrl/↵]
```

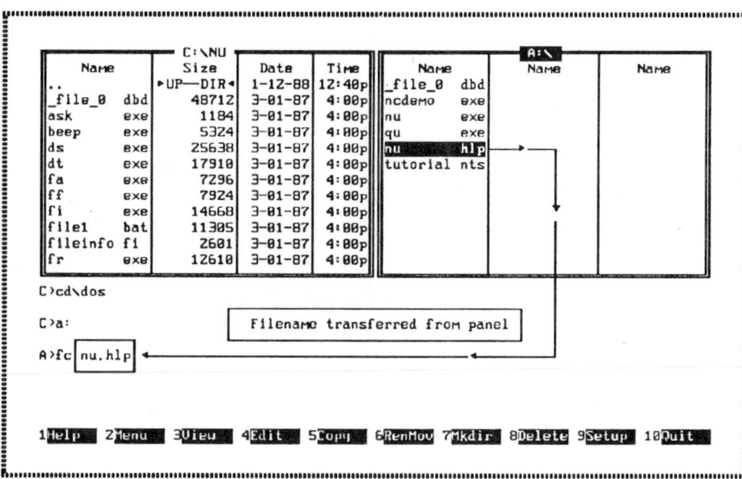

Figure 12-22

The file that you want to compare it to is located in the C:\NU directory. Enter

```
c:\nu\
```

You can have the Commander transfer a second copy of the name into the command at this point. Enter

[Ctrl/]

You have now assembled the complete command. Execute it by entering

↵

The FC program runs and displays a message relating that there are no differences between the files. Therefore, there is no need to copy this file to the hard disk.

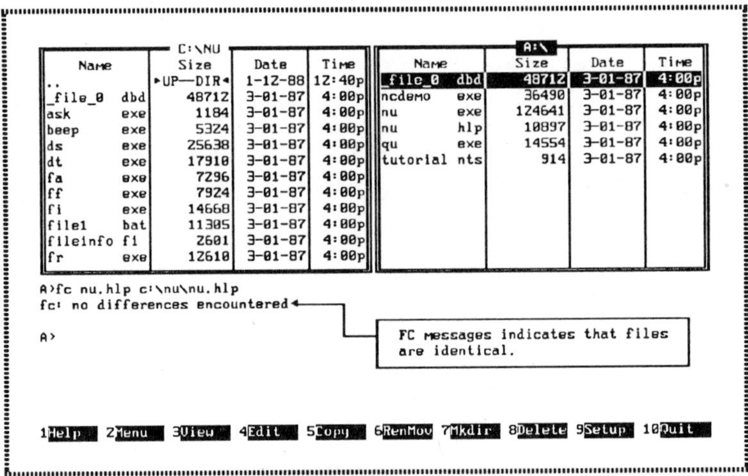

Figure 12-23

The ability to combine manual entry with file pointing is one of the Commander's convenient features. It demonstrates the concept that the Commander supports and enhances DOS without cutting you off from the operating system. Most DOS commands are simple to enter. It is the filenames that present difficulty since they change with each command. The command itself stays the same.

View Files

The [F3] key invokes the **view** command, which gives the Commander the ability to display the contents of files so that you can inspect them.

Most programs are supplied with a **readme** file, which usually contains information about the program that was not included in the printed documentation. The

Norton Utilities program also comes with a readme. To inspect this file with the **view** command, change to the left panel by entering

[Tab]

Locate the **readme** file by entering

[Alt/r]

Display the contents of the file by entering

[F3]

The contents of the file are displayed in a full-screen mode.

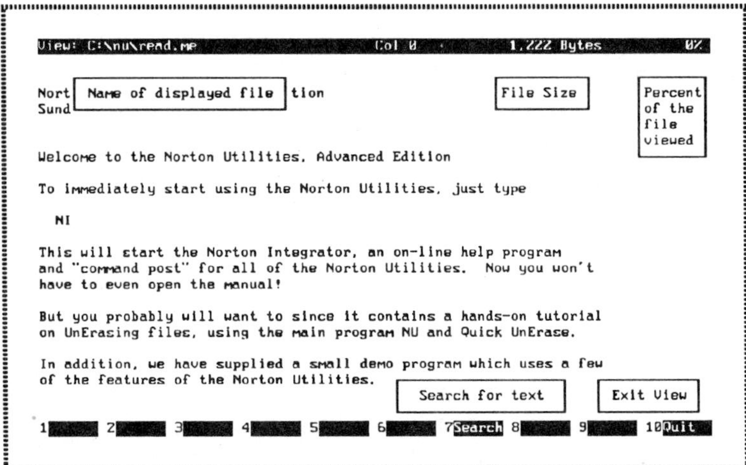

Figure 12-24

You can use the arrowkeys, [Pg Dn] and [Pg Up], to move through the file. [Home] and [End] will move you to the top and bottom of the file respectively.

The view mode also contains a search feature enabling you to locate a specific string in the file. For example, to locate any references to the word **speed**, enter

[F7]

A box appears that allows you to enter the string to search for.

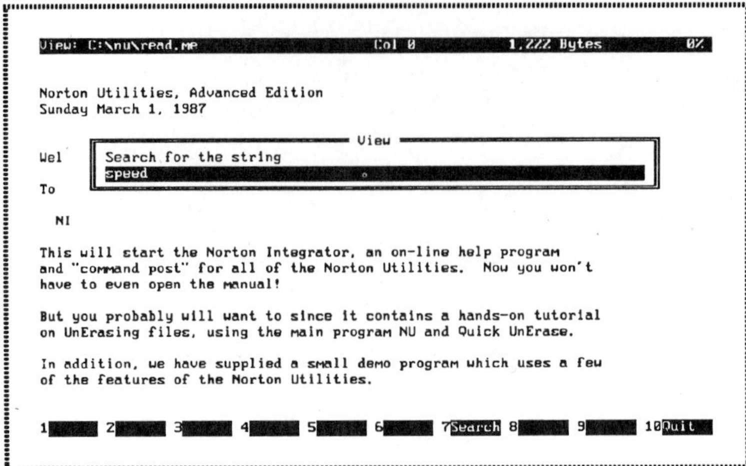

Figure 12-25

Enter the text you want to locate.

```
speed ↵
```

The cursor moves to the first match for that item, if any, in the text file. If you want to continue the search, enter

```
[Shift/F7]
```

The program locates the next match, if any. To exit the view mode, enter

```
[F10]
```

Although the view mode is simple, it is the kind of tool that can save you a great deal of time. You can display batch and text files quickly. When inspecting a computer you've never worked with before, run the Commander and display the AUTOEXEC.BAT and CONFIG.SYS files with [F3] to get some information about the computer setup. Used with the SI (systems information) program from the Norton Utilities, you can get a good idea of what you are dealing with in a few moments.

The DOS alternative to the [F3] command is to use the TYPE command with the MORE filter. Example:

```
type readme|more
```

Of course, you cannot scroll backwards with the TYPE command. If you missed something you must enter the command again. View is limited to files of about 20K.

> The view mode is aimed primarily at text files. Edit can be used on other files, such as 1-2-3 WK1 files. The display of non-text files is similar to that shown in the main Norton Utilities programs in which hex value 00 appears as blank space.

Editing Files

In addition to the [F3], **view** mode, the Commander includes an edit mode, [F4]. The edit mode displays the text of text or batch files and allows you to edit the files. For example, suppose you decide to take the advice offered in the Norton Utilities programs and make the FR/SAVE command part of the AUTOEXEC.BAT for your hard disk. Normally this would call for the use of an editor like EDLIN, or the NORTON EDITOR. But with the Commander running, you can edit text files up to 20K in size with any additional programs. For example, you could alter your AUTOEXEC.BAT to include a command for protecting your hard disk against formatting by using the Edit mode. First locate the AUTOEXEC.BAT.

> FR/SAVE is used to protect your hard disk from accidental reformatting. The FR program is discussed in Section V on survival skills.

Move to the root directory. Enter

```
[Alt \ ]
```

Search for the AUTOEXEC.BAT. Enter

```
[Alt/auto]
```

The highlight will jump to the first file that begins with AUTO. If this file is not AUTOEXEC.BAT, move the highlight until you have located it.

To edit a file, simply press

```
[F4]
```

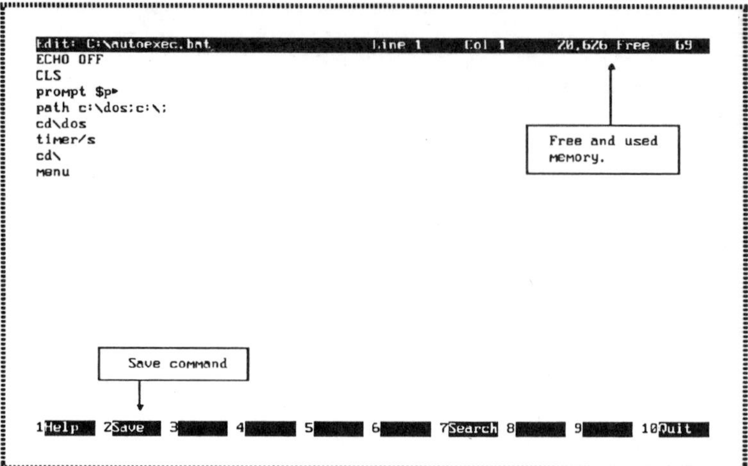

Figure 12-26

The screen for the editor is similar to the view mode, with these additions.

1. The top lines show two values at the right side. The first is the number of characters you can add to the file. The second is the number of characters currently in the file. The total is always 20,700.
2. The Line and column status of the cursor is displayed in the middle of the bar.
3. The [F2] key is assigned the save text function. You must specifically save changes o additions if you want the file updated.

The **AUTOEXEC.BAT** shown in the illustration runs a menu batch program as the last command in the **AUTOEXEC** routine. You should insert the unformat instructions before the MENU command.

The Editor is always in an insert mode. The [Del] key deletes a single character and [Ctrl/y] deletes an entire line. The editor uses commands similar to WordStar for deleting text and moving the cursor.

If your AUTOEXEC.BAT is similar to the example, place the cursor at the beginning of the last line, MENU. Enter

```
cls ↵
cd\nu ↵
fr/save ↵
cd\↵
```

Note that an * appears in the middle of the status line indicating the displayed file has been modified. The file looks like this:

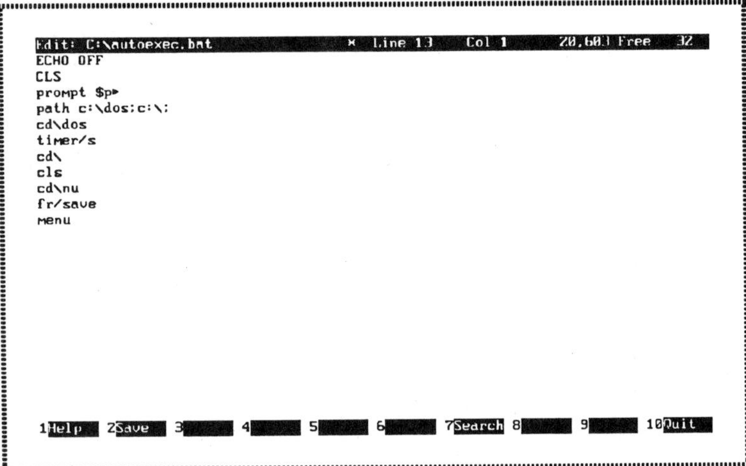

Figure 12-27

Save the modified AUTOEXEC.BAT by entering

`[F2]`
`[F10]`

The ability to edit files is another invaluable tool integrated simply and powerfully into the Commander.

Edit DOS Commands

One further editing facility is offered by the Commander. Like the Norton DOS Editor supplied with the Norton Editor program, the Commander allows you to scroll through a list of previously entered DOS commands.

For example, enter

`chkdsk ↵`

Note that part of the display is covered by the panels. To see the entire display, enter

`[Ctrl/o]`

Suppose that you wanted to run CHKDSK again but using the /F switch. To get the previous command back, enter

`[Ctrl/e]`

The command is redisplayed. You can edit the command. Enter

```
/f ↵
```

Like the Norton DOS Editor, you can scroll backwards in the list to as many commands as can be held in memory by the Commander. Enter

```
[Ctrl/e]
[Ctrl/e]
```

This time the CHKDSK command appears. Execute the command by entering

Note that if you go too far back, [Ctrl/x] will scroll forward in the command list.

Searching the DOS Command List

The Commander has an interesting variation on editing DOS commands. It involves the use of the [Ctrl/↵] combination. If the [Ctrl/↵] is used following a space, the Commander inserts the highlighted filename. However, if you begin a DOS command and do not type a space before you enter [Ctrl/↵], the Commander will take that as a different command. The Commander will search the list of previous DOS commands stored in memory to attempt to find an earlier command that matches the character you entered. For example, you previously entered an FC, file compare command. Enter

```
fc
[Ctrl/↵]
```

The Commander completes the entry with the last command that matches FC. You can accept the command with ↵, edit it, or scroll backwards or forwards to other commands by using [Ctrl/e] or [Ctrl/o]. You can clear the line by entering

```
[Ctrl/y]
```

Return the panel display to its original state by entering

```
[Ctrl/o]
[Ctrl/l]
```

Menus

The Commander has the ability to display user-defined menus. These menus can be superimposed over the display windows or you can turn off the panels to display the menu by itself.

The key to user menus are files called **NC.MNU**. When [F2] is pressed, the Commander is prompted to search for a **NC.MNU** file and use it to control menu display and operation.

The Commander program is supplied with a sample menu file. Erase the sample menu from your hard disk. You can use the WIPEFILE command to search the entire hard disk to make sure that all copies of the sample menu have been removed. An example of the command is shown below:

```
wipefile \nc.mnu/s/n ↵
```

If you are going to construct a menu system using the Commander, you should begin with an NC.MNU file in the root directory. Then, you can edit the file using the Commander editor, [F4]. However, since you erased all the NC.MNU files, you can use a DOS command to create an empty file and then use the Commander editor to expand that file. Enter

```
copy con: nc.mnu ↵
        ↵
      [F6] ↵
```

You have created a file, NC.MNU, with a single blank line. Now, move the highlight to the name NC.MNU so that the Commander can be used to edit the file.

A menu file consists of two types of information.

1. **Menu items.** A menu item is a single line of text that contains the name of the key, if any, used to activate the menu item, followed by a colon. After the colon, you can enter the text you want displayed for the menu item.

   The command keys can be letters, numbers, function keys or [Ctrl] characters. Function keys are entered as **F1, F2, F3,** and so on. [Ctrl] characters are entered as ^A, ^B, ^C, and so forth.

   A menu can display up to 20 menu items at one time. It is not necessary that a menu option be assigned keystroke commands. If no keystroke command is assigned, the option can be executed by moving the highlight to the desired item and pressing ↵.

2. **DOS instructions.** Following each menu item should be a list of the DOS commands needed to carry out the operation. You can list as many commands

as needed after each item. There is a 4000 character limit on the size of the NC.MNU file.

Suppose that you wanted to create a menu that would run three applications, Lotus 1-2-3, dBASE III Plus and WordPerfect. Begin the text file by assigning the [F1] function key to Lotus 1-2-3. Enter

```
F1:
[Tab]
Lotus 1-2-3 Release 2.01 ↵
```

Notice that a space or a [Tab] must separate the key command from the menu item. Now enter the commands you want to execute when this option is selected. In this example, the Norton Utilities TM command is used to keep track of the length of time the program is in use. (See Section II for details on the TM program.) Enter

```
[Tab] CLS ↵
CD\123 ↵
[Tab] 123 ↵
[Tab] CD\ ↵
```

Notice that the last command in the sequence, CD\, returned you to the directory that contains the NC.MNU file. This is important if you intend to create submenus, discussed later in this section. The file looks like this:

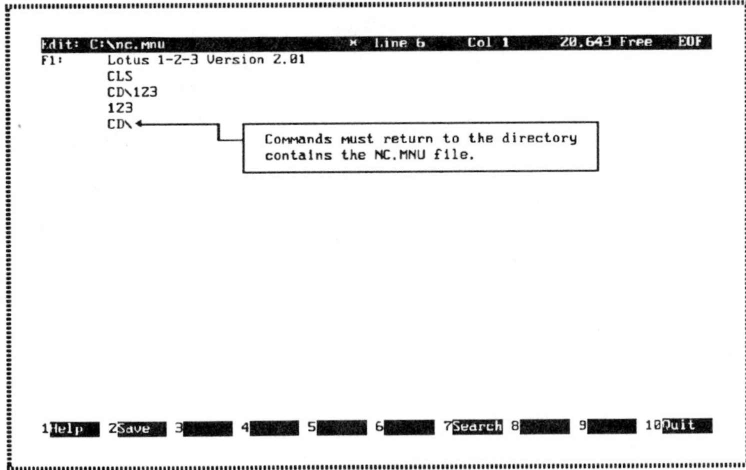

Figure 12-28

Complete the file by adding two more items.

```
Edit: C:\nc.mnu                    *  Line 16    Col 1       20,548 Free   EOF
F1:       Lotus 1-2-3 Version 2.01
          CLS
          CD\123
          123
          CD\
F2:       dBASE III Plus
          CLS
          CD\DB3
          DBASE
          CD\
F3:       WORDPERFECT 4.2
          CLS
          CD\WP
          WP
          CD\






1Help  2Save  3      4      5      6      7Search 8      9      10Quit
```

Figure 12-29

Save this file by entering

[F2]
[F10]

To display the user defined menu, enter

[F2]

The menu appears superimposed over the other Commander panels.

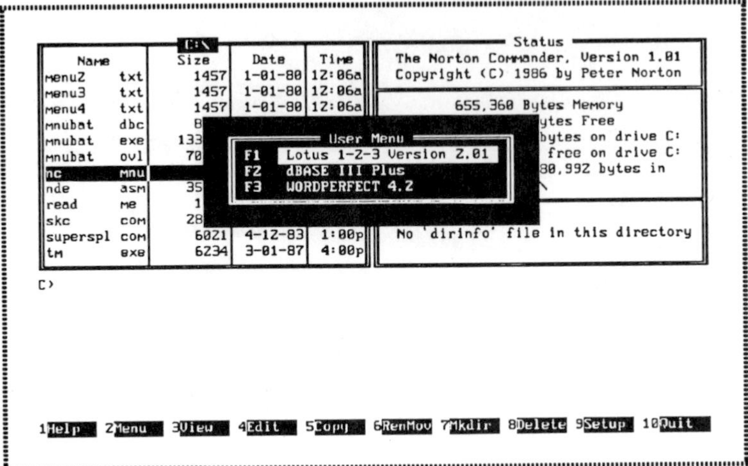

Figure 12-30

There are two ways to activate the options: (1) by using **Command keys** and (2) by **pointing** the highlight at the desired menu item and pressing ↵. Remember that while the menu is displayed, the function keys will not carry out their Commander functions.

Test the menu by running one of the options. Enter

[F1]

Exit 1-2-3. Notice that after the last command executes, the menu is not redisplayed. In order for the Commander system to display the menu all of the time, the setup must be changed. Enter

[F9]

The [F9] command displays a series of options: the top two sections control the display of the panels, while the bottom section controls the screen colors, the function key bar, the user menus and the DOS prompt. Notice that the panel commands can also be controlled from the Commander display using the [Ctrl] commands.

The option that controls menu display is labeled **Automatic user menu**. Set this to YES. Return to the display mode by entering

↵

Notice that the menu is not displayed at this point. You must still manually turn on the menu. Enter

[F2]

Run 1-2-3 and exit it again. This time the menu automatically reappears. If you want to remove the menu and return to the Commander's normal operations, enter

[Esc]

Making a Turnkey System

You can use the Commander menus to create a turnkey system that automatically displays the Commander menu when the computer is booted. First, add a line to the beginning of the menu that will act as a title. Move the highlight to NC.MNU and enter

[F4]

The first line in the menu is not assigned a command key and is not followed by DOS commands. The line is technically part of the menu, but in practice it will function as a heading or label for menu options.

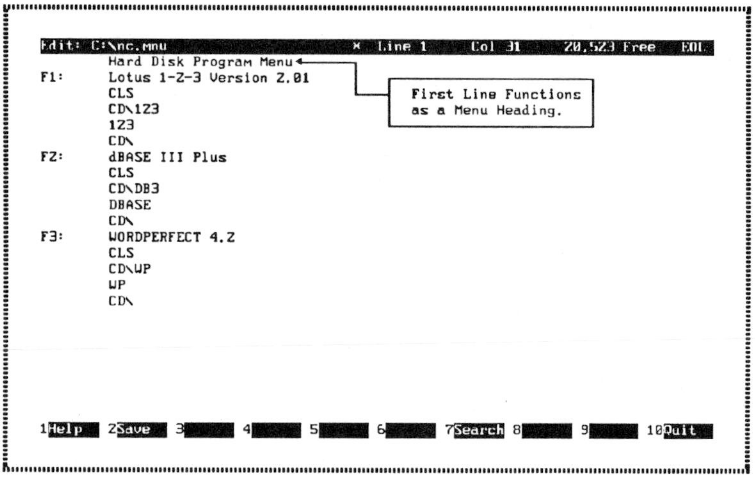

```
Edit: C:\nc.mnu                              *  Line 1    Col 31    20,523 Free   EOL
           Hard Disk Program Menu
F1:        Lotus 1-2-3 Version 2.01
           CLS                               First Line Functions
           CD\123                            as a Menu Heading.
           123
           CD\
F2:        dBASE III Plus
           CLS
           CD\DB3
           DBASE
           CD\
F3:        WORDPERFECT 4.2
           CLS
           CD\WP
           WP
           CD\

1Help  2Save  3  4  5  6  7Search  8  9  10Quit
```

Figure 12-31

Save the revised menu. Enter

[F2]
[F10]

If you are creating a turnkey system, you might want to suppress the display of the function key bar and Commander panels. In effect you are restricting the Commander to functioning as a menu program. While this is only part of the capacity of the command, you may find that other less experienced users will relate better to a clear, uncluttered menu. To turn off these items, enter

```
[Ctrl/o]
[Ctrl/b]
```

If you want the Commander to load and display this way, save this setup, which is stored in a file NC.INI. The INI file, an initialization file, records a set of your preferred default settings. To record the current setting in the NC.INI file, enter

```
[Shift/F9]
```

> If you delete the NC.INI file, the Commander will return to the default settings the next time it is loaded.

The Commander program asks you to confirm your decision to save these settings. Enter

```
s
```

The final step is to add a command that loads the Commander into your AUTOEXEC.BAT on the hard disk. Turn the display panels back on with

```
[Ctrl/o]
```

> The settings that will be used when the program loads again are the last set of settings saved with the [Shift/F9] command, not the last set of settings used with the Commander.

Highlight the AUTOEXEC.BAT and enter

```
[F4]
```

Add the NC command as the last one in the batch file.

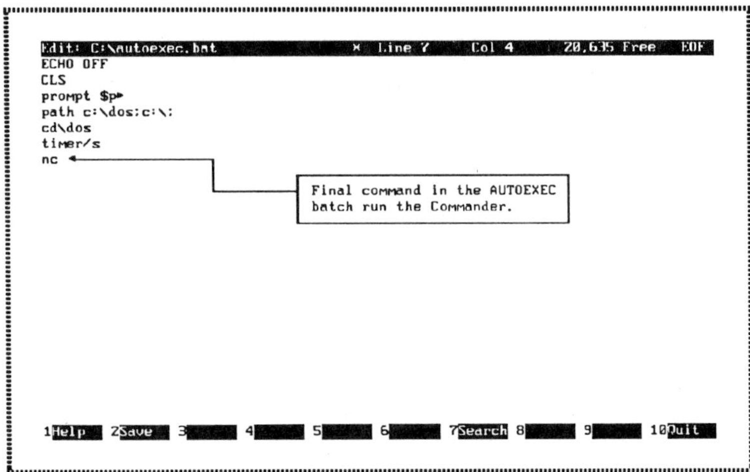

Figure 12-32

Save the file.

[F2]
[F10]

Exit the Commander by entering

[F10] ↵

To start the menu system you can reboot your computer, or, to take a shortcut, enter

`autoexec` ↵

The batch executes the AUTOEXEC routine and finally displays the user menu.

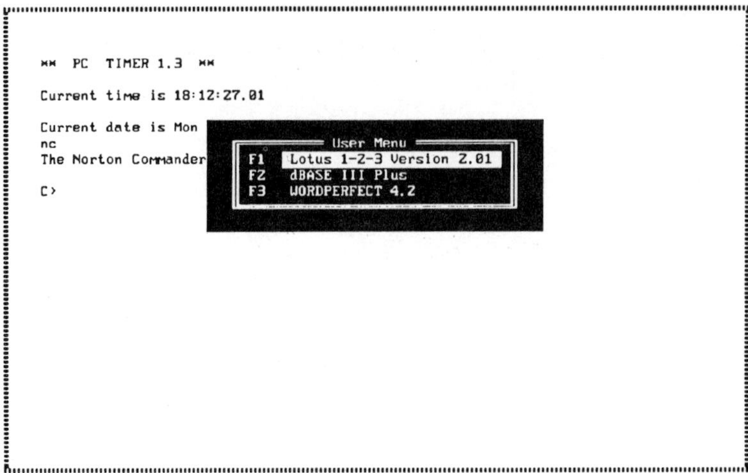

Figure 12-33

To exit the user menu and return to the normal Commander display, enter

```
[Esc]
[Ctrl/o]
[Ctrl/b]
```

Submenus

The concept of user menus can be extended beyond a single menu into a network that can include as varied applications as is possible to construct with DOS batch files. For example, suppose you want to create a submenu of DOS utility operations. The key is to place a file also called NC.MNU in another directory, for example, \DOS. When you change directories, the Commander will search for an NC.MNU file and display the menu option described in the NC.MNU in that directory.

By including options on each menu that change the directories you can create a system of interrelated directories. The first step is to include the submenu option in the main directory stored in the root directory. Move the highlight to the NC.MNU file and enter the edit mode.

```
[F4]
```

Add an option to the end of this menu that changes the directory to \DOS, as shown below.

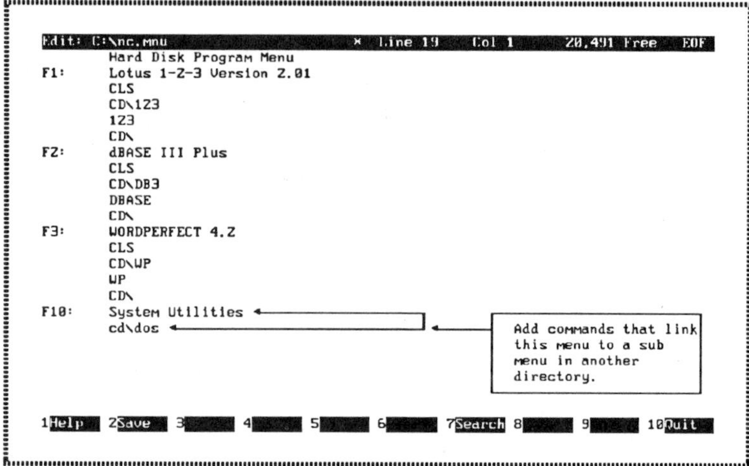

Figure 12-34

Save the revised menu. Enter

```
[F2]
[F10]
```

Change the directory to \DOS by entering

```
cd\dos ↵
```

Create a new file called NC.MNU. Enter

```
copy con: nc.mnu ↵
↵
[F6] ↵
```

In this example, create three commands on this menu plus a fourth that will return you to the main menu in the root directory. The first command is one that formats a floppy disk. Enter

```
F1:
[Tab]
Format a Floppy Disk ↵
[Tab]
format a: ↵
```

The next command is a bit more elaborate. It will use several programs, some DOS, some Norton Utilities, to evaluate the status of your computer system. Enter

```
F2:
[Tab]
Check System ↵
[Tab]
chkdsk/f ↵
pause ↵
si c: ↵
pause ↵
sd/report ↵
pause ↵
```

Notice that the DOS command, PAUSE, was inserted after each operation to allow the user to read the information before the next command wrote data to the screen.

The final command will be used to set a printer characteristic by sending a code or codes to the printer. To take the most common example, the command will send a [Ctrl/o] command to the printer, which will set Epson and IBM graphics printers to the compressed printing Mode. As an additional example, the code for near letter quality print on an IBM Prowriter, [Esc]I6, will be sent also.

The Commander editor is capable of inserting control characters and [Esc] in a file. The Commander uses [Ctrl/q] to allow entry of [Ctrl] characters.

> This is the third variation on this theme mentioned in this book. The EDLIN program uses [Ctrl/v] while the Norton Editor uses [Ctrl/p] for the same purpose.

Enter

```
F3:
[Tab]
Set Printer to Compressed NLQ ↵
[Tab]
ECHO
[space bar]
[Ctrl/q]
[Ctrl/o]
```

The Commander editor displays the IBM PC character set symbol for [Ctrl/o].

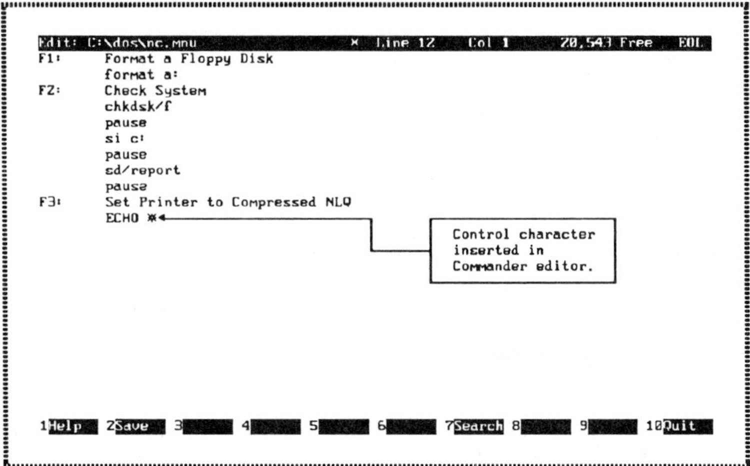

Figure 12-35

Complete the command by entering

```
[space bar]
>PRN ↵
```

Enter another printer command.

```
[Tab]
ECHO
[space bar]
```

This time you need to insert an [Esc] character. Enter

```
[Ctrl/q]
[Esc]
```

The character symbol for [Esc] is inserted. Complete the command by entering

```
Ib >PRN ↵
```

Finally, create an option that returns you to the main menu. Enter

```
F10:
[Tab]
Return to Main Menu ↵
[Tab]
cd\
↵
```

The file looks like this:

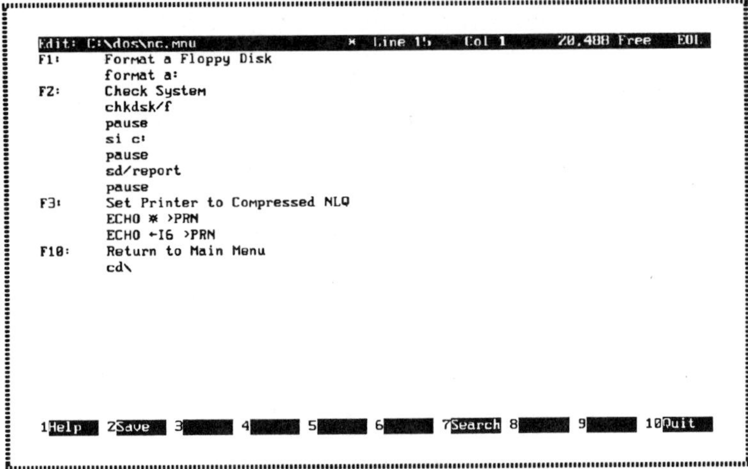

```
Edit: C:\dos\nc.mnu          * Line 15    Col 1      20,488 Free   EOL
F1:     Format a Floppy Disk
        format a:
F2:     Check System
        chkdsk/f
        pause
        si c:
        pause
        sd/report
        pause
F3:     Set Printer to Compressed NLQ
        ECHO * >PRN
        ECHO ←I6 >PRN
F10:    Return to Main Menu
        cd\

1Help  2Save  3  4  5  6  7Search  8  9  10Quit
```

Figure 12-36

Save the file by entering

```
[F2]
[F10]
```

Change back to the root directory and exit the Commander. Enter

```
cd\ ↵
[F10]↵
```

To start the menu system, enter

```
nc ↵
```

The Commander loads the menu automatically because of the settings stored in the NC.INI file. To change to the submenu, enter

[F10]

The submenu appears.

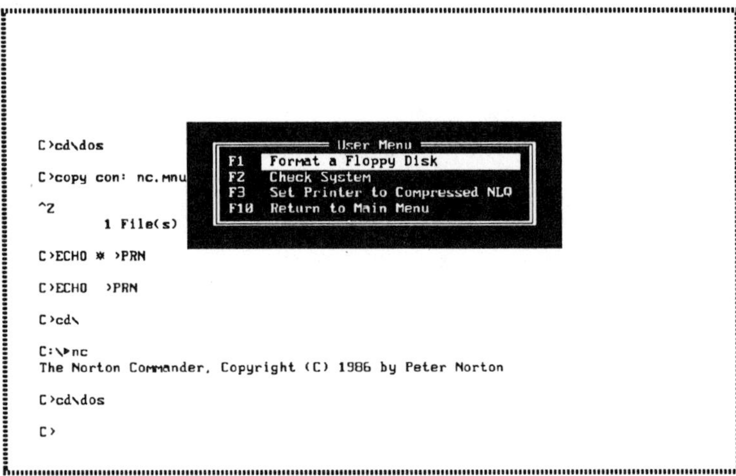
C>cd\dos
C>copy con: nc.mnu
^Z
1 File(s)
C>ECHO * >PRN
C>ECHO >PRN
C>cd\
C:\>nc
The Norton Commander, Copyright (C) 1986 by Peter Norton
C>cd\dos
C>
User Menu
F1 Format a Floppy Disk
F2 Check System
F3 Set Printer to Compressed NLQ
F10 Return to Main Menu

Figure 12-37

Run the options to test that they work. To return to the main menu, enter

[F10]

The Commander can be used to develop a complex system of menus that can handle quite a number of functions for the average user, without them interacting with DOS directly. The Commander menu system is one of the fastest to create. It is even faster to modify because the editing tools needed are built into the Commander. Return the commander to its normal display. Enter

[Esc]
[Ctrl/o]
[Ctrl/b]

Executing Data Files

The normal procedure for running applications from DOS is to enter the name of the EXE, COM or BAT file that corresponds to the application you want to run. The Commander allows you to point at the EXE, COM or BAT files and execute them by pressing ↵. But the Commander goes farther than that. The Commander has the ability to execute an application when data files related to that application are highlighted and selected with ↵. In this regard, programs fall into two classes.

Programs That Accept a File Argument

A program that accepts a file argument refers to programs that will automatically load a specified file as soon as the program is loaded. This is quite common in the word processing field. WordStar, WordStar 2000, WordPerfect and MicroSoft Word all accept file arguments. Multimate does not. For example, the commands listed below will run the specified programs and load the file, TEXT.DOC.

```
ws text.doc

ws2 text.doc

wp text.doc

word text.doc
```

dBASE III Plus will accept a dBASE program name as an argument. The following command will load dBASE and run a program named MENU.

```
dbase menu
```

Programs That Do Not Accept a File Argument

Lotus 1-2-3 will not accept a filename as an argument. For example, the command below will not start 1-2-3 and load the SAMPLE.WK1 worksheet.

```
123 sample.wk1
```

> In fact, the SAMPLE.WK1 will be taken for a driver set name and the program will fail to load.

If you are running an application that accepts a filename argument, you can install the Commander to run the program and load the file, whenever you point and ↵ a filename. If the related application does not accept a file argument, you can still run the program by pointing at a data file, but the application will not automatically load the file.

This effect is achieved by a special text file called NC.EXE. This file contains a list of file extensions and the DOS execution commands that should be related to those extensions. For example, files with a WK1 extension would be related to 1-2-3, DOC files would be related to Word, and DBF files would be related to dBASE.

The NC.EXT file is a normal text file. It contains a list of extensions and the instructions for what program to run if the highlighted file matches one of the extensions. As an example, create an EXT file for the three applications used in the menu example, 1-2-3, dBASE and WordPerfect.

To create a new EXT file, enter

```
copy con: nc.ext ↵
↵
[F6] ↵
```

Highlight the file and load it into the editor with

```
[F4]
```

The EXT file recognizes the ! as a special symbol. The ! is used to indicate what part, if any, of the highlighted file name ought to be used to load the related program.

The EXT file commands have two parts.

1. Extension. The extension tells the Commander what files are related to which loading instructions. You can enter any three character file extensions or use DOS wildcards, * or ?, to represent characters.

2. Loading instruction. The loading instruction tells the Commander what command to enter in order to execute the program. The command can include a file argument if relevant.

For example, Lotus 1-2-3 Version 1A uses the file extension WKS for all of its files. A loading instruction for that program might look like this:

```
WKS:            123
```

Note that the two parts of the commands are delimited by a colon. Release 2 of 1-2-3 can load files with extensions WKS and WK1. To accommodate those files you might use a DOS wildcard character, ?, in the loading instruction.

```
WK?:            123
```

If the program is capable of accepting a file argument, you must use !, which is used as a symbol for the highlighted filename. The ! can be used in the following ways:

! Used by itself, ! tells the Commander to insert the filename, without extension, into the loading command. For example, dBASE assumes that any loading argument will have the standard dBASE program extension, PRG. A loading command for that program would look like this:

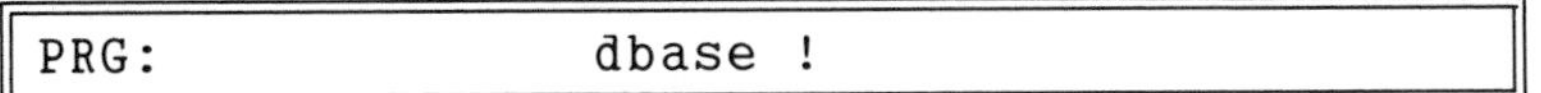

When a file with a PRG extension is selected, the Commander substitutes the filename, without the extension, into the loading command.

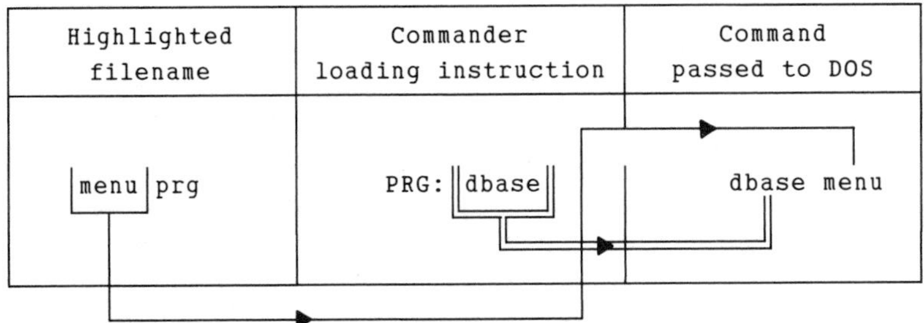

Highlighted filename
Commander loading instruction
Command passed to DOS
menu prg
PRG: dbase
dbase menu

!.! Used in this form the Commander will pass both the filename and extension to the loading command. This command would be used in cases where the application expects one extension but would accept others. dBASE expects a PRG extension for a program file but will accept any other specified extension, FMT, for example.

```
FMT:                    dbase !.!
```

!. This form is used to enter the filename and a period but no extension. This form is used with programs that have a default extension such as PRG with dBASE, or DOC with Word. If you want to load a file that has no extension, then you need to mark that by explicitly using the period.

Loading command syntax	filename assumed to be
word letter word letter.	letter.doc letter

!\ This form is used to insert the current path name into the file specification.

!: This form inserts the current drive specification.

These two can be used when it is necessary to pass the drive and or path to the application along with the filename and/or extension. This type of specification would be a bit unusual since most applications gather this information automatically from memory when they load.

You can now enter the loading instructions for the programs used in this example. Begin with Lotus 1-2-3. Since 1-2-3 uses file extensions and limits them to WK1 or WKS but does not accept a file argument, you can enter

```
wk?
[Tab]
123 ↵
```

> Quatro, which can load 1-2-3 files, does accept a file argument. You could use this for Quatro:
>
> wk? q123 !

dBASE can produce several types of files. PRG files can be used as file arguments. DBF files cannot be loaded but can be related to loading dBASE. In this case, you would enter several specifications for each of the extensions used with dBASE. Enter

```
PRG:
[Tab]
dbase ! ↵
DBF:
[Tab]
dbase ↵
```

WordPerfect poses a different kind of problem. Since WordPerfect does not require any file extensions to be used with its files, the only extension references that could be used are ones that you decide to use. If you assume that files without extensions are probably WordPerfect documents you would enter an empty extension as the criterion for WordPerfect.

```
:
[Tab]
wp ↵
```

Keep in mind that the Commander will search the extension file sequentially. This means that you can create a final option that will operate if no other matches are found. Enter

```
*:
[Tab]
REM Not selected for auto loading
```

Save the file by entering

```
[F2]
[F10]
```

Note that to setup this new extension file the program must be reloaded. Save the current setup by entering

```
[Shift/F9]
```

Exit and reload by entering

```
[F10] ↵
nc ↵
```

Point at the specified extension to see if they run the related application.

> For applications to run, the related files must be stored in the correct directories or else paths should be opened to allow DOS to find the specified programs.

The Commander is a powerful and enjoyable tool with which to work. It can be used simply as a substitute for normal DOS commands or used to implement a full turnkey menu system.

13

THE NORTON EDITOR

The primary difference between an editor and a word processor is that an editor is concerned with creating text files, while a word processing program is concerned with printing text. An editor is useful for creating text files intended to be used as source code for computer programs, or for DOS batch files. DOS operations often entail the creation and editing of text files.

An editor is concerned merely with the features that aid in the entry and revision of text. They are simpler programs than word processors because they do not need features and commands that apply to the paragraph and page formatting requirements of printing. Editors create standard ASCII text files. Word processing programs will usually add special formatting codes to the text that deviates from standard ASCII text format.

The most popular word processing programs, WordPerfect, Microsoft Word, and WordStar, have the ability to store text in an ASCII format if you select the proper option. WordPerfect uses [Ctrl/F5] to load and save text files, Word requires that you turn OFF the Formatted option on the Transfer Save menu to create a text file and WordStar uses the N command to place the program in a nondocument text editing mode.

The advantage of using a text editor over a word processor is one of speed and compactness. Because the editor is not burdened with all the overhead needed in a full-powered word processor, it can provide the necessary editing tools in a simpler, faster, and smaller program. Since the program is smaller it takes up less memory, leaving more memory to use for text, which also enhances the performance. The Norton Editor consists of a single file, NE.COM, which is 32,375 bytes in size. Compare that to word processing programs that are supplied on six or more disks.

The Norton Editor fills a gap that exists between primitive editing programs like EDLIN and full-powered word processing programs. The Editor is a small, fast, text editing program that contains a variety of handy features, all designed to help you produce computer programs or text files as quickly and easily as possible. In addition, the Editor is one of the few text editing or word processing programs on the PC to offer support for a mouse, another great advantage when editing.

Editor Features

The Norton Editor is designed specifically to meet the needs of people who are creating computer programs or other types of structured text files, such as DOS batch files. It makes sense that the features contained in an editor will differ somewhat from those found in a word processing program.

The following section explains some of the features that make the Norton Editor a unique text editing environment.

Editing Features

The Norton Editor contains all of the usual editing features found in word processing programs. The Editor is an **insert-oriented** editor. This means that any text that is typed is automatically added to the file. Insert-oriented editors are the safest type because you cannot accidentally overtype existing information. Editing in an insert-oriented program consists of deleting, moving and copying text.

> Of the major word processing programs, only Multimate defaults to an overtype mode. Insert oriented editing has become the accepted norm, although there is still a core of word processors that prefer overtype mode.

Delete

The Editor provides the following delete commands. Note that [Ctrl] combinations will delete to the left while [Alt] combinations delete to the right.

Table 13.1 Delete Commands in Norton Editor

Backspace and Delete	[backspace]
Delete current character	[Del]
Delete word, left	[Ctrl/w]
Delete word, right	[Alt/w]

(Continued)

Table 13.1 Delete Commands in Norton Editor *(Continued)*

Delete rest of line, left	[Ctrl/L]
Delete rest of line, right	[Alt/L]
Delete entire line, left and right	[Alt/k]
Delete marked block	[F4] d

Undelete

The Editor also includes a simple undelete feature that restores the previous deletion. Note that moving the cursor following a delete clears the undelete buffer. This means that undelete works only immediately after a deletion. Undelete does not work with a block deletion, [F4] d.

Undelete Commands are: [Ctrl/u] or [Alt/u]

Copy and Move

Text can be moved or copied by the use of block markers. Once a block is set, the text can be copied, moved or deleted from the file. Block markers can be set automatically for an entire line, or manually for blocks of any size. To mark a block manually you must set two markers; all the text between the markers is the block. As with WordStar, there can be only one block set at a time.

Table 13.2 Copy and Move Commands

Mark a line as a block	[F4] L
Mark from cursor to end of line	[F4] e
Set individual block marker	[F4] s
Remove block markers	[F4] r
Copy block	[F4] c
Move block	[F4] m
Delete block	[F4] d
Move cursor to block marker	[F4] f

Search and Replace

The Editor provides full search and replace functions, features a programmer cannot be without. The search and replace commands are the same command key. If you enter a second command following the search text, the command becomes a search and replace.

Table 13.3 Search and Replace Commands

Search/Replace towards top of file	[Ctrl/f]
Search/Replace towards bottom of file	[Alt/f]
Continue backwards search	[Ctrl/c]
Continue forwards search	[Alt/c]

Windows

The Editor has the ability to operate in a split-screen mode. The split screen allows you to edit two files at the same time. This is an invaluable aid when working since you can refer to one file without having to save or remove the other. The editor allows you to move or copy text from one window to another. The illustration below shows two dBASE programs being edited at the same time.

```
@ 21,13 Say  "Please Enter number ......" get CHOICE picture "9"
read
DO CASE
        case CHOICE="0"
                EXIT
        case CHOICE="1"
                clear
                menunumber="  "
                ppause=" "
                @ 10,10 to 15,70 double
                @ 11,15 Say "Enter Menu Number or ^Q┘ of Main Menu " get menun»
                read
Line=28    Col=8                A:MNUBAT.PRG           Insert   WW=Off
@ 21,13 Say  "Please Enter number ......" get CHOICE picture "9"
read
DO CASE
        case CHOICE="0"
                EXIT
        case CHOICE="1"
                clear
                menunumber="  "
                ppause="  "
                @ 10,10 to 15,70 double
                @ 11,15 Say "Enter Menu Number or ^Q┘ of Main Menu " get menun»
                read
```

Figure 13-1

You can split the display by entering [F3] x. Once the display is split, the [F3] x command will move the cursor between windows. Other window commands are:

Copy block from other window	[F4] w
Compare text between windows	[F6] t

The Compare command is an interesting one and very useful. The command tells the editor to compare the text in the current window to the text in the other window. This feature enables you to find differences in files that are very close in content. This method is much better than trying to visually inspect a program.

Formatting

As an added feature, the Editor does have some simple formatting features. You can turn on **wordwrap**, which allows the editor to create paragraph-oriented text. The related commands are

Turn on wordwrap, paragraph entry mode	[F5] w
Set line length, i.e., right margin	[F5] L
Re-format paragraph	[F5] f

Files

The [F3] key is used to implement file related commands, as follows:

Save current file and exit editor	[F3] e
Exit without editing	[F3] q
Save text without exiting	[F3] s
Load a new file	[F3] n
Rename current file	[F3] c

The Editor can also edit files that are larger than the available memory. This is done by loading part of the file, saving that part and loading additional text. In this way the Editor can handle files of almost any size. The command keys are:

Write current portion of file	[F3] w
Load next portion of file	[F3] l

The Editor can also append text from one file into the current file being edited. Note that Append always places the next text at the end of the current file regardless of the cursor position at the time of the appending. This feature is not as flexible as file-merge functions in most word processing programs, in which the text is inserted at the cursor position.

The command key is:

Append text file to current file	[F3] a

Printing

While the Editor is designed primarily for editing text files, it does contain printer commands that can produce hard copy. The following are print commands:

Print file	[F7] p
Print marked block	[F7] b
Eject remainder of page	[F7] e
Set page length, in lines	[F7] s
Set left margin for printing only	[F7] m

> Note that if you want to print a program and have line numbers automatically inserted, use the Norton Utilities program LP with the /N switch.
>
> You can run LP without exiting the Editor by using [F9], the DOS access command. First save the current text file: [F3] s y
>
> Then access DOS: [F9]
>
> Run the LP command: LP sample.bat/N ↵
>
> Return to the Editor by entering ↵

Mouse Support

The Editor supports the use of a mouse for cursor location and scrolling. If you have a three button mouse, you can use the middle button to set block markers.

Programmer's Aids

The Editor contains a number of features of special interest to people writing programs, macros, batch files or other types of text files.

1. **Goto line.** The Editor can locate specific lines in a text file. Most word processing programs cannot carry out this function. This command is useful when you want to find a specific line. For example, the Norton Utilities TS (text search) program will supply the line number of matching text found during a text search. With the line number you can use **[F6] g** to move to that line.

   In addition, the Editor will accept a line number as part of the command line when loading a file. Example:

   ```
   ne +15 sample.bat
   ```

   The previous command will load the file **SAMPLE.BAT** and place the cursor on line #15.

2. **Switch case.** The Editor uses [Ctrl/v] and [Alt/v] to change the case of the left or right portions of a line. In most programming languages case is not significant when entering commands. But good form often dictates that certain parts of a command appear in upper or lowercase to improve the readability

   For example, when I publish dBASE programs I always place command verbs, functions, and other reserved words in uppercase and user defined terms in lowercase. The Editor allows me to quickly change the case of items without having to retype. WordPerfect has a similar feature, [Shift/F3], but it operates only in the block mode. The Editor's method is much simpler.

3. **DOS access.** [F9] allows you to access DOS without having to exit the Editor. You can use this access to run DOS commands, DIR, COPY, and so forth, or Norton Utilities programs.

4. **Insert control characters.** Because of the need to use [Ctrl] characters in batch files, the Editor uses a method similar to EDLIN to insert special characters.

   To enter a [Ctrl] character or [Esc], enter [Ctrl/p] followed by the [Ctrl] character or [Esc]. For example, to enter an [Esc] character, enter

   [Ctrl/p][Esc]

   The character appears as ^[in the document.

   You can also use [Ctrl/p] in conjunction with the [Alt]-keypad method to enter control characters by their ASCII decimal value. For example, the following is an alternative method of inserting an [Esc] character.

   [Ctrl/p][Alt/27]

5. **Extended characters.** You can use the [Alt]-keypad method to enter extended ASCII characters into a text file. Note that the characters should be 128 or higher. Characters lower than 128 must be preceded by [Ctrl/p].

> The Editor will not insert character 255 into a text file. The use of this character with the DOS ECHO command, discussed in Section II, is a method by which blank lines can be inserted into a batch file. EDLIN does allow you to enter this character.
>
> However, blank lines can also be created using the ANSI command [Esc][#B, where # is the number of blank lines to insert.

6. **Find matching brackets.** This is a feature that can be a lifesaver if you write programs or macros that require the use of matching sets of ( ), [ ], { } or < >.

   For example, the illustration below contains a line taken from a dBASE program. The purpose of the command is to index names written as first name and last name, in the order of last name then first name. The AT() function searches for spaces to create substring SUBS( ) that reverse the order of last and first names. What is wrong with this command?

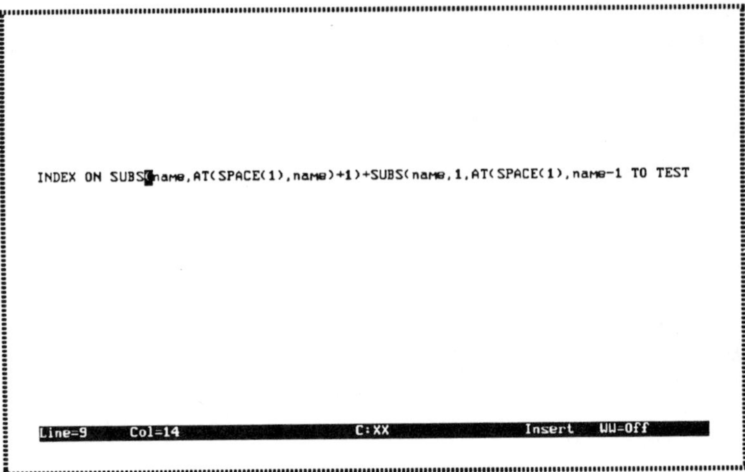

Figure 13-2

Close observation shows that one of the parentheses is missing. But which one? The Norton Editor has a unique feature that locates the matching bracket to any one that you place the cursor on. For example, place the cursor on any (and enter **[F6] M**. The Editor will search for the) that logically matches the highlighted (. This feature makes it much easier to locate missing brackets.

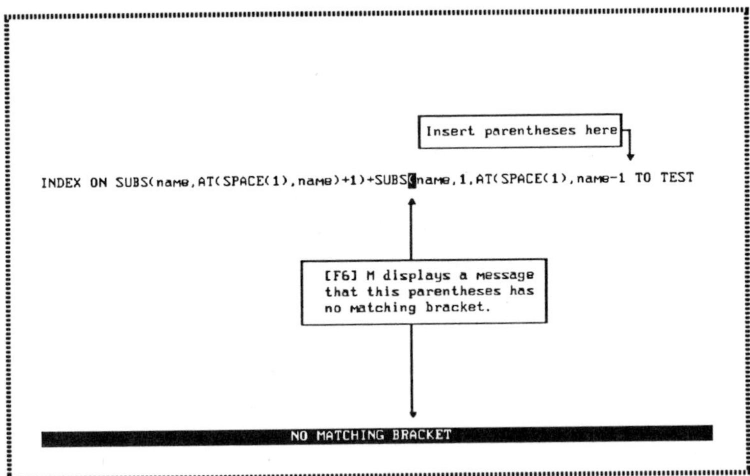

Figure 13-3

7. **Auto-indent.** Indenting programs properly is considered good programming because it makes your programs more readable and easier to understand.

   The Editor has an auto-indent mode, in which successive lines will be indented to the same level following a ↵ instead of placing the cursor at the left margin each time. To increase the indent level, enter [tab]. To decrease the level, enter [backspace].

   Like the matching feature, this one can save you countless keystrokes and speed the process of creating well structured programs.

8. **Suppress details.** The **[F6] C** command causes the Editor to suppress the display of all lines that do not begin with a letter. This means that all intended lines will be suppressed. This feature is a convenient way of suppressing some of the detail in a computer program. The effect of this command will differ with the way the programs are written.

Below is a section of the dBASE program included in Appendix A that creates menus.

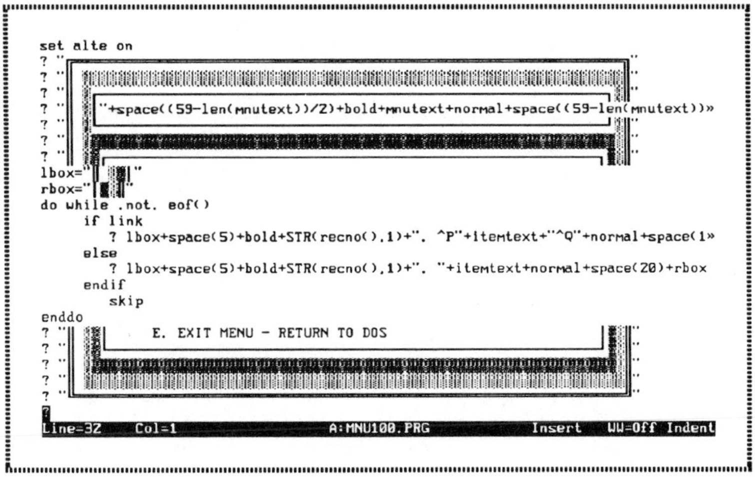

```
set alte on
? "
? "
? "
? "    "+space((59-len(mnutext))/2)+bold+mnutext+normal+space((59-len(mnutext))»
? "
? "
? "
lbox="
rbox="
do while .not. eof()
     if link
        ? lbox+space(5)+bold+STR(recno(),1)+". ^P"+itemtext+"^Q"+normal+space(1»
     else
        ? lbox+space(5)+bold+STR(recno(),1)+". "+itemtext+normal+space(20)+rbox
     endif
        skip
enddo
? "          E. EXIT MENU - RETURN TO DOS
? "
? "
? "
? "
?
Line=32    Col=1              A:MNU100.PRG              Insert   WW=Off Indent
```

Figure 13-4

If the **[F6] C** command is used to suppress lines, the display is reduced to those commands that are not intended. In this example, that allows you to check the DO WHILE and ENDDO loops to see that each pair is correctly matched.

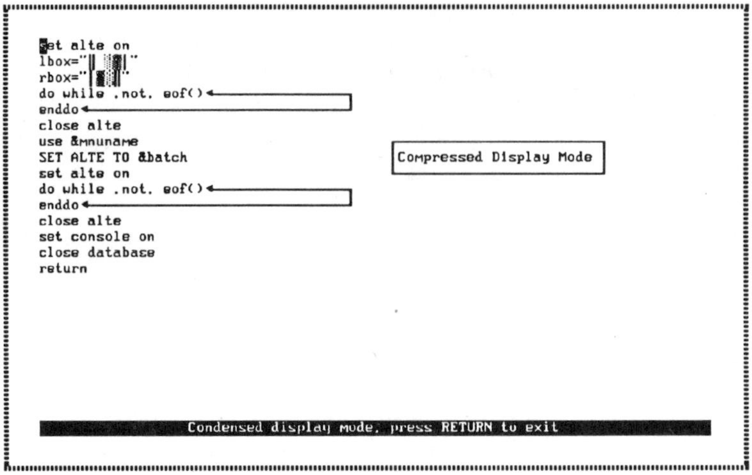

```
set alte on
lbox="▐▌"
rbox="▐▌"
do while .not. eof()
enddo
close alte
use &mnuname
SET ALTE TO &batch
set alte on
do while .not. eof()
enddo
close alte
set console on
close database
return
```

Compressed Display Mode

Condensed display mode, press RETURN to exit

Figure 13-5

Using the Editor with dBASE

If you work with dBASE III Plus you will find that the Norton Editor is an ideal way to create dBASE programs, or to edit memo fields.

dBASE III Plus allows you to select an external word processing program as a substitute for the simple Editor supplied with dBASE. To make this change, you can use the Editor to modify the CONFIG.DB file. CONFIG.DB is a text file that dBASE reads for default settings each time it is loaded. The CONFIG.DB supplied with dBASE III Plus reads:

```
STATUS=ON
COMMAND=ASSIST
```

These two commands turn on the status line and run the Assist command each time dBASE is loaded.

To install the Norton Editor as the dBASE text editor, add the following lines to the CONFIG.DB file.

```
TEDIT=NE
WP=NE
```

Make sure that the NE.COM file is accessible when dBASE is running. This can be done by opening a path to the directory in which NE.COM is stored, or placing a copy in the same directory as dBASE.

DOS Editor

The Norton Editor program disk contains a program called the Norton DOS Editor, which is stored in a directory called **NDE**. A source code is included as well. The program is designed to enhance the command editing template built into DOS. When the Norton DOS Editor is active, you can use the [up arrow] and [down arrow] keys to scroll through a list of previous DOS commands. You can edit the commands and re-execute them. The normal DOS template stores only the last command you entered, while the Norton DOS Editor stores the last 1000 characters worth of DOS commands.

The Norton DOS Editor is a memory resident program that uses about 3K of memory. It uses many of the same editing commands as the Norton Editor to alter commands stored in the memory buffer.

14

THE NORTON GUIDES

The Norton Guides program is really a series of programs like the utilities programs, which enables you to run and create on-line **informational databases**. An informational database should not be confused with a database program, which is a computer application that allows you to enter and retrieve data. An informational database is one that contains a fixed set of information that is referenced, but not altered. It is like a reference book that is implemented as a computer-based source of information as opposed to the conventional printed reference text.

The guides were originally conceived as aids for programmers who needed to remember the specific syntax for commands and functions in a programming language. But most computer users require help in remembering commands, functions, and usages, even if they never write a computer program.

Informational databases, fairly common in todays applications, are usually encountered in the form of help screens built into various applications. The Norton Guides are designed to provide additional means of this type of on-line help. The Guides can be used in one of two ways.

1. The Norton Guides program is currently sold in conjunction with a database, which provides on-line help in specific programming languages, such as BASIC, Pascal, or 8088 Assembly Language.

2. You can use the Norton Guides to create and run your own on-line databases.

This chapter discusses how the Guides can be used to create databases of your own design.

Why Custom-Informational Databases?

If the Norton Guides provide a form of help-screen display, why are custom-informational databases needed? Aren't the help-screen displays provided with the specific applications sufficient? There are three reasons to create a custom-informational database.

Inadequate Help

Even the best help-screen displays provided with standard applications such as word processing or spreadsheets, cover only a fraction of the information you might want or need. This is especially true of powerful and complex programs such as 1-2-3, dBASE III Plus, WordPerfect, and other major applications. In addition, the quality and quantity of these screens vary greatly from product to product. In the end, help screens are viewed as a necessary evil by most software vendors. The Norton Guides allow you to purchase or develop professional level reference guides just as you would purchase reference books about applications.

No Help Available

Not all applications provide on-line help. Many special use programs have no help facility at all. This is true of many programming environments like Turbo Pascal or Quick-Basic.

Another problem is that important information is often hidden while you are working on a different part of the application. For example, most accounting programs assume that you know the chart of account number when you are entering transactions. The common practice is to print out a chart of accounts and keep it by the computer as you are working. The same thing is true for vendor and customer numbers. The Norton Guides provide a means by which you can place that information into an on-line database.

Creating a supporting database with the Norton Guides is helpful to programmers who are developing custom applications. Preparing a Norton Guides database to provide help for those applications means that the code for that help does not have to be written into the applications.

Local Information

In any computer installation you have many choices about how the computers and the applications that run on it, will be setup. It is not uncommon to see post-it notes tagged on computer monitors as a reminder of certain names, or commands that are needed to find your way around the system.

In addition, you may want to create a database with explanations about how your business uses a specific application. For example, you might have an established method of calculating a customer's credit rating. Creating a database explaining that method for a user who is working on a spreadsheet that requires this procedure, would be useful.

A Norton Guides database can be designed that will contain all of this idiosyncratic information. The program provides a means by which you can place a large volume of information about the computer, the application, or a specific office procedure, in one place. Databases can be as simple as a list of customers and account numbers, or a full reference guide about the difference between replace 1A of 1-2-3 and Release 2.

The Norton Guides literally provide a window by which MS-DOS computers can access large amounts of information while running standard applications. Their potential cannot be underestimated. Creating and using on-line guides can be one of the most rewarding ways to better organize your computer usage.

How the Guides Work

The Norton Guides program fall into three separate types.

The Engine

The engine refers to the NG.EXE program. This program is a memory resident application that takes up 65K of memory. The application stays in memory and is activated by a **hot key**, which displays a window on the screen containing information about a specific database file.

The engine is designed to load and unload information from the database, which is a disk-based file. This means that the engine will use only 65K no matter how large a database is being referenced. It also means that the engine can switch database files while still on-line. You can select from several databases stored on the disk without having to reload the engine. The engine is also designed to be removed from memory if the user desires, without having to reboot the computer.

Databases

Databases refer to special files that actually contain the information that the engine will display. The size of the database is limited only by disk space, since the engine loads the section of the database requested for viewing. Databases can contain menus and cross-references as well as data.

Development Tools

If you want to create your own databases, the Norton Guides contains two programs, NGC (Norton Guides Compiler) and NGML (Norton Guides Menu Linker), which will create a database from a series of text files. Like a programming language, the basic information is entered as a text file with special commands inserted into the text. The NGC and NGML programs convert and assemble the text files into a Norton Guides database.

If you have the Norton Guides programs you have all the tools you need to create custom databases. The text files can be prepared by any program that produces standard ASCII text files, such as the Norton Editor or Microsoft Word.

> If you use a word processing program a special technique used to carry your formatting over to the text files, is covered later in this chapter.

Features of Databases

The on-line informational databases that can be created and run with the Norton Guides programs have a number of special features. Like other memory resident programs, the Norton Guides overlay the screen but do not disturb the application with which you are working. When you exit the guide you return to the application you were working with at the exact point where you left it.

Below is a illustration that shows a database for WordPerfect 4.2, called Krumm-On-Line WordPerfect 4.2. It illustrates some of the features of the Norton Guides.

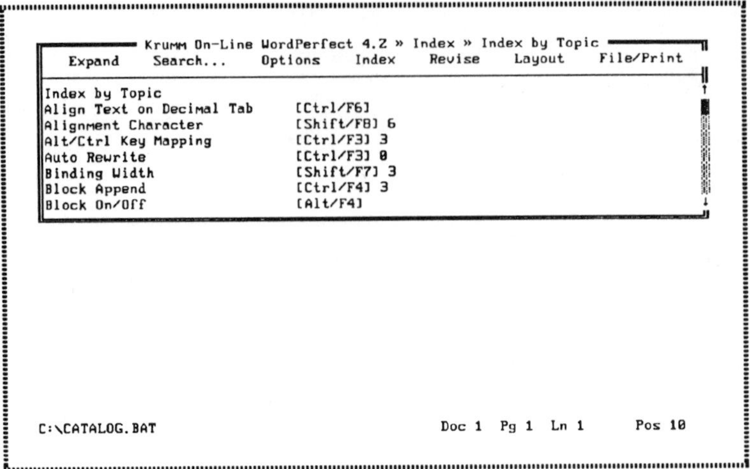

Figure 14-1

Pull-Down Menus

The Norton Guides show a menu bar at the top of the window, which displays a series of pull down menus. The first three options, Expand, Search, and Options, are built into the Norton engine. The last four are user-defined menus and will change with each database that you load. The menus are displayed by moving the highlight with the left or right arrow keys.

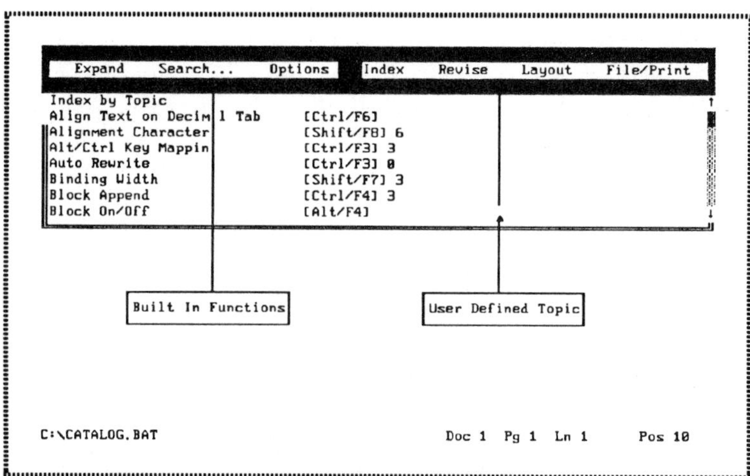

Figure 14-2

A user-defined, pull-down menu can list eight more topics.

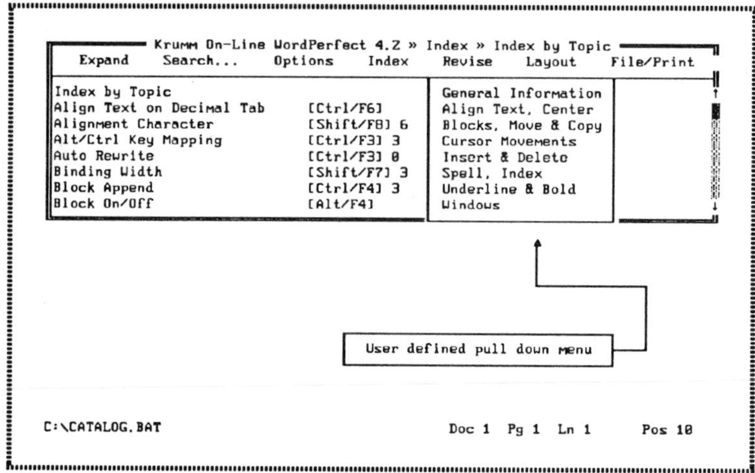

Figure 14-3

Short Topic Listing

Short topics are the headings for full text discussions. These headings form a list within the window. The highlight can be moved from heading to heading using the up and down arrow keys.

On the right side of the window a vertical bar with a highlight appears, to indicate your position in the list of topics. This is helpful in browsing a list of topics that is longer than can be displayed in the window at any one time.

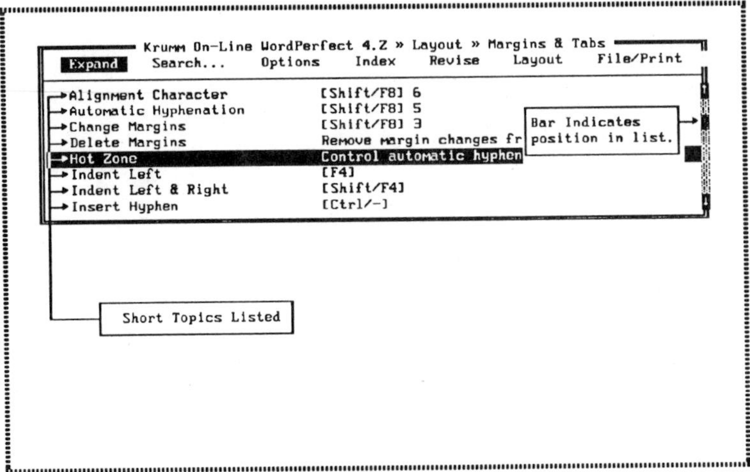

Figure 14-4

Full-Screen Display

The [F9] key toggles the display between half screen, the default, and full-screen display.

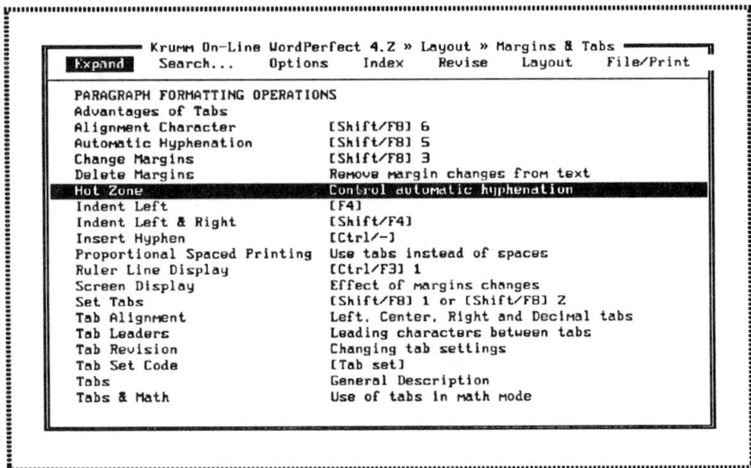

Figure 14-5

Expand Short Topics

Short topics headings displayed in the windows can be expanded to display a full text entry using the Expand command. Expand can be entered by pressing ↵ when you have highlighted the short topic heading of your choice.

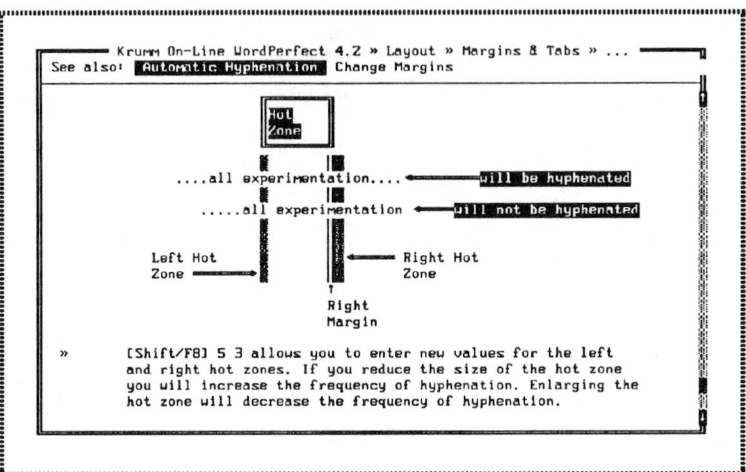

Figure 14-6

Search Short Topics

You can use the **Search** option to locate a key word or text string in the list of short topics. The program moves the highlight to the first short topic that matches the key.

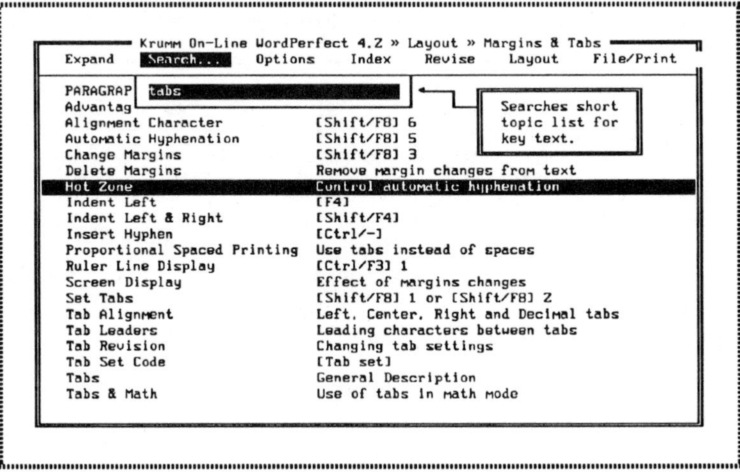

Figure 14-7

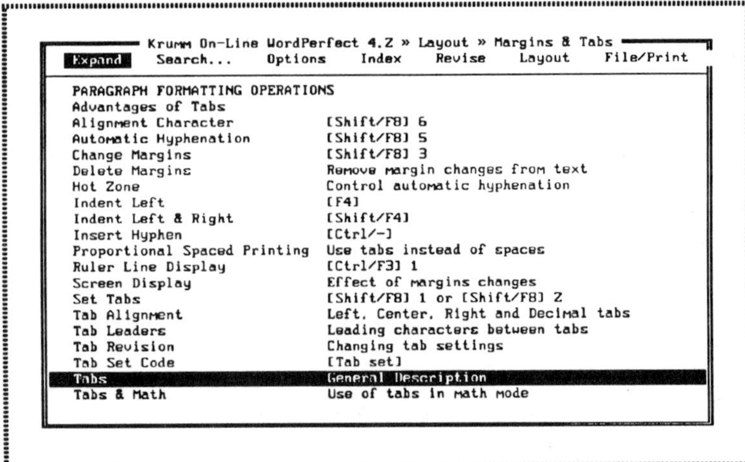

Figure 14-8

Select Database

You can display a list of on-line databases to select. Use this option to switch back and forth between different topics.

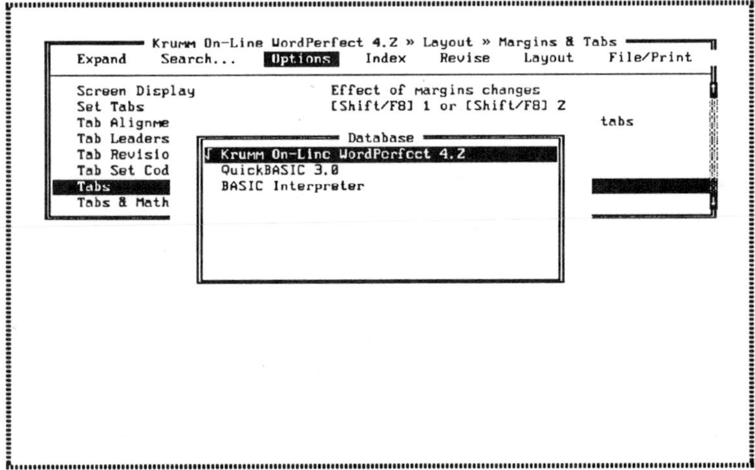

Figure 14-9

Hot Key Selection

The hot key used to activate and deactivate the guide display can be changed at any time. The default hot hey is [SHIFT/F1]. The Krumm On-Line WordPerfect database hot key is set to ['˜], the tilde key, because [SHIFT/F1] is used in WordPerfect for Super/Subscript.

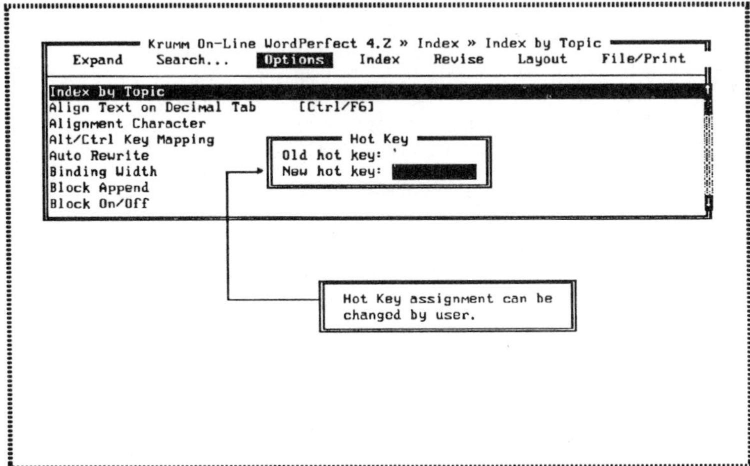

Figure 14-10

See Also References

An expanded entry can contain a list of other topic headings that are related to the displayed topic. The list of topics appears at the top of the window display.

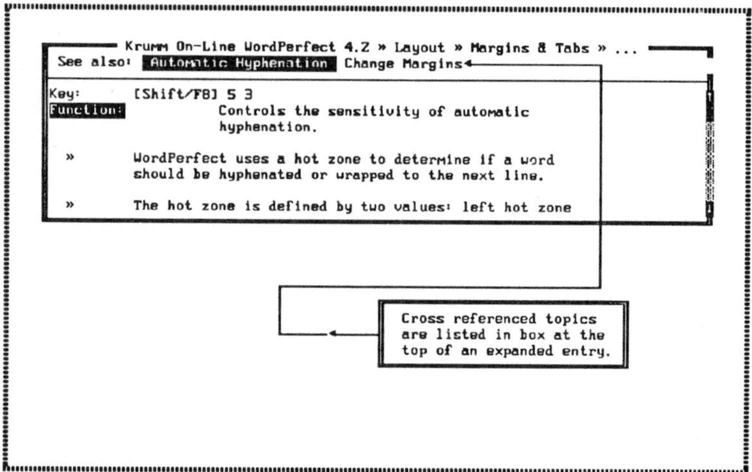

Figure 14-11

You can select a cross-referenced topic by highlighting the topic you want, and pressing ↵. The program then displays the expanded entry for that topic. If the cross-referenced topic also contains cross-references they appear at the top of the window. This system allows the reader to move through all the related entries in a large database in a few moments. It is a much more efficient way to locate data than using an index in a book, since the computer takes care of locating the data for you.

Automatic Lookup

This option prompts the Norton Guides program to highlight the word at the cursor position on the screen when the hot key is pressed. The program then automatically searches the current list of topics to locate a matching entry.

This option is useful for command-driven programs such as dBASE III Plus, or programming languages in which the word you are typing might be a command or function that would be listed as a heading in the database.

The option does not work very well with applications like word processing in which the text on the screen is not usually related to the topic you want to lookup.

Another advantage of Auto-lookup is that the Norton Guides window will display in the top or bottom of the screen opposite the half in which the program cursor is located. This means that the text near the cursor will always be visible when the guide window is displayed.

The Norton Guides program presents a new medium in which information can be brought to the people who need it. Keep in mind that there is no reason to restrict a database to computer-related topics. For example, you might create a database on standard accounting procedures to run in the background of an accounting program.

Creating Databases

In order to realize the full potential of the Norton Guides programs you may want to create a database of your own. Databases can be created for many reasons and the look of the database will vary depending upon your goal.

To learn about database creation, begin with a simple example. Suppose that you are doing financial accounting on your computer. One common problem is that accounting programs, like spreadsheet applications, deal mostly with numbers. For instance, when you create a chart of accounts for your business, the accounts are traditionally assigned numbers; when you enter items into your inventory, you assign each item a number. This is very efficient, except that it is not the way you remember things. It is difficult to remember when entering a transaction that account 50100 is Legal Fees or that Walter La Fish is customer 1034.

> The OneWrite accounting system from Great American Software is one accounting program that will display windows that allow you to list account and vendor numbers.

If you have the Norton Guides programs you can create a database or databases that will display the lists whenever you need them. A list-type database is the simplest type you can create for the Norton Guides. Even though they are simple, most people will find many uses for list displays. Remember that the Norton Guides have a search function that will search the list database to locate an entry.

Preparing a List Database

Norton Guides databases begin with text files. The basic text file is one that contains the data to be displayed in the window when the Norton Guides program is activated. Suppose that you needed to create three lists for your accounting work: a chart of accounts, a list of vendors and a list of customers. Your goal would be to pop-up the Norton Guides database if you couldn't remember an account, vendor or customer number while using your accounting software.

To prepare a text file for the Norton Guides you need a word processor or text editor that will create ASCII text files. You could use the DOS EDLIN program, or better yet, the Norton Editor.

If you are making an extensive database you will probably need to use a full powered word processing program, like the ones discussed later in this chapter. For now, the assumption is made that you are using a standard editor, such as the Norton Editor.

Short Topics

Below is an illustration of how the list database will look when you are finished. The window displays the list of information that you need. The list database that you are creating will consist of a series of short entries. Each short entry will show up in the window as a single line of text.

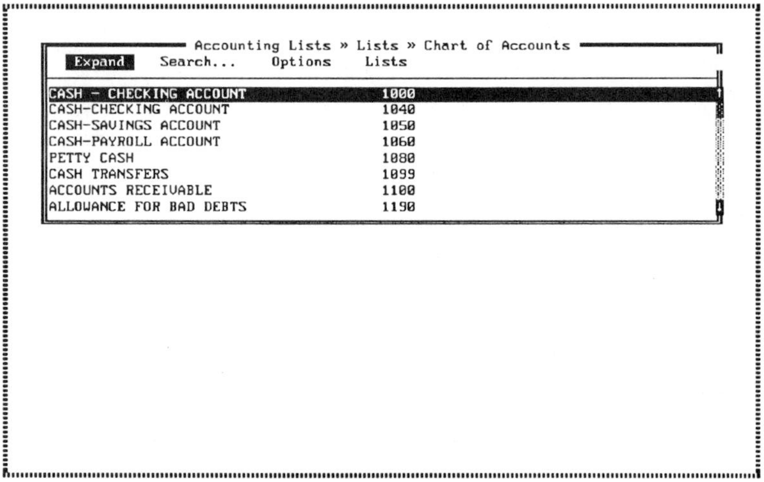

```
Accounting Lists » Lists » Chart of Accounts
Expand    Search...    Options    Lists

CASH - CHECKING ACCOUNT          1000
CASH-CHECKING ACCOUNT            1040
CASH-SAVINGS ACCOUNT             1050
CASH-PAYROLL ACCOUNT             1060
PETTY CASH                       1080
CASH TRANSFERS                   1099
ACCOUNTS RECEIVABLE              1100
ALLOWANCE FOR BAD DEBTS          1190
```

Figure 14-12

The Norton Guides program uses the exclamation point (!) as the beginning of all Norton Guides commands. If the program encounters a ! as the first character on a line, it expects a command to follow. Note that ! used in other locations in the text will be treated as a normal character.

Begin by creating a text file. In this example the file will be called COA.TXT (chart of accounts text). The first line in the database is the one that creates the first line in the display window, CASH – CHECKING ACCOUNT 1000. You would enter

```
!SHORT:CASH - CHECKING ACCOUNT      1000 ↵
```

This line consists of two parts:

```
Command
   word          Text to display
| !SHORT: | CASH - CHECKING ACCOUNT  1000 |
```

Keep in mind that the !SHORT: will not be displayed on the screen. The entire chart of accounts display will consist of a series of !SHORT: entries, one for each item in the list. Below is an example of such a file.

Listing 14.1. COA.TXT File Listing

```
!SHORT:CASH - CHECKING ACCOUNT          1000
!SHORT:CASH-CHECKING ACCOUNT            1040
!SHORT:CASH-SAVINGS ACCOUNT             1050
!SHORT:CASH-PAYROLL ACCOUNT             1060
!SHORT:ACCOUNTS RECEIVABLE              1100
!SHORT:ALLOWANCE FOR BAD DEBTS          1190
!SHORT:INVENTORY                        1200
!SHORT:PREPAID EXPENSES                 1350
!SHORT:LOANS AND EXCHANGES              1400
!SHORT:LAND                             1500
!SHORT:BUILDING                         1510
!SHORT:ACCUM DEPR-BUILDING              1511
!SHORT:EQUIPMENT                        1570
!SHORT:ACCUM DEPR-EQUIPMENT             1571
!SHORT:FURNITURE AND FIXTURES           1580
!SHORT:ACCUM DEPR-FURN & FIX            1581
!SHORT:OTHER FIXED ASSETS               1680
!SHORT:ACCUM DEPR-OTH FIX ASSETS        1681
!SHORT:GOODWILL                         1850
```

Notice that in this file the lines begin with the name of the account. This is because the search feature in the Norton Guides program will search the beginning of each short entry for matching text. Therefore, you should try to place the key word in each entry at the beginning of the line. For example, The key word in CASH-SAVINGS ACCOUNT is the word SAVINGS, it might be better to enter it as SAVINGS ACCOUNT – CASH. That way, searching for SAVINGS would locate the correct item. If the item was left as CASH-SAVINGS ACCOUNT, a search for SAVINGS would skip that entry.

The order in which the items appear in the text file is the order in which they will appear in the database. If you want the names of the accounts to appear alphabetically you must rearrange the text in the correct order. For example, you might enter the chart of accounts as:

```
!SHORT:ACCOUNTS RECEIVABLE                  1100
!SHORT:ACCUM DEPR-BUILDING                  1511
!SHORT:ACCUM DEPR-EQUIPMENT                 1571
!SHORT:ACCUM DEPR-FURN & FIX                1581
!SHORT:ACCUM DEPR-OTH FIX ASSETS            1681
!SHORT:ALLOWANCE FOR BAD DEBTS              1190
!SHORT:BUILDING                             1510
!SHORT:CASH - CHECKING ACCOUNT              1000
!SHORT:CASH-PAYROLL ACCOUNT                 1060
!SHORT:CASH-SAVINGS ACCOUNT                 1050
!SHORT:EQUIPMENT                            1570
!SHORT:FURNITURE AND FIXTURES               1580
!SHORT:GOODWILL                             1850
!SHORT:INVENTORY                            1200
!SHORT:LAND                                 1500
!SHORT:LOANS AND EXCHANGES                  1400
!SHORT:OTHER FIXED ASSETS                   1680
!SHORT:PREPAID EXPENSES                     1350
```

> If you were using a word processor which performs sorting, such as WordPerfect or Word, you can get lists sequenced automatically.

Once you have created this file, you can create similar files for other lists you want to include. Below are two more short sample files, one for vendors and one for customers.

Listing 14.2. VEND.TXT File Listing

```
!SHORT:ACE MACHINING                       147
!SHORT:COMMUNICATIONS SYSTEMS INC          148
!SHORT:DEES EXPORTS                        144
!SHORT:OAKS HARDWARE                       143
!SHORT:PHOTO FAST                          142
!SHORT:R & B TRAVEL                        145
!SHORT:STAMPS & COINS                      146
!SHORT:WORLD EDUCATION CENTER              149
```

Listing 14.3. CUST.TXT File Listing

```
!SHORT:ANDERSON, VAL                    1011
!SHORT:BLADES, SUZANNE                  1012
!SHORT:DEMPSEY, PAUL                    1013
!SHORT:DEMTROLOPULOS, LLOYD             1014
!SHORT:DIAS, KEITH                      1015
!SHORT:FEHR, JAMES                      1016
!SHORT:HAGAN, CHUCK                     1017
!SHORT:KEANE, BILL                      1018
!SHORT:LAIO, BEV                        1019
!SHORT:TOMPKINS, ALEX                   1020
```

This part of the process can continue with the creation of additional lists. At this point, each list is a separate text file with no relationship to any of the other lists created. That will come in the next stage.

The Menu-Link File

Once you have created the files that contain the short entries you want to include in your database you need to create an additional text file called the menu-link. The menu-link file is used by the Norton Guides programs to combine all of the individual text files into a single database. The menu-link file establishes the following for the database:

Database Name

Each database *must* have a name. This name is the one that appears in the list of databases when you select a database for loading, and appears at the top of the window to identify which database is being displayed. Remember that the databases are not listed by their filenames in the selection window, but by the database name. This means that your database name can be up to 40 characters in length.

Pull-Down Menus

This file also contains the name of the pull-down menus that appear on the menu bar at the top of the screen. You must have at least one menu name. You can have as many as 10. Keep in mind that these names are the ones that appear at the top of the display. This means that the number of menus you can display is limited by the total number of characters used in each menu name. If you menu names exceed the display width the menus will still operate but will not be displayed. Each pull-down menu name can contain entries for as many as eight items. Each item in a pull-down menu refers to an entire file of !SHORT entires. This means that you have room to coordinate up to 80 text files worth of data in a single database.

Note that the one to four pull-down menu names can be accessed by typing the first letter of the menu item. To allow this system to work with all menus, make sure that no two menu names begin with the same first letter. Also keep in mind that since the options Expand, Search and Options are always displayed, avoid menu names that begin with E, S or O.

Pull-Down Items

When a pull-down menu is selected, the Norton Guides program displays a box with one to eight topics. The topics and their order is determined in the menu-link file. If you want the items in the pull-down box in a specific order, you must place them in that order in the menu-link file.

Each item in the pull-down box refers to a file of !SHORT entries. However, the name that appears in the pull-down menu box is not the filename of the text file. The menu-link file allows you to assign a description that should be between 1 and 65 characters.

Like the !SHORT entry files, the menu-link file is a text file. In this example a file called **LISTS.TXT** will be created as the menu-link file for the accounting information list files COA.TXT, VEND.TXT and CUST.TXT.

The menu-link file contains only a few lines. The first line is always the !NAME command, which assigns the name to the database. For example, you might call this database **Accounting Lists**. Remember that the name can be up to 40 characters in length. Enter

```
!NAME:Accounting Lists ↵
```

Following the !NAME command, which names the entire database, you will enter a **!MENU** command. This command creates the name of the Pull-down menu. It is not restricted by the program but is limited by the display width of your computer. If you create pull-down menu names that are too wide for the screen, the database will function correctly but the menu displays will be off the screen. As a general rule, the total length of all the menu items should not exceed 40 characters, including spaces. In this case the name Lists should be sufficient.

> As mentioned before, it is best to begin each pull-down menu name with a unique first letter. This enables the person using the database to simply type the letter of the menu to display the option box. Avoid E, S and O as first letters because they would conflict with Expand, Search and Options, which are always part of the menu bar.

Enter

```
!MENU:Lists ↵
```

Following the menu you can list up to eight items. Each item represents a text file that contains your !SHORT entries. For example, suppose you want the chart of accounts list to appear as the first item on this pull-down menu. Enter the name of the menu item and the name of the file that contains the entries.

There is one small change that must be made at this point. In the example, the file that contains the chart of accounts information is COA.TXT. But the name you need to enter is COA.NGO. The extension is different because the Norton Guides program cannot directly incorporate text files into a database. Therefore there is an intermediate step in which the text files are converted into NGO (Norton Guides Object) files. It is these NGO files that are linked with the NGML program, not your original text files. When you prepare a menu-link file remember that it will be NGO, not TXT files that are linked.

To place the chart of accounts as the first item in the Lists menu, enter

```
Chart of Accounts coa.ngo ↵
```

> Keep in mind that there is no basic restriction on the size of the menu item entry. However, as a practical matter, entries over 65 characters will cause the text to be displayed improperly. It is advised that these entries be kept under 65 characters, which will not impose too great a design limitation.

Note that this item is not preceded by a special command. The NGML program assumes that all items listed following a !MENU command belong to the same menu. The assumption continues until another !MENU is encountered.

> The first item in the first pull-down menu has a special significance in the Norton Guides system. This item will, in effect, become the default display item. When a database is first loaded, the program automatically displays this item in the window. If you are creating a complex database, it might be a good idea to create a table of contents or index file and place it as the first item in the first menu. When the database is loaded the user is automatically presented with this table of contents list, which can serve as a guide to rest of the database. This is the technique used in the Krumm-On-Line databases.
>
> If you have a small database, select the most commonly used menu item as the default.

Next, enter the item names and filename of the other two lists:

```
Vendor List vend.ngo ↵
Customer Lists cust.ngo ↵
```

The file now looks like this:

```
!NAME:Accounting Lists
!menu:Lists
Chart of Accounts coa.ngo
Vendor List vend.ngo
Customer List cust.ngo
```

As with the menu bar, consider starting each menu item with a unique letter. Doing so allows you to type the first letter of the entry to activate the option, instead of using the highlight. In this case you have two items, Chart of Accounts and Customer List that begin with the letter C. The Norton Guides program always activates the first C, Chart of Accounts, if C is pressed. Change the first entry to read **Accounts List** to take advantage of the unique letter feature.

```
!NAME:Accounting Lists
!menu:Lists
Accounts List coa.ngo
Vendor List vend.ngo
Customer List cust.ngo
```

If you find that you simply cannot use items with unique letters, you can fudge the difference by adding letters to the menu choice. For example, you might label three entries with the same first letter with A, B, C. Example:

!menu:Formatting

A. Margins mar.ngo

B. Macros mac.ngo

C. Merge mer.ngo

The illustration below relates the text files and commands to their final use in the displayed database.

!NAME Creates name of database.

!MENU Creates pull-down menu names

!SHORT Creates short topics lists that appear in data window.

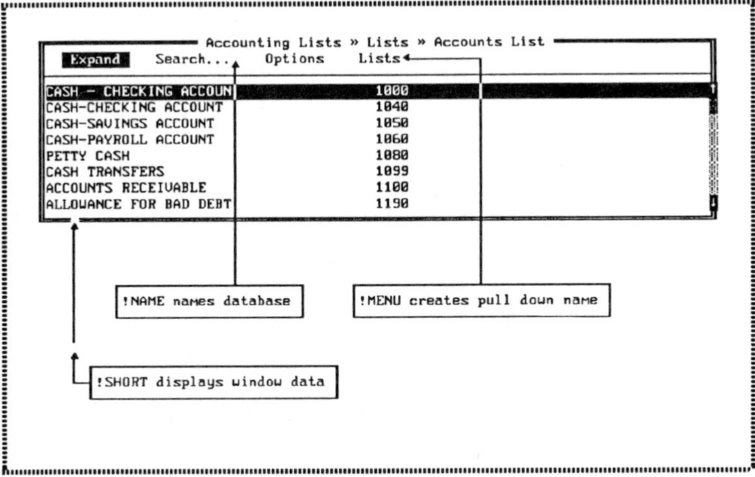

Figure 14-13

Compiling Text Files

Now that you have created the required text files, you can perform the steps necessary to create a database. First you must convert the files that contain the !SHORT commands into NGO (Norton Guide Object) files.

> The term object file is used in programming to represent a binary file produced from a text file. The program is usually written as a text file, which is referred to as the source file or source code file. The compiler program converts each source code file, that is text, to an object file, that is, binary. In programming, source files are compiled to object files. The object files are then linked to form the final program. A similar process takes place in the Norton Guides programs.

The NGC program is used to change text files into NGO files. The program does not change your original text files but creates a new file with the same name, and an NGO extension. For example, to convert the COA.TXT file to an NGO file, enter

```
ngc coa.txt ↵
```

The program displays a list of items showing what it found while compiling the text file.

```
D:\NG>ngc coa.txt

The Norton Guides Compiler, Copyright (C) 1987 by
Peter Norton Computing

  Compiling 'coa.txt'
   Scanning...
   Writing list...
   Writing longs...
   Cross referencing...

32 entries processed
```

If there were problems with the text file, the program would display information about those problems. The most common dilemmas concern cross-referencing, which is covered under the heading Cross-References, later in this chapter.

You can compile more than one file at a time by using several filenames as parameters. Example:

```
ngc vend.txt cust.txt ↵
```

The program will output the statistics for each of the selected files.

```
  Compiling 'vend.txt'
   Scanning...
   Writing list...
   Writing longs...
   Cross referencing...

8 entries processed

  Compiling 'cust.txt'
   Scanning...
   Writing list...
   Writing longs...
   Cross referencing...

10 entries processed
```

If you have a very large number of files to compile, more than eight, you should not place all the names as parameters on a single command. The best solution would be to limit each command to five or six files and create a batch file with a series of NGC commands. When you want to compile your entire database, enter the name of the batch file that contains the NGC commands. You might also add the NGML linking command to the file to compile and link with a single command.

The final step is to use the menu-link file with the NGML program. Notice that the menu-link file is not compiled like the files with the !SHORT commands. Enter

ngml lists.txt ↵

The program displays a list of the NGO files used in the database. Any files that could not be located would also be displayed. Note that the NGML will not write a database, NG file, if one of the specified NGO files cannot be found. All of the NGO files referenced in the menu-link file must exist for a database file, NG, to be produced.

```
  Building 'Accounting Lists'
   coa.ngo...
   vend.ngo...
   cust.ngo...
   Cross referencing...
Created lists.ng
```

You can now load the database into the NG program. Use the **Options Database** command to display the list of databases.

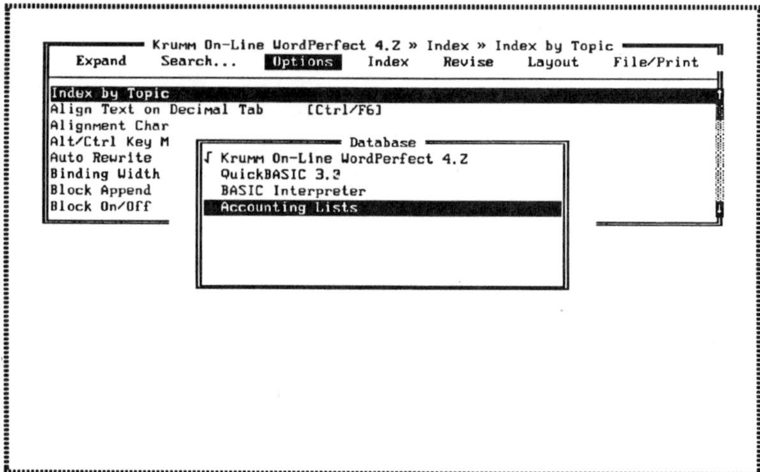

Figure 14-14

Load the database by highlighting the name, and pressing ↵. Pressing **L** displays the pull-down menu, LISTS, which displays three items on the menu.

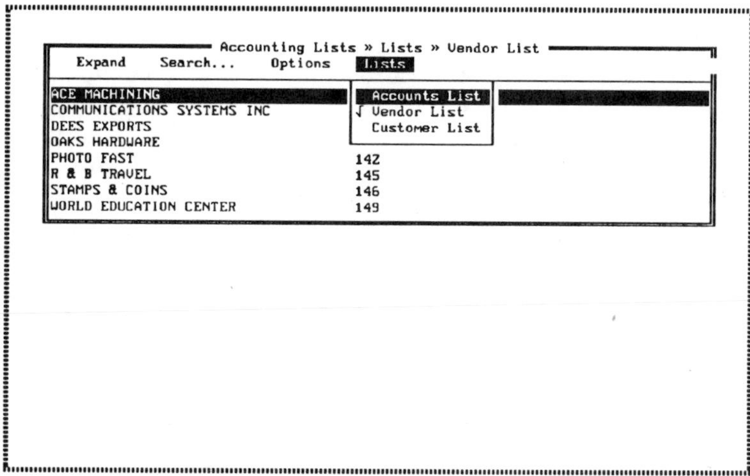

Figure 14-15

To load the vendor file, simply enter V. You can use the search command to locate a specific vendor. Example

```
v
s
stamps ↵
```

The highlight locates STAMPS & COINS.

```
Accounting Lists » Lists » Vendor List
 Expand   Search...   Options   Lists

ACE MACHINING                    147
COMMUNICATIONS SYSTEMS INC       148
DEES EXPORTS                     144
OAKS HARDWARE                    143
PHOTO FAST                       142
R & B TRAVEL                     145
STAMPS & COINS                   146
WORLD EDUCATION CENTER           149
```

Figure 14-16

The database that was created in this section was the simplest type, a list database. But the Norton Guides program can accommodate much more complicated databases. In the next section you will see how the basic list database you have created can be expanded.

Long Entries and Cross-Referencing

The simple list database you have just created functions quite well. However, this type of database is actually just an outline. The Norton Guides allow you to create long entries for one or more of the short **entries** in your text files.

A long entry is simply any type of text you want to associate with a short entry. The only limit imposed on a long entry is that of size: 12,000 characters. If you use an editor or word processor that allows you to enter the extended IBM character set you can create diagrams and drawings as part of your long entry.

Below is a modified version of the VEND.TXT file. Notice that text has been entered below the !SHORT entry for DEES EXPORTS, which represents the long entry for DEES EXPORTS. The text will not be displayed unless DEES EXPORTS is expanded.

```
!SHORT:ACE MACHINING                                   147
!SHORT:COMMUNICATIONS SYSTEMS INC                      148
!SHORT:DEES EXPORTS                                    144
^uProduct:^u
            Women's Shoes
            Goose Down Pillows
^bTerms:^b     Net 30 Days
^rOrders:^r    Call in, 800-555-9292
            Ask for Dave Preston
            Account Number 666-99999
!SHORT:OAKS HARDWARE                                   143
!SHORT:PHOTO FAST                                      142
!SHORT:R & B TRAVEL                                    145
!SHORT:STAMPS & COINS                                  146
!SHORT:WORLD EDUCATION CENTER                          149
```

The Norton Guides program allows you to enhance the text of a long or short entry by using special symbols to indicate different display attributes.

^U Changes the display to underlined text.

^B Changes the text to bold display.

^R Changes the text to reverse display.

The commands are toggles. This means that the first display code turns the attribute on while the next occurrence of the same code turns it off. Make sure that the codes are entered in pairs that bracket the text you want to affect.

> Note that the underline command will be translated as a change in color on a Color/Graphics adapter running a color display. The underline applies only to monochrome displays.

It is important to note that the use of the attribute codes make it more difficult to judge column alignment. If you look at the text of the long entry the items do not appear to line up vertically.

```
^uProduct:^u
            Women's Shoes
            Goose Down Pillows
^bTerms:^b      Net 30 Days
^rOrders:^r     Call in, 800-555-9292
            Ask for Dave Preston
            Account Number 666-99999
```

But when the text is compiled the attribute commands are converted from text to nonprinting instructions. The space they took up as text items is also removed and the final alignment on the database display is correct.

```
Product:
             Women's Shoes
             Goose Down Pillows
Terms:       Net 30 Days
Orders:      Call in, 800-555-9292
             Ask for Dave Preston
             Account Number 666-99999
```

If you want to use these attribute codes, you will have to be content with the alignment problems they cause. A good method is to enter all the text first and get the proper alignment, then add the codes after you are sure that the alignment is correct.

Cross-References

A long entry can be cross-referenced to other long entries by using the **!SEEALSO** command, which should be the last line of a long entry. Its purpose is to list the names of other long entries that are logically related to the one currently displayed.

For example, suppose that there was information in the entries for **OAKS HARDWARE** and under **CHUCK HAGAN** (in the customer file) that was related to **DEES EXPORTS**. A !SEEALSO command could be created that would display those two items for cross-referencing at the top when DEES EXPORTS was expanded.

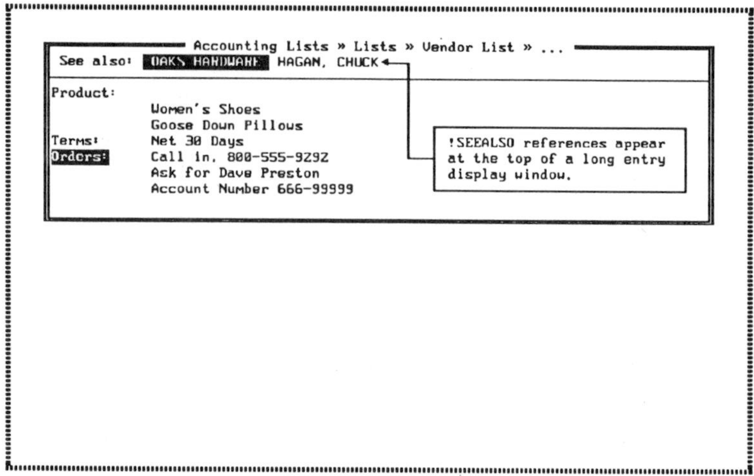

Figure 14-17

A !SEEALSO command sets up an automatic search for a short entry that matches the !SEEALSO reference. If you highlight the reference and press ↵, the program will automatically locate the matching !SHORT reference and display the text of the long entry. Note that cross-referencing will only work when the cross-referenced item !SHORT entry has long entry text associated with it. This makes sense because there would be little purpose in making a cross-reference if all you saw was the short entry topic. The basic purpose of cross-referencing is to eliminate redundant information by linking related items.

The !SEEALSO commands can have one or more references to other !SHORT topics. You can reference any !SHORT topic in the same text file or you can specify a !SHORT topic in some other file in the database. This means that a cross reference can jump to another topic in any menu in the database.

Form of Cross-References

The !SEEALSO syntax is a bit more complicated than the other ! commands. The simplest form of !SEEALSO is shown below:

```
!SEEALSO:OAKS
```

This reference will link the current long entry with a !SHORT entry in the same file that begins with the letters **OAKS**.

Keep in mind that a !SEEALSO will search for a match in the same way that a Search command from the menu bar will search a list of short topics. The match will assume that the !SHORT entry begins the letters OAKS. The case of the text, upper or lower, is not important. But OAKS will not match **SHERMAN OAKS** because the !SHORT entry begins with **SHERMAN**, not OAKS.

To create a !SEEALSO for more than one item, simply add that next item to the list. For example, to cross-reference OAKS and **PHOTO** you would enter.

```
!SEEALSO:OAKS PHOTO
```

Note that the cross-references appear in the order in which they are entered. If you want the reference to have a particular order you must enter them in that order.

You can create references that contain more than one word by enclosing the reference in quotations. The command shown below refers to three short entries: Oaks, Photo Fast, and Stamps. Note that the case of the characters is not significant.

```
!SEEALSO:OAKS "Photo Fast" Stamps
```

> If you use a multi-word reference, take care that you have left only a single space between the word in your reference and your !SHORT entry. If you have accidentally entered two spaces (a common word processing mistake) in either the reference or the !SHORT entry, the program will not locate the cross-reference.

To reference a !SHORT entry in another file, you must precede the reference with the name of the NGO file that contains the !SHORT entry. For example, suppose you wanted to create a cross reference to a specific customer, CHUCK HAGAN, who has a short entry in the **CUST** file. You would enter both the filename and the reference text, separated by a colon. Note that the name is entered as HAGAN, CHUCK because that is the way it is entered in the !SHORT entry in the CUST file.

> Remember that at the time the cross-reference is actually made, the text files will have been compiled into NGO (object) files. The cross-reference must contain a reference to the NGO (object) file, not the original text file.

```
!SEEALSO:cust.ngo:"HAGAN, CHUCK"
```

You can combine cross-references from the same file in the same !SEEALSO, with references to !SHORT entries in the same file. The command below refers to OAKS, in the same file, and HAGAN, CHUCK in the cust file.

```
!SEEALSO:cust.ngo:"HAGAN, CHUCK" OAKS
```

The order is not significant. You can also make references to additional !SHORT entries in other files. The command below refers to an entry in the same file and entries in CUST and COA.

```
!SEEALSO:cust.ngo:"HAGAN, CHUCK"OAKS
```

As with other entries, you are not limited in the number of cross-references you enter. There are some points to consider when creating a !SEEALSO reference.

1. If the text of cross-reference items is wider than can be displayed on a single line, the reference will not appear on the screen display. Note that the length of the displayed references will not include the filenames or other delimiters entered in the !SEEALSO command.

2. When a long entry is displayed, you can move the highlight to a specific cross reference by typing the first letter of the reference. Note this does not activate the cross-reference. You still must press ↵.

3. If you must, place more cross-references in an entry than can be displayed on one line. Those references can be activated by typing the first letter of entry and pressing ↵.

   Since the reader cannot see the name of the reference on the top line, you can include a note in the text of the long entry indicating which letters will activate additional cross reference items.

4. It is not necessary to include a backwards reference to return to the calling reference. For example, if you jump from DEES to OAKS, you would probably want to have a reference that would return you to DEES, which was the original entry you expanded. If you do not place a reference in OAKS for DEES, the program will automatically display a reference called **Previous**. Selecting this option returns the reader to the last !SHORT entry that they expanded.

Below are samples of the file VEND.TXT and CUST.TXT, which now include cross references.

Listing 14.4. VEND.TXT Listing

```
!SHORT:ACE MACHINING                                    147
!SHORT:COMMUNICATIONS SYSTEMS INC                       148
!SHORT:DEES EXPORTS                                     144
^uProduct:^u
             Women's Shoes
             Goose Down Pillows
^bTerms:^b       Net 30 Days
^rOrders:^r      Call in, 800-555-9292
             Ask for Dave Preston
             Account Number 666-99999
!SEEALSO:"OAKS HARDWARE" CUST.NGO:"HAGAN, CHUCK"
!SHORT:OAKS HARDWARE                                    143
^AF0Note:^A07 This company is a branch of DEES
EXPORTS. Please refer all business to DEES
EXPORTS.
!SEEALSO:CUST.NGO:"HAGAN, CHUCK"
!SHORT:PHOTO FAST                                       142
!SHORT:R & B TRAVEL                                     145
!SHORT:STAMPS & COINS                                   146
!SHORT:WORLD EDUCATION CENTER                           149
```

Listing 14.5. CUST.TXT Listing

```
!SHORT:ANDERSON, VAL                    1011
!SHORT:BLADES, SUZANNE                  1012
!SHORT:DEMPSEY, PAUL                    1013
!SHORT:DEMTROLOPULOS, LLOYD             1014
!SHORT:DIAS, KEITH                      1015
!SHORT:FEHR, JAMES                      1016
!SHORT:HAGAN, CHUCK                     1017
This customer does not like shoes from Dee's.
Send him Dee's but tell him you got it somewhere
else. He will never know the difference.
!SHORT:KEANE, BILL                      1018
SHORT:LAIO, BEV                         1019
!SHORT:TOMPKINS, ALEX                   1020→
```

In VEND.TXT a different type of attribute command is used, ^A. The ^A is employed to insert a hexadecimal value, which will be used to affect the screen display. This command allows you to implement some video effects other than the ones possible with ^B, ^U and ^R. If you are using a monochrome system, then you can implement blinking text in normal, bold and reverse video. If you have a color display you can change the color of the foreground and background of the text.

The IBM PC and compatible display adapters use a system in which each bit is assigned a specific meaning, in terms of the effect it will have on the video display. (This is similar to the way individual bits are used to determine the file attributes for each file).

On monochrome displays, the highest bit controls blinking, the next three the background, then bold, and three more for the foreground. A value of 000 produces black, while 111 produces white. Note that a foreground color of 001 will create underlined text.

Suppose you wanted to create a warning that would catch the readers attention. You could use black letters blinking on a white background. The bit settings would be:

blink	Background			bold	Foreground – Under		
1	1	1	1	0	0	0	0

But this is a binary number. To use it with the ^A command it must be converted to hexadecimal notation. (See Chapter 1.) The 1111 in binary coverts to the hex number F, and 0000 converts simply to 0 hex. Thus, to change to black letters blinking on a white background the value hex F0 should be used. Remember that you must explicitly enter another ^A command to return the screen to normal text or else the attribute will continue. The bits for normal white on black text are:

blink	Background			bold	Foreground – Under		
0	0	0	0	0	1	1	1

Because 0000 is hex 0 and 0111 is hex 7, the value to return to normal text is hex 07. In the example the word Note: will appear flashing black letters on a white background because it is entered as:

```
^AF0Note:^A07
```

Keep in mind that the ^A07 is used to return the rest of the text to normal video.

On a color display, you can control the individual red, green and blue components to create the full eight color palate available on the color/graphics adapter. To create blinking red letters on a white background you would need to set the bits in the following way (note that in additive color systems, such as the color/graphics adaptor, turning on red, green and blue create white; green and blue create cyan; green and red, yellow-brown, and red and blue, magenta:)

	Background				Foreground		
Blink	Red	Green	Blue	Bold	Red	Green	Blue
1	1	1	1	0	1	0	0

This translates to hex F4. To create the warning you would enter

```
^AF4Note:^A07
```

Note that white on black text is 07 for color and monochrome systems.

> The color operations are complicated by the fact that the Norton Guides programs provide a color option that automatically selects specific colors for the text, highlights, and menus. If you are running a database under the color option, and you enter a specific color combination, like the one above (red on white), you will want to return to normal color use by the color option, which is cyan letters on a blue background, not white on black. The value for the cyan on blue is binary 00011011, which is 1B hex. Instead of ^A07 you would use ^A1B to return to normal text.
>
> Running hex color 1B on monochrome will produce bold white on black text.

To alter the database, all the altered files must be recompiled and re-linked. When that is done you can try out the cross-referencing feature you placed in the data base. To compile, enter

```
ngc vend.txt cust.tct ↵
ngml lists.txt ↵
```

> Note that the Norton Guides program will automatically load the new version of the database if you replace the file, LISTS.NG, with a new file of the same name.

If you display DEES on the vendor list you will see the cross-references appear at the top of the window.

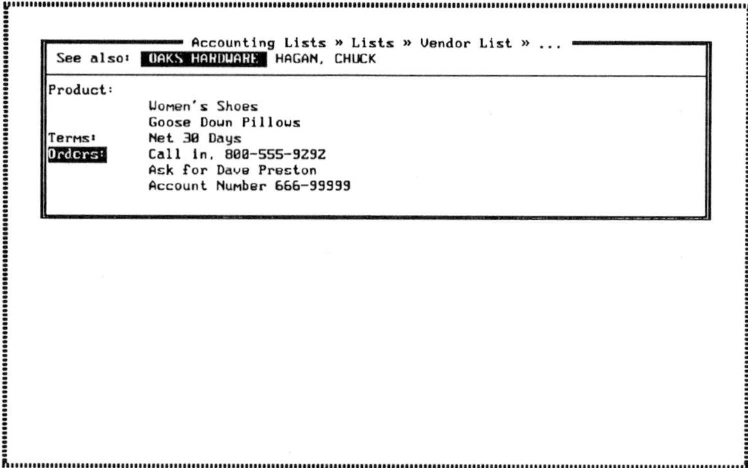

Figure 14-18

You can access the HAGAN entry by entering

h↵

The text of the entry now appears in the window. If you look at the top line of the display you will see that the current menu topic has changed to the Customer List. The Norton Guides automatically inserts a Previous cross reference that will take you back to the calling topic.

Nesting Lists

The Norton Guides also contain a feature that allows you to have a !SHORT entry expand into another file, instead of a long text entry. This is very useful when the information that falls under a given !SHORT can be presented better as list than as text entry. The advantage of lists of !SHORT entries over long text entries is that they can be searched quickly to find specific data.

When a list entry calls a list rather than a long text entry, it is called nesting. Nesting lists within lists allows you to create an outline structure in which a !SHORT entry is a category and the file that it displays is a list of subtopics. For example, the current chart of accounts listing contains four cash account entries.

```
!SHORT:CASH - CHECKING ACCOUNT            1000
!SHORT:CASH-CHECKING ACCOUNT              1040
!SHORT:CASH-SAVINGS ACCOUNT               1050
!SHORT:CASH-PAYROLL ACCOUNT               1060
```

You might consider, storing this detail in a separate file and showing only a general topic in the display called CASH ACCOUNTS.

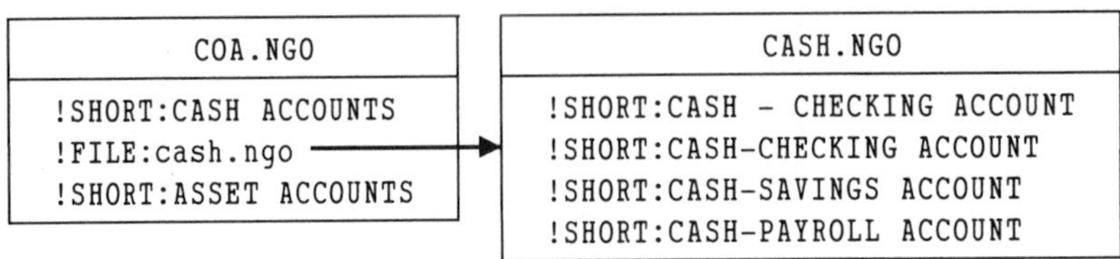

The **!FILE** command is used to link a !SHORT entry with another file that contains an additional list of !SHORT entries, creating the expanding outline effects.

As an example, create a file called CASH.TXT that contains the first four lines of the COA.TXT file. If you are using a word processor you can simply copy those lines to a new file. Then alter the COA.TXT file to read as below. Note that the cash accounts are replaced by a single !SHORT entry, which is then followed by a !FILE reference to the CASH.NGO file. The NGO extension is used, not TXT, because the link will be created after the compiling process creates the object files.

Listing 14.6. CASH.TXT Listing

```
!SHORT:CASH - CHECKING ACCOUNT          1000
!SHORT:CASH-CHECKING ACCOUNT            1040
!SHORT:CASH-SAVINGS ACCOUNT             1050
!SHORT:CASH-PAYROLL ACCOUNT             1060
```

Listing 14.7. Revised COA.TXT Listing

```
!SHORT:CASH ACCOUNTS
!FILE:cash.ngo
!SHORT:ACCOUNTS RECEIVABLE              1100
!SHORT:ALLOWANCE FOR BAD DEBTS          1190
!SHORT:INVENTORY                        1200
!SHORT:PREPAID EXPENSES                 1350
!SHORT:LOANS AND EXCHANGES              1400
!SHORT:LAND                             1500
!SHORT:BUILDING                         1510
```

(Continued)

Listing 14.7. Revised COA.TXT Listing *(Continued)*

```
!SHORT:ACCUM DEPR-BUILDING              1511
!SHORT:EQUIPMENT                        1570
!SHORT:ACCUM DEPR-EQUIPMENT             1571
!SHORT:FURNITURE AND FIXTURES           1580
!SHORT:ACCUM DEPR-FURN & FIX            1581
!SHORT:OTHER FIXED ASSETS               1680
!SHORT:ACCUM DEPR-OTH FIX ASSETS        1681
!SHORT:GOODWILL                         1850
```

Compile and link the new files into a revised database. Remember that you must compile all files that have been changed, COA.TXT and CASH.TXT.

When you load the new database you will see the entry for CASH ACCOUNTS.

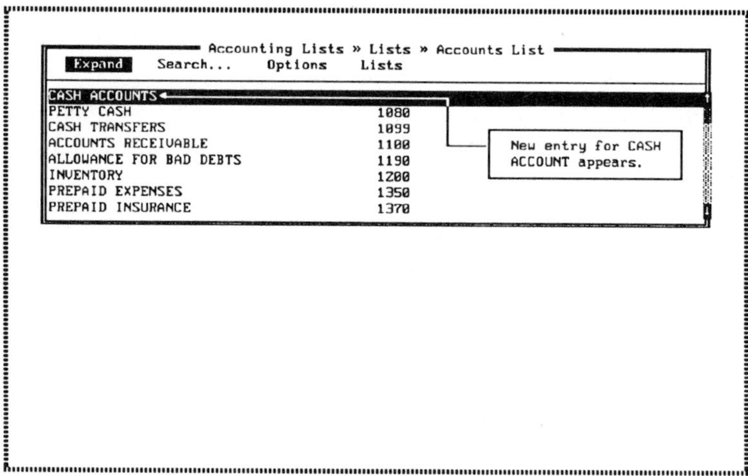

Figure 14-19

Enter

↵

The entry expands to display the sublist from the CASH file.

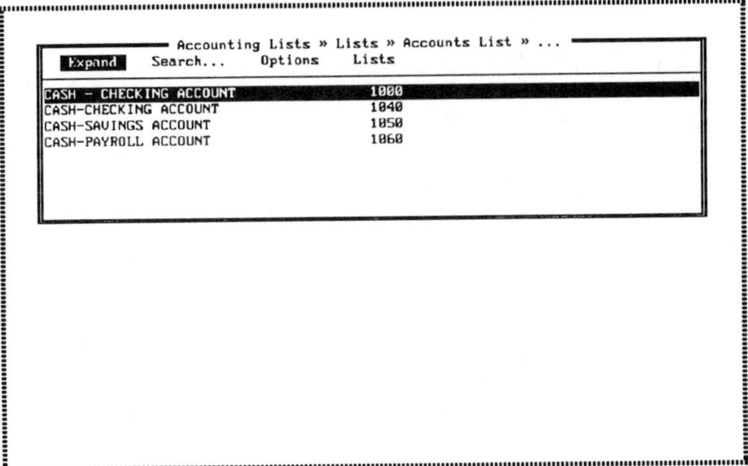

Figure 14-20

The Norton Guides provide a few simple but powerful tools. If you plan to construct a database it is probably a good idea to first create an outline of the files and the names that you will use. An outlining program like Ready or Think-tank, or an outlining word processor like Word are helpful. Remember that good planning makes it much easier to write !SEEALSO commands because your plan will contain the names of the files and key reference words you will need to cross reference the database.

Word Processing and Text Files

If you are going to create large databases that contain a great deal of text, use a word processing program as opposed to a text editor like the Norton Editor. Word processing programs such as WordPerfect and Word provide spelling checking and synonym help, both of which are always useful in writing text.

In addition, word processing programs can help you quickly format text by setting margins, indents, centering and other special effects that will enhance the look of your database display. For example, you can set the margins on your word processor to 80 columns wide to allow you to type lines that are as wide as the screen display. Remember that this text is not destined for the printer, but the screen.

Most of the popular word processing programs, including WordPerfect and Word, provide a means to save text in ASCII text format. But you should remember what that option actually means in terms of the specific word processor you are using. For instance, when you save a file as text, the word processor strips out all the formatting codes that are contained in the file. This includes settings for margins, centering, indents, and overhangs.

When you are creating text for the long entries in a database these formatting features allow you to create more readable text. But if you save the text as a text file, the word processor will remove those indent and margin changes.

The [Ctrl/F5] command in WordPerfect, and the Transfer Save option in Word, create text files that lose the formatting displayed on the word processing screen. However, there is another way to create the ASCII text file and retain all of the formatting advantages displayed on the word processing screen.

This method involves the use of a printer file rather than a text file. A printer file is one that captures the output that is normally sent to the printer. This output contains the formatting shown on the screen because that is the way the word processor prints it. Not all word processing programs have this option. Word and WordPerfect do because they use printer description files to assign formatting techniques specific to each printer. The trick is to select a printer that changes the formatted word processed text into ASCII standard text, in which all of the margin, indents and overhangs are implemented with spaces. The effect is that the text looks the same in the Norton Guides display as it does on the word processor screen.

Printing Text to a File with Word

To create a formatted text file with Word, first locate a file called **PLAIN.PRD**, provided on one of the printer disks. This file implements a standard ASCII output when text is printed. Once you have this file, use the **PO** (**P**rint **O**ptions) command to select **PLAIN** printer name.

Then use the **PF** (**P**rint **F**ile) command to create a printer file from the text. Enter an appropriate filename, for instance, xxxx.txt, and Word will create a standard ASCII text file in which margins, centering, indents and overhangs are implemented as space characters. This creates a formatted text file that can be compiled with the Norton Guides program into a database.

If you are using Word 4.0, this procedure will include any line drawings or paragraph boxes displayed on the screen. The outline and style sheet features of Word 4.0 make it easy to print out databases in one style for the printer and another for the text file.

Printing Text to a File with WordPerfect

WordPerfect also allows you to create formatted files, but its method of doing so is more limited than Word. WordPerfect contains two default printer definitions that create standard text output. You can display a list of printer definitions by entering [Shift/F7] 4 3.

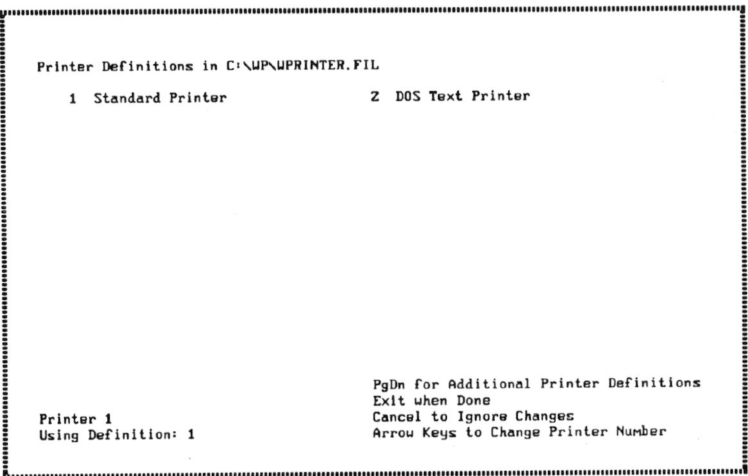

Figure 14-21

Select DOS Text Printer as the printer. For example, enter 2 ↵. This will display options for the printer port to use. To direct the text to a text file rather than a printer, select 8, then enter the name of a file, for instance, TEST.TXT.

```
Printer Port
     0 - LPT 1     1 - LPT 2     2 - LPT 3
     4 - COM 1     5 - COM 2     6 - COM 3     7 - COM 4
     8 - Device or File Pathname = TEST.TXT
Selection: 8
```

Figure 14-22

When you want to print, use [Shift/F7] 1 to select the printer assigned to the DOS Text Printer/Text File definition. This creates a text file that contains the centering and margin formats. Note that WordPerfect does not implement line drawing with these printer definitions so that line draw items will not be included in these files.

Database Commands

The commands used in database text files are listed below:

Table 14.1. Menu-Link File Commands

!NAME	This command is used to create the name of the database that will appear in the database selection menu. It also appears at the top of the menu window.
!MENU	Creates a pull-down menu on the main menu bar. You can usually create four pull-down menus, each one containing 8 menu items. Menu items should begin with unique letters avoiding E, S and O.

Table 14.2. Database Topic Files

!SHORT	Creates a short, one line entry in the database window. The short entry can be followed by up to 12,000 characters of text called a long entry.
!SEEALSO	Use this as the last line of a long entry. It creates a cross-reference to the text of a another short entry. The short entry can be in the same file or any other file used in the database.
!FILE	This command can be used to substitute a list of short entries for a long entry. Following a short entry with !FILE causes the specific short entry file to be displayed when the current short entry is expanded.

Summary

In addition to the Norton Utilities program discussed earlier, there are three other products in the Norton line discussed in this section that are useful tools for anyone serious about computers:

The Commander provides a powerful, visual extension to DOS

The Norton Editor is a small but powerful text editing program with features specifically designed for program writing.

The Norton Guides have the vast potential for creating user-defined informational databases and are among the most exciting utilities developed for the PC in recent years. They provide a fascinating and accessible means by which information can be placed into a computer system and recalled when and where it is needed. They provide a link between the necessary reference material and the computer user who needs it.

APPENDIX

A dBASE III PLUS PROGRAM

This appendix contains a program created with dBASE III Plus that can be used to generate menu batch files similar to the ones created in Section II. The program takes advantage of the Norton Utilities ASK and TM programs.

This program, though not a menu program, generates menu batch files, saving you the trouble of writing menu batch files from scratch. Each menu allows eight user-defined operations and automatically includes an exit to DOS.

The program begins with a single main menu called MENU. It can then create up to 99 submenus numbered 1 through 99. The menus can be used to run programs, DOS commands or send codes to the printer. You can also link menus together to form a system of submenu.

The program requires:

1. dBASE III Plus or a compatible program like DBXL.

2. Norton Utilities programs ASK and TM.

The program can be compiled, with Quicksilver for example.

Database Files

The program requires you to create a database called MENU.DBF with the following structure.

```
Structure for database: C:menu.dbf
Number of data records:        8
Date of last update    : 12/22/87
Field  Field Name  Type        Width     Dec
    1  ITEMTEXT    Character      30
    2  DIRECT      Character      30
    3  C01         Character      50
    4  C02         Character      50
    5  C03         Character      50
    6  C04         Character      50
    7  C05         Character      50
    8  LINK        Logical         1
    9  PSQ         Logical         1
** Total **                      313
```

Field 1—Contains menu items that will be displayed for the user.

Field 2—Contains the name of the directory in which the program is stored.

Fields 3 through 7—Contain DOS commands to be carried out for that item.

Field 8—If true, item is a link to another menu.

Field 9—If true, menu item is a printer code command.

Use the APPEND BLANK command to insert eight blank records into the file. This file will be the model for all the menus that the program creates.

The Program Files

The program consists of three program files and one format file.

```
MENUFORM.FMT
MNU100.PRG
MNU200.PRG
MNUBAT.PRG
```

Format File

Create a format file, MENUFORM.FMT, which will be used as the screen layout for entering data into the menu database files. The data will then be used by the MNU100.PRG program to generate DOS batch files.

Listing A.1. MENUFORM.FMT Listing

```
@ 0,0 say "Menu "+substr(dbf(),1,8)
@  2,  3  SAY "DEFINE MENU ITEM          Item "+STR(recno(),1)+" of
                                         "+STR(reccount(),1)
@  6,  4  SAY "Menu Item Text:"
@  6, 20  GET  MENUFORM->ITEMTEXT
@  8,  4  SAY "Commands to"
@  9,  4  SAY "execute for      [Example: to run WordPerfect enter WP]"
@ 10,  4  SAY "menu item:   1."
@ 10, 20  GET  MENUFORM->C01
@ 11, 17  SAY "2."
@ 11, 20  GET  MENUFORM->C02
@ 12, 17  SAY "3."
@ 12, 20  GET  MENUFORM->C03
@ 13, 17  SAY "4."
@ 13, 20  GET  MENUFORM->C04
@ 14, 17  SAY "5."
@ 14, 20  GET  MENUFORM->C05
@ 16,  4  SAY "Directory where"
@ 17,  4  SAY "commands should"
@ 18,  4  SAY "execute:"
@ 18, 13  GET  MENUFORM->DIRECT
@ 18, 45  SAY "[Example: \WP ]"
@ 20, 13  SAY "Is this a link to a submenu?    " get link picture "Y"
@ 21, 13  SAY "Is this a Printer Code Command? " get psq picture "Y"
@ 22,0 say  " Press [Pg Dn to Display the Next Menu Screen "
@  1,  0  TO  3, 21    DOUBLE
```

Program Files

This file is a simple loop that allows you to edit the eight records in each menu file.

Listing A.2. MNU200.PRG

```
clear
go top
do while .not. eof()
        set format to menuform
        read
        skip
enddo
close format
close database
return
```

The next program is one that actually creates the text files. It takes advantage of the SET ALTERNATE commands in dBASE that redirect screen output to a text file. By printing the lines with the alternate file open, you are in effect creating DOS batch files. The lines beginning with * are comments. They do not have to be written in the program.

Listing A.3. MNU100.PRG

```
set talk off
* create variables for ANSI screen attribute commands
bold=chr(27)+"[1m"
normal=chr(27)+"[0m"
blink=chr(27)+"[5m"
set console off

* assign filename to alternate file
* this file will be the menu text file
textfile=TRIM(mnuname)+".txt"
batch=TRIM(mnuname)+".bat"
set alte to &textfile
set alte on
* create menu text file by printing data stored in itemtext field
```

(Continued)

Listing A.3. MNU100.PRG *(Continued)*

```
? "                                                         "
? "                                                         "
? "  "+space(25)+bold+mnutext+normal+space(35-LEN(mnutext))+"
? "                                                         "
? "                                                         "
lbox="  "                                                   "
rbox="
do while .not. eof()
     if link
        ? lbox+space(5)+bold+STR(recno(),1)+".►"+itemtext+
          "◄+normal+space(18)+rbox
     else
        ? lbox+space(5)+bold+STR(recno(),1)+"."+itemtext+normal+
          space(20)+rbox
     endif
        skip
enddo
? "         E. EXIT MENU - RETURN TO DOS                    "
? "                                                         "
? "                                                         "
? "
?
?
close alte
* open text file for menu batch file
use &mnuname
SET ALTE TO &batch
set alte on
* print text of menu batch file
? "ECHO OFF"
? "CLS"
? "TYPE "+textfile
? 'ASK "Enter your choice'+chr(27)+'[5m►'+chr(27)+'[0m",123456789E'
? "IF errorlevel 9 GOTO program9"
? "IF errorlevel 8 GOTO program8"
? "IF errorlevel 7 GOTO program7"
? "IF errorlevel 6 GOTO program6"
? "IF errorlevel 5 GOTO program5"
? "IF errorlevel 4 GOTO program4"
? "IF errorlevel 3 GOTO program3"
? "IF errorlevel 2 GOTO program2"
? "IF errorlevel 1 GOTO program1"
do while .not. eof()
```

(Continued)

Listing A.3. MNU100.PRG *(Continued)*

```
* check to see if menu item is a link to a submenu
IF LINK
    ? ":program"+str(recno(),1)
    ? c01
ELSE
* check to see if menu item is a printer code
* if true create ECHO to Printer DOS command
IF PSQ
      ? ":program"+str(recno(),1)
      setstr=TRIM(c01)
      ? "ECHO "+&setstr + " >PRN"
      ? mnuname
  ELSE
      * normal menu item
      ? ":program"+str(recno(),1)
      ? "CLS"
      ? "ECHO "+chr(27)+"[7B"
      ? "ECHO "+chr(27)+"[5mLoading"+chr(27)+"[0m "+itemtext
      ? "ECHO "+chr(27)+"[7B"
      ? "ECHO Please Wait...................."
      ? "cd"+direct
      ? "TM START C2N"
      IF c01#space(10)
              ? TRIM(c01)
      ENDIF
      IF c02#space(10)
              ? TRIM(c02)
      ENDIF
      IF c02#space(10)
              ? TRIM(c03)
      ENDIF
      IF c04#space(10)
              ? TRIM(c04)
      ENDIF
      IF c05#space(10)
              ? TRIM(c05)
      ENDIF
      ? "c:"
      ? "cd\"
      ? "CLS"
      ? "SET program="+TRIM(itemtext)+" in use for "
      ? "ECHO "+chr(27)+"[7B"
      ? 'TM STOP "%program%" /C2/L/N'
```

(Continued)

Listing A.3. MNU100.PRG *(Continued)*

```
                ? "ECHO "+chr(27)+"[7B"
                ? "PAUSE"
                ? mnuname
              ENDIF
             ENDIF
             skip
             * goto next records
             * repeat until end of file
     enddo
     * implement exit to DOS as last option on all menus
     ? ":program9"
     ? "CLS"
     ? "ECHO "+chr(27)+"[7B"
     ? "ECHO  Menu Terminated by user - DOS now active !"
     ?
     * close files and return to main program MNUBAT.PRG
     close alte
     set console on
     close database
     return
```

The final program, the MNUBAT.PRG program, is a menu program that ties together the other files.

The menu display has four options.

1. Allows you to enter menu information into the files.
2. Allows you to create additional menus, 1 through 99.
3. Displays a list of the existing menu options.
4. Compiles the data stored in the menu database files and creates the batch files.

Listing A.4. MNUBAT.PRG Listing

```
SET TALK OFF
SET STATUS OFF
needcomp=.f.
itloops=.T.
DO WHILE itloops
CLEAR
IF needcomp
    1,40 say "[Menus need to be compiled]"
endif
@  4, 20  SAY "Modify Hard Disk Menus"
@  5, 13  SAY ""
@  6, 21  SAY "1. Change Menu"
@  7, 21  SAY "2. Add Menu"
@  8, 21  SAY "3. List Menu Summary"
@ 11, 13  SAY ""
@ 12, 21  SAY "4. Compile Menus in Dos Batch Files"
@ 13, 21  SAY "0. Exit Program"
@  3, 13  TO  5, 56
@  5, 13  TO 11, 56
@ 11, 13  TO 14, 56
@  5,13 SAY "├"
@  11,13 say "├"
@  5,56 SAY "┤"
@  11,56 SAY "┤"
choice=" "
@ 21,13 Say  "Please Enter number ......" get CHOICE picture "9"
read
DO CASE
        case CHOICE="0"
                EXIT
        case CHOICE="1"
                * ask for number of menu to edit
                * return will select main menu
                clear
                menunumber="  "
                ppause=" "
                @ 10,10 to 15,70 double
                @ 11,15 Say "Enter Menu Number or ↵ for Main Menu "
                get menunumber
                read
                menuname="menu"+TRIM(menunumber)+".dbf"
                * check to see that file exists
                IF file(menuname)
```

(Continued)

Listing A.4. MNUBAT.PRG Listing *(Continued)*

```
                * file exits edit by running MNU200
                needcomp=.t.
                USE &menuname  ALIAS MENUFORM
                DO MNU200
        ELSE
               * file does not exit
                @ 10,10 to 15,70 double
                @ 11,15 Say "Menu Number "+menunumber
                @ 12,15 say "Has not been created!"
                @ 13,15 say "Use Option #2 to Create New Menu"
                @ 14,15 say "Press ◄┘" get ppause
                read
        ENDIF
case CHOICE="2"
        * ask for menu to create
        clear
        menunumber="  "
        ppause=" "
        @ 10,10 to 15,70 double
        @ 11,15 Say "Enter Menu Number or ◄┘ for Main Menu "get
        menunumber
        read
        menuname="menu"+TRIM(menunumber)+".dbf"
        * check for existing file
        IF .not.(file(menuname))
                * if not existing, create file
                clear
                @ 10,10 to 15,70 double
                @ 11,15 Say "Creating Menu "+menunumber
                USE menu
                copy stru to &menuname
                use &menuname
                do while reccount()<8
                        append blank
                enddo
        ELSE
                * if conflict, display warning
                clear
                @ 10,10 to 15,70 double
                @ 11,15 Say "Menu Number "+menunumber
                @ 12,15 say "Already Exits"
                @ 14,15 say "Press ◄┘ " get ppause
                read
```

(Continued)

Listing A.4. MNUBAT.PRG Listing *(Continued)*

```
                ENDIF
        case CHOICE="3"
                * list items in database
                USE MENU
                clear
                ? "Main Menu"
                List itemtext
                wait
                menunumber=1
                restof=.t.
                DO WHILE restof
                        menuname="MENU"+LTRIM(STR(menunumber,2))+".DBF"
                        IF FILE(&menuname)
                                USE &menuname
                                 Clear
                                ? menuname
                                List itemtext
                                wait
                               menunumber=menunumber+1
                        else
                                exit
                        endif
                ENDDO
        case CHOICE="4"
                *compile databases into batch files
                clear
                @ 10,10 to 12,70
                @ 11,12 say "Creating Menu Files...."
                create main menu
                USE MENU ALIAS MENUFORM
                mnuname="menu"
                mnutext="Main Menu"
                DO MNU100
                menunumber=1
                moretodo=.t.
                * loop for each existing database
                DO WHILE moretodo
                        menuname="MENU"+LTRIM(STR(menunumber,2))+".DBF"
                        IF FILE(menuname)
                                USE &menuname ALIAS MENUFORM
                                mnutext="Sub Menu"+LTRIM(STR(menunumber,2))
                                mnuname="menu"+LTRIM(STR(menunumber,2))
                                DO MNU100
```

(Continued)

Listing A.4. MNUBAT.PRG Listing *(Continued)*

```
                                  menunumber=menunumber+1
                         else
                                  exit
                         endif
                   enddo
                   @ 11,12 say "Menus Created          "
                   @ 15,0
                   wait "               Press Any Key to Continue"
                   needcomp=.f.
     ENDCASE
   ENDDO TRUE LOOP
   return
```

When the program is run, it will display this menu.

```
Modify Hard Disk Menus
--------------------------------------
 1. Change Menu
 2. Add Menu
 3. List Menu Summary

--------------------------------------
 6. Compile Menus in Dos Batch Files
 0. Exit Program
```

Use option 1 to exit the existing menu database. The program begins with one file, MENU.DBF. Option 2 creates a new menu database. Make sure that you create databases consecutively. Option 3 displays a quick listing of the database items.

The Menu Screen

Option 1 will display a menu option entry screen. There are three ways to fill out this screen.

Normal Menu Item

```
Menu C:menu.d

 DEFINE MENU ITEM             Item 2 of 8


    Menu Item Text: Lotus 1-2-3 Version 2.01

    Commands to
    execute for       [Example: to run WordPerfect enter WP]
    menu item:    1. lotus
                  2.
                  3.
                  4.
                  5.

    Directory where
    commands should
    execute: \123                          [Example: \WP ]

            Is this a link to a submenu?      N
            Is this a Printer Code Command?   N
Press [Pg Dn] to Display the Next Menu Screen
```

In a normal menu item you fill in three things: the text of the item that should appear on the menu display, the command or commands (up to five) that you want executed, and the name of the directory that contains the program you want to run. The entry above is for Lotus 1-2-3.

Link to Another Menu

This is a special item that is used to change to a different menu.

```
Menu C:menu.d

 DEFINE MENU ITEM            Item 8 of 8

    Menu Item Text: Utility Menu

    Commands to
    execute for        [Example: to run WordPerfect enter WP]
    menu item:     1. menu1
                   2.
                   3.
                   4.
                   5.

    Directory where
    commands should
    execute:                                  [Example: \WP ]

             Is this a link to a submenu?     Y
             Is this a Printer Code Command?  ?
Press [Pg Dn] to Display the Next Menu Screen
```

In this type of option you need only enter the text for display and the name of the menu that you want to link to. The names are always MENU1, MENU2, MENU3 etc. Also enter Y for the prompt **Is this a link to a submenu?**.

If you are working on a submenu, you should include an option to return to the main menu, as shown below.

```
Menu C:menu1.

 DEFINE MENU ITEM            Item 8 of 8

    Menu Item Text: Return to Main Menu

    Commands to
    execute for        [Example: to run WordPerfect enter WP]
    menu item:     1. menu
                   2.
                   3.
```

```
                4.
                5.

    Directory where
    commands should
    execute:                                 [Example: \WP ]

            Is this a link to a submenu?     Y
            Is this a Printer Code Command?  ?
  Press [Pg Dn] to Display the Next Menu Screen
```

Printer Codes

The menu item below shows how a printer code is implemented through the menu. Notice that the string entered is similar to a BASIC string as shown in most printer manuals with the exception that dBASE uses CHR( ) not CHR$( ) to implement ASCII values that are not standard characters. The entry below is for [Esc] X 1, the code that set the IBM Proprinter into NLQ mode.

```
Menu C:menu2.

  DEFINE MENU ITEM              Item 1 of 8

    Menu Item Text: Set Printer

    Commands to
    execute for        [Example: to run WordPerfect enter WP]
    menu item:    1. CHR(27)+"X1"
                  2.
                  3.
                  4.
                  5.

    Directory where
    commands should
    execute:                                 [Example: \WP ]

            Is this a link to a submenu?     N
            Is this a Printer Code Command?  Y
  Press [Pg Dn] to Display the Next Menu Screen
```

Index

About the Author

Rob Krumm's writing career began in 1982 when he opened his own private school in Walnut Creek, California, called microCOMPUTER SCHOOLS, Inc. He found that students learned faster, and retained more, when they worked at the microcomputer with a detailed step-by-step learning guide in the application they were studying. This first "learning guide" was popularized in the best-selling Brady Book, *Understanding and Using dBASE II.*

Since that time, Rob's writing career has blossomed. One of the industry's most prolific authors, Rob has used his detailed "hands-on" style in several successful computer books covering such subjects as spreadsheets, word processors, utilities, and the dBASE II, III, and III Plus products. His columns and commentaries have appeared in the *San Francisco Examiner* and in several popular computer magazines and journals. In addition, his semi-monthly column, "The Bottom Line," can be read in the Berkeley-based *Computer Currents.*

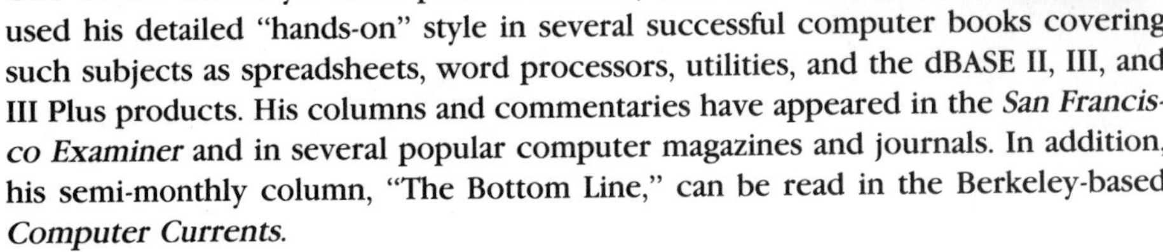

Place
First Class
Postage
Here
Post Office
Will Not
Deliver
Without Postage

Brady Books
One Gulf+Western Plaza
New York, NY 10023